GLOBALIZATION AND LABOUR
IN THE ASIA PACIFIC REGION

Dedication

for Jean Rowley

without whose unselfish and ceaseless support
nothing would have been possible

STUDIES IN ASIA PACIFIC BUSINESS
1369-7153

Editors: Robert Fitzgerald, Chris Rowley and Paul Stewart

Management in China: The Experience of Foreign Businesses
Edited by Roger Strange

Greater China: Political Economy, Inward Investment and Business Culture
Edited by Chris Rowley and Mark Lewis

Beyond Japanese Management: The End of Modern Times?
Edited by Paul Stewart

**Human Resource Management in the Asia Pacific Region:
Convergence Questioned**
Edited by Chris Rowley

Korean Businesses: Internal and External Industrialization
Edited by Chris Rowley and Johngseok Bae

China's Managerial Revolution
Edited by Malcolm Warner

East Asian Direct Investment in Britain
Edited by Philip Garrahan and John Ritchie

Managed in Hong Kong: Adaptive Systems, Entrepreneurship and Human Resources
Edited by Chris Rowley and Robert Fitzgerald

90 0452704 8

This book is to be returned on
or before the date stamped below

Globalization and Labour in the Asia Pacific Region

Editors

Chris Rowley
City University Business School, London

John Benson
University of Melbourne

FRANK CASS
LONDON • PORTLAND, OR.

First published in 2000 in Great Britain by
FRANK CASS PUBLISHERS
Newbury House, 900 Eastern Avenue, London IG2 7HH

and in the United States of America by
FRANK CASS PUBLISHERS
c/o ISBS, 5804 N.E. Hassalo Street
Portland, Oregon 97213-3644

Website www.frankcass.com

British Library Cataloguing in Publication Data

Globalization and labour in the Asi Pacific. – (Studies in
Asia Pacific business; no. 8)
1. Labor market – Asia 2. Labor market – Pacific Area
3. International economic relations 4. Deregulation – Asia
5. Deregulation – Pacific Area
I. Rowley, Chris, 1959 – II. Benson, John, 1945 July 23 –
331.1'2'095

ISBN 0 7146 5035 8 (cloth)
ISBN 0 7146 8089 3 (paper)
ISSN 1369-7153

Library of Congress Cataloging-in-Publication Data:

Globalization and labour in the Asia Pacific / editors, Chris Rowley, John Benson.
    p.cm. – (Studies in Asia Pacific business, ISSN 1369-7153)
"This group of studies first appeared in a special issue of 'Asia Pacific business review,
ISSN 1360-2381', vol. 6, nos. 3&4 (Spring/Summer, 2000)" – T.p. verso.
    Includes bibliographical references and index.
    ISBN 0-7146-5035-8 (cloth) – ISBN 0-7146-8089-3 (pbk.)
        1. Foreign trade and employment – Asia. 2. Foreign trade and employment
– Pacific Area. 3. Labor market – Asia. 4. Labor market – Pacific Area. 5.
Free trade – Asia. 6. Free trade – Pacific Area. 7. Globalization. I. Rowley,
Chris,1959 – II. Benson, John, 1948 – III. Series.

HD5710.75.A78 G58 2000
331.12'095–dc21   00-031563

This group of studies first appeared in a special issue of
Asia Pacific Business Review [ISSN 1360-2381], Vol.6, Nos.3&4
(Spring/Summer, 2000) published by Frank Cass and Co. Ltd.

Printed in Great Britain by Antony Rowe Ltd., Chippenham, Wilts.

Contents

1

Global Labour?
Issues and Themes

CHRIS ROWLEY and JOHN BENSON

The lexicon of globalization continues to be one of the most fashionable and is in common usage in a range of areas – even though globalization's exact meaning and effects remain contested. Our examination and analysis of globalization is in terms of its impacts on labour and its organization, and the possible responses, in the Asia Pacific region.

This focus suggested itself for a variety of reasons. First, there was the obvious drive of intellectual curiosity. Second, there was something of a rebalancing need. There is now a disparate barrage of work on globalization from a broad range of angles and subjects. Even within the area of business and management a variety of literature has appeared. Yet, these have twin drawbacks. On the one hand many accounts are naïve and simplistic, universalistic and deterministic, while on the other the focus is generally on managerial issues and so neglects the impacts on workers and their organizations. This bias is being rectified to some extent (see Bauman, 1998). For instance, the adverse effects of globalization on unskilled workers and the need for governments to provide social insurance has been examined (Rodrik, 1997), while a recent *Financial Times* report was titled 'Globalization "is bad for health"' (Williams, 1999). Even more crucially, labour's role in the processes, and tactics and strategies for responding, has been relatively ignored, although there is some useful recent work in this area (see Leisink, 1999; Mehmet *et al.*, 1999). Third, the particular regional focus provided a range of 'types' of economy and labour organization in various contexts and stages of development. It was the unevenness and contrasts in the way globalization impacts on labour and its organization, and how in turn it might be mediated, which were critical. These points forged the main contours of the template for our call for contributions to this volume.

This introduction begins by attempting to locate and define globalization. The emphasis in this section is on its meaning for labour and the key questions it raises in relation to its impacts on the state, labour markets and labour organization. A typology and grouping of the contributions is followed by a broad overview of each chapter. A short conclusion ends this piece.

GOING GLOBAL? LOCATIONS AND VIEWS

A number of key points concerning globalization need to be emphasized at the outset. Globalization needs to be grounded and located as part of several wider debates, and these are common to much of the work in this collection. First, there are the perennial 'universalism' and 'convergence' issues. These views are not new (see Rowley, 1997), although they may take on fresh (dis)guises, such as post-Fordism, flexible specialization, lean production, Japanization, and so on. For instance, Cox (1994) suggests globalization accelerated the emergence of a new model of production (from Fordism to post-Fordism). Some of the more universalistic and deterministic nostrums on globalization can be seen within such perspectives. Second, globalization can be seen as part of the ongoing debates revolving around foreign direct investment (FDI) and its impacts and locations, and competition for it. This is often linked to a view that globalization encourages 'regime shopping', 'social dumping' and a 'race to the base', with a global subordination of labour (including poor pay and standards) seen to flow from such trends. These areas are integral to our interest and that of several of the authors in this collection. Third, common threads are the roles of government in deregulation, privatization and enticement of capital through pursuing flexible labour policies, along with the demise of the nation state and the accompanying inability of national governments to regulate/control multinational corporations (MNCs). This last point is evident in the following statistics. Some 70 per cent of world trade is managed by 500 corporations (Korten, 1995), while 70 of the largest MNCs have revenues bigger than the gross national product of Cuba (Handy, 1998). Korea's then second largest *chaebol* Daewoo, following its relentless expansion abroad (and before its recent dismantling), had assets greater than the gross domestic product of the Philippines (Burton, 1999). A fourth area concerns trade union strategies, such as level of organization and the difficulties of international coordination and cooperation in response to such changes.

Getting a grip on globalization?

There are a variety of ways of viewing globalization. It can be taken as involving both macro and micro aspects. On one hand there is a process of integration of national economies, while on the other there is significant change in markets (product and financial), assisted by their common liberalization and deregulation. As with many concepts, trying to more tightly pin down globalization's 'meaning' is problematic (Amin and Thrift, 1996). For some it is a 'process of extending interdependent cross-border linkages in production and exchange' (Kozul-Wright, 1995: 139). For Harcourt,[1] it is the integration of national economies in terms of trade and investment, with erosion of barriers (including to FDI and 'outsourcing') increasing capital mobility. It is the global pressure on these barriers that, according to Benson and Debroux, represents the key challenge to policymakers. Burgess states that globalization indicates the internationalization of production, trade and markets and the integration of domestic economies into global economies. For Zhu and Fahey, globalization reflects the three integration processes of: (1) financial and currency markets; (2) production, trade and capital formation across national boundaries; (3) functions of global governance partially regulating national economic, social and environmental policies. Also, as Hadiz points out, globalization is associated with growing internationalization of the processes of production and finance with the decline of states and the importance of 'national politico-economic entities'. Importantly, Bhopal and Todd remind us of the need to distinguish between financial and manufacturing globalization because of the latter's lower mobility, longer term focus and more direct impacts on employment.

As a simple, broad, encompassing working definition we would suggest globalization be seen as the erosion of the political, social and economic boundaries of nation states and markets. This does not attach reasons for globalization but does point to a number of key issues addressed by this volume. These are the: influence of

MNCs (via FDI, etc); limitations of national laws to protect labour; a power shift towards capital; difficulties for unions in attempting to influence the process; and the level at which action needs to be taken.

What does globalization mean for labour?

If globalization means the reduction in influence of the nation state, then this will have a number of implications for trade unions that generally have been able to protect, at least to some degree, their members through national political means. Of course, the level of protection has been uneven across location (that is, developed versus developing economies), time (strength of unions in developed economies in the 1970s compared to the 1990s), sector (manufacturing versus services, metals versus textiles, public versus private), and membership (gender divisions, level of migrant labour).

For labour, globalization raises a number of key questions. These are:

• What are its effects on wages, job security, conditions and patterns of work?

• Has it created a 'new' set of problems for labour, such as the cheap import of workers, deskilling, and patterns of control and subordination?

• How have national economies attempted to regulate these effects, and how successful have they been? Alternatively, is the state unable to influence the direction and effect of globalization?

• What types of strategies have trade unions adopted to protect members against the impacts of globalization? Alternatively, are unions powerless in their ability to influence the globalization process and thus will be simply subordinated to global forces?

• At what level do workers need to act, and is it possible for unions to develop transnational perspectives and structures?

• How can workers be mobilized, and how can worker solidarity be achieved across firms, sectors, economies and cultures?

The answers to these questions will raise other significant questions. For example, if it is concluded that workers have to operate at regional and global levels, then what type of structures are appropriate and is it firms or governments that require lobbying and where? One only has to look at the movement of some UK unions towards views that the European Union (EU) is the increasingly important policy arena to witness this. This has led them to open offices in Brussels and to lobby at this level.

Newness and state power?

Definitional difficulties are only one problematic area. Even the newness of globalization is debated, as is its impact on the power and position of the state. For one group, globalization is new, at least in terms of ending national economies and capitalism (Petrella, 1996). There is an 'end of the nation state' in a 'borderless world', with a belief in market mechanisms reigning over state intervention (Ohmae, 1990, 1995). Globalization increasingly subordinates national institutions and policies to international ones (Thurow, 1996). In short, the dramatic decline of states in the national economy and society has been promulgated (Strange, 1996).

In contrast to this camp, a variety of commentators have argued that globalization is not new and does not necessarily weaken states. Thus, international economic integration was important in the late nineteenth and early twentieth centuries (Kozul-Wright, 1995). For some commentators, states, especially in Asia, even have the capacity to exploit opportunities presented by globalization (Weiss, 1997). Hirst and Thompson (1996) robustly refute some naïve nostrums – arguing globalization is a myth and that one of its key elements – the impotence of national governments over the seemingly universal and omnipotent global winds of change – is largely self-imposed through political choice. Others imply a similar message (see, *inter alia*, Boyer and Drache, 1996).

Hall and Harley argue that governments have not simply been rendered powerless in the face of global economic activity as states can still act decisively and strategically. For instance, in Australian labour–capital relations the state has exercised a critical degree of autonomy from the forces of international capital. Yet, this is less the case for other economies in the region. This suggests that while globalization has significant disruptive potential, 'What is also clear is that some types of institution – and national system – are more vulnerable than others' (Ferner and Hyman, 1998: xv).

Therefore, determinism is less applicable, and a more nuanced and contingent perspective is needed in this area. This type of grounded and historical perspective is unfashionable, and unpalatable in some of the more myopic and anaemic subject areas. Part of the problem is that there is an all too common concern and fetish to focus on changes rather than possible continuities.

Labour markets

Another key element of globalization concerns its impacts on labour markets. There is a fear of eroding regulatory capacities of states, the victims of 'regime shopping' by MNCs and the stern criteria of fiscal rectitude within financial markets (Ferner and Hyman, 1998: xviii). For Abbott, developing countries often seek to underpin economic growth via FDI attracted by cheap and compliant labour. As Bhopal and Todd put it, belief in free markets produces 'regime shopping' by MNCs and 'regime competition' amongst states, and the driving down of regulatory frameworks to lower levels. They also note that dependency theorists see MNC investment in dependent states resulting in the suppression of trade unionism as MNCs seek lower labour costs and weaker labour markets. For Hadiz, globalization in Indonesia has produced a fear that there is some form of zero-sum competition for investment in which easily mobile capital ceaselessly searches for sources of cheap and weakly organized labour both in internal (that is, local unemployed) and external (China, Vietnam) competition. Others, such as Chan on China, make similar points of the 'threat' to investment if wage costs are not kept down.

Neither is this simply a case of developing economies competing with each other in the vortex of deregulating labour markets. It also has an impact on 'developed' economies. For example, Harcourt notes that globalization can be seen in relation to, on the one hand wage depression, and on the other, consequent job security erosion in industrialized countries. Without adequate rules and regulations, unfair labour practices centred on the exploitation of the weak and vulnerable are globalized. It is argued that globalization is producing increasingly dysfunctional labour markets as capital mobility expands exploitation, discrimination and unfair employment practices (Mehmet *et al.*, 1999). This is via a 'race to the bottom', in which mobile capital seeks cheap labour in regimes willing to erode social codes and labour standards due to 'capital–labour asymmetry' – capital freely moves across national boundaries taking jobs and incomes with it, and leaving adjustment and welfare costs in its wake as labour is less mobile (ibid.). Such processes can be seen, for instance, in Australia where forces include differences in regional industrial relations (IR) systems (see Lambert, 1999). For Burgess, globalization in Australia has resulted in: (1) pressure on employment conditions via threats of relocation, import substitution, and so on; (2) policy responses exalting labour flexibility and boosting non-standard employment while attacking traditional working conditions; (3) a union reply embracing globalization and legitimizing the neoliberal response.

The determinism debate again resonates. Burgess argues that in Australia globalization is regarded as inevitable, with a 'globalization imperative' dominating the policy agenda and the neoliberal response (of downward pressure on employment conditions and union presence) presented as the only one. Similarly, Hall and Harley argue that the Australian policy response to globalization was neoliberal, of labour market reform and IR decentralization. Yet, they believe that this was not an inevitable agenda, but rather reflected a particular interpretation of challenges. In short, it was the commensurate policy shifts rather than globalization *per se* that attacked the IR environment. Thus, trade liberalization and deregulation have been justified in terms of global economic forces and assuring international competitiveness, but those policies resulted from conscious choices by governments keen to appeal to financial capital and sustained by neoliberal ideology.

Labour and its organization

Another key area is the impact of globalization on labour and its organization. Some commentators believed globalization could benefit labour by increased internationalism (Levison, 1974; Labour Research Association, 1984). However, in reality globalization has often raised rivalry between labour movements at both national and industrial levels, so reinforcing a global division of labour (Jenkins, 1984; Southall, 1988; Olle and Schoeller, 1987). This conflict can also occur between industrial sectors and groups of workers within the one economy. Benson and Debroux highlight this problem where, in Japan, deregulation resulting from global pressures has resulted in a divided union movement. Moreover, as Ng and Rowley found, the deregulation of immigrant labour in Hong Kong resulted in a 'split consciousness' within the labour movement.

Various contributors note the erosion of labour power under the impacts of globalization. For Burgess, the globalization agenda in Australia produced trade union decline, attacks on standard employment and increased non-standard work as such arrangements are less regulated and generally outside the union domain. Hall and Harley also note the problem for unions from globalization for a relatively small and vulnerable economy with a trading profile dominated by exports of commodities and high levels of protection for domestic manufacturers.

Again, universalism and deterministic perspectives need to be added to. Winters (1996) noted that the bargaining position of labour was impacted on by variations in capital mobility. This is borne out by our contributors. Harcourt argues that there is not just one model of the global economy that all have to follow, and that the unions should try to shape more worker-friendly international economic institutions.

In short, globalization is neither universal nor deterministic, either in its impacts or across locations and sectors. It can be that '"economic imperatives" may be contradictory in their implications, and are likely to be mediated – or indeed obstructed – by political contingencies at national level' (Ferner and Hyman, 1998: xix). We would support the position of commentators who argue that 'the pressures of internationalization are real and substantial, but neither unilinear nor overwhelming in their industrial relations consequences' (ibid.: xv), and that the idea of globalization 'can be both a rhetorical device and a self-fulfilling prophecy in its logic of fatalism' (ibid.)

These issues run through this volume, and are categorized in Table 1. This typology also allows for a quick reference of each of the contributions. The chapters can also be put into a fourfold classification, as outlined below.

CONTRIBUTIONS

This volume is composed of contributions by internationally diverse authors on a range (in terms of industrial and economic development, suppliers and receivers of FDI and labour organization) of economies. The chapters can be roughly grouped

TABLE 1

GLOBALIZATION AND UNION STRATEGY

Impacts	Focus		
	Individual unions	*Peak union bodies*	*Regional associations*
Work organization	Burgess Kim *et al.* Chan	Bhopal and Todd	Price Hadiz
Labour markets	Harcourt Ng and Rowley	Yuen and Lim	
Labour organization	Hall and Harley Zhu and Fahey Lawler and Suttawet	Benson and Debroux	Abbott

into four: regional perspectives; work on Australia, in some ways the most 'Western-like' economy; more 'developed' countries/economies, such as Japan, Korea, Singapore and Hong Kong; and 'developing' countries/economies, such as Thailand, Malaysia, Indonesia, China and Vietnam.

Regional perspectives

For Abbott, the sub-global regional 'context' in which trade unions operate presupposes the types of 'imperatives' that dominate their existence and activities. These are taken to operate along one of three dimensions – industrial, political and ideological – and evolve in accordance with the 'logic of spill-over' in regional integration processes. Using this interpretation, the contrasting experiences of regional trade unions operating within the Asia Pacific and EU are utilized to account for why they are primarily confined to promoting a particular view of trade unions in society.

Notwithstanding this pessimistic outlook, Price suggests that unions can confront globalization at the regional level by participating in regional bodies such as the Asia Pacific Economic Cooperation (APEC) forum. This body has established a Human Resource Development Working Group that now allows a new regional union body to meet with management and government representatives, and so to have some influence in the development of regional policy. Nevertheless, Price concludes the prospect for the promotion of labour's agenda within the wider APEC group is at present extremely tenuous.

Australia

For Hall and Harley, Australian governments responded to global markets by expanding international trade with policies of deregulation, labour market reform and IR decentralization. This produced major challenges for all trade unions, but the differential impact of policy on sectors and the labour market meant these varied significantly by union. The degree to which particular types of unions favour specific strategic orientations show systematic differences between blue-collar and production industry unions, and white-collar and service sector unions.

Harcourt concentrates on the response of the Australian trade union movement to globalization. The effects of globalization on labour markets, wage inequality, employment security and collective bargaining are outlined. The strategic response to this is analysed in terms of trade policy, international labour cooperation and traditional industrial campaigns on globalization issues. It is suggested that unions can employ a combination of international and domestic strategies to deal with globalization.

In the context of neoliberal policy responses to globalization in Australia, Burgess explores the impact of the growing non-standard workforce on trade union membership and policy. It is no coincidence that Australian union density fell as the share of non-standard employment rose. The characteristics of these jobs and their workers are largely outside the unions' traditional domain. One challenge unions face is to make themselves more relevant for such employees and to increase their recruitment among them.

Developed countries/economies

For Benson and Debroux, globalization generated substantial pressure on the Japanese employment regime and, in turn, upon the industrial union system. While not all changes can be directly attributed to globalization, the success of Japanese firms in exports and overseas production made the economy reliant on a strong world economy. The economic downturn in a number of countries in the 1990s, and in particular Asia, weakened the demand for Japanese exports. This, in combination with the Japanese banking and financial crises, created pressure for an overhaul of the employment system.

Kim *et al.* review the background of Korean IR and analyse more recent changes with a focus on the 'two faces' of globalization's effects. There was a positive impact in terms of enhanced basic worker rights to meet global standards, but also a negative impact on working conditions and employment practices. The latter brought substantial setbacks for unions and workers and rapidly eroded the power basis of organized labour. This negativity clearly appeared after the recent Asian economic crisis and its virulent Korean variant.

Yuen and Lim examine globalization and the effects on the labour market in Singapore. They discuss the responses of the government and the trade union movement to globalization. Citing government policies in dealing with the recent economic crisis, the concept of 'managed flexibility' is highlighted. They also examine the changing role of unions.

Ng and Rowley analyse globalization in Hong Kong in terms of labour market deregulation and the paradoxical outcomes for policies and trade unions. They locate this within globalization via two-way migration flows: Hong Kong capital to mainland China, and a countercurrent of Chinese labour to Hong Kong. This movement had critical impacts on workers and labour organization in terms of the dilemma of protecting simultaneously both 'local' and 'guest' workers. Such parochialism is more widely applicable for other labour movements and may not help pan-national union responses to global capitalism.

Developing countries/economies

Bhopal and Todd examine MNCs (American, Japanese and Australian) and organized labour in Malaysia. They conclude that despite the predictions of globalization theorists, the legacy of MNCs' 'home' context is carried into the 'host' country. Country of origin characteristics interact with local contexts to inform management strategies towards unions. Nevertheless, while there are substantial differences between MNCs in their approaches to unions, there is also a degree of conformity as they all embrace the restrictive intent of the state's union regulatory environment, thereby curtailing labour's power.

Similarly, Lawler and Suttawet argue that globalization, with its accompanying privatization and deregulation, has severely eroded the viability of the labour movement in Thailand. Part of the reason for this relates to historical factors and the underdeveloped nature of trade unions. These authors conclude that the recent movement towards democracy will not actually produce a stronger union movement. Worryingly, this will also mean that there will be little social or industrial pressure against further changes demanded by globalization.

Hadiz examines globalization in Indonesia. He argues that mobile capital 'demands' favourable investment climates, thereby increasing pressure on states to restrict organized labour. While in the advanced industrial countries the enhanced bargaining position of capital has created problems, newly emerging labour movements in 'late industrializing' countries like Indonesia are especially disadvantaged because of the global context characterized by the weakened bargaining position of labour. Nevertheless, labour strife has increased, despite long-established state control mechanisms legitimized by reference to supposedly authentic 'Indonesian values' that eschew conflict.

Globalization in China is the focus of Chan, who analyses labour and trade unions in an era of changing economic contexts, market reforms and worsening terms and conditions in many workplaces. She argues that deregulation has not produced a 'free' labour market, but one that in reality remains 'unfree'. While the earlier constraints of allocating people to jobs under a command economy have eroded, many workers remain restrained in a different way – they have to 'buy' their jobs and in so doing become 'bonded labour'.

Zhu and Fahey examine China in comparison with Vietnam in the context of globalization and market-orientated economic reform. They identify challenges and opportunities for trade unions in the areas of policy formation at the national level, and participation in collective bargaining and dispute mediation at enterprise level. It is argued that unions in both countries will have a significant role on a wide range of social issues under their special political, social and economic systems in the transition era as they undergo a social experiment, and diverge and attempt transition to a 'social market economy'.

CONCLUSION

We have introduced and outlined the problematic nature of globalization, its newness, and some of its impacts and effects in relation to the state, work and labour organization. In short, there is a threat from globalization to national economic regulation as national governments and organized labour may be rendered powerless when faced with global economic integration, internationalization, marketization and neoliberal deregulation (Gray, 1996). However, these are varied and may not be deterministic as industrial relations systems vary.

It is such important areas that our contributors now cover in depth. They will show the complexity that lies behind eponymous globalization.

NOTES

1. From now on, unqualified references to authors refer to their particular contributions in this collection.

REFERENCES

Amadeo, E. and Horton, S. (eds) (1997) *Labour Productivity and Flexibility*. London: Macmillan.

Amin, A. and Thrift, N. (eds) (1996) *Globalization, Institutions and Regional Development in Europe*. Oxford: Oxford University Press.

Bauman, Z. (1998) *Globalization: The Human Consequences*. Cambridge: Polity Press.

Boyer, R. and Drache, D. (eds) (1996) *States against Markets: The Limits of Globalization*. London: Routledge.

Burton, J. (1999) 'Daewoo discovers it is not too big to be allowed to fail', *Financial Times*, 17 August, p. 4.

Clegg, S., Ibarra-Colado, E. and Bueno-Rodriguez, L. (eds) (1999) *Global Management: Universal Theories and Local Realties*. London: Sage.

Cox, R. (1994) 'Global Restructuring: Making Sense of the Changing International Economy', in R. Stubbs and G. Underhill (eds), *Political Economy and the Changing Global Order*. New York: St Martin's Press, pp. 45–59.

Felstead, A. and Jewson, N. (eds) (1999) *Global Trends in Flexible Labour*. London: Macmillan.

Ferner, A. and Hyman, R. (1998) 'Introduction: Towards European Industrial Relations?', in A. Ferner and R. Hyman (eds), *Changing Industrial Relations in Europe*. Oxford: Blackwell Publishers, pp. xi–xxv.

Gray, J. (1996) *After Social Democracy*. London: Demos.

Handy, C. (1998) *The Hungry Spirit*. London: Arrow.

Hirst, P. and Thompson, G. (1992) 'The Problem of Globalization: International Economic Relations, National Economic Management and the Formation of Trading Blocs', *Economy and Society*, Vol. 24, No. 4.

Hirst, P. and Thompson, G. (1996) *Globalization in Question*. Cambridge: Polity.

Jenkins, R. (1984) 'Divisions over the International Division of Labour', *Capital and Class*, Vol. 22, pp. 28–57.

Korten, ?. (1995) *When Corporations Rule the World*. San Francisco: Brett-Koehler.

Kozul-Wright, R. (1995) 'Transnational Corporations and the Nation State', in J. Mitchie and J. Grieve-Smith (eds), *Managing the Global Economy*. Oxford: Oxford University Press, pp. 135–71.

Labour Research Association (1984) *Labour Confronts the Transnationals*. New York: International Publishers.

Lambert, R. (1999) 'Australia's Historic Industrial Relations Transition', in P. Leisink (ed.), *Globalization and Labour Relations*. Cheltenham: Edward Elgar, pp. 212–48.

Leisink, P. (ed.) (1999) *Globalization and Labour Relations*. Cheltenham: Edward Elgar.

Levison, C. (1974) *International Trade Unions*. London: Allen and Unwin.

Mehmet, O., Mandes, E. and Sinding, R. (1999) *Towards a Fair Labour Market: Avoiding a New Slave Trade*. London: Routledge.

Ohmae, K. (1990) *The Borderless World: Power and Strategy in the Interlinked Economy*. New York: Harper.

Ohmae, K. (1995) *The End of the Nation State: The Rise of Regional Economies*. New York: Free Press.

Olle, W. and Schoeller, W. (1987) 'World Market Competition and Restrictions upon International Trade Policies', in R. Boyd, R. Cohen and P. Gutkind (eds), *International Labour and the Third World*. Aldershot: Avebury.

Petrella, R. (1996) 'Globalization and Internationalization: The Dynamics of the Emerging World Order', in R. Boyer and D. Drache (eds), *States against Markets: The Limits of Globalization*. London: Routledge.

Rodrik, D. (1997) *Has Globalization Gone Too Far?* Washington, DC: Institute for International Economics.

Rowley, C. (1997) 'Comparisons and Perspectives on HRM in the Asia Pacific', *Asia Pacific Business Review*, Vol., 3, No. 4, pp. 1–18.

Rowley, C. (1998) 'Manufacturing Mobility? Internationalization, Change and Continuity', *Journal of General Management*, Vol. 23, No. 4, pp. 21–34.

Strange, S. (1996) *The Retreat of the State*. Cambridge: Cambridge University Press.

Southall, R. (1988) 'Introduction', in R. Southall (ed.), *Trade Unions and the New Industrialization of the Third World*. London: Zed Books.

Thurow, L. (1996) *The Future of Capitalism*. Sydney: Allen & Unwin.

Weiss, L. (1997) 'The Myth of the Powerless State', *New Left Review*, 225, pp. 3–27.

Williams, F. (1999) 'Globalization "Is Bad for Health"', *Financial Times*, 10 June, p. 5.

Winters, J. (1996) *Power in Motion: Capital Mobility and the Indonesian State*. Ithaca, NY: Cornell University Press.

2

Why Ideology Dominates Regional Trade Unionism in the Asia Pacific

KEITH ABBOTT

Since the end of the 1980s there has been a significant increase in the number of regional integration projects throughout the world. The prolongation of the General Agreement on Tariffs and Trade (GATT) Uruguay Round, failure of the newly created World Trade Organization (WTO) to deliver expected benefits, and general uncertainties surrounding the globalization of finance, trade and communication networks, to name a few, have all had an important influence in encouraging national governments to look more favourably upon multilateral economic and political arrangements. This has been reflected in the acceleration of the European Union's (EU) Single Market programme, the expansion of the Association of South East Asian Nations (ASEAN), the formation of the North American Free Trade Association (NAFTA), the initiation of large-scale multilateral economic projects like the Asia Pacific Economic Cooperation (APEC) and the Free Trade Area of the Americas (FTAA), and proposals to set up interregional integration arrangements such as the Transatlantic Free Trade Area (TAFTA) and Asia Europe Meeting (ASEM) (Dieter, 1997: 19–20). It is against the background of these 'globalizing' developments that the following discussion is struck.

Most theories of trade unions are confined to explaining the characteristics and behaviour of organized labour in a national context (for extensive reviews of such theories see Poole, 1981; Martin, 1989). Theories of trade unions operating at a global or international level have an extremely sparse literature (though see Lorwin, 1953; Levison, 1972; Logue, 1980; Busch, 1983; Cohen, 1987). There are good reasons for this division of attention. As units of study, national trade unions are more numerous, deal more directly with day-to-day workplace industrial relations, and have traditionally been far more accessible to research than their international counterparts. It has also been far easier to distinguish and attribute the major causal influences that shape the character and development of trade unions operating within the limited geopolitical confines of the nation-state. Theories of trade unions operating at a sub-global or regional level[1] are almost non-existent. Hence the purpose of this chapter, which takes a few steps towards filling this research void by drawing on neo-functionalist models of sub-global integration and institutional theories of national trade union organization to posit a theory of regional trade union development and behaviour.

In terms of the central theme of the present volume, it is hoped that such a theory will assist our understanding of this type of organization in two fundamental ways: first, by accounting for why sub-global regional trade unions function in the way they do under different forms of globalization; and second, by accounting for why this function changes as the processes of globalization unfold. To the extent that the theory provides a fair and reasoned reflection of these phenomena, a supplementary understanding should emerge from this chapter about the relative power and influence these organizations are capable of wielding under different conditions of globalization. It is organized in the following way.

The discussion first argues that the type of sub-global regional 'context' in which regional trade unions operate determines the types of 'imperatives' that come to dominate their concerns and activities. In so doing, it asserts that ideological imperatives have historically dominated international and regional trade union thinking, with the important exception being the regional trade unions operating in Western Europe. The discussion draws on this exception as a means of providing a theoretical interpretation of how the imperatives that determine the support and activities of regional trade unions develop as the regional context in which they operate changes. The discussion then applies the theory to regional trade unions operating in the Asia Pacific, and concludes with a brief comment about their future prospects.

SUB-GLOBAL 'CONTEXTS' AND REGIONAL TRADE UNION 'IMPERATIVES'

Much of the industrial relations literature fails to distinguish between the organizational characteristics and primary objectives of different types of trade union. The functions and concerns of national industry and occupation trade unions, for instance, are often taken as similar to those of national trade union confederations (see, for example, Ball and Millard, 1986: Chapter 4; Jackson, 1980: Chapter 3). The assumption that all components of a trade union movement share common objectives and modes of action, however, cannot be sustained. Employees organized at the level of industry invariably act and hold concerns that are different to those undertaken and held by representative trade unions organized at the national level. National trade unions similarly act and hold concerns that differ from those of national trade union confederations (see, for example, Martin, 1980). Were it otherwise there would be few reasons for the division of responsibility that invariably comes to exist within the hierarchy of trade union relationships (Crouch, 1982). It is thus worthwhile to first distinguish regional trade unions from other types of trade union. To this end we can reformulate the Webbs' classic definition (1894: 1) to suggest that a regional trade union is a transnational organization that affiliates trade unions within a sub-global regional area for the purpose of maintaining or improving the conditions of employment for workers. They differ from other types of trade union organizations in that they affiliate trade unions operating within a definable sub-global region of transnational proportions. They differ also in that they affiliate nationally organized occupation and industry trade unions (hereafter simply referred to as national sectoral trade unions), national trade union confederations (or national confederations), regional occupation and industry trade union federations (or regional sectoral federations), or some combination of these. They are finally distinguished, though in a less definitive way, by the types of 'imperatives' that dominate their concerns and activities. These imperatives could be argued as operating along three dimensions.

The first is where a sub-global industrial context exists, which can be distinguished as a region in which the majority of multinational corporations (MNCs) operating therein are willing and able to engage trade unions on a transnational basis. In such circumstances the activities and concerns of a regional trade union will be dominated by *industrial* imperatives. By this it is meant that its existence and support will be predicated upon its ability to achieve material gains for members through cross-border bargaining relations held with MNCs operating in the region. Where no such context exists, other imperatives will be apparent. Thus, a second dimension is where a sub-global political context exists, which can be identified as a region in which the majority of constituent countries have ceded certain aspects of their domestic political sovereignty to a transnational polity. In this instance a regional trade union's existence and support will be primarily predicated upon its ability to achieve political gains through the type of relations it holds with the transnational polity. In short, its existence and support will be dominated by *political* imperatives. A third dimension is where no sub-global industrial or political contexts exist, in which case a regional trade union's existence and support will be based upon less concrete imperatives. These can be termed as *ideological*, in the sense that they are aimed at attracting and galvanizing members around a particular vision of trade unions in society. This can involve calling public attention to perceived injustices committed by national governments or employers within a sub-global region. It may also involve appealing to the wider international community to exert moral pressure on behalf of some labour-related cause or on behalf of an affiliated organization, or the provision of financial and other forms of assistance to strengthen the position of member trade unions that share the philosophical views the regional organization represents. (The concept of 'context determined' used here draws on a theoretical characterization of collective bargaining hierarchies formulated by Clegg, 1976).

Highlighting these distinctions is not to suggest that the existence and concerns of regional trade unions will be dominated by any one imperative to the exclusion of others. Like all trade unions, they will inevitably subscribe to some form of ideological conviction, hold expectations of developing substantive relations with MNCs, and aspire to exert political influence where possible. The point to be taken is that the prevalence of sub-global industrial or political contexts, or lack of them, can be expected to promote one imperative over others as the foundation upon which a regional trade union's principal activities, concerns and support will be based.

A second element to this schema, and one that seems capable of lending its applied interpretation a degree of dynamism, draws on the literature relating to regional integration. The most elaborate and most criticized theory in this area is neo-functionalism, which came to prominence in the 1950s and 1960s as a means of explaining the early economic and political development of the EU. It fell out of favour during the 1970s and early 1980s when this development stalled, but has since re-emerged in a number of studies seeking to explain the EU's recent drive to implement its Single Market project (see Transholm-Mikkelsen, 1991). For present purposes, a modified version of the original neo-functionalist theories provided by Haas (1958) and Lindberg (1963) will suffice. The basic thesis of these two writers is that integration within one sector will provide its own impetus and spread to others, such that transnational institutions established to coordinate and/or administer specific tasks will set in motion economic, social and political pressures for further integration. Called the 'logic of spill-over', the process is said to begin with various forms of 'functional spill-over', in which the technical characteristics of economic tasks undertaken in developing industrial societies become so interdependent that it becomes impossible to treat them in isolation. Attempts to integrate the tasks lead to economic problems, which can only be solved by integrating more and more tasks, beginning at the national level and eventually spilling over to the transnational level. As the process unfolds, 'negative' forms of integration are put in place (that is, the removal of economic barriers between nation states), which are later supplemented by the establishment of more complex forms of 'positive integration' (that is, the adoption of coordinated and common policies).

The need to manage the problems associated with these developments in turn leads to a 'political spill-over', as government leaders and other public officials undergo a learning process which culminates in the collective perception that the interests of their respective countries are better served by seeking transnational rather than national solutions. This perception is made possible as processes of 'bureaucratic interpenetration' and informal 'cooptation' emerge from the efforts of political elites seeking to manage the problems of functional spill-over. This leads to the establishment of intergovernmental political institutions, and eventually to the foundation of supranational institutions.[2] As these institutions develop and grow they are said to generate new pressures that lead to a 'cultivated spill-over'. In this final stage, the traditional expectations and loyalties of political and business elites are ultimately transformed, leading them to call for ever-more comprehensive forms of integration between member states and the establishment of ever-more powerful supranational institutions to govern their processes.

HOW REGIONAL TRADE UNION 'IMPERATIVES' CHANGE

In so far as the development of the EU can be taken as a model of regional integration that broadly conforms with these processes, coupling the 'logic of spill-over' with the notion of regional 'contexts' offers a means of understanding how regional trade union 'imperatives' evolve. This interrelationship can be elaborated in the following way. Ideological imperatives have undoubtedly dominated global and regional trade union thinking for much of the present century (Busch, 1983). For the most part, MNCs have long been successful at resisting the cross-border activities of trade unions, such that transnational industrial contexts, either regionally or globally, have been weak or non-existent. The same can also be said of transnational political contexts. The Trade Union Advisory Committee of the Organization for Economic Cooperation and Development (TUAC-OECD) and the International Labour Organization (ILO), for example, have for years been moribund as agencies for advancing the transnational interests of workers, whilst the regional polities of continental America, Africa and the Asia Pacific have been confined to dealing with commercial and trading matters only, and had few powers to deliberate on social and labour issues of any substance. Under these transnational business and political circumstances, it is hardly surprising that both global and regional trade unions seeking to attract or maintain membership support have had little option but to act as standard-bearers for one of the major international working class ideologies: democratic socialism, communism or social Catholicism.

Regional organizations operating in Western Europe are an important exception to this general rule. The European Trade Union Confederation (ETUC), for example, affiliates national confederations in a sub-global region (that is, Western Europe) where there exists a sub-global political context (that is, the EU) of some *significance*. It is significant in the sense that the EU has a legal identity where settled legislation is binding and often comes into existence without necessarily passing though the political apparatus of member states. It is significant, also, in that the governing institutions of the EU have a mandate which extends beyond purely trade and commercial matters to include issues such as political union and social cohesion. In the absence of any substantive industrial context, the ETUC has to some extent always depended upon the promotion of a particular vision of trade unionism, in this case the cause of social democratic trade unionism (see below), but it has also depended upon the ability to act as a political intermediary between its member organizations and the institutions of the EU (see, for example, Kirchner, 1977). Over the course of its history, however, the nexus between ideological and political imperatives has been far from balanced. Ideological imperatives, for instance, were prominent during the period surrounding the ETUC's foundation in 1973, both as a means of determining the criteria for membership and for the settlement of organizational policies (Windmuller, 1976: 44–5). Political imperatives were of secondary importance, not least because the integrative processes of the EU at this time had stalled (Williams, 1990: 299–300), and only came to the fore during the mid-1980s in response to the EU's moves to implement its Single Market programme and improve the democratic dimensions of its institutions (Abbott, 1997: 473–7).

This shift has since been reflected in what can only be described as a developing symbiotic relationship between the ETUC's internal political relations and the type of external political relations it has been able to develop with the institutions of the EU. As the ETUC's 'imperatives' have come to rest more squarely on political objectives specified in claims made upon EU legislators, there has been an implied demand made on its part for increasing levels of political authority from affiliates to speak and act on their behalf. The generally favourable reactions of European legislators to such claims, evidenced most notably in the policies of inclusion under the Val Duchesse and Social Protocol processes (see European Communities, 1992), has seen the ETUC's external political legitimacy (or its external political imperative, if you like) steadily grow. This, in turn, has seen the ETUC's internal political authority (or its internal political imperative) similarly grow as affiliated organizations have come to perceive that its claims are being increasingly recognized by European legislators (derived from

Martin, 1980: Chapter 1). In short, the accelerated integrative processes of the EU over the past decade has extended the logic of spill-over beyond government and business elites to include the leadership of this important representative of European labour, with member organizations coming to rely more and more upon it as a political intermediary for advancing their interests at the national level (Marginson and Sisson, 1996: 11).

From this brief synopsis it can be argued that as the 'globalizing' processes of regional integration unfold an impetus is provided for regional trade union 'imperatives' to undergo a transition. In the case just referred to, the transition has been from the ideological to the political, and has been predicated upon the existence (or developing existence) of a *significant* sub-global political 'context'. To put it in more general theoretical terms, the 'imperatives' of regional trade unions may be historically, or in the first instance, dominated by ideological concerns, but as the processes of regional cooperation and integration unfold in a manner consistent with the 'logic of spill-over' there will be a transition to political concerns. The course and timing of this transition, however, will be dependent upon two factors. It will first be contingent upon where the loci of effective political authority reside in the administration of a transnational polity at any given time; and second, it will be dependent upon the type of matters governed by the polity. If, for example, the structure of authority is dominated by intergovernmentalism and the matters administrated are limited to commerce and trade (for example, conditions that marked EU political processes prior to the mid-1980s), then the regional trade union will be disposed to rely on its affiliates and their national channels of action to support what will ostensibly be its labour and social demands. Its internal political authority will be low as a consequence of this reliance, which in turn will be to the detriment of its ability to influence the governance and outcomes of the transnational polity. In such circumstances, ideological imperatives will more likely dominate the regional trade union's basis of support and appeals for membership action, with political imperatives being of secondary importance. If, however, the structure of political authority is dominated by supranationalism and the matters administered extend to labour and social issues (for example, conditions which reflect recent trends in EU political processes), then the converse set of conditions are likely to be more operable, with political imperatives coming to the fore and ideological concerns being relegated to a lower level of importance. It follows from this that if the 'logic of spill-over' unfolds as expected, or in a manner consistent with the historical development of the EU, then the movement in trade union imperatives will be from the ideological to the political.

It remains to say something about sub-global industrial contexts and regional trade unions whose existence and activities are dominated by industrial imperatives. In this regard there is little in terms of precedent upon which to make any definitive statements, theoretical or otherwise. Few, if any, transnational trade unions, whether regionally or globally organized, can claim their existence and support is principally based upon the ability to achieve material gains through cross-border bargaining relations held with MNCs. The only real evidence of an industrial context that might be said to satisfy the criteria necessary for this to occur yet again refers us to regional organizations operating within the EU, in this instance to the European industry committees of International Trade Secretariats (ITSs) (see below). Even here it is only to an embryonic industrial context with uncertain influence on trade union imperatives to which we refer. What can be said is that over the past decade there has been a rapid expansion of transnational information and consultation forums established within MNCs operating in the region (EIRR, 1993a, 1993b; Bonneton et al., 1996), and that European industry committees have been integral in negotiating the implementation of such forums (ETUI, 1993). Whilst this offers an exceptional instance of regional trade unionism dominated by industrial imperatives, it needs to be weighed against the fact that the powers of these information and consultation forums in the decision structures of MNCs are minimal, and that ongoing trade union involvement in their processes is negligible (Streeck, 1997: 325–38). The establishment of such forums also owes much to the political desire of the EU to implement its Single Market programme in a socially acceptable manner. The passing of the European Works Council Directive in 1994 was a reflection of this desire, and paved the way for European industry committees by making it a legal requirement for European MNCs to engage workers and their representatives in negotiations over the implementation of transnational workers' councils (see Abbott, 1998; EIRR, 1994).[3]

What this suggests is that the establishment of a substantial sub-global political context appears to be a necessary precondition for the emergence (or maintenance) of a sub-global industrial context. Thus, just as a nexus could be said to exist between the ideological and the political in the way regional trade unions deal with the existence or non-existence of a transnational polity, so also could it be argued that a nexus seemingly exists between the political and the industrial in the way regional trade unions deal with significant and insignificant sub-global political contexts. *Significant* here means a context in which a transnational polity has supranational powers to deliberate on labour and social matters of some substance, as opposed to *insignificant*, where the transnational polity is governed by intergovernmentalism and confined to dealing with commercial and trading matters only. It follows from this that the movement in regional trade union 'imperatives' will typically run from the ideological to the political, and *only* then from the political to the industrial. This thesis is depicted in Table 1, with the most likely transition of *Dominating Imperatives* moving typically from top to bottom as *Regional Contexts* change in accordance with the 'logic of spill-over'.

TABLE 1
REGIONAL CONTEXTS AND DOMINATING IMPERATIVES

Regional contexts	Dominating imperatives
No industrial or political contexts	Ideological
Insignificant political context	Ideological (primary) / political (secondary)
Significant political context	Political (primary) / industrial (secondary)
Industrial context	Industrial

REGIONAL TRADE UNIONISM IN THE ASIA PACIFIC

It is with this theoretical interpretation in mind that one can start to make sense of the development and behaviour of regional trade unions operating in the Asia Pacific. Before looking at these organizations, however, it is first necessary to comment on the global trade union movement more generally. This is because regional (or sub-global) trade unions covering the Asia Pacific are either branches of, or have close ties with, global trade unions. The structure of organized labour at the international level is divided by three competing visions of trade unionism. The first is represented by the World Federation of Trade Unions (WFTU), which has historically subscribed to the view that trade unions should support national and international political endeavours to raise workers to a level of revolutionary class-consciousness. This organization has traditionally drawn the bulk of its membership from former eastern bloc countries, and it directly controls a number of Trade Union Internationals (TUIs). The WFTU has long rejected moves towards economic and political integration amongst capitalist economies, and thus denied the need to organize unions on a sub-global or regional basis. Its ideological predilection towards revolutionary politics has mellowed since the collapse of the Soviet Union; however, its class conflict perception of workplace relations and lack of organization of trade unions at a regional level still persists (Upham, 1993). It is not considered further here, although it should be noted that the WFTU and its TUIs affiliate a number of important national confederations and sectoral unions in China and other parts of Asia, which compete for membership against unions organized on the basis of non-communist ideals (Longman International Reference, 1989: 451–5).

The second vision is represented by the World Confederation of Labour (WCL), which subscribes to a Catholic socialist form of trade unionism and affiliates national confederations that support, amongst other things, the ideals of class collaboration, the spiritual welfare of workers, co-determination in industry and private property ownership. It draws the bulk of its membership from Western Europe and South America, and coordinates the activities of several Trade Internationals (TIs). Both the WCL and TIs operate regional committees, the most important of which are the WCL's ODSTA (*Organisation Democratique Syndicale des Travailleurs Africains*), which covers Africa; CLAT (*Central Latinoamericana de Trabajadores*), which covers South America; and BATU (Brotherhood of Asian Trade Unions), which covers Asia (WCL, 1998). With the possible exception of CLAT's role in Latin America, for the most part the activities and influence of these regional organizations are circumscribed by a lack of resources, negligible support, and limited coverage of the workforces in the countries they represent. They also are not considered further, though again it is worth bearing in mind that their existence provides competition for membership among national trade union movements throughout the Pacific and in certain parts of Asia (Longman International Reference, 1989: 449–50).

The third vision is represented by the International Confederation of Free Trade Unions (ICFTU). This organization is by far the largest, wealthiest and most important in terms of its global coverage and influence. It affiliates 206 national confederations from 141 countries and territories and has a total indirect membership of 125 million workers. As an organization that subscribes to the ideals of democratic socialism, the ICFTU supports the concepts of independent trade unionism, human rights, industrial and political democracy, and welfare capitalism. It holds close associations with ITS, which affiliate social-democratic inspired national sectoral unions, and its most important regional organizations are OBIT (*Organizacion Regional Interamerica de Trabajadores*), which covers North and South America; AFRO (African Regional Organization), which covers Africa; and APRO (Asia Pacific Regional Organization), which covers Asia and South Pacific Countries (ICFTU, 1998). The ETUC, which represents trade union interests in Europe, is organizationally independent of the ICFTU, though it is closely aligned in sharing the same ideals and regional aspirations – indeed, the two organizations share the same building in Brussels.

It is the ICFTU's APRO which is of principal concern here, it being the foremost regional representative of the global trade union with the widest coverage and greatest potential for exerting influence in the Asia Pacific.[4] The argument is that APRO is dominated by ideological imperatives, that political imperatives are of secondary importance, and that industrial imperatives play almost no part as a basis for the organization's action and support. In terms of the theory set out in the previous section, the inference here is that the Asia Pacific is a region where little or no political and industrial 'contexts' are apparent. We will return to make the linkages set out here later, but for the moment let us look at the evidence of ideology as dominating APRO's role in the region.

APRO groups national confederations from 29 countries and represents around 33 million workers in the Asia Pacific (ICFTU/APRO, 1998). It has no bargaining role with national industries or MNCs, which rules out industrial imperatives as the primary basis for its support and action. In assessing what imperatives do predominate, it is to APRO's parent international that one must turn, not least because the objectives pursued by the organization essentially replicate those of the ICFTU. The priority policy areas identified by the ICFTU at its 1995 World Congress essentially dealt with four issues: (1) the need to develop more comprehensive strategies to assist member organizations to monitor trade union rights in countries violating international labour standards; (2) the need to organize more effective local campaigns to raise the number of ratifications of ILO conventions; (3) the need to explore avenues of cooperation with other non-governmental organizations that share the ICFTU's values, such as Amnesty International, Greenpeace and Anti-Slavery International; (4) and the need to find ways to strengthen links with ITs and improve cooperative relations with the WCL (*Free Labour World*, 1996: 1–3). The strategy used to galvanize and lend substance to these aspirations aimed to link trade union rights to international trade and commercial agreements. To this end, the ICFTU has devoted considerable time and attention to promoting the merits of the concept amongst its member organizations, urging them to lobby their respective national governments to support the inclusion of a social clause into such agreements.[5] It has also worked in unison with international human rights groups to exert moral pressure on countries where trade union rights are violated (which are typically found in the underdeveloped and developing worlds), and sought to attract international attention to such violations through highly publicized missions seeking the release of incarcerated trade union leaders or changes in national labour laws which disallow workers to organize and bargain collectively without state intervention (*Free Labour World*, 1997: 3–4).

These efforts reflect an ideological predilection which holds the existence of independent trade unionism to be synonymous with the preservation of basic human rights, the import of which, in the absence of any substantive international industrial or political contexts, has long been the fundamental basis upon which the ICFTU's existence has rested. Linked to the issue of international trade and commerce, it is a predilection which has combined, so to speak, to define the political role of the ICFTU in its current relations with international bodies such as the ILO, OECD, WTO, IMF (International Monetary Fund) and the WB (World Bank). The problem that confronts the development of these relations, and thereby the potential realization of social clauses being included in international trade and commerce agreements, is that these bodies are intergovernmental and, with the exception of the ILO, have little or no mandate to deliberate on human and trade union rights. It is for this reason that the political role of the ICFTU remains, as it always has, largely subsidiary to its ideological role.

The point to be made is that APRO pursues almost similar objectives at the regional level, and confronts almost the same set of obstacles as its parent international in trying to exert political influence. Indeed, if anything, the regional context in which the organization operates makes the deference of the political to the ideological even more pronounced. Like the ICFTU, APRO equates the maintenance of independent trade unionism with the preservation of human rights, but pursues this objective in a region where the existence of such independence and the recognition of such rights are more the exception than the rule – the exceptions, of course, being Australia, New Zealand, Japan, Canada and the USA. It similarly tries to secure and protect the rights of member organizations to organize and bargain collectively at the level of industry, but does so in a region dominated by governments that have an active interest in curtailing such rights for the purpose of attracting foreign investment in the pursuit of high growth industrial development strategies (Mauzy, 1997: 210–30). It also tries to encourage transnational trade and commercial bodies to include social clauses in their trade and commerce agreements, but does so in a region where such bodies are made up of countries who view demands of this type as being fundamentally against their cultural and economic well-being (Haworth and Hughs, 1997: 179–95; see also ICFTU-APRO, 1997, 1998). In this regard, also, the two most important regional polities – ASEAN and APEC[6] – are both politically constituted and operate under the same intergovernmental mode of governance and limited commercial and trading mandates as many of their international counterparts. Unlike their international counterparts, however, neither body has permanent bureaucratic infrastructures or committee systems that formally incorporate trade union delegates or systematically recognize trade union representations (Acharya, 1997: 329, 337–8). The weak political context this presents for the political development of trade unions at the regional level is compounded by the fact that APEC includes countries not covered by APRO (that is, from North and South America) – a problem which has required the ICFTU to establish an interim body known as the Asia Pacific Labour Network.

What this means is that although the priorities and activities of the ICFTU and APRO are similar, it is especially difficult for the latter to establish a transnational political role for itself in a region which is politically against, and organizationally benign towards, conferring this role on trade unions. In terms of the theoretical interpretation set out in the last section, it is the absence of a significant sub-global political context within the Asia Pacific region that undermines the prospects of APRO establishing a symbiotic, self-generating internal and external political dynamic of the type noted earlier in the case of the ETUC. It is this absence, also, that accounts for the similar objectives pursued by the ICFTU and APRO, as well as for the lack of active membership support for APRO's regional political objectives within national frameworks of action. It is this absence, finally, which explains why APRO relies predominantly on ideological imperatives as the basis for its existence and support. Its main role is accordingly one where the bulk of the organization's time and attention is directed towards such things as the provision of training programmes to create trade union elites capable of discouraging grassroots political struggles of the type advocated by the WFTU. In the same vein, it is also directed towards encouraging member organizations to focus on economic issues and to support governments willing to guarantee trade union rights. These and other similar activities are essentially ideological in the sense that they aim to promote a particular vision of trade unions – one that holds them to be appropriately constituted only when they are independent of political parties, avoid revolutionary political activism and support welfare capitalism.

CONCLUSION

The predominant form of globalization in the Asia Pacific conditions sub-global regional trade unions like APRO to function in a particular way. The present lack of industrial and political contexts means it is presently confined to the role of providing moral, logistical and educational support to member organizations. The inability to act industrially and politically in any substantive sub-global institutional environment, in turn, means that APRO's member organizations are unwilling to cede the authority and resources necessary for it to coordinate cross-border campaigns.

There is, thus, no organizational mechanism within, or 'globalizing' integrative stimulus from outside, which will enable the regional trade union movement to bring organized pressure and influence to bear on MNCs and transnational polities operating in the Asia Pacific.

This situation seems unlikely to change in the foreseeable future. Regional globalization processes in the Asia Pacific may be driven by commonly held 'free-market' ideals and notions of minimal state action, but the reality of entrenched national parochialisms still persists as a major constraint upon the possibility of supranational institution-building (Snitwongse, 1990; 56). At the same time, the preservation of trade union inabilities to act transnationally remains highly desirable among powerful economic and political interests in the region. Business interests in developed countries (such as Australia, New Zealand, Japan, Canada and the USA) see the possibility of greater cost efficiencies to be gained in more open trading and commercial regimes which allow for the relocation of capital and operations to underdeveloped and developing countries (such as Korea, Taiwan, Indonesia and Malaysia) where trade union activities are tightly controlled and labour standards are kept low as a matter of state policy. Conversely, political interests in underdeveloped and developing countries see the possibility of underwriting rapid economic growth through foreign investment attracted by cheap and compliant labour (Palmujoki, 1997: 271).

So long as these circumstances remain, the assumed automatism of the neo-functionalist model will be perpetually suspended. This being the case, it is hard to see the role of APRO, or that of any other regional trade union organization operating in the Asia Pacific, transiting along the trajectory hypothesized in the earlier theoretical section. Indeed, for such a trajectory to occur would require the region's globalization processes to proceed beyond their present low level commercial and trading interfaces. Moreover, it would require a higher degree of adherence among Asian Pacific states to the principle of 'indivisibility' and the emergence of conditions in which the costs and benefits of regional integration are more evenly spread both geographically and functionally. Indeed, it is only when cross-border factor mobility comes to hinge less on the intra-system differences that one might begin to expect national parochialisms to diminish and the technical problems of industrialization noted by neo-functionalists to have a chance to manifest in a way that encourages business and political elites to see the need for more comprehensive forms of supranational regional governance. On the argument presented here, it is only then that regional trade unionism in the Asia Pacific will move beyond its present ideological concerns.

ACKNOWLEDGEMENTS

For helpful comments on earlier drafts of this paper I am grateful to Ross Martin, Willy Brown, Chris Rowley and Jenny Rowe. The usual disclaimers apply.

NOTES

1. The terms 'regional' and 'sub-global' are used to denote transnational arrangements, relations and/or organizations pertaining to, or covering, two or more nation-states within a definable geographic area. They are to be distinguished from the terms 'international' and 'global', which are used to describe arrangements, relations and/or organizations pertaining to, or covering, large numbers of nation-states dispersed across the world.

2. As used here, a supranational regional structure is where sovereign political authority is concentrated within a single transnational polity with the power to enforce legally binding policy measures on member states and whose governmental decisions are based on simple or qualified majority voting procedures. An intergovernmental regional structure is where sovereign political authority is dispersed across a federally constituted transnational polity with no power to enforce agreed policy measures on member states and whose governmental decisions are based on unanimous voting procedures or informal consensus.

3. It is of interest to the argument that even prior to the passing of this Directive, many MNCs were moved to engage the European industry committees in the hope of reaching non-binding outcomes as a means of proving to European policymakers that legislation pertaining to transnational worker participation councils was unnecessary (Marginson and Sisson, 1996: 12–13).

4. It is worth noting that there are other trade union bodies of lesser note operating in the region, such as the ICFTU's Asia Pacific Labour Network and the Regional Women's Committee for Asia and the Pacific, the Asia Pacific Trade Union Coordination Committee (APTUCC), and the Australian-sponsored South Pacific and Oceanic Council of Trade Unions (SPOCTU). There are also several regional committees run by various ITs. For reasons of space these organizations are ignored, though their primary activities, support and concerns can be considered as broadly similar to those of APRO.

5. The 'social clause' is based on five ILO international labour Conventions singled out in the declaration of the 1995 Copenhagen Social Summit. They include: freedom of association for workers and employers to establish and join organizations of their own choosing without previous authorization (Convention 87); the right to organize and bargain collectively (Convention 98); freedom from forced labour (Conventions 29 and 105); minimum age for the employment of children (Convention 138); and freedom from discrimination in employment and occupation on the grounds of race, sex, religion, political opinion, etc. (Convention 111). (*Asian Labour Update*, 1995: 4).

6. APEC is made up of 18 member states from Asia, Australasia, and North and South America. ASEAN is made up of Cambodia, Brunei, Indonesia, Laos, Malaysia, Myanmar, Philippines, Singapore, Thailand and Vietnam.

REFERENCES

Abbott, Keith (1997) 'The European Trade Union Confederation: Its Organisation and Objectives in Transition', *Journal of Common Market Studies*, Vol. 35, No. 3, September, pp. 465–81.

Abbott, Keith (1998) 'The ETUC and Its Role in Advancing the Cause of European Worker Participation Rights', *Economics and Industrial Democracy*, Vol. 19, No. 3, November, pp. 605–31.

Acharya, Amitav (1997) 'Ideas, Identity, and Institution-building: From the "ASEAN Way" to the "Asia-Pacific Way"?', *Pacific Review*, Vol. 10, No. 3, pp.319–40.

Asian Labour Update (1995) 'What Rights are in the Social Clause', Issue 20 (Nov. 1995 March 1996).

Ball, Alan and Millard, Frances (1986) *Pressure Politics in Industrial Societies*. London: Macmillan Educational.

Bonneton, P., Carley, M., Hall, M. and Krieger, H. (1996) *Analysis of Existing Agreements on Information and Consultation in European Multinationals*. Luxembourg: Office for Official Publications of the European Community.

Busch, Gary (1983) *The Politics of the International Trade Unions*. London: Macmillan.

Clegg, Hugh (1976) *Trade Unionism under Collective Bargaining: A Theory Based on Comparisons of Six Countries*. Oxford: Basil Blackwell.

Cohen, Robin (1987) 'Theorising International Labour', in R. Boyd and P. Gutkind (eds), *International Labour and the Third World: The Making of the New Working Class*. Aldershot: Avebury, pp. 3–25.

Crouch, Colin (1982) *Trade Unions: The Logic of Collective Action*. London: Fontana.

Dieter, Heribert (1997) 'APEC and the WTO: Collision or Co-operation', *Pacific Review*, Vol. 10, No. 1, pp.19–38.

European Communities (1992) 'Treaty on European Union, Together with the Complete Text of the Treaty Establishing the European Community', *Official Journal of the European Communities*, Vol. 35, No. C224, August, *passim*.

EIRR (1993a) 'Information and Consultation in European Multinationals – Part One', *European Industrial Relations Review*, No. 228, January, pp. 13–19.

EIRR (1993b) 'Information and Consultation in European Multinationals – Part Two', *European Industrial Relations*, No. 229, February, pp. 14–20.

EIRR (1994) 'Farewell, European Works Councils?', *European Industrial Relations Review*, No. 242, pp. 13–15.

ETUI (European Trade Union Institute) (1993) *European Industry Committees and the Social Dialogue*. Brussels: ETUI.

Free Labour World (1996) 'ICFTU Aims to be at the Centre of a Worldwide Social Movement', No. 7/8, July–August, p. 1.

Free Labour World (1997) 'Asia's Anti-Union Governments', No. 1, January, p. 5.

Haas, Ernst (1958) *The Unity of Europe: Political, Social and Economic Forces, 1950–57*. London: Stevens and Son.

Haworth, Nigel and Hughes, Stephen (1997) 'Trade and International Labour Standards: Issues and Debates', *Journal of Industrial Relations*, Vol. 39, No. 2, June, pp. 179–95.

ICFTU (International Confederation of Free Trade Unions) (1998) 'Membership'. Internet website, http://www.icftu.org/

ICFTU/APRO (1997) 'Omnibus Resolution' (statement issued by ICFTU/APRO 69th Regional Executive Board Meeting). Internet website, http://singnet.com.sg/icftu/doc_reb69.html

ICFTU/APRO (1998) 'Building Recovery in Asia, Heading Off Global Recession and Preventing Currency Crisis' (statement adopted by the ICFTU/APRO Forum on the Asian Economic Turmoil, Singapore, 10–11 February). Internet website, http://singnet.om.sg/-icftu/doc_frm_state.html

Jackson, Michael (1980) *Industrial Relations*. London: Croom Helm.

Kirchner, Emil (1977) *Trade Unions as a Pressure Group in the European Community*. Farnborough: Teakfield.

Knutsen, Paul (1997) 'Corporatist Tendencies in the Euro-Polity: The EU Directive of 22

September 1994, on European Works Councils', *Economic and Industrial Democracy*, Vol. 18, No. 2, May, pp. 289–323.

Levison, Charles (1972) *The International Labour Movement*. New York: Harper and Brothers.

Lindberg, Leon (1963) *The Political Dynamics of European Economic Integration*. Stanford, CA: Stanford University Press.

Logue, John (1980) *Toward a Theory of Trade Union Internationalism*. Publication No. 7. Gothenburg: University of Gothenburg Press.

Longman International Reference (1989) *Trade Unions of the World: 1989–1990*, 2nd edn. London: Longman.

Lorwin, Lewis (1953) *The International Labour Movement*. New York: Harper and Brothers.

Marginson, Paul and Sisson, Keith (1996) 'European Collective Bargaining: A Virtual Prospect' (revised paper). Paper presented at the IREC Conference 'Industrial Relations in Europe: Convergence or Diversification?' University of Copenhagen, September.

Martin, Ross (1980) *TUC: The Growth of a Pressure Group: 1868–1976*. Oxford: Clarendon Press.

Martin, Ross (1989) *Trade Unionism: Purposes and Forms*. Oxford: Clarendon Press.

Mauzy, Diane (1997) 'The Human Rights and "Asian Values" Debate in Southeast Asia: Trying to Clarify the Key Issues', *Pacific Review*, Vol. 10, No. 2, pp. 210–30.

Palmujoki, Eero (1997) 'EU–Asean Relations: Reconciling Two Different Agendas', *Contemporary Southeast Asia*, Vol. 19, No. 3, December, pp. 269–85.

Poole, Michael (1981) *Theories of Trade Unionism: A Sociology of Industrial Relations*. London: Routledge and Kegan Paul.

Snitwongse, K. (1990) 'Meeting the Challenges of Changing Southeast Asia', in R. Scalapino (ed.), *Regional Dynamics: Security, Political, Economic Issues in the Asia Pacific Region*. Jakarta: Centre for Strategic and International Studies.

Streeck, Wolfgang (1997) 'Neither European nor Works Councils: A Reply to Paul Knutsen', *Economic and Industrial Democracy*, Vol. 18, No. 2, May, pp. 325–37.

Transholm-Mikkelsen, Jeppe (1991) 'Neo-Functionalism: Obstinate or Obsolete? A Reappraisal in the Light of the New Dynamism of the EC', *Millennium: Journal of International Studies*, Vol. 20, No. 1, Spring, pp. 1–22.

Upham, Martin (1993) *Trade Unions and Employer Associations of the World*. Harlow, Longman Current Affairs.

WCL (World Confederation of Labour) (1998) 'Membership'. Internet website, http://www.cmt-wcl.org/en/regorganis.html

Webb, Sidney and Webb, Beatrice (1894) *The History of Trade Unionism*. London: Longman.

Williams, Shirley (1990) 'Sovereignty and Accountability in the European Community', *Political Quarterly*, Vol. 61, No. 3, September, pp. 299–317.

Windmuller, John (1976) 'European Regionalism: A New Factor in International Labour', *Industrial Relations Journal*, Vol. 7, No. 2, summer, pp. 36–48.

3

Challenging APEC: The Asia Pacific Labour Network and APEC's Human Resource Development Working Group

JOHN PRICE

In September 1997, ministers of human resource development (HRD) from 18 members of the Asia Pacific Economic Cooperation (APEC) gathered in Seoul, South Korea (Korea from now on) to discuss APEC's work related to labour force development. The basis for their discussions was a concept paper provided by Korea that focused on linking learning and work, improving skill development, and involving labour and management in human resource development (Republic of Korea, Ministry of Labour, 1997). Ministers endorsed many of the views in the concept paper, which one Canadian educator and activist claimed were 'filled with cliches, false promises, and identification of the interests of the people with the interests of capital' (Kuehn, 1998: 48–62). This criticism notwithstanding, in a somewhat surprising development for APEC – an organization many non-governmental organizations (NGOs) had roundly condemned for its inaccessibility – the ministers called for the participation of labour in APEC's activities:

> We direct the HRD Working Group, under the existing networks, to develop a project in which representatives of labour, management, and government from member economies can exchange views on best practices on training, skills development, the use of technology, and other human resources development related issues in the workplace, avoiding duplication of work undertaken in other forums. (APEC, 1997c)

This initiative represented the first time that an official APEC body had recognized the labour movement and called for its participation as a legitimate actor in the APEC process. While some mused that such an initiative might not survive the scrutiny of higher level APEC bodies, in fact, at the official APEC summit that November, trade and foreign ministers officially endorsed the initiative, recognizing that 'the roles and contributions of labour and management in attaining APEC's objectives of promoting sustainable growth and the overall well-being of the people in the region are important' (APEC, 1998b: 8). The initiative also allowed APEC ministers to claim that they were making progress in 'APEC's engagement with broader sectors of society that are affected by impacts of economic growth and liberalization' (APEC, 1998b: 10).

As a result of the ministerial resolutions, the Canadian government subsequently submitted a proposal for a tripartite project that would 'focus on how the three communities can work more effectively together in areas such as training and skills development as outlined in the 1997 Ministerial statement' (NEDM Coordinator, 1998). The proposal was endorsed by APEC national delegations in the Network for Economic Development Management (NEDM), a sub-group of APEC's Human Resources Development Working Group (HRD WG), at a meeting held in Bali, Indonesia, in January 1998.

The developments described above pose a number of questions. What is the relationship between APEC and civil society including the labour movement? How does HRD fit in to APEC's agenda? Why did APEC ministers call for and ratify labour participation in APEC's HRD activities? And finally, what challenges might labour organizations face should they decide to participate in the HRD WG? This chapter attempts to answer these questions by examining the interaction of the international labour movement with APEC, with particular focus on APEC's HRD WG. It concludes by attempting to summarize the problems and potential for labour organizations working within APEC.

APEC AND CIVIL SOCIETY

A regional body founded in 1989, APEC currently consists of governments of 21 states in the Asia Pacific: Australia, Brunei, Canada, Chile, China, Hong Kong, Indonesia, Japan, Korea, Malaysia, Mexico, New Zealand, Papua New Guinea, Peru, the Philippines, Russia, Singapore, Taiwan, Thailand, the USA and Vietnam.[1] It has, in its own words, become 'the primary regional vehicle for promoting open trade and practical economic cooperation' (APEC, 1997d: 1). Policy decisions are taken at the annual meetings of APEC, but it has a far flung and often virtual network of policy research and project development. At APEC's 1993 meeting, the annual summit adopted the tri-tier process that begins with senior officials' meetings (SOM), is followed by a formal meeting of trade and foreign affairs ministers, and concludes with a meeting of government leaders.

The meeting of government leaders at Blake Island (near Seattle) during APEC's 1993 summit adopted a vision statement that embraced the recommendation of the Eminent Persons Group (EPG) for the creation of a free trade zone in the Asia Pacific (APEC, 1993). A special body, the Committee on Trade and Investment, was established to provide substance to the vision. Finally, leaders called for the creation of a Pacific Business Forum to ensure high level input from the business community. At the Bogor summit the following year, APEC set the achievement of free trade by 2010 for industrialized countries and 2020 for developing countries as a concrete objective. In 1995, APEC leaders endorsed the creation of the APEC Business Advisory Council (ABAC) as the official conduit between big business and APEC. As Canadian government representative James Lambert put it: 'While APEC was conceived as a government-to-government forum, it has from the outset viewed service to the business community in the region as one of its primary objectives' (Lambert, 1997: 200). Even though APEC has had limited success in actually moving forward on its agenda, there is general agreement that in its formative period up to 1995, APEC consolidated around a free trade agenda promoted particularly by the USA as well as by Canada, New Zealand and Australia.

Criticism of APEC

On the surface at least, the decision to incorporate labour organizations into APEC activities, at least within the HRD WG, appears to constitute a significant departure in APEC's relations with civil society. APEC has gained the reputation of being hostile to civil society participation in its deliberations and of doggedly pursuing an agenda of trade and investment liberalization to the exclusion of other issues.[2] Beginning in 1993 at the Seattle summit, NGOs, including labour organizations, began to organize to protest against APEC's agenda (Price, 1998). Subsequent to demonstrations at Seattle, major parallel protest meetings and demonstrations occurred in Japan (1995), the Philippines (1996), Canada (1997) and in Malaysia (1998). The Kyoto declaration, adopted in 1995, has guided much of the parallel NGO movement: 'However, we unanimously reject the basic philosophy, framework and assumptions of the model of free market and trade liberalization embraced by the APEC agenda. This model does not lead to freedom; it negates the development and democratic aspirations of the people.'

APEC's higher profile subsequent to the Seattle summit also drew the attention of the international labour movement. The International Confederation of Free Trade Unions (ICFTU) has a regional organization for its affiliates in Asia, the Asia Pacific Regional Organization (APRO). However, its geographical parameters do not include the east side of the Pacific, the Americas, and unions from that region are organized in their own regional body. Because neither of these regional bodies incorporated unions from all of the members of APEC, the ICFTU had to create a new regional association. Thus in September 1995, affiliates of the ICFTU in Chile, Mexico, USA, Canada, New Zealand, Australia, Papua New Guinea, Singapore, Malaysia, Philippines, Thailand, Hong Kong, Chinese Taipei, Korea and Japan, and sectoral groupings from the international trade secretariats (international industrial federations), gathered to create the Asia Pacific Labour Network (APLN) with the specific purpose of monitoring and lobbying APEC. On 7 October, APLN representatives met with then prime minister Murayama Tomoichi, host of the 1995 Osaka APEC summit, to press for changes in APEC's agenda. The following month, NGOs in Japan organized a parallel APEC meeting in which at least one APLN affiliate, the Canadian Labour Congress, participated. The following summer, the ICFTU held its 1996 convention at which it announced its support for the APLN and its intention to intervene in the APEC process: 'The ICFTU, in conjunction with the host countries' unions, will devote attention to assuring that labour and social matters are brought onto the agenda for those [APEC] meetings and to achieving a high profile for the ICFTU Asia Pacific Labour Network over the coming years' (Sixteenth World Congress of the ICTFU, 1996: 42). The ICFTU also resolved at the Congress to work with NGOs with whom they had shared objectives.

At the same time as the international labour movement began to actively monitor APEC, a number of affiliates also exerted pressure on the national level. The immediate upshot of these developments was that both the US and Philippine governments included labour representatives (AFL-CIO and TUCP) in their delegations to the Manila HRD ministerial meeting in January 1996. A few months later, the Pacific Economic Cooperation Council (PECC), which has official observer status within APEC, invited labour representatives to its meetings in Brunei and called for all its members to include labour representatives in their delegations. And although the Korean government did not include representatives of the labour movement in its APEC delegation, it was eager to promote labour–management cooperation as part of its quest to gain entry into the Organisation of Economic Cooperation and Development (OECD), which requires that members meet certain social criteria. Korea was also desperately soliciting support for its labour laws which would allow employers to lay off workers more easily, a move which it hoped labour would endorse but which in fact backfired, leading to a major labour protest in December 1996 (see Bae *et al.*, 1997).

In the run up to the 1996 APEC summit in the Philippines, the APLN organized another international forum at which time it developed a more comprehensive agenda regarding APEC that was outlined in the statement 'A Trade Union Vision for APEC' (Asia Pacific Labour Network, 1996). According to this statement, the aim of the APLN was to 'harness the APEC objective of the internation-alization of markets to the improvement of the conditions of work and life of the citizens of our populous region'. While embracing what it perceived as the reality of globalization and APEC's objective of 'internationalizing markets', the APLN statement pointed out that increased competition could drive down wages and living standards; that economic change could only be managed with the involvement of trade unions; and that unions have a significant role in the development of best practice/high performance industries and enterprises. The APLN called for an equal partnership with socially responsible employers and governments on the basis of International Labour Organization (ILO) principles of tripartism and respect for union rights; for sustainable development through increased employment, education and training, and improvements in the quality and remuneration of employment; and for progressive HRD measures as well as measures to eliminate commercial exploitation of children. It concluded that, since the 1995 Osaka Summit, unions had been invited to participate in APEC HRD WG activities and that the APLN wanted representation on selected APEC committees, continuation of annual meetings with the host of the APEC leaders' summit, and the creation of an APEC Labour Forum as an advisory body to APEC. An APLN delegation subsequently met with Philippine president Ramos.

With the APEC summit moving to Vancouver in 1997, the Canadian government also began to make overtures to the Canadian labour movement, including representatives of the Canadian Labour Congress in its delegations to senior official and ministerial meetings in Canada. On the regional level, the Public Service International (PSI) convened an Asia Pacific meeting on APEC in September. For that meeting, the PSI, which represents 20 million public sector workers worldwide, commissioned a general study on APEC and a second one on APEC's infrastructure policies and how they contributed to the threat of privatization of electrical utilities (Ranald, 1997). In October, representatives of regional trade unions gathered for the annual APLN meeting in Ottawa. Hosted by the Canadian Labour Congress, the network attempted to take advantage of the increasing emphasis on economic and technical cooperation within APEC, and the APLN statement pointed to the positive tone of the leaders' declaration in 1996. The network called for:

- trade union participation in select APEC committees;
- regular contacts between the network and the APEC secretariat;
- inclusion of union representatives in national delegations;
- regular annual meetings between the APLN and the host of the APEC summit;
- implementation of a proposed APEC HRD joint labour-management project on workplace best practices;
- creation of an HRD subgroup on APEC's social dimension;
- creation of an HRD WG labour management advisory council and inclusion of core standards on the HRD agenda;
- endorsement of the principle of an APEC Labour Forum. (ICFTU Asia Pacific Labour Network, 1997)

The Canadian Labour Congress also invited members of the APLN to attend the parallel People's Summit, which it was helping to organize. APLN representatives then pressed their demands in a meeting with Canadian prime minister Jean Chretien. It was in this meeting that the Canadian government assured the APLN of support for a labour–management project within APEC's HRD WG. Canada then used its position as APEC SOM chair for 1997 to ensure that the November ministerial meeting officially endorsed the project.

There are two significant moments from the preceding information that require further investigation. The first is that there appear to be substantive differences between the approach of the NGO parallel movement regarding APEC and the international labour movement's approach, an issue which we will return to in the conclusion. The second matter is the importance of the HRD WG, which is the only area in which the APLN has achieved any progress at all in implementing its agenda.

THE HUMAN RESOURCE DEVELOPMENT WORKING GROUP

Understanding the origins and development of the HRD WG is essential in order to evaluate the significance of the APEC decision to promote a labour–management project within that working group and to understand the associated potential for any substantive change within APEC.

Background

In his analysis of the Korean concept paper prepared for the second meeting of HRD ministers, Kuehn (1998) concluded that the APEC's HRD orientation was misguided because it advocated: recasting education as preparation for work as opposed to preparation for citizenship; excessive business involvement in determining education priorities; inappropriate emphasis on vocational programmes that undercut the social sciences and humanities; unrealistic expectations that training and education activities will resolve unemployment problems. We will attempt to examine the evolution and dynamics of the HRD WG within APEC, keeping in mind Kuehn's hypothesis.

From its inception in 1989, APEC conceived its training and education activities as a component of HRD. In its founding meeting in 1989, APEC designated HRD as a strategic area for programme development in so much as it related to investment and technology transfer. Meeting in Singapore in 1990, APEC ministers directed the creation of the HRD WG along with three associated subgroups, the Business Management Network (BMN), the HRD for Industrial Technology Network (HURDIT), and the NEDM. Two other sub-groups were added: the Education Forum (EdFor) in 1992–93, and the Labour Market Information (LMI) group in 1996.

The HRD WG structure is complex and subject to numerous influences. The key decision making body is the WG plenary which is composed of representatives from the national delegations (beginning in 1996, union representatives became members within the national delegations of a number of countries). Coordination of the WG is through a 'lead shepherd', a position that Canada filled from 1996 to June 1998 at which time China took over. The sub-groups or networks are free to pursue research topics subject to the priorities developed by the WG. The group as a whole has three 'cross-cutting' themes: sustainable development, small and medium enterprises (SMEs), and lifelong learning. In January 1997 the WG defined eight medium term priorities including:

> Increasing access to quality basic education; developing labour market analysis and information; developing of managers and entrepreneurs in key sectors (including training for small and medium-sized enterprises and management of sustainable development); improving skills development and lifelong learning; increasing quality of education and training providers, methods, curriculum, material; facilitating mobility of qualified persons through mutual recognition of qualifications/ skills; enhancing quality, productivity, efficiency, and equitable development of labour forces and workplaces; and strengthening cooperation in education and training in support of trade and investment liberalization-facilitation. (Canada, Department of Foreign Affairs and International Trade, 1996: 2)

Decisions from ministerial meetings are also important in that they define the priorities at a higher level. Two HRD ministerial meetings have taken place, one in the Philippines in 1996, and the second in Seoul in September 1997. The USA hosted a third HRD ministerial meeting, in 1999.

While it is beyond the scope of this piece to thoroughly document and analyse the activities of the networks, a brief overview of each is provided below:

BMN: One of the original networks, the BMN is mainly concerned with business management issues, 'identified through in-depth dialogue with business'. This network has identified five thematic areas: management for sustainable development; cross-cultural management; executive education and development; management of SMEs; management of organizational change. Between May 1997 and January 1998, the network was involved in 21 projects in five thematic areas (APEC, 1998a). Completed projects include economic development zones, senior managers' training, a trade and investment insurance training programme and a programme on international quality assurance systems. On the whole its activities are mainly educational, focusing on business management issues such as 'change management' and entrepreneurship, cross-cultural issues including dispute resolution, and technical training related to information technology, total quality management and insurance. It also participated in a literacy project. The BMN is also involved in institution-building, however, and a major project is aimed at developing an Asia Pacific network of chief human resource officers. It is particularly interested in developing projects linked to trade and investment liberalization and deepening its ties with business, and with ABAC in particular.

NEDM: This network has acted as the host for the tripartite successful practices project and, therefore, is quite important. One of the original networks created in 1990, it is devoted to issues related to macroeconomic development and is less tied to a neoliberal agenda. For example, in the past the network has sponsored projects related to gender and education, as well as education and poverty alleviation. NEDM is currently focusing on labour market issues, workplace and labour productivity issues, and gender and equity. Recent initiatives include a review of HRD WG projects with respect to women's participation in project activities. The network is also the sponsor of a Task Force on the Human Resource and Social Impacts of the Financial Crisis (consisting of

Indonesia, Malaysia, Philippines, Thailand and the USA) that appears to be on a fast track within the working group (HRD WG, 1998: items 62–5) Women active in this network have worked closely with the 'Women Leaders' Network from APEC Economies', which has become an unofficial lobby for certain feminist issues in APEC.[3] The network also worked to establish a link between the WG and the APEC Women's ministerial held in October 1998.

HURDIT: The network has identified five priorities for future work, including promoting labour force mobility in technical and vocational education and training; identifying best practices in basic education and lifelong learning; enhancing HRD in SMEs for technological change; strengthening institutions that train and educate youth, women and impaired persons facing unemployment or under-employment; facilitating scientific and technical changes, currently in Internet and electronic communication. The network has played an important role in developing the issue of lifelong learning, one of the WG's cross-cutting themes, and sponsored the Lifelong Learning Conference in Taipei, November 1997.

EdFor: The EdFor group came into existence with the convening of an APEC education ministerial meeting in August 1992 and was placed under the jurisdiction of the HRD WG on recommendation from APEC senior officials (APEC, 1992). It is mainly concerned with developing the means 'to monitor the performance of education systems, provide high quality instruction in key subjects, like mathematics and natural sciences, and facilitate mobility of students, trainees, teachers, professionals, and information' (APEC Secretariat, nd: 2). While APEC ministers stated that in general it was not desirable or possible to define common educational standards across the region, they stated that in certain areas such as mathematics, the natural sciences and some technical areas it might be possible to develop comparable standards. The USA has played an important role in EdFor and it has been deeply engaged in capacity building. For example, the University of Washington, as part of the APEC Leaders Education Initiative, recently announced the creation of an APEC Internet Collaboration Center (ICC) that will supposedly 'redefine how international policy is formulated'. The USA and New Zealand will be among the first to use the new network to promote the complete liberalization of agricultural markets. Using the ICC, over 300 decision makers around the Pacific Rim will be sharing ideas, co-writing proposals and generating recommendations to present to APEC officials. The network will also focus on a meeting of education ministers which is scheduled to take place in Singapore in 2000.

LMI Group: The purpose of this group, established subsequent to the first meeting of HRD ministers in the Philippines in 1996, is to create a labour market information database for the Asia Pacific.

Most of the work of the HRD WG is conducted through these five networks, each of which has a coordinating institution. Estimates vary regarding the quantity and scope of HRD WG activities. According to the APEC Secretariat, in 1997 the WG was engaged in about 40 projects, had completed another 30, and had 20 in preparation. Table 1 captures the extent of project development in each network:

TABLE 1

PROJECTS BY NETWORK (HRD WORKING GROUP PROJECTS, 1992–1996)

	Business management network	Education forum	Industrial technology	Labour market information group	Network for economic development management
No. of projects	21	14	18	1	12

Source: Gibb (1998: 5).

This brief overview indicates that the HRD WG is a vast network of virtual projects. Most of these projects are not directed at trade and investment liberalization *per se*, although the BMN has promoted a number of such activities. However, the scope of activities is much wider and includes substantial work on the issue of gender and development, for example, and recently labour-related issues have gained some prominence. The task force on the economic crisis in Asia, established in Bali in 1998, was also an important activity that may well contradict the general thrust of APEC's neoliberal agenda. There is thus some evidence that not all of the HRD agenda within APEC conforms to Kuehn's (1998) critique, which was focused on a single concept paper prepared for a ministerial meeting. Much does, however, and the activities of EdFor deserve much closer scrutiny in that regard.

Another factor for consideration is the fact that the structure and processes of the HRD WG may put substantial limits on what might be done within the confines of this type of organization. Although in theory networks are free to pursue whatever topic they desire, in fact the process itself can screen out or limit the type of activity undertaken. There are many levels to this filtering system. First, projects are screened and shaped through the national delegation selection process. Because APEC is by its very nature a governmental organization, the respective APEC governments exercise absolute control over labour's participation, or not, within their delegation. Second, the effectiveness of any given project may be limited because it only involves a select number of states. Third, if independent funding for a project does not exist then the project must be funded through a national government or APEC. In the case of the latter, the APEC funding process requires that first a network and then the HRD WG as a whole should prioritize projects. Furthermore, the general direction of network activities is also shaped by the HRD WG, which has the specific mandate to undertake policy discussions and formulate policy recommendations to SOMs. Ministerial meetings shape the agenda by identifying strategic themes which are then incorporated into HRD WG strategic goals.

LABOUR INFLUENCE IN THE HRD WG

Given the HRD WG's organizational maze and the elaborate screening mechanism, how was it that it decided to undertake a tripartite project within APEC despite objections from a number of countries? In fact, the decision was the culmination of a process that began in 1996. This process involved an increase in the direct and indirect influence of labour within the HRD WG, a broadening of the mandate of the WG to include labour issues, and subsequently a concerted effort to have the WG approve a project that would facilitate broader labour participation. At least four countries, the Philippines, Korea, Canada and the USA, played an instrumental role in promoting labour issues within the HRD WG.

In early 1996, the US Department of Labor took over responsibility for coordinating US participation in the HRD WG.

Because of its history of close collaboration with the AFL-CIO and for financial reasons (labour representatatives had alternative funding sources for APEC participation), the US Department of Labor authorized the participation of labour representatives within the US delegation to the HRD WG, despite opposition from the State Department who feared labour participation would upset other APEC member states. As a result, AFL-CIO representative Lynn MacDonald attended the Wellington, New Zealand, meeting of the working group in January 1996.

At about the same time, in preparation for the 1996 leaders' summit scheduled for Subic Bay in November, the Philippine government convened the first meeting of APEC HRD ministers on 10–11 January. At that time, APEC members first recognized that 'government, employers and workers have their respective role to play' (APEC, 1996). In mid-1996, at the Brunei meeting of the HRD WG, the US and Philippines delegations worked to introduce a health and safety project into the mix.

According to a number of observers, the turning point for labour issues within the working group came at the 15th HRD WG meeting held in Sydney, Australia, in January 1997. At that time the Philippines and US delegations proposed projects related to wages and productivity as well as workplace health and safety. Korea introduced a proposal to involve unions and employers in a dialogue on training in the workplace. Subsequently, Korea began to push labour–management cooperation as a key issue and it was incorporated into the concept paper that led to the proposal for a labour–management project. Earlier attempts to introduce labour issues had been vetoed by Japan and Singapore, who argued that labour issues should be restricted to discussion in the ILO. Most significantly, the Sydney meeting also debated and adopted strategic goals for the working group. In the context of that discussion, the HRD WG identified 'enhancing quality, productivity, efficiency, and equitable development of labour forces and workplaces' as one of eight medium-term strategic priorities for HRD (Canada, Department of Foreign Affairs and International Trade, 1996: 2). This further opened the door to introducing labour-related issues within the WG.

With Canada designated as host of the 1997 leaders' meeting, the HRD WG's mid-year session took place in Montreal in May. Representatives from the Canadian Labour Congress and the AFL-

CIO attended that meeting as part of their country delegations. Canada and the USA backed a Korean proposal for a project to examine best practices in tripartite cooperation related to training and education for the workplace. At the same meeting, the Philippines introduced the idea that APEC should have a trade union advisory body similar to the Trade Union Advisory Council (TUAC) in the OECD. While this idea was a non-starter, it highlighted the continued push by some countries to raise labour-related issues within the WG. A final development in Montreal was the decision to broaden the mandate of the NEDM to include labour isues. The second APEC HRD ministerial meeting took place in Seoul in September. At that time, those lobbying for a tripartite project within the WG exerted pressure to have ministers promote the project. As a result, the Seoul ministerial declaration (cited at the beginning of this chapter) not only endorsed the project but 'directed' the HRD WG to make it happen. The momentum for a tripartite project carried through into the APLN meeting with Canadian prime minister Jean Chretien in Ottawa in October and the tripartite proposal was then endorsed by trade and foreign ministers at their ministerial meeting just prior to the APEC leaders' meeting in Vancouver.

Subsequent to Vancouver, the HRD WG convened its 17th regular meeting in Bali, Indonesia, at which Canada introduced the tripartite (labour–management–government) project (HRD WG, 1998). At Bali, the HRD WG also decided to convene a special Task Force on the Human Resource and Social Impacts of the Financial Crisis, which was the focus of a special symposium at the working group's 18th meeting in Taipei in June 1998. As a result of an organizational review in Bali, the HRD WG abolished coordinating committees for cross-cutting themes and replaced them with 'focal points'. The USA would handle sustainable development, the Philippines would deal with small and medium enterprises, and Canada took responsibility for lifelong learning. What may be disconcerting for labour was that in the priorities for the following year, the group identified education and skill building, school to work transitions, and participation of women and youth as priorities, with no mention of labour–management participation in HRD as a major theme (HRD Working Group, 1998: item 57).

The pressure from labour organizations at the national and international levels for labour-related projects and a broader HRD mandate for the WG led to the changes in the HRD WG described above and to the eventual adoption of the tripartite project. The potential for labour issues being including within APEC poses some significant challenges for the labour movement.

CHALLENGES FOR THE LABOUR MOVEMENT

Based on the history and process described above, clearly APEC is dealing with issues that are not purely economic. Education, training, environmental issues, and gender are all being discussed within APEC. One may well make the argument, as Kuehn (1998) does, that these issues are being subordinated to a neoliberal agenda. But it is wrong to assume that APEC is a purely business-dominated organization focused uniquely on trade and investment liberalization. One of the reasons that APEC deals with social issues is because the APEC mandate includes a more traditional form of international cooperation; that is, economic and technical cooperation.

Somewhat paradoxically, APEC's economic and technical cooperation activities have also gained increasing prominence since the 1995 Osaka summit, and this has created the context for new initiatives such as the proposed labour–management project in HRD. This second stream within APEC is quite distinct from the trade and investment liberalization agenda. According to APEC (Economic Committee, 1996: 13–22), its economic and technical cooperation activities are aimed at:

- achieving sustainable growth and equitable development in the Asia Pacific region;
- reducing economic disparities among APEC economies;
- improving economic and social well-being; and
- building an Asia Pacific community.

There are two forces propelling this apparently contradictory dynamic within APEC. The first is the rather hesitant acquiescence of developing countries and Japan in the liberalization agenda promoted by the USA with the support of other Eastern Pacific countries. Some have suggested that:

> most Asian governments have largely united behind the Japanese geo-economic counterstrategy of talking up free

trade and free markets but in practice, blunting and eventually killing the move towards an APEC free trade area. This strategy of attrition, with its smokescreen of free trade verbiage and its emphasis on consensus, is presented, so as to disarm the 'Anglo-Saxon' competition as the 'Asian Way'. (Bello and Bullard, 1997: 30)

However, even industrialized countries such as Canada and the USA do not necessarily perceive social issues as being exclusive from trade and investment liberalization and, as demonstrated in the labour and environmental side agreements attached to NAFTA, they recognize the necessity for at least lip service to social issues. This recognition is closely related to the fact that both the Liberal party in Canada and the Democratic party in the USA came to power in competition with the Mulroney–Reagan regimes, the archetypes of neoliberalism. While many would argue that both these governments have been converted to neoliberalism, the fact remains that they remain politically sensitive to the criticism of globalization and generally promote neoliberalism with a human face. It is the intersection between this tendency, and the previously described emphasis on economic and technical cooperation by Southern countries and Japan, that is creating a certain space within APEC for issues or views that may contradict APEC's general neoliberal approach. This same intersection also creates other contradictions, and thus we find that opposition to the introduction of labour issues into APEC comes from certain developing countries, who fear labour issues might undermine their comparative advantage, or from industrialized countries that are dyed in the wool neoliberal in their orientation. As a result, the prospect particularly for the promotion of labour's agenda within APEC is extremely tenuous.

CONCLUSION: PROBLEMS AND POTENTIAL

As part of its programme for working within APEC, the ICFTU/APLN endorsed the concept of a labour–management project articulated at the second HRD ministerial meeting in Seoul. This project received the blessing of APEC foreign and trade ministers in Vancouver and appears to be moving forward within the HRD WG. However, the project that was accepted was only a small part of the APLN programme. Given this and the particular dynamics of the WG, the labour movement could adopt a range of positions regarding this project. One might be to consider the project as a limited but symbolically important first step in a process to achieve labour's objectives within APEC, a small beach head on which to establish a labour presence. The other perspective might be to consider the project an example of tokenism, that given the lack of progress on other APLN demands and given the fact the project is but one of 70 or so, there has been no real commitment on APEC's part to come to grips with labour issues. To make matters even more complicated, there is a perception that this type of project is like pinning a labour tail on a free trade 'donkey'; that is, it will make little difference to APEC's overall thrust and only lend legitimacy to an otherwise unsustainable agenda.

One of the factors that will have to be considered is the nature of the project and the HRD WG itself. The project, although yet to be fully developed, is limited to best practices based on labour–management cooperation. In many cases, cooperative efforts in training and education have resulted from the labour movement promoting and fighting for an independent agenda. The nature of the HRD WG as a composite of national delegations means that there will be a strong screening process that could limit the case studies to be chosen and also limit labour's ability to coordinate its activities on a multilateral basis. The process may also be limited by the decision, if confirmed, of the HRD WG to minimize labour-management issues as a priority for its activities. On the other hand, this particular WG has displayed a certain flexibility; and the creation of the task force on the effects of the economic crisis and recent approval of a project on wages and productivity, and another on paid and unpaid labour, all of which allow for labour participation, could be opportunities to promote a labour perspective and to build bridges with certain developing countries.

The other factor to consider is the general content of the HRD WG activities. While it is clear that there is some diversity in the networks and the politics of various projects, there is so far little evidence that contradicts Kuehn's (1998) assessment that APEC's HRD policy is fundamentally going in the wrong direction and there is much that confirms it. The issue is further complicated by the fact that the inclusion in the working group of EdFor, which is looking at general education and teaching systems, widens the scope of work group activity far beyond workplace issues. Is it within the capacity of individual national labour federations to successfully deal with this issue? Will the APLN or its affiliate the Education International, the particular trade secretariat concerned with this issue, be involved in monitoring and intervening in the HRD WG, and do they have the resources to devote to such a project? If so, what mechanisms need to be developed to assure the coordination necessary for an effective labour presence?

Also important is the relationship between the international labour movement and the broader movement that has grown up to challenge APEC and its agenda. While a decision by the APLN or its affiliates to participate in the HRD WG is entirely consistent with its programme to date, there remain serious differences of opinion regarding the labour movement's 'social dimension' perspective on trade and investment liberalization. These differences exist both within the labour movement and between the labour movement and the broader NGO movement that has grown up in opposition to APEC's vision. In the end, whichever route is chosen, the labour movement will need to expend considerable energy to assure that its affiliates and NGO allies understand the direction being taken.

In conclusion, the successful introduction of a project examining successful practices in the workplace, that explicitly allowed for the participation of organized labour, was the result of intensive lobbying at the WG and ministerial level. It required strong promotion by an APEC member and gained the acquiescence if not agreement of other countries in APEC. Only the future will tell whether this represented the first step in a process of transformation of APEC or a token gesture to appease the northern countries.

ACKNOWLEDGEMENTS

Catherine Griffiths provided invaluable research assistance for this project. I would like to thank Heather Gibb, Larry Kuehn, Stephen Benedict, Bob Baldwin, Stewart Goodings, Lynn MacDonald, Robert B. Shepard and Nigel Haworth for their advice and insights on issues discussed in this chapter. The opinions expressed and responsibility for errors rests entirely with the author. Funding for this research was generously provided by the Labour Education and Training Research Network based at the Centre for Research on Work and Society, York University.

NOTES

1. For detailed examination of APEC's history see Ranald, 1997; Atkinson, 1995; Bello and Bullard, 1997; Gallant and Stubbs, 1997; Garnaut and Drysdale, 1994; IBON, 1996; Kelsey, 1996; Lambert, 1997; Manila People's Forum on APEC, 1996; Minden, 1997; Pacific Asia Resource Center, 1995; Price, 1998.
2. Most NGOs, including trade unions, criticize APEC for its exclusion of civil society. Sensitive domestically to this criticism, the Canadian government, as SOM chair in 1997, commissioned and tabled with APEC senior officials a study on civil society participation in multilateral organizations. See APEC, 1997b.
3. This network organized a conference in Ottawa-Hull in September 1997. For background information on APEC and gender see Gibb, 1997.

REFERENCES

APEC (1992) 'Toward Education Standards for the Twenty-First Century', APEC Education Ministers, Washington, DC, 6 Aug.

APEC (1993) 'APEC Leaders' Economic Vision Statement', Blake Island, Seattle, 20 Nov.

APEC (1996) 'Joint Ministerial Statement: Call for Action on Human Resource Development', APEC – Human Resource Development Ministers, Manila, 11 Jan.

APEC (1997a) *Asia Pacific Economic Cooperation 1997*. Singapore: APEC Secretariat.

APEC (1997b) 'Engagement with Civil Society Organizations to Multilateral Organizations', APEC SOM Chair Office.

APEC (1997c) 'Joint Ministerial Statement', APEC – Human Resource Development Ministers, Seoul, 26 Sept.

APEC (1998a) 'Summary Record of 11th BMN General Meeting', APEC HRD, Business Management Network, Bali, Indonesia, 19–20 Jan.

APEC (1998b) 'Joint Statement', APEC Ninth Ministerial Meeting, Vancouver, 21–22 Nov., p. 8.

APEC Secretariat (nd) 'APEC Human Resources Development Working Group', APEC Secretariat.

Asia Pacific Labour Network (1996) 'A Trade Union Vision for APEC', Manila, November.

Atkinson, Jeff (1995) *APEC – Winners and Losers*. Australian Council for Overseas Aid Development, Dossier 34, Oct.

Bae, J., Rowley, C., Kim, D.H. and Lawler, J. (1997) 'Korean Industrial Relations at the Crossroads: The Recent Labour Troubles', *Asia Pacific Business Review*, Vol. 3, No. 3, pp. 148–60.

Bello, Walden and Bullard, Nicola (1997) 'APEC and the Environment'. A report commissioned for the Rio + 5 Forum, Rio de Janeiro, Brazil, 13–19 March.

Canada, Department of Foreign Affairs and International Trade (1996) 'APEC and Human Resource Development'.

Economic Committee (1996) *The State of Economic and Technical Cooperation in APEC*. Singapore.

Gallant, Nicole and Stubbs, Richard (1997) 'APEC's Dilemmas: Institution Building around the Pacific Rim', *Pacific Affairs*, Vol. 70, No. 2, pp. 203–18.

Garnaut, Ross and Drysdale, Peter (eds) (1994) *Asia-Pacific Regionalism: Readings in International Economic Relations*. Pymble: HarperEducational.

Gibb, Heather (1997) *Gender Front and Centre*. North–South Institute / CIDA / UNIFEM.

Gibb, Heather (1998) *Report on the 'stocktaking' of APEC Human Resource Development Working Group Projects with respect to Women's Participation*. North–South Institute, Prepared for NEDM, APEC HRD WG, Ottawa.

HRD Working Group (1998) 'Summary Conclusions, 17th APEC HRD Working Group Meeting', Bali, Indonesia, 19–20 January.

IBON (1996) *The APEC and Globalization*. Manila: IBON Special Release.

ICFTU Asia Pacific Labour Network (1997) *Building the Social Dimension of APEC*. Ottawa.

Kelsey, Jane (1996) 'Demystifying APEC'. Paper presented to the People's Conference against Imperialist Globalization, Manila, 21–23 Nov.

Kuehn, Larry (1998) 'Schools for Globalized Business: The APEC Agenda for Education', *Our Schools, Our Selves*, Vol. 9, No. 1, pp. 48–62.

Lambert, James (1997) 'Institution-Building in the Pacific – Canada in APEC', *Pacific Affairs*, Vol. 70, No. 2, pp. 195–202.

Manila People's Forum on APEC (1996) *APEC: Four Adjectives in Search of a Noun.* Manila: Focus on the Global South.

Minden, Karen (1997) 'Canada's Role in APEC', in Hampson *et al.* (eds), *Asia Pacific Face-Off.* Ottawa: Carleton University Press, pp. 119–44.

NEDM Coordinator (1998) 'Progress Report', 12th APEC-HRD NEDM Network Meeting, Nusa dua, Bali, Indonesia, 19–20 Jan.

Pacific Asia Resource Center (1995) *AMPO: A Monster in the Asia Pacific, NGOs Confront APEC*, Vol. 26, No. 4.

Price, John (1998) 'International Alliance-Building: Non-Governmental Organizations (NGOs) Confront APEC', *Asian Perspectives*, Vol. 22, No. 2, pp. 21–50.

Public Sector Research Centre (1997) 'APEC and Electricity Privatization', Sydney: University of New South Wales.

Ranald, Pat (1997) 'GATT, APEC and the Labour Movement', Sydney: Public Sector Research Centre.

Republic of Korea, Ministry of Labour (1997) 'The Provisional Themes for the 2nd APEC HRD Ministerial Meeting', 16 May.

Sixteenth World Congress of the ICFTU (1996) *The Global Market – Trade Unionism's Greatest Challenge.* Brussels, 25–29 June.

4

Organized Labour in the Borderless World: Globalization, Deregulation and Union Strategy in Australia

RICHARD HALL and BILL HARLEY

In recent years Australia, along with other economies, has faced an increasingly complex and challenging economic environment. In the face of broadening global markets and expanding international trade and commerce, recent Australian federal governments have adopted a new and distinctive, but broadly neoliberal, policy stance of financial sector deregulation, trade liberalization, labour market reform and industrial relations decentralization. This policy agenda was by no means inevitable, but reflected a particular interpretation of the challenges facing Australia; one in which the goal of improving Australia's international trade competitiveness was uppermost and the means by which this was to be achieved was a fundamental restructuring of industry, trade and financial regulations and industrial relations practices. These policy shifts, rather than globalization or internationalization *per se*, have dramatically altered the environment for Australian unionism.

Government policy alone does not determine the environment in which unions operate. Nonetheless, the approach adopted by successive federal governments has contributed to a situation in which unions face unprecedented challenges. The increasing exposure of Australian industry to greater international competition has led to the loss of jobs in highly unionized manufacturing and blue-collar sectors, with jobs growth concentrated in lowly unionized white-collar and services sectors. Together these factors have undermined the traditional membership base of unions. Concurrently, labour market deregulation, industrial relations decentralization and, more recently, anti-union policy and legislation, have made it difficult for unions to operate effectively.

The future of the Australian labour movement will be very much dependent on the strategies that it adopts in response to these challenges. We acknowledge that union strategy and behaviour are structured and constrained by political, institutional, economic and industrial forces, but we also recognize that unions are constituted by their members. The characteristics and predicament of the membership imparts a critical influence on union behaviour and strategy. Thus, in exploring union strategy, we seek to integrate consideration of environmental factors and membership characteristics in the context of the recent transformation of the Australian economy and industrial relations system.

We divide our discussion[1] into three main parts. In the first, we provide an overview of the connections between global economic forces and economic policy development in Australia over the past 15 years. In the second part we analyse the strategic response of Australian unions to the challenges facing them. We construct a framework that contrasts union strategic orientations on two major dimensions: the emphasis on either narrow sectionalism or articulation with the broader labour movement; and the extent to which unions adopt traditional industrial tactics or a range of innovative practices associated with a 'service' model. Using this framework we analyse data from our 1996 Australian National Trade Union Survey (ANTUS) to identify systematic links between the different industries and occupations covered by unions on one hand, and their strategic orientations on the other. We conclude that different types of unions have indeed engaged in different kinds of strategies in response to the challenges thrown up by environmental change. In the final part of the chapter, we consider the future of Australian unions in an era of globalization and make inferences about the likely patterns of union strategy that will emerge in the future.

THE CHANGING ENVIRONMENT OF AUSTRALIAN UNIONS: GLOBALIZATION AND DEREGULATION

In Australia, as in other Anglophone economies, governments have portrayed deregulation as a necessary response to globalization. According to this scenario, Australia has been forced to deregulate finance, trade, wage setting and industrial relations more in order to become internationally competitive. But the Australian economic record since deregulation commenced in 1983 suggests that deregulation has been far from successful (Bell, 1997: 171–7), and the comparative experiences of other economies indicates that there are alternatives to deregulation (Soskice, 1990; Thurow, 1992; Walter, 1996: Chapter 6). Since the early 1980s, Australia has endured deindustrialization, escalating foreign debt, wastage of capital on financial market speculation at the expense of productive investment, high interest rates and chronically high unemployment (Carroll and Manne, 1992; Mahony, 1993; INDECS, 1995; Bell, 1997).

The programme of trade liberalization and deregulation has been justified in terms of global economic forces and the imperative of assuring Australia's international competitiveness. However, those policies have resulted from conscious choices taken by a series of governments keen to appeal to finance capital and sustained by the ideology of neoclassical economics.[2] Globalization *has* profoundly affected labour–capital relations in Australia, but the effects have been mediated by the state, which has exercised a critical degree of autonomy from the forces of international capital. Perhaps the most important insight from recent debates about globalization and the nation state is that governments have not simply been rendered powerless in the face of increasing international or global economic activity. International pressures *have* increased but governments can still act decisively and strategically.

Similarly, our analysis suggests that unions remain strategic and potentially decisive actors. The Accord arrangements which characterized the period 1983–96 provided the union movement with *some* influence over policy setting.[3] Since the election of the conservative Coalition Government in March 1996, conditions for organized labour in Australia have deteriorated further.[4] Nevertheless, the union movement will continue to exert an influence on the industrial and political landscape and to explore different strategic options.

While there has been considerable research into the strategic role of the Australian union movement throughout the Accord years and since (Ewer *et al.*, 1991; Beilharz, 1994; Evatt Foundation, 1995; Costa and Hearn, 1997), there has been relatively little analysis of the different strategies pursued by individual unions or sections of the union movement. Has it been the case that significant strategic development and action has been conducted principally at the confederal level, that of the Australian

Council of Trade Unions (ACTU),[5] or have individual unions pursued distinct and divergent strategies as well? Moreover, in a period where Australian industrial relations has increasingly shifted to the workplace, and where the influence of the ACTU is probably weaker than at any time since 1983, is it not likely that the strategies of individual unions have now become even more important?

Just as the more critical contributions to the globalization debate have warned that the importance of nation states should not be prematurely dismissed (Hirst and Thompson, 1992, 1995, 1996), our analysis suggests that unions still enjoy some room to manoeuvre and capacity to exercise strategic choices.

Internationalization, Deregulation and the Environment for Australian Unionism

The Labor years (1983–96) provided the Australian union movement with both threats and opportunities. While the environment for unionism was becoming more challenging, unions and the ACTU enjoyed an unprecedented position as a result of the Accord. The ACTU was given access to policymaking via tripartite institutions and was able to negotiate national wage bargains and agreements designed to increase spending on social welfare (Singleton, 1990; Beilharz, 1994; Hampson, 1996).

However, by 1986, the social democratic promise of the Accord was beginning to fade. In exchange for the intensification of work, reduced job security and dramatic improvements in productivity across most industries[6], unions were able to secure only modest wage gains under the Accord (Stilwell, 1991). Moreover, from 1987 wage rises were, in part, forgone in exchange for tax cuts as part of the government's commitment to fiscal restraint and low inflation.

The tensions between the corporatist impulse of the Accord and the economic rationalist character of virtually all other areas of economic policy resulted in a difficult and contradictory environment for unionism. Rather than arising simply from industrial relations deregulation and decentralization or the eventual limitations of the Accord process, the most profound challenges to unions were caused by the brand of economic rationalism pursued by Hawke, and then Keating, justified by the imperative of globalization and the overriding goal of international competitiveness.

Almost every aspect of the economic and industrial transformation orchestrated by the Labor governments of the 1980s and 1990s created problems for the unions. Financial and trade deregulation caused deindustrialization and loss of jobs in the highly unionized manufacturing sector. Restructuring and rationalization hit other highly unionized industrial sectors as well. Fiscal restraint meant savage public sector cutbacks resulting in the loss of jobs in other traditionally strongly unionized sectors (Whitfield and Ross, 1996: 190–1; Bell, 1997: 110–14).

Simultaneously, other technological and economic shifts affected patterns of jobs growth and decline. Most significant have been shifts from full-time, secure jobs to casual and part-time jobs, from blue-collar to white-collar work and from high-wage jobs to low-wage jobs (Bell, 1997: 111–15). These trends have involved jobs being lost in areas conducive to union membership and gained in areas that are difficult to organize.

The decentralization of the labour market and the industrial relations system created new responsibilities and obligations for unions while simultaneously encouraging certain sectionalist tendencies where some strong unions were able to pursue generous enterprise specific bargains. Enterprise bargaining, first introduced as a principle to guide federal industrial negotiations in 1991, encouraged individual unions and branches of unions to pursue enterprise specific deals irrespective of the broader interests of other unions or the union movement. Further, under Labor, non-union enterprise bargains or 'enterprise flexibility agreements' allowed workplaces to introduce non-union agreements as an alternative to the highly centralized award system.

These deregulatory trends marked a critical departure from the traditional practice of Australian industrial relations, most notably the setting of working conditions through awards. Awards were determined by the Industrial Relations Commission (then the Conciliation and Arbitration Commission) through arbitral hearings and applied to all employees in specific occupations and industries *whether or not they were union members*. In the event of a dispute or a wage claim unions brought a case before the Commission and awaited a decision in the form of an award. Thus, the arbitration system gave unions relatively direct access to the authoritative settlement of industrial disputes and a critical and guaranteed institutional role in the system of industrial relations (see Deery *et al.*, 1997: Chapter 5; Gardner and Palmer, 1997: 155–76). Enterprise bargaining, industrial relations decentralization and labour market deregulation have placed greater burdens on union resources and eroded a number of the institutional supports that have previously assisted unions.

The election of the Coalition government in March 1996 further deepened the crisis facing Australian unions. The government has taken an explicitly anti-union approach to industrial relations policy while intensifying economic rationalist approaches in other areas of economic policy. The Workplace Relations Act 1996 has marginalized the award system encouraging firms to negotiate certified agreements (with or without a union) or non-union, individual Australian Workplace Agreements (McCallum, 1997), and has made unions much more vulnerable to prosecution for taking industrial action and reduced their capacity to meet with or negotiate on behalf of workers (Costa, 1997).

Australian unionism is now confronting the most challenging environment since the Labor Party split over allegations of communist influence in the union movement in the 1950s. Union membership has been declining, the advantages for unions of the centralized system have been eroded, the experience of the Accord has left many sceptical of the virtues of close union–party ties, and unions have to deal with the perception of some members that unions have lost touch with their membership.

To summarize the preceding discussion, globalization has had multiple effects on Australian unionism. Principally, these are based on the economic effects of globalization on a relatively small and vulnerable economy with a trading profile that has traditionally been dominated by the export of commodities and a high level of protection for domestic manufacturing. The internationalization of trade and investment, in particular, has had a significant impact on the Australian economy (see Bell, 1997, and Evatt Foundation, 1995, for detailed figures).

However, these economic effects of globalization have been mediated by deliberate government policies. These policies have created a series of prodigious challenges for unions: (1) the exposure of Australian industry to greater international competition has led to the loss of jobs in highly unionized manufacturing and blue-collar sectors; (2) jobs growth has been concentrated in lowly unionized sectors: white collar, services, part-time and casual work; and (3) labour market deregulation, industrial relations decentralization and, more recently, anti-union policy and legislation have made it more difficult for unions to effectively organize and mobilize. In the next section of the chapter, we consider the strategic responses of unions to the range of challenges confronting them.

ENVIRONMENTAL CHANGE AND UNION STRATEGY

It is difficult to be sanguine about the future of Australian unionism. Nonetheless, unions are far from being the passive victims of changes in their environment. The extent to which unions are willing and able to adopt appropriate strategies is likely to be of fundamental importance in determining their continued viability.

In seeking to make sense of how unions respond to change, we acknowledge the difficulty of defining, let alone understanding, union 'strategy' (see Gardner and Palmer, 1997: 111–19). Accordingly, we prefer to use the more modest concept of 'strategic orientation'. By this we mean *a tendency to employ concurrently a number of discrete practices which together constitute a recognizable and distinct approach to dealing with membership, administrative and industrial issues.*

It is difficult to capture the many facets of strategy, especially when using the type of large-scale survey method that this study employs. It is less problematic, however, to gather information that describes unions' patterns of behaviour. Thus, our concept of strategic orientation emphasizes the side of strategy which is 'a pattern … [or] consistency in behaviour' (Mintzberg, 1994: 23), which reflects at least to some extent a consciously formed plan on the part of union officials and/or members.

In constructing our conceptual framework, we identify two dimensions of union strategic orientation (Figure 1). The first draws on our earlier work, which identified two opposing orientations, designated 'articulated institutional unionism' and 'militant economistic unionism' (Hall and Harley, 1997: 36–7). An articulated institutional orientation entails the integration of unions or sections of unions with other unions, union confederations or peak bodies and with the ALP and pursuit of ends through political/institutional means as well as industrially. Militant

FIGURE 1

UNION STRATEGIC ORIENTATIONS ON TWO DIMENSIONS

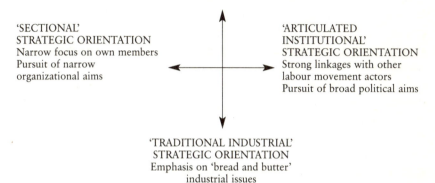

'MANAGERIAL SERVICE'
STRATEGIC ORIENTATION
Provision of non-traditional services
Members as customers
Surveying members
Employment of specialist staff

'SECTIONAL'
STRATEGIC ORIENTATION
Narrow focus on own members
Pursuit of narrow
organizational aims

'ARTICULATED
INSTITUTIONAL'
STRATEGIC ORIENTATION
Strong linkages with other
labour movement actors
Pursuit of broad political aims

'TRADITIONAL INDUSTRIAL'
STRATEGIC ORIENTATION
Emphasis on 'bread and butter'
industrial issues

economistic unionism emphasizes sectionalism and a narrow concern with the affairs and membership of one's own union or section. Thus, the first dimension of union strategic orientation that we consider is the relative extent of integration[7] or sectionalism.

The second dimension is based in part on Heery and Kelly's (1994) claims about the emergence of managerial unionism in the UK. We identify 'managerialist service unionism' as a strategic orientation involving the adoption of a 'service' orientation to members, manifested in features such as the provision of a range of non-industrial services, surveying members to determine their needs, and employing specialist officers (see Hall and Harley, 1998, for a detailed discussion). We suggest that a key dimension that differentiates the strategic orientation of unions is whether, and to what extent, they adopt the practices associated with managerial service unionism (as opposed to more traditional approaches).

We do not classify unions as being exclusively sectionalist or articulated, or as exclusively traditional or managerial service. Rather, we argue that a given union will fall somewhere along each continuum. Further, we see no reason to suppose that the positions of unions on either dimension will be systematically associated with their positions on the other.

Nonetheless, we suspect that the strategic orientations adopted by individual unions or sections (on either dimension) will be influenced by the specific circumstances in which they find themselves. While there is no *necessary* link between environment and strategy, clearly unions are organizations that have the capacity to adopt particular policies and practices as means to deal with specific environmental pressures and challenges (see Delaney *et al.*, 1996). The specific challenges facing unions are likely to differ depending on the industries in which they operate and the occupations that constitute their membership. Thus, we expect that there will be systematic relationships between circumstances and orientations, though the precise nature of these associations is difficult to predict.[8]

The significant losses of blue-collar jobs in manufacturing and other traditionally unionized parts of industry, which can be expected to continue over the next decade (DEETYA, 1995), might lead to an increasingly articulated orientation by unions which organize in these occupations and industries. Such a strategy would represent a means to maintain a 'critical mass' of labour organizations, even as membership of individual unions fell. On the other hand, it seems equally plausible that individual unions would seek to shore up their own positions by aggressive sectionalism and concentration on the needs of members and potential members at a local level.

In the growing, but traditionally lowly unionized, service sector there is no *a priori* reason to suppose that either sectionalism or articulation would represent a more rational response to environmental pressures. On one hand, a concerted, articulated approach might represent an efficient means to maximize economies of scale in seeking to organize and recruit employees in a part of the economy which is not traditionally unionized and many of whom are employed on a part-time or casual basis. On the other hand, it seems equally plausible that a narrow sectional approach will emerge in these areas, as unions seek to maximize their share of this growing section of the labour market.

Turning to our other dimension of strategic orientation, accounts of managerial service unionism have presented it as significantly a white-collar service sector phenomenon (see Heery and Kelly, 1994). The essential argument is that white-collar service sector employees are significantly different in their orientations from blue-collar employees in other industries, and that unions must provide more than just improved pay and conditions if they are to attract such workers. Yet there seems little reason to suppose that the provision of additional benefits would be any less attractive to other employees. Indeed, recent calls for a greater service orientation by Australian unions have been by no means restricted by sector or occupational representation (see, for example, ACTU, 1995; Costa, 1992; Easson, 1994).

Our view, therefore, is that individual unions might conceivably adopt any combination of the two strategic orientations regardless of the sector in which they operate or the occupations that they organize. In the next section we examine evidence in an attempt to identify associations between the impact of globalization and deregulation and the approaches adopted by unions in different parts of the economy and the labour market.

EVIDENCE FROM THE AUSTRALIAN NATIONAL TRADE UNION SURVEY

In order to explore associations between environment and strategic orientation, we employ data drawn from the 1996 ANTUS. The population on which the survey is based comprises 'union organizations' rather than 'registered trade unions' and includes, therefore, both registered unions *and* sections within unions – typically, functionally distinct branches or divisions.

As the survey is one of union organizations, the questionnaire was directed to the most senior union official primarily responsible for the management of the union organization. In most cases, these officials were designated as Secretaries, Assistant Secretaries or General Secretaries. Although the survey respondents were therefore senior union officials, it must be emphasized that the unit of analysis for this survey is the union organization rather than the union official. Necessarily, the views and attitudes of the relevant union official impinge on the responses given; many require the exercise of some judgement or evaluation. Nevertheless, questions invariably asked the official to make a judgement from the perspective of the union as an organization rather than from the perspective of the official as a union manager, and respondents were directed to answer on behalf of their union. Valid responses were received from 363 of the defined population of 575 union organizations resulting in a response rate of 63.1 per cent. Full details of the survey can be found in Hall and Harley, 1998.

Operationalizing Strategic Orientations and Union Characteristics

Using data from the survey it was possible to construct indicators of the two strategic orientations that allow us to assess the extent to which union organizations tend towards either end of the two scales. The first, INTSCALE (Degree of Integration), was constructed using a series of responses to questions about factors influencing:

- decisions about whether to amalgamate with another union or unions;

- the choice of industrial strategies; and

- approaches to recruitment

For each of these three areas respondents were asked: 'How important were the following ... in determining this section's[9] approach ...?'. The question then listed:

- 'The views/policies of other sections of the union'
- 'The views/policies of the Australian Labor Party'
- 'The views/policies of the ACTU'
- 'The views/policies of the Trades and Labor Council/TLC'
- 'The views/policies of an associated union federation'
- 'The views/policies of other unions'

Respondents were asked to rate the importance of each factor on a Likert scale, with a range from 1 ('not important') to 5 ('very important').

To construct INTSCALE the responses to these items were summed, giving a scale with a possible range from 18 to 90. The scale has good internal consistency (Alpha = 0.89) and an actual range from 18 to 82. The mean value is 44.6 and the median is 44.0. The higher the score on the scale, the more a union tends towards integration, while a lower score indicates a more sectionalist approach.

The second indicator, MSSCALE (Extent of Managerial Service Unionism) was also constructed as a scale. The scale was the sum of a number of dummy variables. The first was scored so that if respondents reported that their section's membership had increased and that 'More effective provision of non-traditional services' was either 'important' or 'very important' (on a five-point Likert scale) in contributing to this increase then a value of 1 was assigned. The second was based on a question that asked: 'When recruiting members how important is the promotion of [the union's] provision of non-industrial services?', which was scored in the same way as the first dummy. The remainder of the items that constitute the scale were based on simple 'yes/no' questions which asked whether the union had the following features:

- provision of subsidized general goods and services for members;

- discount credit for members;

- a computerized membership information management system;

- a programme for improving standards of responses to telephone queries;

- surveying of members' opinions, attitudes or needs;

- surveying of non-members' opinions, attitudes or needs; and

- an increased proportion of expenditure on advertising over the past five years.

An affirmative answer to any of these was scored as 1 and a negative answer as 0. Thus, the scale has a possible (and actual) range from 0 to 9. It's internal consistency is not as good as that of INTSCALE (Alpha = 0.55). The mean value is 3.8 and the median is 4.0. The higher the score on the scale, the more a union organization can be said to tend towards a managerial service strategic orientation, while a lower score is indicative of a more traditional approach.[10]

In addition to indicators of strategic orientation, our analysis required the construction of variables that could be used to identify unions on the basis of the industries in which they operate and the occupations that they organize. To allocate union organizations to occupational categories, we utilized a question that asked respondents to identify the main occupational group covered by their section. The categories they were given to choose from were the Australian Standard Classification of Occupations (First Edition) Major Groups (see ABS, 1997, for details of this classification).

We made a decision to group union organizations by occupation. With a relatively small number of respondent organizations (n = 363) it was necessary to devise a simple division so as to ensure reasonable cell counts. Accordingly, we allocated respondents to one of three groups. If their main occupation was 'Managers and administrators', 'Professionals', 'Associate professionals', 'Advanced clerical and service workers', 'Intermediate clerical and service workers' or 'Elementary clerical and service workers', the union organizations were designated 'White collar'. If they identified 'Tradespersons and related workers', 'Intermediate production and transport workers' or 'Labourers and related workers', they were designated 'Blue collar'. Those who did not identify a main occupational group were designated 'Other'. Such a simple grouping glosses over important occupational differences, but nonetheless the categories of 'blue' and 'white' collar capture the main occupational difference necessary for our analysis of the impact of globalization.

Similarly, respondents were asked to identify the main industry in which their union organization operated and were provided with the Australian and New Zealand Standard Industry Classification (ANZIC). On the basis of this response they were assigned either to 'Services' (Wholesale trade, Retail trade, Accommodation, cafes and restaurants, Communication services, Finance and insurance, Property and business services, Government administration and defence, Education, Health and Community services, Cultural and recreational services, or Personal and other services), or 'Production' (Agriculture, forestry and fishing, Mining, Manufacturing, Electricity, gas and water supply, Construction, or Transport and storage). Again, those who failed to identify a main industry were assigned to the category of 'Other'. The rationale for this grouping is essentially the same as that for the occupational groupings.

Results of the Analysis

As a means to assess our earlier claim that strategic orientation is likely to be systematically associated with circumstances, we conducted simple correlation analyses of the two scales with the industry and occupation variables. Initial bivariate correlation analysis (Kendall's tau_b) showed that the integration scale was correlated positively with the production industry dummy ($0.14**$)

and the blue-collar occupation dummy (0.15**) and negatively with the service industry dummy (–0.19**) and the white-collar occupation dummy (–0.23**). This suggests a relative tendency on the part of blue-collar and production unions towards integration and on the part of white-collar and service sector unions towards sectionalism.

On the other hand, the managerial service union scale was correlated negatively with the production industry dummy (–0.24**) and the blue-collar dummy (–0.19**) and positively with the service industry dummy (0.16**). Only the white-collar dummy failed to pass the test of statistical significance when correlated with the managerial service unionism variable (0.01). On this basis we can infer that blue-collar and production unions tend towards a more traditional industrial approach than service sector unions.

These results are generally consistent with the claim that the tendency towards a particular strategic orientation is systematically associated with the main occupational group organized and the main industry in which the union organization operates. There is, however, a high degree of correlation between 'collar colour' and industry, rendering it problematic to ascertain the potential role of each factor in influencing strategic orientation. Accordingly, we conducted partial correlation analysis. Table 1 shows the correlations between the strategic orientation variables and the industry variables, controlling for the occupational variables.

TABLE 1

PARTIAL CORRELATION COEFFICIENTS FOR STRATEGIC ORIENTATION AND INDUSTRY, CONTROLLING FOR OCCUPATION

	Production	Services
Integration (INTSCALE)	0.10	–0.14*
Managerial service (MSSCALE)	–0.18**	0.12*

* = significant at the 0.05 level
** = significant at the 0.01 level

While none of the coefficients is large, all but one is significant. Moreover, the directions of the associations are the same as in the earlier bivariate analysis, with service industry unions tending towards the managerial service orientation and away from integration. Production unions tend away from the managerial service orientation. While the association between production unions and integration is positive, it is not statistically significant and on that basis we regard it as questionable.

Table 2 shows the partial correlations between the orientation variables and the occupation variables, controlling for industry. Here only one of the associations, that between white-collar unions and integration, is statistically significant. It is negative, as was the association in the bivariate correlation analysis, indicating that unions that organize mainly white-collar staff are less likely to be integrated than are other unions. These results lead us to infer that the industry in which a union operates is likely to be a more important determinant of strategic orientation than is the main occupation comprising its membership.

TABLE 2

PARTIAL CORRELATION COEFFICIENTS FOR STRATEGIC ORIENTATION AND
OCCUPATION, CONTROLLING FOR INDUSTRY

	Blue collar	White collar
Integration (INTSCALE)	0.06	–0.19**
Managerial service (MSSCALE)	–0.08	–0.10

* = significant at the 0.05 level
** = significant at the 0.01 level

While much work remains to be done before we can claim to understand the complex interplay between globalization, deregulation and union strategy, nonetheless the simple analyses presented here allow us to reach some important conclusions. It is clear that there are systematic associations between where unions operate and whom they organize, on one hand, and their strategic orientations on the other. Unions that organize predominantly blue-collar production workers appear more likely to pursue strategies that involve a relatively high level of integration with the rest of the labour movement and less likely to attempt a managerial-service strategy. There are a number of possible explanations for this. The employee base of these unions is currently being eroded through industrial restructuring. In such a climate, integrating with other unions, labour movement institutions and the Labour Party might be a particularly attractive defensive strategy. Blue-collar unions also tend to have a much more radical, collectivist and industrially focused historical tradition than white-collar unions. These ideological and cultural traditions might tend to predispose those unions to stick with more traditional strategies and tactics and reject a managerial-service orientation that depends on the provision of new, non-industrial services and researching the attitudes and preferences of their members.

White-collar unions and those that organize in the services sectors are even more distinctive in terms of strategic orientation than the production and blue-collar unions. Unions primarily representing workers in services are less likely to report a significant degree of integration with the rest of the movement and they are more likely to pursue managerial-service strategies. White-collar unions are also unlikely to be highly integrated, though they are not significantly more likely to pursue managerial-service unionism. Globalization and the restructuring of Australian industry undertaken by recent Australian governments have been much kinder to these unions than blue-collar and production unions: the pool of potential union members has been growing. Under these circumstances it is understandable that these unions are more amenable to new strategies as a means of attracting new members. Secondly, it might be thought that the white-collar character of their members suggests the virtue of appealing beyond immediate industrial interests, to their broader and more diverse interests. It is also possible that a managerial-service approach is more important where the union membership is quite diverse and where the interests and issues affecting the membership are more varied and, possibly, difficult to infer.

CONCLUSION: THE FUTURE OF AUSTRALIAN UNIONS

What then is the future for Australian unions? We have stressed the importance of government policy responses to globalization, rather than any direct and unmediated impact of globalization, as the key determinant of the predicament facing unions. Further, we have stressed that these impacts are felt quite differently in different parts of industry and the labour market. Our analysis of the ANTUS data shows clearly that different kinds of unions – as defined by the industries and occupations – adopt systematically different strategic orientations. To the extent that this allows us to make inferences about the links between globalization and union strategy, we can make some informed judgements about the particular strategies that are likely to be pursued in future.

As is to be expected, blue-collar and production unions appear to favour more traditional industrial tactics and might be more likely to seek the support of other sections of the labour movement. The new legislative regime is specifically designed to counter these strategies. The proscription of preference clauses that previously allowed *de facto* closed shops to operate, the granting of equal rights to non-unionists, the encouragement of non-union agreements and individual contracts and, most importantly, the prohibition of secondary boycotts and other industrial action supported by increasingly severe penalties threaten the power resources of unions and jeopardize their ability to take united action.

Moreover, there appears little reason to suppose that there will be any significant change to government policy settings in the near future, suggesting that we are likely to witness a continuing decline in blue-collar production employment and a corresponding drain on membership for blue-collar unions. Our prediction is that in this situation there is likely to be an intensification of the use of traditional industrial tactics among such unions and an increasing emphasis on solidaristic approaches.[11]

Many white-collar and services unions are in a different predicament. With typically lower coverage rates it might be thought that these unions have less to lose and more to gain in the new environment. At least these unions tend to be organizing in areas of the economy where there has been, and will continue to be, jobs growth. It appears that these unions are more prepared to market themselves to their actual and potential membership as service orientated organizations looking to respond to the diverse interests of a more varied membership base. While this might constitute a more modern approach more in tune with enterprise level bargaining and the need to actively attract and retain members, it remains to be seen whether it can deliver the industrial benefits and protections demanded by members.

The logical outcome of the contemporary trends of labour market deregulation, decentralization of the industrial relations system and the weakening of union power, is dramatically increased downward pressure on wages in Australia. For unions and workers the 'bottom line' of globalization and the imperative to make Australia more competitive is the repeated allegation that Australian labour costs are too high. This provides the justification for employers and the government to argue the need for lower wages and/or greater productivity. With the dismantling of the centralized arbitration system and the weakening of closed shop arrangements and provisions, the path is open for non-unionists on individual non-union contracts and agreements to undercut existing wages and conditions. Under the new legislation, unions, whether white-collar or blue-collar, are less able to resist these threats through united industrial action. On the other hand, it is difficult to see how a managerial-service approach is able to better facilitate the mobilization of collective strength at the workplace and across the labour market. This highlights the potential importance of concerted and united political action that draws on the resources and strengths of the labour movement as a whole and on the capacity of individual unions to see themselves as part of a political movement.

NOTES

1. Authors' names are listed alphabetically. Each author made an equal contribution.
2. The term 'deregulation' is used throughout. However, we acknowledge and endorse the argument of Buchanan and Callus (1993) that so-called labour market deregulation does not involve the elimination of regulation as much as the introduction of different forms of regulation based on a neoclassical view of economics and a unitarist view of industrial relations. In particular, they argue that the 'deregulation' of work relations in the Australian case has in fact involved the substitution of various forms of *external* regulation by forms of *internal* regulation emphasizing, for example, managerial prerogative rather than collective labour law.
3. Between 1983 and 1996 the ruling Labor governments negotiated a series of national level wages and social policy agreements with the Australian Council of Trade Unions. Each of these agreements as to wage rises, government undertakings as to policy and institutional development and the basis for collective bargaining, was referred to as an Accord. There were eight Accords in all, the last few being relatively indistinguishable from incomes policies where the terms for productivity bargaining were set down. (See Ewer *et al.*, 1991; Hampson, 1996; Beilharz, 1994).
4. Australian politics is dominated by two major party groupings: the Australian Labor Party (ALP), established in the late nineteenth century as the parliamentary representative of the trade union movement, and the Coalition of the Liberal Party of Australia and the National Party. The former, and dominant, Coalition partner was formed in the 1940s as the advocate of business interests and 'free enterprise', while the latter, the National Party, is the modern form of the Australian Country Party which has always relied on a rural vote and has sought to represent the interests of farmers, graziers and the primary industries more generally. The Coalition was in government in 1975–83 and was re-elected in 1996. The ALP formed the government in the interim period, 1983–96.
5. The ACTU, formed in 1927, is the sole trade union confederation representing the vast majority of Australian unions. Since the 1970s the ACTU has had a leading role in presenting National Wage Cases and other major wage cases and in coordinating the

union movement more generally. During Labour's last period in office (1983–96) it was the ACTU that was signatory to the Accords with the government.

6. From 1987 it became customary for at least some part of wage increases to be justified in terms of demonstrated productivity improvements or the elimination of inefficient work practices. For aggregate figures on productivity growth see INDECS, 1995: 70–7.

7. Our conception of 'integration' owes much to the conceptions of 'solidaristic unionism' and 'inclusive unionism' used by a number of European commentators (Visser, 1990; Korpi, 1983).

8. We recognize that there are numerous other factors (such as ideological orientation, historical patterns of behaviour, inter-union rivalry, etc.) which are likely to influence union strategic orientation. Nonetheless, we expect environmental pressures to remain important influences on orientation.

9. 'Section' is used throughout the questionnaire to refer to the union, or section of the union, to which the questionnaire was administered.

10. As a means to test our assumption that a union organization may exhibit a number of strategic orientations concurrently, we measured correlation between the two scales. The coefficient was small (–0.02) and not statistically significant. On this basis, we conclude that there is no association between the strategic orientations and infer that union organizations may tend towards one, both or neither of them simultaneously.

11. A case in point is the maritime dispute that gripped Australian ports in mid-1998, during which the Maritime Union of Australia (MUA), with the support of other unions and the ACTU, was able to shut down a number of Australian ports in response to attempts by employers to use non-union labour. Paradoxically, in this case globalization acted in the union's favour in the sense that their capacity to exert pressure on employers rested largely on their capacity to interfere with international trade.

REFERENCES

ABS (Australian Bureau of Statistics) (1997) *ASCO: Australian Standard Classification of Occupations*, 2nd edn. Canberra: AGPS (Cat. No. 1220.0).

ACTU (Australian Council of Trade Unions) (1995) *Congress Reports and Resolutions*. Melbourne: ACTU.

Bell, S. (1997) *Ungoverning the Economy: The Political Economy of Australian Economic Policy*. Melbourne: Oxford University Press.

Beilharz, P. (1994) *Transforming Labour: Labour Tradition and the Labour Decade in Australia*. Melbourne: Cambridge University Press.

Buchanan, J. and Callus, R. (1993) 'Efficiency and Equity at Work: The Need for Labour Market Regulation in Australia', *The Journal of Industrial Relations*, Vol. 35, No. 4, March, pp. 515–37.

Carroll, J. and Manne, R. (eds) (1992) *Shutdown: The Failure of Economic Rationalism and How to Rescue Australia*. Melbourne: Text Publishing.

Costa, M. (1992) 'Mythology, Marketing and Competition: A Heretical View of the Future of Unions', in M. Crosby and M. Easson (eds), *What Should Unions Do?* Sydney: Pluto Press.

Costa, M. (1997) 'Union Strategy post the Workplace Relations Act', *Australian Bulletin of Labour*, Vol. 23, No. 1, pp. 48–58.

Costa, M. and Hearn, M. (eds) (1997) *Reforming Australia's Unions*. Sydney: Federation Press.

Deery, S., Plowman, D. and Walsh, J. (1997) *Industrial Relations: A Contemporary Analysis*. Sydney: McGraw-Hill.

Delaney, John T., Jarley, Paul and Fiorito, Jack (1996) 'Planning for Change: Determinants of Innovation in US National Unions', *Industrial and Labour Relations Review*, Vol. 49, pp. 597–614.

DEETYA (Department of Employment, Education, Training and Youth Affairs) (1995) *Australia's Workforce 2005: Jobs in the Future*. Canberra: AGPS.

Easson, M. (1994) 'The ACTU Executive', *Workplace*, Summer, p. 21.

Evatt Foundation (1995) *Unions 2001: A Blueprint for Trade Union Activism*. Sydney.

Ewer, P., Hampson, I., Lloyd, C., Rainford, J., Rix, S. and Smith, M. (1991) *Politics and the Accord*. Sydney: Pluto Press.

Gardner, M. and Palmer, G. (1997) *Employment Relations: Industrial Relations and Human Resource Management in Australia*, 2nd edn. Melbourne: Macmillan.

Hall, R. and Harley, B. (1995) 'The Australian Response to Globalization: Domestic Labour Market Policy and the Case of Enterprise Bargaining', in P. Gollan (ed.), *Globalization and Its Impact on the World of Work*, ACIRRT Working Paper 38. Sydney: ACIRRT.

Hall, R. and Harley, B. (1996a) 'Trade Union Aims, Structures and Strategies in a Changing Environment', in T. Bramble and B. Harley (eds), *Trade Unionism in Australia and New Zealand: Roads to Recovery*, Graduate School of Management Monograph. St Lucia: The University of Queensland.

Hall, R. and Harley, B. (1996b) 'Australian Trade Unions and the Interpretation of Change', in G. Griffin (ed.), *Contemporary Research on Unions: Membership, Organization, Marginalization and Non-Standard Employment*, NKCIR Monograph No. 7/8. Melbourne: National Key Centre in Industrial Relations.

Hall, R. and Harley, B. (1997) *Towards a New Classification System for Australian Unions*, ACIRRT Working Paper No. 46. Sydney: ACIRRT, 56pp.

Hall, R. and Harley, B. (1998) *Managerialist-Service Unionism in Australia: Evidence from the 1996 Australian National Trade Union Survey*, Department of Management Working Paper. Parkville: The University of Melbourne.

Hampson, I. (1996) 'The Accord: A Post-mortem', *Labour and Industry*, Vol. 7, No. 2, pp. 55–77.

Heery, E. and Kelly, J. (1994) 'Participative and Managerial Unionism: An Interpretation of Change in Trade Unions', *Work, Employment and Society*, Vol. 8, No. 1, pp. 1–22.

Hirst, P. and Thompson, G. (1992) 'The Problem of "Globalization": International Economic Relations, National Economic Management and the Formation of Trading Blocs', *Economy and Society*, Vol. 21, No. 4, pp. 357–96.

Hirst, P. and Thompson, G. (1995) 'Globalization and the Future of the Nation State', *Economy and Society*, Vol. 24, No. 3, pp. 408–42.

Hirst, P. and Thompson, G. (1996) *Globalization in Question*. Cambridge: Polity Press.

INDECS (1995) *State of Play: 8*. Sydney: Allen and Unwin.

Korpi, W. (1983) *The Democratic Class Struggle*. London: Routledge and Kegan Paul.

McCallum, R. (1997) 'Australian Workplace Agreements – An Analysis', *Australian Journal of Labour Law*, Vol. 10, No. 1, pp. 50-61.

Mahony, G. (ed.) (1993) *The Australian Economy under Labour*. Sydney: Allen and Unwin.

Mintzberg, H. (1994) *The Rise and Fall of Strategic Planning*. New York: The Free Press.

Singleton, G. (1990) *The Accord and the Australian Labour Movement*. Melbourne: Melbourne University Press.

Soskice, D. (1990) 'Reinterpreting Corporatism and Explaining Unemployment: Coordinated and Non-Coordinated Market Economies', in R. Brunetta and C. Dell Aringa (eds), *Labour Relations and Economic Performance*. London: Macmillan.

Stilwell, F. (1991) 'Wages Policy and the Accord', *Journal of Australian Political Economy*, Vol. 28, pp. 27–53.

Thurow, L. (1992) *Head to Head: The Coming Economic Battle among Japan, Europe and America*. Sydney: Allen and Unwin.

Visser, J. (1990) *In Search of Inclusive Unionism. Bulletin of Comparative Labour Relations*, No. 18. Deventer, Netherlands: Kluwer.

Walter, J. (1996) *Tunnel Vision: The Failure of Political Imagination*. Sydney: Allen and Unwin.

Whitfield, K. and Ross, R. (1996) *The Australian Labour Market*, 2nd edn. Sydney: Harper Educational.

5

Last Line of Resistance or a Golden Opportunity: Australian Trade Union Responses to Globalization

TIM HARCOURT

Is 'globalization' the key to economic prosperity for all, or yet another device to further advance international capital at the expense of workers? The globalization debate has become important in international policy circles in the Asia Pacific region. The debate came to the fore as a result of the Asian financial crisis, which began in July 1997 with the large capital outflow and devaluations of the key Asian currencies and later spread to Russia and Latin America. It has influenced domestic politics in countries harmed most by the currency crisis and has also affected domestic elections in industrialized countries.

This chapter is in two parts. First, it assesses the current state of research on the effect of globalization on the welfare of workers. Second, it outlines some Australian trade union strategies to deal with the impact of globalization. These range from international union efforts to have labour issues included in trade policy to domestic campaigns by unions on globalization issues and labour market adjustment.

WHAT IS GLOBALIZATION?

Whilst globalization is a contemporary term, the issue of how national economies integrate has been controversial in economics since Adam Smith's *Wealth of Nations* (1776). In Australia, too, the 'free-trade versus protection' debate had enormous impact on the development of national politics in the late nineteenth and early twentieth centuries. At Federation in 1901, the main political parties were either 'free trade' or 'protectionist', with the emerging Australian Labor Party having elements of both positions in its ranks (see Costa, 1991).

Now, at the beginning of the twenty-first century, we have the controversy of 'globalization', which has a number of competing definitions. Ohmae has enthusiastically written about the 'borderless world' and the 'end of the nation state' (see Ohmae, 1990, 1995). Ohmae (1990:11–13) supports market mechanisms over government intervention (preferring 'innovators' to 'regulators'). He regards globalization as a modern phenomenon whereby previously closed economies become open. Yet, as Kozul-Wright (1995: 139–42) points out, international economic integration was important in the 1870–1913 period (a 'Golden Age' of international integration). Kozul-Wright (1995: 139) defines globalization as:

> a continuous process of extending interdependent cross-border linkages in production and exchange, pursued by firms, many of which by definition are transnational, with the aim of advancing their particular interests, and regulated by states (and other institutions) with the aim of ensuring the potential benefits are obtained by wider communities.

Hirst and Thompson (1992: 357–9) use the term 'globalization of economic relations'. They examine the importance of trading blocs within the international economy, how these blocs relate to each other and how this might affect the management and coordination of the world economy overall. Other analysts, such as Holland (1987), note the emergence of global 'mesoeconomic' power by multinational corporations (MNCs) in the world economy. Rodrik (1997) has written about the adverse effects of globalization on unskilled workers and the need for governments to provide social insurance.

This chapter focuses on 'economic globalization' – that is, the integration of national economies in terms of trade and investment. It distinguishes between the effects of trade liberalization and other globalization effects that increase capital mobility. Trade liberalization refers to the removal or minimization of trade barriers through the process of the World Trade Organization (WTO) and the Asia Pacific Economic Cooperation (APEC) forum. The WTO process often receives the most public scrutiny as it involves direct policy decisions by national governments to reduce trade barriers. This received much publicity in Australia because in the 1980s the government considered itself a leader in the trade liberalization process, especially given its role in the formation of the Cairns Group and APEC (see Garnaut, 1994; Hawke, 1992; Oxley, 1990).

Other globalization effects refer to developments other than the erosion of trade barriers that increase capital mobility. This includes the removal of impediments to foreign investment and the increased ability of firms to 'outsource' part of their business to subcontractors in other countries. With international capital becoming more mobile, investment flows have outstripped world trade flows in recent decades (see Kozul-Wright, 1995).

Contemporary globalization has caused some unusual political alliances. For instance, some on the extreme left of politics oppose globalization because they oppose the power of international capital over sovereign national governments. The extreme right opposes globalization as it is against all things 'foreign' – capital, governments, people (including immigrants). Many labour market problems are blamed on globalization for popular appeal, especially at election time. For instance, Patrick Buchanan, a US Republican Party Presidential contender in 1996, was quick to blame globalization and the US trade deficit with Japan for wage and job losses for American workers in manufacturing (see Rodrik, 1997: 69). However, Buchanan did not have such pro-worker views on minimum wage legislation and collective bargaining. Ironically, some pro-globalization advocates on the right do not object to the influence of Geneva in the form of the WTO, but they may object to the same Geneva influence in the form of the International Labour Organization (ILO) .

However, not all participants are simply 'pro' or 'anti' globalization. Some believe that globalization is inevitable and it is a question of how a nation positions itself in an ever-changing world. A nation can revert to isolationist economic strategies or use social policy to build up its stock of human capital to minimize the adverse social effects of globalization (see Rodrik, 1997; Latham, 1998). This pragmatic policy approach has been adopted by Tony Blair's 'New Labour' in the UK and social democratic parties in Europe and Australia (see Latham, 1998).

DOES GLOBALIZATION HURT WORKERS AND THEIR TRADE UNIONS? WHAT IS THE ECONOMIC EVIDENCE?

Trade Liberalization and Wage Inequality

Most attention in economics has been on the effect of trade liberalization on relative wages. The advocates of trade liberalization and globalization usually argue about the 'efficiency gains', 'gains from trade', 'comparative advantage' and the elimination of 'dead weight losses'. There is typically little reference made to the distributive consequences of policy advice based on international trade models, despite the warnings from bodies like the Organization for Economic Cooperation and Development (OECD) that 'though freer trade is likely to generate welfare gains for a nation as a whole its distributional effects need to be considered' (OECD 1997: 122).

Much of the theoretical debate has focused on the effects of trade on developed country wages in response to fears that trade with low-wage developing countries will depress wages in industrialized countries. Economic theory offers several competing theories on the link between trade and wages. The most influential are the 'Heckscher–Ohlin' and 'Stolper–Samuelson' models of the 1940s (see Belman and Lee, 1997: 67; Stolper and Samuelson, 1941; Rodrik 1997: 14–16). The Hecksher–Ohlin theorem predicts that free trade equalizes commodity prices between countries sharing the same technology and producing the same commodities, which in turn equates wages and rents in both countries. In contrast, the Stolper–Samuelson theorem says that any interference with trade that drives up the local import price must unambiguously benefit the productive factor used intensively in producing the import-competing goods. In the Stolper–Samuelson model the scarce factor of production, labour, was expected to be less scarce in the absence of trade barriers. This explained why labour would benefit from tariff protection in terms of real wages.

With the increase in unemployment and wage inequality in industrialized countries in the 1980s and 1990s, the Heckscher–Ohlin and Stolper–Samuelson models were revisited by various economists, including Wood (1995). Wood argued that international trade in this period between 'first world' and 'third world' had hurt unskilled workers in the first world. The debate centred on the questions 'Does trade with the third world hurt (unskilled) workers in the first world?' and 'If so, by how much?' Many economists argue that trade is but a small factor in the decline of wages and employment prospects of first world unskilled workers (see Bhagwati and Kosters, 1994; Lawrence, 1994; Slaughter and Swagel, 1997; Burtless, 1995; Freeman, 1995).

Wood (1995) argues that in industrialized countries, the demand for unskilled labour has fallen substantially over the past two decades at a time of rapid growth in imports from developing countries of low-skilled intensive manufactured goods. Wood believes that the evidence shows that trade has hurt unskilled workers. Freeman (1995: 31), though, is sceptical about trade being the main culprit in the plight of unskilled workers. Freeman sees other forces at play, including technological advances and political events. He explains that domestic labour market conditions are more important than trade in determining pay for a large segment of the labour force. Accordingly, Freeman is sceptical that trade agreements, such as the North American Free Trade Agreement (NAFTA) or the European Union (EU) arrangements, will have a large effect on wages and employment (ibid.: 31–2).

The debate about trade liberalization and wage inequality is also associated with the debate about trade liberalization and the growth of average wages. Is trade to blame for real wage decline or are other factors at play? Some economists have argued that stagnation in US real wages merely reflects a productivity decline. This is more difficult to ascertain in Australia because of other factors, such as the institutional effects of incomes policies like the prices and incomes Accord between the Australian Council of Trade Unions (ACTU) and the Hawke–Keating Labor governments of 1983 to 1996 (analysed in Chapman, 1998).

The debate about the impact of trade liberalization on wage inequality is a hotly contested one in the empirical literature and in economic theory. However, three assessments can be made: first, skilled workers tend to fare better from the effects of trade liberalization than unskilled workers. Second, there is an effect of trade on relative wages, but there is debate about its magnitude. Third, whatever their views on the effects of trade on relative wages, most economists prefer a labour market policy response, such as raising the skill level of unskilled workers, to a trade policy response, such as raising tariffs or quotas in industries that employ unskilled workers. Other economists, such as Singh (1997) and

Galbraith (1996), reject the model implicit in how conventional trade economists treat the labour market. They also reject the developed/developing world or 'North–South' dimensions of the trade and labour markets debate, seeing this as a device for creating a 'wedge' between first world and third world workers in order to benefit the policy 'elites' in both types of economies.

Trade Liberalization and Employment Insecurity

The debate about trade liberalization and employment insecurity is a spin-off of the debate about trade liberalization and relative wages. The essential argument between Wood (1995) and other economists concerns the reduction in the demand for unskilled labour in developed countries because of trade with the developing world. This reduction in demand, it is argued, shows itself either in the form of a reduction in the relative wage of the unskilled or in job losses. It is argued that the USA has been affected by the trade impact through wage inequality whilst Europe has suffered employment losses. Much of this debate concerns the efficacy of US labour market institutions relative to those of Europe (the labour market 'flexibility' argument). The conventional wisdom is that American labour market institutions produce lower unemployment than Europe's 'inflexible' institutions. This argument has been discredited by Solow (1997), who finds that factors outside the labour market are responsible for Europe's unemployment rates. Overall, the debate about trade liberalization and employment insecurity is almost identical to that about trade liberalization and relative wages in that economists disagree as to the magnitude of the effects of trade liberalization relative to other factors such as technology.

However, there are other relevant indirect effects on the labour market to be considered. For example, industrial relations institutions can be affected by trade liberalization in a way that has implications for employment security and other labour market outcomes. Belman and Lee (1997) analyse some important studies on the impact of trade liberalization on manufacturing employment, jobs quality and average wages, as well as relative wages and overall labour market conditions. The survey also notes the spillover effects of the 'loss of wage leadership from the manufacturing sector . . . which may also be a source of poor wage performance throughout the economy' (ibid.: 78). This, however, does not consider other reasons for wage deterioration – such as the erosion of US labour market institutions. These effects are also important in Australian industrial relations given the historical role played by the metal industry's 'fitter's rate' in Australian wage determination. If trade liberalization harms Australian manufacturing and reduces the demand for labour and wage growth in the metal engineering industry, then this affects bargaining in other sectors. The ultimate pattern of wage settlements in the labour market depends on the role of the leading sectors, be it 'over-award' bargaining in the past or enterprise bargaining in recent years.

Increased Capital Mobility and Bargaining Power

Whilst economists have engaged in a vigorous debate about the effects of trade liberalization on workers, there are other (potentially) more important globalization effects that trade unions need to be aware of. For instance, Australian trade unions should be concerned if, by campaigning purely on the protection versus free trade debate, they completely miss the effects of increased capital mobility (including outsourcing and contracting-out overseas). The inequality of bargaining power between employer and workers stemming from capital mobility is a major policy issue for trade unions (see Thorpe, 1997). However, conventional trade models do not always model alternative transmission mechanisms that affect workers. These include the threat of employers outsourcing or moving plants offshore in the face of wage claims (see OECD, 1997; Belman and Lee, 1997: 91–6; Brofenbrenner, 1997); the movement of capital to low-wage countries that do not comply with ILO conventions; and the movement of displaced workers from the tradeable goods sector to the non-tradeable or domestic goods sector, causing a reduction in real wages in both sectors.

The OECD (1997) has surveyed the trade and 'other' effects, including the role of technology in the globalization process. Whilst it is difficult to distinguish the effects of trade from those of technology on the labour market, the survey notes that the majority of the studies conclude that trade has played a 'small role' in labour market outcomes. Notably, one study by Machin *et al.* (1996) mentioned the importance of labour market institutions in lessening the impact of globalization on workers. The study notes that 'labour market institutions play an important role', and that in the USA and UK industries with 'higher unionization levels experienced less downgrading of the relative wages and employment of unskilled workers' (OECD, 1997: 116).

This evidence shows that unions can protect workers in the face of globalization. If unions can prove their 'worth' to workers who are fearful of the effects of globalization, this could have a positive influence on union recruitment drives. However, it also depends on the influence of globalization on the resources of unions. There is substantial evidence that unions protect workers' jobs by improving the productivity and international competitiveness of companies (Mishel and Voos, 1992). If unions can 'prove' that they are a positive influence on the employer's ability to compete in the global economy, this may also assist union recruitment.

WHAT HAVE AUSTRALIAN TRADE UNIONS DONE ABOUT GLOBALIZATION? HAVE THEY BEEN SUCCESSFUL?

Trade unions have a number of strategies available to them to deal with the adverse effects of globalization on workers. These include both international and domestic strategies.

International Strategies

International Labour Cooperation: Advocates of international labour cooperation suggest that like corporations, trade unions can organize internationally. There is a widespread literature on international labour cooperation, including the work of Levinson (1972), Gunter (1972), Weinberg (1978) and Bendiner (1987). In an overview of the literature on international trade union cooperation, Ramsey (1996: 3–8) classifies the schools of thought into 'Evolutionary Optimism', the 'Managerial Sceptics', the 'Left Pessimists' , 'National Alternativism', and 'Contingency Theories'. Ramsey traces the impediments to international labour cooperation, especially in terms of internationally coordinated bargaining in MNCs. With major difficulties in the European context there would seem little hope for labour cooperation in a wider global sphere.

Because of the disadvantage that labour faces compared to MNCs in terms of resources and influence over government, how much can labour gain by cooperating across national borders?

Whilst international union action, if threatened excessively and repeatedly, can be deemed ineffective if not supported by solid action by the membership (the 'cry wolf' scenario), it can be crucial for unions, particularly those in small countries, subject to state oppression. For instance, Fiji TUC President Michael Columbus[1] said that if it were not for the Australian and New Zealand transport union responses to blockade Fiji at the time of the military coup in 1987, the Fiji union movement would have been finished with drastic consequences for the liberty of its officials.

Another example is the ACTU's long lasting campaign against apartheid. Support for the African National Congress (ANC) and non-racial South African trade unions over the long years of apartheid included industrial action against South African sports teams, support for economic sanctions and financial support for trade unions in South Africa (see ACTU, 1995a). This action assisted the successful struggle against apartheid and brought benefits in turn for Australian unions. The Congress of South African Trade Unions (COSATU) reciprocated when it lent support to the Western Australian Trades and Labour Council (WATLC) in its fight against state government legislation in 1995 and to the Maritime Union of Australia (MUA) campaign against Patrick Stevedores in 1998.

The MUA's waterfront industrial campaign in 1998 received support from transport unions all over the world. This follows strong support from the MUA for seafarers in Burma, the Philippines and elsewhere who have had their human rights violated. The 'Ships of Shame' campaign by the MUA and International Transport Workers' Federation (ITF) has been instrumental in improving the welfare of seafarers in developing countries (see Commonwealth of Australia, 1993; ITF, 1998). Regular Australian assistance has also been provided by airline unions to their Papua New Guinea and Fijian counterparts. Australian unions have also supported their counterparts in the Republic of Korea in the 1997 showdown in Seoul over industrial legislation (see Bae et al., 1997, for an analysis of this conflict).

The ACTU is active in the ICFTU and various regional union bodies. Similarly, Australian unions belong to their respective international trade secretariats (ITS). However, it is difficult for under-resourced trade union bodies to take on the well-resourced global MNCs. Nonetheless, there are advantages in terms of information exchange and selective intervention at crucial stages in industrial disputes. International action in support of the MUA, for example, was taken very seriously by the Federal government, because of Australia's position as a small open economy.

While it is difficult for unions to take on global capital 'head to head' there is the case of the campaign against Rio Tinto, the international mining conglomerate. The Australian unions, together with the International Federation of Chemical, Energy, Mine and General Workers' Unions (ICEM), conducted a high profile campaign against Rio Tinto, who have aggressively tried to union-bust and replace collective regulation with individual contracts. The campaign against Rio Tinto was launched in Johannesburg in February 1998 at a meeting hosted by South African President Nelson Mandela and former Australian Prime Minister Bob Hawke (see ICEM, 1998a, 1998b).

International Trade Instruments: Australian unions have also followed the example of their US and European counterparts in trying to influence trade policy. This has often been unsuccessful as unions have had to compete against powerful business interests and the realities of geopolitics. This is difficult for Australia as a small industrial nation with a 'European past' in the emerging Asia Pacific region. Unions also have to make decisions about international resources and have typically relied on the ACTU and their ITS to represent them on international issues generally, including issues of trade policy. However, the ACTU, directly and through the ICFTU, has attempted to provide a labour voice in trade policy institutions such as the WTO and APEC.

Since the inception of the General Agreement on Tariff and Trade (GATT) in 1948, the international trade union movement has attempted to place labour standards on the international trade agenda. This was to ensure that countries did not undertake a 'race to the bottom'. Australian unions have supported the ICFTU in the campaign for a 'social clause' – that is, providing access to trade agreements on the basis that nations meet 'core labour standards' set by the ILO. The issue of the social clause also faces opposition because it is regarded as 'protectionist' by developing countries who regard low-cost labour as their only 'comparative advantage'. Also, the threat of trade sanctions is controversial (even if it is only a last resort) because of uncertainty concerning how it would be enforced (and who would enforce it).

In response, trade union advocates argue a number of points on the social clause. First, it is an 'insurance policy against protection' as it ensures that trade is fair and that better labour standards accompany the growth in trade that comes from liberalization. It is argued that trade liberalization will get more support if countries know it cannot be used to reduce social protections and living standards. Second, it is argued that the WTO is an appropriate mechanism to deal with labour standards as it can be done via the multilateral process rather than one nation accusing another of unfair labour practices, as can occur under the USA's Generalized System of Preferences (GSP). Third, it is argued that it is not about wages or relative labour costs but about labour standards and workers' rights – safety and non-discrimination – that assist productivity and economic growth (see OECD, 1995: 21). Fourth, those who oppose labour have attempted to form a 'North–South' or 'developed–developing country' wedge on the issue of the social clause. In fact, the interests of the North and South are not necessarily opposed, and deregulation solutions often hurt workers in both types of economies. Finally, it is argued that there should be more 'carrot' than 'stick' in the social clause. Instead of threatening sanctions, it could instead be framed in such a way that market access be offered to countries that make demonstrated efforts to raise labour standards.

The ACTU was successful in lobbying the previous Labor government on setting up a Tripartite Working Party on Labour Standards in the Asia Pacific region (see Commonwealth of Australia, 1995, the 'Duffy Report'). However, for the most part both Australian governments have not supported labour standards provisions in the WTO. Australia has been hamstrung by its size and lack of bargaining strength in world trade and its geopolitical need to 'fit in' with Asia, despite historical differences. It cannot use trade policy as leverage in the same way as the USA, given that there is no GSP but a need for Australia to retain Asian markets for export. Australia is a small voice in the WTO and supports the multilateral trade system as being in Australia's national interest.

Whilst the WTO mechanism has become a way of putting labour standards on the international trade agenda, it has been suggested that APEC, as a consensus-based institution, had more potential to effectively promote labour standards. In fact the Duffy Report suggested that the APEC forum be used in this way to the Keating Labor government in 1995. In its recommendations, the Report said that it will 'be necessary for APEC to address labour standards issues as it develops as a forum for broad based economic cooperation' (ibid.: 72–3). The Report suggested that Australia, with its commitment to trade in the region and its key role in international labour forums in the past, would be a good 'honest broker' in any discussion of labour issues in APEC. However, the union impact in APEC has been limited because of the lack of formal recognition for independent trade unions in Asia and the fact that APEC is only a fledging economic policy institution (see ACTU, 1997a).

Unions in other countries have used trade agreements to protect labour standards. Key examples are NAFTA and the EU's 'Community Charter for the Fundamental Social Rights of Workers' (the 'Social Charter'). Assessments of NAFTA and the 'side agreement' on labour standards have not been positive. For example, a study of the NAFTA 'side agreement' by Bronfenbrenner (1997) found that 'NAFTA has created a climate that has emboldened employers to more aggressively threaten to close, or actually close their plants to avoid unionization' (ibid.: 3).

There is no NAFTA equivalent in Australia. The Closer Economic Relationship (CER) agreement between Australia and New Zealand contains no side clause on labour, even though the unions do cooperate occasionally in industrial campaigns, such as in the airline industry. In terms of the EU Social Charter, Australia has no equivalent but unions have looked closely at their European counterparts in terms of social and labour adjustment (see Public Services International, 1997).

Another instrument supported by the Australian unions has been the Codes of Conduct. Part of the ICFTU's approach in trade policy has been to encourage the adoption of such codes for investment in the global economy. Examples include the promotion of the ILO's Tripartite Declaration of Principles concerning Multinational Enterprises and Social Policy and various consumer-union Codes involving MNCs like Reebok and Levi Strauss. Whilst many of the guidelines are voluntary, some that target a company's market and image as a good 'corporate citizen' can have some effect (see Commonwealth of Australia,

1995: 14–17). Similarly, the ACTU, together with the ICFTU, campaigned for 'no child labour' products to be used in the 1998 World Cup in France and 2000 Olympic Games in Sydney (see ACTU, 1997c).

Domestic Strategies

Domestic Industrial Campaigns on Globalization Issues: There is some scope for campaigning on globalization issues, particularly where there have been job losses as a result of some of Australia's less successful trade and industry policies. A good example is the 'fair wear campaign' by the Textile, Clothing and Footwear Union of Australia (TCFUA) on outwork. It has been argued that companies in the industry used outworkers in order to avoid paying minimum wages and meeting minimum conditions in the relevant industry awards. Outworkers are typically migrant women who work at home as 'subcontractors' for companies. They are typically poorly paid and often subject to intimidation. The TCFUA has attempted to regulate out the worst aspects of outwork. The fair wear campaign puts consumer pressure on employers to sign a 'code of conduct' that they will pay fair minimum wages and conditions. As a result of the campaign, a number of retailers agreed to sign the TCFUA's code of conduct on outwork. This provides a legal and fair basis for outwork (see ACTU, 1996, 1997d).

The TCFUA also ran a campaign with respect to tariff policy. In Australia, the Productivity Commission (PC) holds public inquiries into certain industries and reports to the Federal government. The PC and its predecessors have typically called for tariff reduction and the elimination of other forms of industry regulation. The TCFUA made submissions to the PC inquiry into the textile, clothing and footwear (TCF) industries and also successfully lobbied the Federal government to reject the PC's recommendations for a further reduction in tariff protection on the grounds that tariff reductions would further reduce employment (see Commonwealth of Australia, 1997a).

Similar inquiries have been held into the automotive industry, the aviation industry, competitive tendering and other matters subject to scrutiny. Australian unions play an active role in influencing the course of inquiries and the Federal government's response to the PC recommendations. Some recent efforts have been successful, such as the automotive industry inquiry and the TCF inquiry, cited above (see Commonwealth of Australia, 1997b). However, for much of the 1980s the union campaigns were not successful as the Australian Labor government reduced tariffs. One difficulty is that unions are often 'captured' by the industry position when they join forces politically with employers. If the employers are not sufficiently strong in terms of their lobbying capacity (such as the Australian TCF employers), the union is forced into a losing strategy. Rodrik (1997: 76) suggests that unions should distance themselves from the protectionist lobby. Fortunately for the TCFUA, there were supplementary strategies in place, such as the fair wear campaign and award restructuring, that could be used to partially protect their members' interests.

Domestic Labour Market Responses: Domestic labour market responses to globalization are based on the rationale that unions should do what unions do best – protect workers' welfare in the labour market. Unions have neither the resources to be instant trade policy experts nor the commercial power to affect investment. However, unions can represent workers to 'cushion' the effects of globalization. Examples of this include the 'award restructuring' policy devised by the ACTU in 1989 (see Belchamber, 1992). The rationale was to raise the skill levels of workers, particularly in low paid areas, and to provide career paths to workers who previously had no access to promotion and progression in their jobs. At the same time, the improved skill levels and work practices would provide productivity benefits to employers competing with fierce international competition (see also Rowley and Lewis, 1996; Rowley, 1997; Rowley and Bae, 1998, for other examples). Australia's improved average productivity levels in the 1990s, compared to the 1980s, can be traced to award restructuring and associated workplace reforms (see ACTU, 1998a: 117–22). This 'high skill, high wage, high productivity' approach of Australian unions in the face of globalization contrasts strongly with the 'concession bargaining' approach of American unions in the late 1970s and early 1980s.

Award restructuring allowed the Australian workforce to prepare for increased globalization in the 1990s by improving skill levels. Policies that anticipate such changes are beneficial. However, because no policy body has perfect foresight, it is necessary to have supplementary labour market adjustment schemes when 'external shocks' do harm to industry sectors.

Assessment of the Strategies

Australian trade unions have used a combination of strategies to deal with the problems of globalization with a varying degree of success (see Table 1). International labour cooperation has been successful in certain industrial disputes (such as the Waterfront dispute of 1998) and where there is a major political issue (apartheid in South Africa). However, there are still major resource constraints facing Australian unions who rely heavily on their international affiliations.

TABLE 1

MATCHING GLOBALIZATION PROBLEMS AND TRADE UNION STRATEGIES

Policy problem	Trade union strategy
Wage inequality due to trade liberalization	Labour standards in international trade agreements ('social clause') Domestic industrial campaigns on globalization Domestic labour market responses (e.g. award restructuring – to increase the skills of low paid workers)
Employment insecurity due to trade liberalization	Labour standards in international trade agreements ('social clause') Domestic industrial campaigns on globalization Domestic labour market responses (e.g. labour market adjustment programmes).
Increased capital mobility affecting bargaining power and labour standards	Labour standards in international trade agreements ('social clause') International labour cooperation Domestic industrial campaigns on globalization

The use of international trade instruments, while limited to date, may well become more important in the future. The Asian financial crisis has caused policymakers to reassess the international economic institutional framework set up by Bretton Woods and there is now an opportunity to include labour issues in the reform process. The International Monetary Fund (IMF) and World Bank have indicated that there is a role for labour in the new institution-building (see Camdessus, 1998; World Bank, 1995). This shows that there is not just one model of the global economy that all have to follow and that unions should try to shape more worker-friendly international economic institutions.

The domestic agenda, however, should not be ignored. Some domestic industrial campaigns on globalization issues are effective, such as the TCFUA's fair wear campaign. However, campaigns that allow unions to be trapped in a broader political agenda may not help (for example, in the tariff debate). The failure of the tariff campaign in the 1980s left the TCFUA with no option but to run the fair wear campaign, but the problems of outworkers and the avoidance of award responsibilities by employers need to be highlighted, whatever the state of trade policy.

Domestic labour market responses are often underrated but can be effective. They should not be regarded as substitutes for international strategies, but as powerful complements. Award restructuring and labour market adjustment programmes whilst seemingly out of the sphere of trade policy are actually important, and have assisted Australian workers in dealing with the adverse effects of globalization. These policies are consistent with calls by economists for a labour market, rather than a trade policy, response to help unskilled workers. Whilst Wood (1995) and others called for labour market subsidies for the low skilled, the policies of award restructuring may be more effective as there is an industrial relations focus with benefits for both employers and workers.

CONCLUSION

This contribution has outlined the current debate on the effects of globalization on workers and has provided examples of trade union strategies in Australia used to deal with those effects. The evidence shows that the advocates of trade liberalization have not been able to overwhelmingly convince opinion makers that benefits will automatically flow from globalization and trade liberalization. Some economists do not deal adequately with income distribution questions, while others admit that there will be 'winners and losers' and instead make policy recommendations on how losers can be compensated. Alternatively, those opposing globalization have not always identified whether it is globalization or other elements that cause harm to workers and the community. Furthermore, many anti-globalization advocates are unable to show why the 'closed economy' counterfactual would have been more beneficial.

Australian trade unions have attempted a combination of strategies to deal with globalization. The international strategies include labour cooperation across borders and lobbying for labour standards in trade policy instruments. These strategies can be limited, given the resource constraints of unions compared to governments and business and the fact that geopolitical forces can work against unions. Whilst sympathetic to trade unions on international labour standard issues, the Hawke–Keating Labor governments did not want to cause diplomatic problems with Asia Pacific neighbours because of foreign policy objectives. The international strategies are also considered too 'big picture' and remote from usual trade union business. However, unions with international traditions, such as the coal miners and transport workers, have shown that international support can work in practical ways to win major industrial disputes. The domestic strategies too are often underrated. Campaigns on globalization issues can work to unions' advantage, and labour market strategies that raise skill levels and assist job security can be effective.

Globalization has become part of the bargaining challenge that trade unions face in advancing their members' interests. Hard-headed analysis is needed, together with a comprehensive set of strategies, to enable globalization to be treated as both a challenge and opportunity for workers.

ACKNOWLEDGEMENTS

This article was written in Melbourne, Australia and Cambridge, Massachusetts. I would like to thank Jane Howard of the ACTU and Jo Bosben of the Australian APEC Study Centre for their assistance with the preparation of the article. I benefited from comments from Jo Bosben, John Benson, Geoff Harcourt, Chris Rowley and anonymous referees. I was assisted by conversations on this issue with Elaine Bernard, Richard Freeman, Dani Rodrik, Robert Solow and David Weil. All errors and omissions are mine.

NOTES

1. In conversation with the author.

REFERENCES

ACTU (1994) *Trade in the Asia Pacific Region: An ACTU Guide*. Melbourne: ACTU.
ACTU (1995a) *Policy Information for South African Trade Unions*. Melbourne: ACTU.
ACTU (1995b) *APEC – What Should Unions Do?* Melbourne: ACTU.
ACTU (1996) *Australian Senate Inquiry into Garment Industry Outworking: ACTU Submission*. Melbourne: ACTU.
ACTU (1997a) *Trade Unions and APEC*. Melbourne: ACTU.

ACTU (1997b) *Australia in Relation to APEC*. ACTU Submission to Australian Senate Inquiry into APEC. Melbourne: ACTU.

ACTU (1997c) *International Strategy and Key Objectives Resolution, ACTU 1997 Congress*. Melbourne: ACTU.

ACTU (1997d) *Outwork Protest Turns to Celebration*. ACTU Media Release, 21 July. Melbourne: ACTU.

ACTU (1998a) *Living Wage 1997/98*. ACTU Written Submission. Melbourne: ACTU.

ACTU (1998b) *Sydney Olympics Promote Fair Labour Standards*. ACTU Media Release, 24 Feb. Melbourne: ACTU.

AFL-CIO (1997) *NAFTA Expansion: Off the Fast Track, on the Right Track*. Washington, DC: AFL-CIO.

Australian Services Union (1998) *Submission to the Industry Inquiry into International Air Services*. Melbourne: Australian Services Union.

Bae, J., Rowley, C., Kim, D.H and Lawler, J. (1997) 'Korean Industrial Relations at the Crossroads: The Recent Labour Troubles', *Asia Pacific Business Review*, Vol. 3, No. 3, pp. 148–60.

Belchamber, G. (1992) *A Decade of Change: Australian Trade Unions and Global Free Trade*. Melbourne: ACTU.

Belman, D. and Lee, T. (1997) 'International Trade and the Performance of US Labour Markets', in R. Blecker (ed.), *US Trade Policy and Global Growth: New Directions in the International Economy*. New York: M.E. Sharpe, pp. 61–107.

Bendiner, B. (1987) *International Labour Affairs: The World Trade Unions and the Multinational Companies*. Oxford: Clarendon Press.

Bhagwati, J. and Kosters, M. (1994) *Trade and Wages: Levelling Wages Down?* Washington, DC: AEI Press.

Bronfenbrenner, K. (1997) *The Effects of Plant Closing or Threat of Plant Closing on the Right of Workers to Organize*. Report submitted to North American Commission for Labour Co-operation, Cornell University, Ithaca, New York.

Burtless, G. (1995) 'International Trade and the Rise in Earnings Equality', *Journal of Economic Literature*, Vol. 33, June, pp. 800–16.

Camdessus, M. (1998) 'Is the Asian Crisis Over?' Address to the National Press Club, Washington, DC, 2 April. IMF Internet site.

Canadian Labour Congress (1996) *The Social Dimensions of North American Economic Integration*. Ottawa: Canadian Labour Congress.

Costa, M. (1991) 'Protectionism, Neo-Mercantilism and Free-Trade Labour', in M. Costa and M. Easson, *Australian Industry: What Policy?* Sydney: Pluto Press, pp. 107–22.

Chapman, B. (1998) *The Accord: Background, Changes and Aggregate Outcomes*. CEPR, Australian National University, Canberra.

Commonwealth of Australia (1993) *Ships of Shame*. Report from House of Representatives Standing Committee on Transport, Communications and Infrastructure, Parliament House, Canberra: AGPS.

Commonwealth of Australia (1995) *Report of Labour Standards in the Asia Pacific Region*. Report of the Tripartite Working Party on Labour Standards. Canberra: AGPS.

Commonwealth of Australia (1997a) *The Textiles, Clothing and Footwear Industries: Report of the Industry Commission*. Report No. 59, Sept., Melbourne.

Commonwealth of Australia (1997b) *The Automotive Industry: Report of the Industry Commission*. Report No. 58, May, Melbourne.

Freeman, R. (1995) 'Are Your Wages Set in Beijing?' *Journal of Economic Perspectives*, Vol. 9, No. 3, Summer, pp.15–32.

Galbraith, J.K. (1996) 'Uneven Development and the Destabilization of the North: A Keynesian View', *International Review of Applied Economics*, Vol. 10, No. 1, pp.107–20.

Garnaut, R. (1994) 'Options for Asian Pacific Trade Liberalization'. Paper presented to Institute of South East Asian Studies, Singapore.

Gunter, H. (1972) *Transnational Industrial Relations*. IILS, Geneva.

Hawke, R.J.L. (1992) 'APEC or Regional Agreements – the Real Implications', *Australian Quarterly*, Vol. 64, No. 4, Summer, pp. 339–49.

Hirst, P. and Thompson, G. (eds) (1992) 'The Problem of "Globalization": International Economic Relations, National Economic Management and the Formation of Trading Blocs', *Economy and Society*, Vol. 21, No. 4, Nov., pp. 357–94.

Holland, S. (1997) *The Global Economy: From Meso to Macroeconomics*. London: Weidenfeld and Nicolson.

ICEM (1998a) '"Defend Collective Bargaining", Mandela Tells World's Rio Tinto Unions', *ICEM Update* No. 7, 8 Feb.

ICEM (1998b) 'Rio Tinto: World's Unions Launch Action Network', ICEM Update No. 8, 9 Feb.

ITF (1998) 'Global Union Action Halts Australian Strike Breaking Mercenary Scheme', ITF Internet site. London: ITF.

Kozul-Wright, R. (1995) 'Transnational Corporations and the Nation State', in J. Michie and J. Grieve Smith (1995) (eds), *Managing the Global Economy*. Oxford: Oxford University Press, pp. 135–71.

Latham, M. (1998) *Civilizing Global Capital: New Thinking for Australian Labour*. Sydney: Allen and Unwin.

Lawrence, R. (1994) 'Trade, Multinationals and Labour', in Lowe, P. and Dwyer, J. (eds.), *International Integration of the Australian Economy*. Sydney: Reserve Bank of Australia.

Levinson, C. (1972) *International Trade Unionism*. London: George Allen and Unwin.

Machin, S., Ryan, A. and Van Reenan, J. (1996) *Technology and Changes in Skill Development: Evidence from an International Panel of Industries*. Centre for Economic Performance Discussion, Paper No. 297. London: London School of Economics.

Mishel, Lawrence and Voos, Paula (eds) (1992) *Unions and Economic Competitiveness*. New York: M.E. Sharpe.

OECD (1995) *Trade and Labour Standards: A Review of the Issues*. Paris: OECD.

OECD (1997) *Employment Outlook*. Paris: OECD.

Ohmae, K. (1990) *The Borderless World: Power and Strategy in the Interlinked Economy*. New York: Harper Business.

Ohmae, K. (1995) *The End of the Nation State: The Rise of Regional Economies*. New York: The Free Press.

Oxley, A. (1990) *The Challenge of Free Trade*. Melbourne: Harvester Wheatsheaf.

Public Services International (1997) *International Trade Agreements and Trade Unions: Briefing Notes*. France: Public Services International. .

Ramsey, H. (1996) '"Solidarity At Last?" International Trade Union Theory and the Prospects for Trans-Europe Collective Bargaining Approaching the Millennium'. Unpublished mimeo. Glasgow: University of Strathclyde.

Rodrik, D. (1997) *Has Globalization Gone Too Far?* Washington, DC: Institute for International Economics.

Rowley, C. (1997) 'Reassessing HRM's Convergence', *Asia Pacific Business Review*, Vol. 3, No. 4, pp. 198–211.

Rowley, C. and Bae, J. (1998) 'Korean Business and Management: The End of the Model', *Asia Pacific Business Review*, Vol. 4, No. 3, pp. 130–9.

Rowley, C. and Lewis, M. (1996) 'Greater China at the Crossroads? Convergence, Culture and Competitiveness', *Asia Pacific Business Review*, Vol. 2, No. 3, pp. 1–22.

Singh, A. (1997) 'Expanding Employment in the Global Economy: The High Road or the Low Road?', in P. Arestis, G. Palma and M. Sawyer (eds), *Markets, Unemployment and Economic Policy: Essays in Honour of Geoff Harcourt*, Vol. 1. London: Routledge, pp. 405–18.

Slaughter, M. and Swagel, P. (1997) 'Does Globalization Lower Wages and Export Jobs?', *Economic Issues*, No. 11, Washington, DC: International Monetary Fund, pp. 1–12.

Smith, A. (1776) *The Wealth of Nations*. London: Penguin.

Solow, R. (1997) 'What Is Labour Market Flexibility ? What Is It Good For?' Keynes Lecture to the British Academy, 30 Oct., London.

Stolper, W. and Samuelson, P. (1941) 'Protection and Real Wages', *Review of Economic Studies*, Vol. 9, pp. 58–73.

Thorpe, V. (1997) *Globalization and Social Policy*, ICEM Info 4. Brussels: ICEM.

Weinberg, P. (1978) *European Labour and Multinationals*. New York: Praeger Publishers.

Wood, A. (1995) 'How Trade Hurt Unskilled Workers', *Journal of Economic Perspectives*, Vol. 9, No. 3, Summer, pp. 57–80.

World Bank (1995) *Workers in an Integrating World: World Development Report 1995*. Washington, DC: Oxford University Press.

6

Globalization, Non-Standard Employment and Australian Trade Unions

JOHN BURGESS

Trade unionism is in crisis in many countries as high unemployment rates persist, workforces are dramatically restructured, the public sector is downsized and a coalition of hostile employers and conservative governments enact anti-union legislation. This at least is the picture emerging in the Anglo-Saxon OECD (Organization for Economic Cooperation and Development) economies of Australia, New Zealand, the USA and Canada (Anderson, 1991; Edwards, 1993; Taylor, 1994). Many publications and conferences in Australia have discussed the theme of the future of trade unionism and even whether unionism has a future (Berry and Kitchener, 1988; Crosby and Easson, 1992; Griffin, 1996). It seems that all the conditions that trade unions accrued over many years of struggle are now under threat. It is not only unionism that is being challenged; it is the traditional employment paradigm with preset conditions and entitlements of employment. Employers and governments are directly challenging these conditions, and in the process the rationale for trade unions as protectors of employment standards is also being challenged.

The Political Threat against Australian Trade Unions

In Australia trade unions have been under direct legal and political challenge for over a decade as militant employer groups, right wing think tanks, the media and successive state governments have attacked unionism and the supporting institutional framework, including the conciliation and arbitration process, awards and centralized wage determination (Dabscheck, 1995). At the state level, legislation has been enacted which makes it difficult for unions to organize and eases the path of employers towards workforce de-unionization and facilitates the shift from collective awards to individual employment contracts (Hearn, 1997). This process reached its zenith with the election of the conservative (Liberal Party and National Party) coalition parties to Federal government in 1996 and 1998. They enacted the 1996 Workplace Relations Act that facilitated non-union agreements and individual employment contracts; it also contained numerous regulations and sanctions governing trade union behaviour (Pocock and Wright, 1997).

Changing Workforce Composition Adverse to Unionism

Against these direct political threats, Australian trade unions have had to also contend with unfavourable structural shifts in the composition of the workforce. Employment shares have shrunk in traditional union sectors of manufacturing and utilities while they have expanded in the lowly unionized private service sectors (Lipsig-Mumme, 1997). In addition to this, the public sector has been shrinking through 'fiscal consolidation' and the privatization of public sector business enterprises. These structural shifts require new recruitment and bargaining strategies on behalf of trade unions. Indeed, the peak union body, the Australian Council of Trade Unions (ACTU), has been conscious of declining union densities and the need to implement a range of recruitment strategies among workers (such as youth) who have been outside of or ignored by trade unionism in the past (Gahan, 1997). Nevertheless, recruitment and retention challenges facing trade unions in Australia are considerable (Berry and Kitchener, 1988; Crosby and Easson, 1992; Evatt Foundation, 1995; Costa and Hearn, 1997).

The Rapid Decline in Australian Trade Union Density and Membership

Australian trade union membership data support the view that trade unionism is under serious threat. Between August 1990 and August 1997 trade union density fell from 40.5 per cent to 30.3 per cent; even more alarming for trade unions is that membership declined from 2.66 million to 2.11 million, a loss of over half a million members (Australian Bureau of Statistics (ABS), Catalogues 6325.0 and 6310.0). This cannot solely be attributable to a hostile Federal government bent on destroying trade unionism, but it can in part be attributable to the rapidly changing workforce structure where new and permanent full-time jobs are a rarity. For example, in the two years between August 1995 and August 1997, the net employment increase in Australia was 37,000. However, full-time jobs declined by 80,000 while part-time jobs increased by 117,000 (ABS Catalogue 6203.0). The absence of full-time job growth points to one of the important issues that has confronted trade unions across the OECD for the past two decades, the growth in so-called non-standard employment (Brosnan and Campbell, 1995).

The Growing Non-Standard Share of Employment

There has been a rapid expansion in non-standard employment in Australia over the past two decades. The characteristics of non-standard workers often place them outside of trade union representation. The dilemma confronting trade unions is that non-standard employment conditions are being directly and indirectly used to undermine standard employment conditions, and in the process contribute to a declining union density. This chapter discusses the intersection between the globalization imperative, the growing non-standard workforce and declining trade union density in Australia. It concludes with an outline of possible trade union strategies towards the recruitment and retention of non-standard workers. The theme is that if trade unions are to remain relevant they must directly address the needs of the non-standard workforce that accounts for over 75 per cent of the new jobs created.

GLOBALIZATION AND AUSTRALIA

Globalization is a catch-all term that has been applied to institutions, processes and outcomes across national economies and across the international economy. It has been applied in different contexts and it has different meanings in these contexts. There is extensive debate over what globalization means and what it constitutes (Amin and Thrift, 1996). In addition there is debate over whether in fact globalization is a new or homogeneous process (Hirst and Thompson, 1996). As a descriptive term of economic change it indicates the internationalization of production and trade, the internationalization of all markets and the integration of domestic economies into global economies. Thurow (1996: 115) describes globalization as a process whereby any product can be produced anywhere for consumption anywhere.

Globalization has also been used to describe the process of systems change and transformation (Sklair, 1996). In this context there are three distinct meanings: the end of the Fordist production model and the development of post-Fordist production (Reich, 1991); the end of the Cold War and the demise of the communist production and distribution model, together with the global ascendancy of capitalism (Thurow, 1996); and the end of the post-1945 welfare state in OECD economies supported by Keynesian measures to maintain full employment, and the ascendancy of minimalist models of government intervention and welfare support (Catley, 1996). Globalization is also a process in which national institutions and policies are increasingly subordinated to international institutions and policies, and as such it is part of the challenge to national identity and national policy sovereignty (Thurow, 1996). In this context globalization also describes the ascendancy of international capital, in particular the international corporation, over domestic capital, or what Reich (1991: 110) labels as the transnational 'global web'. It also describes the impact of information technology in transforming communications and providing for instantaneous links between economies and markets (Amin and Thrift, 1996: 3). Finally, it is an ideological process that demands certain types of policies and certain types of responses to the inevitability of globalization pressures (Bell, 1997: Chapter 4). The ascendancy of neoliberal policy frameworks is in part a response to the belief in the inevitability of globalization together with the view that there is only one way public policy can respond to these pressures. This view is reinforced by national policy institutions such as central banks, and by international policy institutions such as the IMF (International Monetary Fund) (Thurow, 1996).

Globalization has had an extreme impact on Australia, not least because a globalization paradigm has emerged as the basis for public policy design. Since the mid-1980s there has been a globalization imperative in Australian public policy that has not only transformed policy institutions but also the operation of public policy (Bell, 1997; Catley, 1996). At a superficial level it can be argued that globalization is occurring in Australia through the spread of information technology, the increase in international tourism and in international trade and finance, and as a result of the industrial restructuring of the economy. However, developments in trade, finance and industrial structure do not represent something that is decisively different from the past. Information technology is decisive in terms of the breadth and depth of its impact across sectors; it can transform communications, internationalize production and significantly change the process of production. Yet, technological change in itself does not signify the need for a wholesale evaluation of the role of the state and a policy programme that is based on the premise of the inevitability of globalization. This is where Australia has been most affected by globalization: it is taken as unavoidable and with proscribed policy responses. The only policy debates are about how far and how fast the neoliberal policy response should be instituted and what institutions are necessary in a post-globalization economy, together with debate over how much domestic policy sovereignty is still available in such a context (Catley, 1996).

Sklair (1996) and Bramble (1996) have directly and indirectly promulgated this thesis. Sklair (1996) catalogues the influences of the globalizers in Australian business, political parties and policy institutions such as the Federal treasury and the reserve bank. It is hardly coincidental that the neoliberal agenda has been so influential in Australia since the early 1980s. These views also extend to influential trade unions, with Bramble (1996) outlining the demise of the collectivist and protectionist labourist project and its replacement by what he calls the 'globalization agenda', which embodies unions accepting the inevitability of a shift towards an open economy, the redefining of the role of the state and the end of the social democratic agenda (full employment, redistribution and state ownership). As a consequence, a 'globalization hegemony' has evolved in Australia that is based on three assumptions: that globalization is inevitable, that there is a definite policy response to globalization, and that impediments to the globalization agenda should be removed.

For labour the impact of globalization has come via three processes. First, the process of internationalization of production and markets has placed pressure on employment conditions. There is the continuing threat of plant relocation and import substitution for domestic production. Benchmarking, best practice and international competitiveness have become descriptors of the downward pressure on employment conditions over the past decade emanating from increasing international competition (Amin and Thrift, 1996). Second, the policy response, based on the neoliberal paradigm, has exalted labour flexibility and in the process has attacked many traditional employment conditions (such as job protection and overtime payments) as being impediments to the effective operation of the market mechanism and to free trade. Under the guise of labour flexibility, award conditions, minimum wages, centralized wage determination and trade unionism have been under constant political and legislative pressure (Campbell, 1993). Within this context, non-standard employment arrangements are encouraged since they exhibit both numerical and functional flexibility, and because they largely operate outside of employment regulations (ibid.). Thirdly, the trade union response to the globalization agenda has involved strategies that largely embrace globalization and legitimize the neoliberal policy response (Bramble, 1996).

Trade unions have been placed in a contradictory position within the globalization imperative context. By attempting to protect employment conditions and rights they are represented as opponents to modernization, internationalization and globalization. They are depicted as being stuck in an earlier Fordist production era and within the context of an earlier Keynesian policy paradigm (Clark, 1992). On the other hand, through accommodating globalization trade unions have implicitly legitimized the neoliberal agenda and they have become incorporated into an agenda that has required the transformation of employment conditions. This last observation is nowhere more pertinent than with respect to the post-1988 industrial relations decentralization phase of the Prices and Incomes Accord, a corporatist policy arrangement between the ACTU and the Labour Federal government (Bramble, 1996; Dabscheck, 1995).

STANDARD AND NON-STANDARD EMPLOYMENT

There is no universal definition of what constitutes standard and non-standard employment. Indeed, even the terminology is confusing, with references being made in the literature to 'precarious' (Rodgers, 1989), 'atypical' (Robinson, 1991), 'peripheral' (Payne and Payne, 1993) and 'contingent' (Polivka and Nardone, 1989) employment. This discussion will use the term 'non-standard' as a catch-all for those employment arrangements that to different degrees are either unregulated or outside of the traditional forms of employment regulation. The exact nature of standard employment is imprecise, often being proscribed through employment law, collective agreements, custom and practice, and trade union policy. For this reason, the definition and measurement of standard employment is dependent upon national regulatory systems and will, therefore, differ across countries. Standard employment is associated with a normal employment contract involving continuity and regularity of employment, mutuality and security in employment, and access to defined non-wage employment benefits (Leighton, 1986: 504). As a consequence, non-standard employment embodies a range of employment arrangements that deviate from the standard employment form, but in themselves are disparate. This catch-all concept includes part-time employment, self-employment, fixed-term employment, outworking, working unsociable hours, temporary employment and casual employment. It also includes several ambiguous employment forms such as home-working and agency working. These employment types differ in many respects, such as income, award coverage, status and security. It can range from self-employed professional workers located at the upper end of the income distribution profile to casual workers with irregular and unpredictable hours, income and employment continuity.

For the above reasons, estimating employment categories for Australia is a very approximate exercise. As a starting point the standard workforce can be argued to include all full-time, permanent employees. Full-time employee arrangements generate a weekly income above the prescribed minimum. Employees are subject to inclusion within industrial awards that establish legally binding minimum conditions of employment including hours, wage rates and non-wage benefits. Employees can also access trade union membership. Permanent employees have rights to notice, protection from unfair dismissal and a range of non-wage benefits such as sickness benefits (Campbell and Burgess, 1997). In Australia it is possible to obtain estimates for the following divisions within the workforce: employees and non-employees, full-time and part-time workers, and permanent and casual employees.

Non-employees represent a very disparate group of workers (Burgess, 1990) who share employment arrangements that are largely unregulated and unprotected, and as such they can be considered as non-standard workers. Part-time workers are also regarded as non-standard since they often receive less than a full-time minimum weekly income, and around a third are involuntary in terms of wishing to work longer hours (Mitchell and Burgess, 1998). Casuals do not require notice of termination, have very little protection against dismissal and do not qualify for a range of non-wage benefits such as holiday pay (Campbell and Burgess, 1997).

An approximation for the non-standard workforce in Australia can be obtained by summing non-employees, part-time employees and full-time casual employees. Such an exercise is presented in Table 1. The table tracks the inexorable demise of the standard workforce and with it the rise in non-standard employment. The relative growth in the non-standard workforce is largely attributable to the related growth in part-time and casual employees. The share of non-employees in the workforce has remained stable. Over the 1982–97 period the non-standard employment share increased from 0.33 to 0.46; that is, by nearly 40 per cent. If we were to consider other non-standard employment arrangements not captured in the official labour force estimates, then estimates of the size and share of the non-standard workforce would expand further. Such employment arrangements as multiple job holdings, employment experience over the year, external workers, seasonal workers, outworkers, temporary workers, fixed-term workers, incorporated and salaried business owners, and unrecorded work are not included in the estimates contained within Table 1. Their inclusion would push the non-standard workforce above 50 per cent of the Australian workforce. Non-standard employment growth is not purely a manifestation of structural shifts in the workforce. It is not being generated just because of the rise in service sector employment, or because of the growing female share of employment or because of the relative decline in the occupational share of trade and craft workers. By the same token it is also not a one-off or temporary phenomenon; the rise in non-standard employment has persisted over at least the past two decades in Australia. The evidence suggests that the growth in non-standard employment is occurring across the spectrum of industries, occupations, gender groups, age groups and workplace sizes.

TABLE 1

STANDARD AND NON-STANDARD WORKFORCE IN AUSTRALIA
(RATIO OF TOTAL WORKFORCE)

Year	Std workforce	Non-std workforce	Part-time permanent employees	Full-time casual employees	Part-time casual employees	Non-employees
1982	0.67	0.33	na	na	na	0.16
1986	0.63	0.37	na	na	na	0.17
1988	0.63	0.37	0.05	0.04	0.11	0.16
1989	0.63	0.37	0.05	0.04	0.12	0.16
1990	0.62	0.38	0.05	0.04	0.12	0.17
1991	0.60	0.40	0.06	0.04	0.12	0.17
1992	0.59	0.41	0.07	0.05	0.12	0.17
1993	0.58	0.42	0.07	0.05	0.12	0.16
1994	0.56	0.44	0.07	0.06	0.14	0.17
1995	0.57	0.43	0.07	0.05	0.14	0.17
1996	0.55	0.45	0.07	0.07	0.15	0.16
1997	0.54	0.46	0.08	0.07	0.15	0.16

Source: ABS (Catalogues 6203.0, 6310.0, 6310.0.40.001 and 6334.0).

NON-STANDARD EMPLOYMENT AND AUSTRALIAN TRADE UNIONS

In Australia there has been a dramatic decline in trade union members, densities and numbers. At the same time the average membership size of trade unions is increasing through a process of ACTU sponsored amalgamations (Dabscheck, 1995: 117–39). The reasons for the diminishing membership of trade unions are varied and complex and include the effects of industry structural change, the failure of trade union policy, direct legislative attack by employer groups and governments together with populist attacks by the media. This broader discussion of the reasons for the falling trade union density in Australia, while critical, is outside of the scope of this chapter (see Crosby and Easson, 1992; Griffin and Svenson, 1996; Peetz, 1996).

The causal relationship between decline in trade union density and growth in non-standard employment in Australia is not clear-cut. Falling union densities are likely to open up the possibilities for non-union recruitment and to place pressure on existing employment conditions. Non-standard employment growth makes it difficult for trade unions to recruit workers who have few benefits or protected conditions, especially casual employees. However, non-standard employment growth is one reason why trade union densities are falling. The impact on trade unions of growing non-standard employment is not uniform across the different forms of non-standard employment arrangements.

Consider the relationship between non-employees and trade unions. With few exceptions, non-employees have very low trade union densities. Their very status would superficially appear to be incompatible with trade unionism. The award system in Australia basically protects the wages and conditions of employees, and membership of a trade union would enhance the likelihood that workers are located under the umbrella of award protection. Non-employees are composed of a disparate group of workers including the self-employed and employers, and account for around 16 per cent of the Australian workforce. Recent innovative employment practices (Bennet, 1995: 147), while aimed at removing workers from the protection of awards, do not necessarily remove their right to belong to a trade union (Underhill and Kelly, 1993). Indeed, a large minority of self-employed contractors is contracted to only one agency or one employer (Vandenheuval and Wooden, 1995); they have ambiguous employment status and rights in terms of award coverage and trade union membership.

Part-time and/or casual employees have traditionally lower trade union membership as compared to full-time employees (Lewis, 1990: 22, 31; Plowman, 1992: 272). For example, in 1997 the full-time union density was 34 per cent, the part-time union density was 21 per cent, the permanent employee density was 35 per cent, while the casual employee density was 14 per cent (ABS Catalogue 6310.0). The lower density for part-time and/or casuals partly represents structural features (high proportion of females, young workers, service sector employees, small business workplaces), but it also reflects other factors associated with part-time and casual workers, including high employment turnover, the difficulty in organizing and the associated high costs of recruitment, the past neglect/hostility of trade unions towards such workers (Campbell, 1992), and their vulnerability to employer coercion, especially in small businesses. Groups with a high incidence of part-time and casual employment have relatively low trade union densities, especially younger employees (18 per cent for 15–19 year olds) and females (22 per cent). However, the problem with part-time/casual employees is that they are often located outside the traditional organizational, industrial and demographic domains of trade unions. It is not that part-time employees, for example, have less need of trade union membership than do full-time employees; it is just that they have not been part of the traditional union membership profile or they have not been working in traditional workplaces in which trade unions were located (Ellem, 1992).

If the share of the non-standard workforce continues to increase in Australia, then in the absence of any significant institutional or policy changes, the density of trade unions will continue to fall as a consequence of the structural features associated with non-standard employment. The issues confronting trade unions in terms of non-standard workers have been addressed elsewhere by Bray (1991a: 199–201), who identifies four potential responses from trade unions to non-standard workers: (1) ignore, (2) exclude and oppose, (3) limit their numbers and regulate, and (4) recruit and integrate.

In the past, the traditional Australian trade union response has been to see non-standard employment as a potential threat to standard employment conditions, hence strategies (1) to (3) represented the range of responses by unions towards non-standard workers (Lever-Tracy, 1988; Campbell, 1992; Ellem, 1992). However, the numbers of non-standard workers together with the increasing political and legislative attacks on trade unions have forced unions to move increasingly towards strategy (4), even though such strategies are often costly and face opposition both within trade unions and from employers (Crosby, 1992). The discussion now turns towards the type of strategies trade unions require in order to attract non-standard workers.

TRADE UNION STRATEGIES: POSSIBILITIES AND PROSPECTS FOR THE NON-STANDARD WORKFORCE

In a static environment there are profound problems confronting trade unions. In a dynamic environment nearly all the anticipated changes in the workforce and at the workplace are potentially adverse for trade unions. While the 1996 Federal Workplace Relations Act was designed in part to reduce the influence of trade unions at the workplace and to further erode their collective representation (Gahan, 1997; Pocock and Wright, 1997), the legislative attack is only one dimension of the overall hostile environment facing unions. Non-standard employment will continue to increase its workforce share; the thrust of labour market deregulation is towards removing all those conditions that support standard employment and to dilute standard employment conditions. There is an uneasy and contradictory relationship between the non-standard workforce and trade unions; non-standard employment growth contributes to declining trade union density, which in turn provides more discretion and opportunity for employers to dilute standard employment conditions and to extend the non-standard workforce.

Part of the appeal for employers of non-standard workers may lie with their non-union membership. Notwithstanding this, the falling density of trade unions places them under political pressure. How representative are they of employees? What legitimacy do they possess in negotiating with employers? Are the rights accorded to trade unions, union officials and union members still relevant in such a context?

By its very nature non-standard employment is fragmented, has high turnover rates, is often located in small enterprises and is largely outside the traditional interests and focus of trade unions. However, unless trade unions begin to assess how they can recruit and expand membership among non-standard workers their political position will continue to be eroded. There are many ideas and strategies (see, for example, Evatt Foundation, 1995: Chapter 12), but so far they have failed to be effectively implemented.

While there is evidence of some deliberate employer policies to circumvent trade unions by changing workforce status from employee to self-employed or salaried managerial staff (Underhill and Kelly, 1993; Bennet, 1995; Vandenheuval and Wooden, 1995), in the main the bulk of non-standard workers fall outside the traditional interests and domains of trade unions. Recruitment could be assisted if there were a conscious attempt to reduce workforce casualization, especially for those who have ongoing employment arrangements. Trade unions have to modernize their image, actively advertise their advantages and services, offer membership inducements, and utilize public relations (Bolt, 1993; Evatt Foundation, 1995). All these suggestions have been canvassed, but the problem is that trade unions have been slow to react to the rapid structural developments in the workforce. Also resources have been diverted to other agendas, including the union amalgamation process of the mid-1980s (Dabscheck, 1995). Moreover, their position will continue to be under legislative threat from Coalition governments, militant employers, innovative employment practices and the prevailing libertarian policy regime which views trade unions as a market imperfection (Budget Statements, 1996).

Developing a trade union response to non-standard employment presumes an underlying context about the aims, functions and strategies of unions. Do they perform simple agency functions? Are they catalysts for societal change? Are they compradors with business and the state? Whose interest do they represent? How should they be organized? These questions are fundamental, but they are beyond the scope of this chapter (see Hall and Harley, 1996). Nevertheless, the presumption of the following analysis is that trade unions must increase their recruitment and retention of non-standard workers if they are to retain any collective representational legitimacy in the Australian workforce.

How then can trade unions more effectively recruit, retain and represent non-standard workers? For its part the ACTU is aware of these trends and has instituted a programme of action to recruit new members, to increase membership among non-standard workers and to more effectively represent non-standard workers (ACTU, 1992, 1995; Gahan, 1997). The Evatt Foundation (1995) published an extensive report on trade union reforms and activism designed in part to address the decline in union densities and address non-standard workers: key strategies identified were modernization and building a recruitment culture. Nevertheless, there are no easy answers to the recruitment and representation questions. However, any trade union strategy for non-standard workers should consider the following possibilities:

- Imposing a short-term fee levy on all members to be used in promoting trade unionism. Unions can more actively and aggressively promote the virtues of their 'product' and directly 'advertise' for members. Increasingly, traditional recruitment strategies are going to become more difficult to implement in the face of legislation, such as the 1996 Workplace Relations Act, that attempts to exclude trade unions from the workplace. Mail order and telephone recruitment strategies and other modern marketing techniques have to be contemplated in order to avoid many of the obstacles being placed in the way of direct recruitment (Plowman, 1992).

- Placing more resources into regional and workplace

organization. The industrial relations system has successively become more decentralized and decollectivized in Australia, yet over the 1980s trade unions promoted a more centralized structure through the expensive and acrimonious strategy of amalgamations (Dabscheck, 1995: Chapter 4; Costa, 1997). Organizers are fully occupied in coping with enterprise bargaining and all its complexities, thus there is insufficient time or resources being devoted to workplace recruitment and representation. To what extent are non-standard workers consulted with respect to enterprise bargains? The suspicion is that it is not simply a question of recruitment, but also a question of maintaining contact and monitoring the concerns of non-standard workers (Burgess *et al.*, 1997).

- Develop different administrative and logistical support. For example, through flexible fee structures and by providing accessibility beyond 9 am to 5 pm, Monday to Friday.

- Enterprise bargaining is very resource intensive for trade unions, but it is also resource intensive for employers. Blanket union representation allows employers to bargain with one employee representative only, often across multiple workplaces in the case of large businesses. By diluting union membership employers face the prospect of more multiple union presence, more militant and fragmented unionism, inter-union rivalry at the workplace and extensive transaction costs associated with enterprise bargaining and with individual employment contracts. Moreover, the new Australian Workplace Agreements clearly open up non-union representation and non-union bargaining agents. This is not necessarily all to the advantage of employers: it potentially increases their transaction costs and makes the employment arrangement potentially more complex and legalistic.

- More flexible trade union structures and greater inter-union cooperation. Many non-standard workers have low levels of attachment and are often isolated and vulnerable, for example in small businesses or in home based employment. Union membership could be portable across unions, with unions adopting a more cooperative approach towards recruitment and representation (on a 'fee for service' basis, say) in the case of small business enterprises, or isolated and regional/rural workplaces.

- Effectively preventing exploitation. In the main, non-standard workers are vulnerable and subject to potential exploitation. Casual employment conditions apply to workers who have ongoing employment; managerial and non-employee status is used to avoid award conditions and trade union access. Preventing exploitation is difficult in a country that has very few (and declining) regulations placed over non-standard employment. Unions could attempt to enforce existing regulatory requirements. Also, workforce re-regulation is a policy response trade unions could more actively pursue where they can demonstrate that non-standard employment arrangements are a means of avoiding employment rights and conditions (Brooks, 1991; Buchanan and Callus, 1993; ACTU, 1995).

- Endeavour to establish the concerns of non-standard workers, especially with respect to enterprise bargaining. These may not be identical, or even compatible, with those of standard workers. Trade unions increasingly face a very disparate membership in terms of their employment conditions, attachment and aspirations. No longer can it be assumed that all union members have identical employment arrangements and concerns (Ellem, 1992).

- Product labelling and the pressure of consumerism. Identify those products that are produced by a regulated and unionized workforce. Consumerism has been one of the few international forces behind the enforcement of basic labour rights, including the abolition of slavery and child labour (Nowicka, 1996). Unions could mount a campaign, in consort with consumer groups, to identify those companies that do enforce employment regulations and do employ trade union labour. These responses can be global through linking these programmes with international consumer, human rights and trade unions, and may in fact assist trade unions in their battles with transnational corporations and governments with an anti-collectivist agenda.

The above list of suggestions is not exhaustive, nor should it be taken to understate the recruitment and retention task facing unions. No one strategy will provide the answer: conditions do vary considerably across industries, workplaces and between different forms of non-standard employment. To date the response has been largely fragmented and isolated, despite the calls by the ACTU (1995) for a national strategy. From the above list the strategies that have been apparent have been the devolution of resources to the workplace, attempts to secure blanket coverage (despite the illegality of closed shops) in some sectors with a high incidence of non-standard employment (such as supermarkets), and the occasional victory in securing improved conditions for non-standard workers (such as fixed-term contract lecturing staff).

Overall there is an increased trade union awareness of the problems and challenges posed by a growing non-standard workforce. Over the longer term the decentralization of the industrial relations system will force trade unions to devote more resources to the workplace in order to directly address the issues of recruitment and representation for all workers. While current industrial relations legislation seeks to proscribe and limit trade union workplace activity and encourage non-union bargaining, there remains scope to more effectively recruit at the workplace under an industrial relations regime that does strengthen managerial prerogatives.

RESPONDING TO THE GLOBAL IMPERATIVE

The challenge that non-standard employment poses for Australian trade unions is part of the broader issue of how Australian trade unions should respond to those pressures that have been labelled as globalization. Non-standard employment has been allowed to expand, in part, because trade unions have protected traditional core or standard employees and either ignored or excluded non-standard workers. Non-standard employment growth is consistent with the neoliberal policy response to globalization, since non-standard employment arrangements are by their very nature less regulated or unregulated, and generally outside the domain of trade unions.

This is part of the dilemma faced by Australian trade unions. They are faced with falling densities, a hostile political environment, stagnant labour market conditions (including high rates of unemployment) and constant pressure on employment conditions. The neoliberal policy response to accommodate and promote globalization encourages non-standard employment arrangements and discourages trade unions and labour regulation. The dilemmas surrounding a response to globalization pressures and the rise in non-standard employment were highlighted by the *Unions 2001* discussion paper (Evatt Foundation, 1995). It detailed the erosion of employment conditions, falling trade union densities and the hostile political environment faced by trade unions. In this report globalization was largely seen as a distinctive issue in terms of the internationalization of capital and the potential threat to labour standards (ibid.: Chapter 11), not part of the overall neoliberal policy context in which unions find themselves. Likewise, non-standard employment received only cursory attention. It was never addressed in detail in terms of analysis and consequences, nor was it placed in the broader context of systems change.

Trade unions still have choices, despite declining membership and pressure on financial resources. They do have a choice in terms of how they respond to globalization and how they respond to non-standard employment growth. The emerging neoliberal hegemony is neither legitimate, nor in the long run very effective. Indeed, Thurow (1996) suggests the eventual demise of capitalism if inequality and exclusion are allowed to expand at current rates.

There has been discussion and debate in Australia over the trade union response to globalization (Bramble, 1996; Bryan, 1995). Non-standard employment can, however, be incorporated into the mainstream concerns of trade unions, including recruitment, protection and representation. This would constitute a starting point, but by no means would it be sufficient in itself as a response to the neoliberal policy agenda that continues to create many more opportunities for workforce fragmentation together with the erosion of employment conditions.

CONCLUSION

Globalization in the context of this analysis is presented as a policy framework, containing both prediction and prescription. Globalization is regarded as inevitable and it requires a specific policy response from the state. There is a globalization imperative that dominates the Australian policy agenda. Neoliberalism is continuously presented as the only effective response to globalization. This agenda places downward pressure on employment conditions and systematically attempts to reduce trade union presence in the workplace. Furthermore, independently of the policy agenda, trade unions have experienced falling densities and membership in Australia and they have had to contend with the rapid growth in employment arrangements that are largely located outside the traditional or standard employment parameters and concerns that have set trade union policy in Australia.

Declining trade union densities and non-standard employment growth pre-dated the globalization agenda in Australia. Nevertheless, there are linkages between these concurrent developments. First, the neoliberal policy framework is in general antagonist to trade unions (as a market imperfection) and supportive of deregulated and flexible employment arrangements characteristic of many forms of non-standard employment. Second, trade union legitimacy is under pressure not only from legislation that promotes non-union workplace agreements and individual employment contracts, but also from the growing number of non-standard workers outside trade unions. Third, the system of centralized and collective arrangements that was characteristic of the industrial relations system until the mid-1980s was premised on the primacy and continuation of the standard employment model as the basis for the domain of trade union activity. Subsequent developments in both employment policy and in employment restructuring have largely circumvented this model.

While the future for Australian trade unions does look bleak there are a number of strategies that trade unions can pursue in order to strengthen their representation among non-standard employees. The challenges confronting unions extend beyond the non-standard workforce. However, there is the broader challenge of confronting the globalization imperative and the neoliberal policy hegemony. Non-standard employment has been allowed, even encouraged, to flourish within this context. Dealing with the context and the policy agenda will require that trade unions also confront the employment model on which much of their activity over the past century has been based.

ACKNOWLEDGEMENT

The author thanks the editors and the anonymous referees for their assistance. The usual caveats apply.

APPENDIX

Australian Bureau of Statistics Labour Force Data cited in the text (Catalogue Numbers and frequency):

- 6203.0 The Labour Force, monthly
- 6310.0, Distribution of Weekly Earnings, annual
- 6310.40.001, Distribution of Weekly Earnings of Employees, irregular
- 6323.0, Trade Union Statistics, annual
- 6325.0 Trade Union Members, annual
- 6334.0 Employment Benefits, annual, discontinued 1994

REFERENCES

Anderson, G. (1991) 'Deregulating Labour Law: New Zealand's Employment Contracts Act 1991', *Current Affairs Bulletin*, Vol. 68, No. 1, pp. 24–6.

ACTU (Australian Council of Trade Unions) (1992) 'The ACTU Policy on the Organization, Resources and Services of the Trade Union Movement', in M. Crosby and M. Easson (eds), *What Should Unions Do?* Sydney: Pluto Press, pp. 371–88.

ACTU (1995) *Casual Employment and Industrial Regulation: What Should Unions Do?* Discussion Paper, ACTU, Melbourne.

Amin, A. and Thrift, N. (1996) 'Living in the Global', in A. Amin and N. Thrift (eds), *Globalization, Institutions and Regional Development in Europe*. Oxford: Oxford University Press, pp. 1–22.

Bell, S. (1997) *Ungoverning the Economy: The Political Economy of Australian Economic Policy*. Melbourne: Oxford University Press.

Bennet, L. (1995) 'Bargaining Away the Rights of the Weak: Non-Union Agreements in the Federal Jurisdiction', in P. Ronfelt and R. McCallum (eds), *Enterprise Bargaining, Trade Unions and the Law*. Sydney: Federation Press, pp. 120–53.

Berry, P. and Kitchener, G. (1988) *Can Unions Survive?* Canberra: Building Workers' Industrial Union.

Bolt, C. (1993) 'Unions: The Struggle for Relevance', *Australian Financial Review*, 19 March, p. 14.

Bramble, T. (1996) 'Globalization, Unions and the Demise of the Labourist Project', *Journal of Australian Political Economy*, No. 38, pp. 31–62.

Bray, M. (1991a) 'Unions and Owner-Drivers in NSW Road Transport', in M. Bray and V. Taylor (eds), *The Other Side of Flexibility: Unions and Marginal Workers in Australia*. Australian Centre for Industrial Relations Research and Teaching (ACIRRT), Monograph No. 3. University of Sydney, pp. 142–67.

Bray, M. (1991b) 'Conclusions', in M. Bray and V. Taylor (eds), *The Other Side of Flexibility: Unions and Marginal Workers in Australia*. ACIRRT, Monograph No. 3. University of Sydney, pp. 190–205.

Brooks, A. (1991) 'Marginal Workers and the Law' in M. Bray and V. Taylor (eds), *The Other Side of Flexibility: Unions and Marginal Workers in Australia*. ACIRRT, Monograph No. 3. University of Sydney, pp. 44–74.

Brosnan, P. and Campbell, I. (1995) 'Labour Market Deregulation in Australia: Towards New Forms of Workforce Division'. Conference of the International Working Party on Labour Market Segmentation, Sienna, Italy.

Bryan, D. (1995) 'International Competitiveness: National and Class Agendas', *Journal of Australian Political Economy*, No. 35, pp. 1–23.

Buchanan, J. and Callus, R. (1993) 'Efficiency and Equity at Work:The Need for Labour Market Regulation in Australia', *Journal of Industrial Relations*, Vol. 35, No. 4, pp. 515–38.

Budget Statements (1996), Statements 1–4, 1996/97. Canberra: AGPS.

Burgess, J. (1990) 'Non Employee Status in Australia: Trends and Issues', *Australian Bulletin of Labour*, Vol. 16, No. 4, pp. 233–53.

Burgess, J. (1994) 'Restructuring the Australian Labour Force: From Full Employment to Where?', *Journal of Australian Political Economy*, No. 34, pp. 103–27.

Burgess, J., Strachan, G., Keogh, P., Macdonald, D., Morgan, G. and Ryan, S. (1997) 'Participation, Equity and Outcomes: Enterprise Bargaining in Three Female Dominated Workplaces', *Journal of Interdisciplinary Gender Studies*, Vol. 2, No. 1, pp. 77–92.

Campbell, I. (1992) 'The Casualization of Labour: A Challenge for Trade Unions'. Industry Adjustment Group Seminar, University of Newcastle.

Campbell, I. (1993) 'Labour Market Flexibility in Australia: Enhancing Management Prerogative?', *Labour and Industry*, Vol. 5, No. 3, pp. 1–32.

Campbell, I. and Burgess, J. (1997) 'National Patterns of Temporary Employment: The Distinctive Case of Casual Employment in Australia'. Conference of the International Working Party on Labour Market Segmentation, Porto, Portugal.

Catley, R. (1996) *Globalising Australian Capitalism*. Melbourne: Cambridge University Press.

Clark, D. (1992) 'How to Save Australian Trade Unions from Extinction: A Three Point Radical Reform Plan', in M. Crosby and M. Easson (eds), *What Should Unions Do?* Sydney: Pluto Press, pp. 20–9.

Costa, M. (1997) 'Super Unions: Dinosaurs of the Information Age', in M. Costa and M. Hearn (eds), *Reforming Australia's Unions*. Sydney: Federation Press, pp. 69-72.

Costa, M. and Hearn, M. (eds) (1997) *Reforming Australia's Unions*. Sydney: Federation Press.

Crosby, M. (1992) 'Organising a Mobile Workforce', in M. Crosby and M. Easson (eds), *What Should Unions Do?* Sydney: Pluto Press, pp. 332–8.

Crosby, M. and Easson, M. (eds) (1992) *What Should Unions Do?* Sydney: Pluto Press.

Dabscheck, B. (1995) *The Struggle for Australian Industrial Relations*. Melbourne: Oxford University Press.

Edwards, R. (1993) *Rights at Work: Employment Relations in the Post Union Era*. Washington, DC: Brookings Institute.

Ellem, B. (1992) 'Organising Strategies for the 1990s. Targeting Particular Groups: Women, Migrants, Youth', in M. Crosby and M. Easson (eds), *What Should Unions Do?* Sydney: Pluto Press, pp. 347–61.

Evatt Foundation (1995), *Unions 2001: A Blueprint for Trade Union Activism*. Sydney: Evatt Foundation.

Gahan, P. (1997) 'Strategic Unionism in Crisis? The 1997 ACTU Congress', *Journal of Industrial Relations*, Vol. 39, No. 4, pp. 536–56.

Griffin, G. (1996) *Contemporary Research on Unions: Theory, Membership, Organization and Non-standard Employment*. National Key Centre in Industrial Relations Research, Monograph No. 9. Melbourne: Monash University.

Griffin, G. and Svenson, S. (1996) 'The Decline of Australian Trade Union Density: A Review', in G. Griffin (ed.), *Contemporary Research on Unions: Theory, Membership, Organization and Non-standard Employment*, Vol. II. National Key Centre in Industrial Relations, Research Monograph No. 9. Melbourne: Monash University, pp. 226–73.

Hall, R. and Harley, B. (1996) 'Australian Trade Unions and the Interpretation of Change', in G. Griffin (ed), *Contemporary Research on Unions: Theory, Membership, Organization and Non-Standard Employment*. Melbourne: National Key Centre for Industrial Relations, Research Monograph No.9. Melbourne: Monash University, pp. 32–62.

Hearn, M. (1997) 'The Australian Labour Movement and Industrial Relations, 1986–1996', in M. Costa and M. Hearn (eds), *Reforming Australia's Unions*. Sydney: Federation Press, pp. 1–11.

Hirst, P. and Thompson, P. (1996) *Globalization in Question*. Cambridge: Polity Press.

Leighton, P. (1986) 'Atypical Employment: The Law and Practice in the United Kingdom', *Labour Law Journal*, No. 3, pp. 34–50.

Lever-Tracy, C. (1988) 'The Flexibility Debate: Part-time Work', *Labour and Industry*, Vol. 1, No. 2, pp. 210–41.

Lewis, H. (1990) *Part-time Work: Trends and Issues*. Canberra: Department of Industrial

Relations, AGPS.

Lipsig-Mumme, C. (1997) 'The Politics of the New Service Economy', in P. James, W. Veit and S. Wright (eds), *Work of the Future: Global Perspectives*. Sydney: Allen and Unwin, pp. 109–25.

Mitchell, W. and Burgess, J. (1998) 'Eight Propositions about Unemployment: An Australian Perspective'. Conference of the Study Group on Unemployment. International Industrial Relations Association World Conference, Bologna, Italy.

Nowicka, H. (1996) 'Oxfam Presses Retailers', *Guardian Weekly*, 26 May, p. 20.

OECD (1996) *Employment Outlook*. Paris.

Payne, J. and Payne, C. (1993) 'Unemployment and Peripheral Work', *Work, Employment and Society*, Vol. 7, No. 4, pp. 513–34.

Peetz, D. (1992) 'Union Membership and the Accord', in M. Crosby and M. Easson (eds), *What Should Unions Do?* Sydney: Pluto Press, pp. 171–210.

Peetz, D. (1996) 'Workplace Co-operation, Conflict, Influence and Trade Union Membership', in G. Griffin (ed.), *Contemporary Research on Unions: Theory, Membership, Organization and Non-standard Employment*, Vol. II. National Key Centre in Industrial Relations Research, Monograph No. 9. Melbourne: Monash University, pp. 309–46.

Plowman, D. (1991) 'Whither Australian Trade Unions?', *Economic and Labour Relations Review*, Vol. 2, No. 2, pp. 25–44.

Plowman, D. (1992) 'Arresting Union Decline: Membership and Recruitment Strategies', in M. Crosby and M. Easson (eds), *What Should Unions Do?* Sydney: Pluto Press, pp. 266–88.

Pocock, B. and Wright, P. (1997) 'Trade Unionism in 1996', *Journal of Industrial Relations*, Vol. 39, No. 1, pp. 120–36.

Polivka, A. and Nardone, T. (1989) 'On the Definition of Contingent Work', *Monthly Labour Review*, Dec., pp. 9–16.

Reich, R. (1991) *The Work of Nations: A Blueprint for the Future*. New York: Simon and Schuster.

Robinson, O. (1991) 'The Atypical Workforce: Raising the Status of Part-time Employment in Canada', *Industrial Relations Journal*, Vol. 22, No. 1, pp. 46–58.

Rodgers, G. (1989) 'Precarious Work in Western Europe: The State of the Debate', in G. and J. Rodgers (eds), *Precarious Jobs in Labour Market Regulation*. Geneva: ILO, pp.1–16.

Romeyn, J. (1992) *Flexible Working Time: Part-time and Casual Employment*. Industrial Relations Research Monograph No. 1. Canberra: Department of Industrial Relations.

Sklair, L. (1996) 'Who Are the Globalizers?', *Journal of Australian Political Economy*, No. 38, pp. 1–30.

Taylor, R. (1994) *The Future of Trade Unions*. London: André Deutsch.

Thurow, L. (1996) *The Future of Capitalism*. Sydney: Allen and Unwin.

Underhill, E. and Kelly, D. (1993) 'Eliminating Traditional Employment: Troubleshooters Available in the Building and Meat Industries', *Journal of Industrial Relations*, Vol. 35, No. 3, pp. 398–422.

Vandenheuval, A. and Wooden, M. (1995) 'Self-Employed Contractors in Australia: How Many and Who Are They?', *Journal of Industrial Relations*, Vol. 37, No. 3, pp. 263–80.

7

Japanese Trade Unions at the Crossroads: Dilemmas and Opportunities Created by Globalization

JOHN BENSON and PHILIPPE DEBROUX[1]

A major reason why the Japanese post-war economy experienced rapid growth up to the 1990s, and had little unemployment compared to the other industrialized countries, was the stability of the industrial relations system (Dertouzos *et al.*, 1989). During these years, companies negotiated directly with their workforce through its enterprise union. In exchange for employment security and real wage increases, unions would guarantee cooperative behaviour by their members (Inohara, 1990). Human resource management was thus associated with high organizational commitment, labour flexibility and a willingness to embrace change. Firm specific problems were easier to resolve as unions were organized at that level and were ready to work with management to achieve enterprise success and growth (Mouer, 1989).

Despite its success, this labour management system has been periodically attacked and its demise announced by commentators with the occurrence of each economic downturn (Narikawa, 1997: 12). Management responded by limiting the scope of the system in several ways: by not extending employment guarantees beyond age 55; by shifting the key wage criteria from age to seniority; and by introducing an increasingly dominant skill component into wage composition. In the late 1970s, management became aware of a looming labour shortage. This, coupled with high production costs, led to an expansion of overseas investment in the 1980s. This process was hastened by the rapid currency appreciation of the Japenese yen. Nevertheless, the system revealed enough flexibility to accommodate the adverse and new circumstances presented in the early part of the 1990s (Benson, 1998).

However, by 1998 a number of factors had emerged and consolidated, and this has forced management to reassess their labour practices and strategies. The Asian financial crisis, involving Thailand, Korea, Malaysia and Indonesia, has had a major impact as these four countries were key export destinations for Japanese investment and capital goods. In addition, the dynamics of globalization revealed the rigidities of the Japanese business system. This led to increasing pressure from the USA, the World Trade Organization and the European Union for the liberalization of the Japanese markets. The problem was compounded by the bursting of the financial bubble in the late 1980s that entailed massive stock and asset deflation, pushing Japan into a long period of economic stagnation. Apart from a momentary respite in the mid-1990s, caused primarily by Japanese fiscal policy, the Japanese economy is again in a period of sustained economic downturn. As at October 1998, Japan's gross domestic production had recorded four consecutive quarters of negative growth (*The Economist*, 5 December 1998: 132).

For many, the negative features of the Japanese form of capitalism were seen as the primary cause of these economic difficulties. This has led to an acknowledgement by the Japan Federation of Employers (*Nikkeiren*), the key employer group (Nikkeiren, 1995), the bureaucracy (MITI, 1995) and many private companies that a shift away from an enterprise-centred, and towards a more market-driven, approach is now necessary. This chapter[1] examines the impact of these forces on the industrial relations system and the trade union response to such changes. Before considering the response by labour to this situation it is necessary to locate such an analysis within the wider issue of globalization.

GLOBALIZATION AND THE JAPANESE ECONOMY

The post-war Japanese economy has been built on international trade. Trade policy became, in fact, the 'point of contact for Japan's external relationships' (MITI, 1998: 13). The pace of economic reconstruction relied primarily on the export of consumer goods to the mass markets of the USA and Europe. As Japan's exports grew Japanese firms launched offshore production centres, first in their major market regions of the USA and Europe and then in the emerging Asian market. The increasing exports to the Asian market and the development of Asian operations hastened the process by which Japanese firms were increasingly being integrated into the global economy.

These developments took place in a period of strong domestic and international demand, and a shortage of skilled labour in Japan. Thus, the move to set up operations offshore had little impact on domestic production or the Japanese labour management system. Yet, limits to economic growth were clearly evidenced by the 1980s (Nakamura, 1981: 54) and it was becoming increasingly difficult for Japanese policymakers to insulate Japan from external events. The weak Japanese domestic economy was prevented from entering an earlier recession by the strong growth occurring in other Asian countries. In particular, the decline in the international demand for Japanese consumer goods was offset by an increasingly strong global market for Japanese capital goods.

Initially, the globalization of the Japanese economy was seen in a positive light. Trade flows did not have a negative, but rather a positive, influence on the Japanese trade balance. The direct impact on production and employment was also, until recently, positive. This situation began to change after 1993, particularly with the increased Japanese investment in Asia. As expected, more capital intensive production was a substitute for the more labour intensive processes that were shifted abroad (MITI, 1997a). Unlike much of the investment in Europe and North America, more than 70 per cent of Japanese investment in Asia involved new production facilities or an expansion of existing capacity (MITI, 1996).

At about the same time, smaller companies belonging to the industrial groups were increasingly put into competition with foreign suppliers. In addition, for supplier companies that followed their larger Japanese clients into Asia, the decline in the Asian domestic markets has placed many of these firms on the brink of bankruptcy. The only solution for these companies was to cut their domestic production and to re-import their Asian production to Japan. All these factors have had a negative impact on direct and indirect employment in Japan, not only for the reasons cited above but also due to reduced consumer demand in Japan (MOF, 1998).

Running parallel to these developments has been a substantial decline in competitive advantage of a number of key sectors of the Japanese economy. Previously, the trade structure of Japan had been characterized by a high export concentration on a limited number of goods. It was these products that accounted for most of the Japanese trade surplus. This situation is now increasingly under threat (MITI, 1997b). By international comparison, Japan's export structure is in industrial sectors with a low growth potential. Thus, even if Japanese export firms can maintain their competitive advantage as a whole, the Japanese economy faces a loss of its relative share of the global market (Legewie, 1997). Existing competitive advantages of Japanese industries are, however, being increasingly eroded by low wage countries. Only 15 per cent of Japanese exports in 1992 fell into categories with negligible competition from developing countries. This compared to figures of between 25 to 30 per cent for other industrialized countries. In contrast, more than 50 per cent of Japanese exports faced relatively high competition, which was substantially more than in any other country (MITI, 1997b).

It is the effects of globalization that Japan's policymakers are now facing. Initially, globalization was seen as synonymous with international trade. As world trade expanded the Japanese economy similarly expanded. This presented few difficulties for the Japanese bureaucracy, apart from the occasional criticism concerning access to the Japanese market. More recently globalization has been linked with the demise of the nation state as the most effective base for the organization of economic activity (Petrella, 1996). In this scenario, Japanese policymakers will need to focus on the barriers to international trade, the improvement of enterprise flexibility, and the elimination of institutional rigidities in financial and labour markets (MITI, 1998). It is these last two aspects that have potential to significantly affect employment, trade unions and the industrial relations system.

One of the manifestations, for example, of the recent Japanese economic stagnation has been the steady rise in unemployment. The focus so far has been on the decline of the manufacturing sector that has seen over one million job losses since 1991 (MITI, 1997a). Government forecasts indicate that this trend will continue (Iwase, 1997a: 21). Part of the reason for this decline has been Japanese enterprise offshore investment in search of cheaper production costs. This has raised the fear of a deindustrialization or, as it is commonly referred to, a 'hollowing out' of Japanese industry. As in Western countries, this concern is based on the belief that shifting production abroad results in fewer exports from, and more imports to, Japan and thus leads to a delocalization of domestic production and employment (Seki, 1997).

These issues have led to all sections of society, including trade unions, to look for economic solutions that are both politically and socially feasible. It is now widely accepted by enterprise management and public authorities that Japanese industry must restructure and move into new industrial sectors that are able to secure domestic production and employment over the long term. This will allow for the reallocation of resources, the export of capital and intermediate goods, and improved access to foreign markets. The level of delocalization of Japanese industry as a whole, except for the automotive and electronics industries, is still much lower than that of the other developed countries. It can, therefore, be expected that, despite the current problems, the pace of globalization of Japanese industry will hasten and that resources will be transferred to more competitive production activities. However, it is likely that these new production activities will require fewer workers, so a further decline in manufacturing employment will occur, although this may be partially offset by increased employment in the service sector.

Finally, an emerging issue resulting from globalization is the increasing pressure for a restructuring of corporate governance. Up to recently, the pursuit of profit has not been the key corporate objective but rather the means to enable the company's growth and long-term survival. This is becoming less the case. Many large Japanese companies now intend to raise capital through the domestic and foreign capital markets. Some firms already have on their boards foreign institutional investors who give priority to shareholders' value. As a consequence, the balance between interdependent partners is increasingly difficult to maintain because the stakeholders no longer have the same objectives. This undermines the basis of the traditional multiple stakeholder system and places in question the role of enterprise based trade unions.

TRADE UNIONS' RESPONSE TO GLOBALIZATION

Managerial Change and Strategy

It is in the above context that the current debates within the trade union movement concerning the relationships with the other key players (companies, government, bureaucracy) and the policies it can develop must be located. Since the 1960s, unions have focused primarily on achieving higher real incomes and maintaining job security for their members. However, as outlined above, the lengthy period of low growth and fewer job opportunities in the 1990s has placed considerable pressure on trade unions. This has forced them to reassess their strategies at the company, industry and national levels.

In the present low growth and competitive environment, many companies want to control their labour costs. Part of their strategy has been to employ more part-time and temporary workers. A survey conducted by *Nikkeiren* of large enterprises found that these forms of employment will continue to increase in the future (Iwase, 1997b: 29). Furthermore, an increased amount of work is now being outsourced. A further strategy employed by large firms, which have subsidiaries and subcontractors, is to adopt group-wide personnel management to enable them to shift employees from one place to another rather than dismiss them. A third component of this cost control strategy is to link wages to some performance criteria. This has led to a questioning of the traditional wage system and the way such wages are determined.

Many of the firms in the electronics and information technology sectors are at the forefront of these changes. Firms such as Sony, Hitachi, Fujitsu and NEC are now fully fledged multinational corporations and make management decisions according to global world standards. In short, their worldwide corporate strategy cannot be subordinated to the idiosyncrasies of their Japanese-based operations. Fujitsu, for example, has abolished its long-standing seniority-based pay system and has switched to a performance-based pay system that applies to all workers (*Nikkei Business*, 27 April 1998: 14–23). Similarly, Hitachi plans to reduce the share of pay based on seniority from 60 per cent to 40 per cent over the next three years. This will apply to all 30,000 of its white-collar employees. Although such changes are more likely to occur in the faster growing and more internationally competitive industries, traditional industries such as textile, steel and automobiles are also affected (*Shakai Keizai Seisansei Shimbun*, 5 July 1998).

Key Issues for Trade Unions

In response to these trends, trade unions' stance on compensation is changing. At the Japanese Trade Union Confederation (*Rengo*) there is a broad acceptance of the need to move away from a wage system centred on seniority and equality. Rengo has stated that a wider wage differential would not be a setback to workers. Rather, this should be seen as a positive incentive for employees and, for many, should lead to higher wages (*Shakai Keizai Seisansei Shimbun*, 25 August 1998: 2). The declaration of Rengo reflects the stance adopted by a number of key industrial unions. For example, the Japanese Electrical, Electronic and Information Union (*Denki Rengo*) has adopted a policy accepting merit pay at their convention in Okinawa on 8 July 1998. This is an important change and demonstrates a break with its previous strong commitment to seniority-based promotions and gaining standard pay increases for all employees. Moreover, the union is considering dropping future seniority-based wage demands and instead requesting the specification of a minimum wage for each work classification. The president of the union, Katustoshi Suzuki, is quoted as saying 'Labour and management both end up being losers if their company can not beat back the competition. Results-oriented pay is the wave of the future' (*Shakai Keizai Seisansei Shimbun*, 25 August 1998: 3).

Clearly, the labour movement has begun to accept the idea that the Japanese economy has to integrate more fully into the international system and that this process will have a substantial impact on workers. The practice of lifetime employment, for example, is expected to fundamentally change. *Nikkeiren* has suggested the future firm will need to adopt a core/specialist/flexible model with only the core workers enjoying lifetime employment (Naruse, 1997: 18). This model is similar to the proposal by the Economic Council of the Government to increase the use of the external labour market. Such proposals have been severely criticized by Rengo as doing little to improve labour productivity (Narikawa, 1997: 12). Nevertheless, over time it is expected that those employees enjoying lifetime employment will fall to about 60 per cent of the average firm's labour force.

The high unemployment and personal dislocation resulting from the current economic crisis and globalization are again raising the issue of welfare policy. Since the 1950s welfare benefits have been primarily an enterprise responsibility. There was in the 1970s a push by unions, backed up by the political left, to develop a welfare state. The Spring Wage Offensive (*Shunto*) was seen as a mechanism that could evolve from the narrow objective of wage increases towards a 'People's Offensive' that would ultimately lead to socio-economic changes. Little came out of this campaign, primarily because of the strength of the Liberal Democratic Party (LDP) and the divisions within the Japanese socialist party. By the end of the decade this push, due to the impact of the second oil shock, had been replaced by a new commitment towards economic efficiency.

A similar context to that prevailing in the 1970s existed in the late 1990s. In the 1970s, the debate was focused on the necessity of providing some leisure time and a stronger emphasis on the quality of life. It was advocated by the trade unions in a society that had concentrated almost single-mindedly on economic performance over the previous 20 years. On the other hand, the bureaucracy and government, together with companies, were adamantly opposed to the development of a welfare state. At this time such a move was seen as constituting a potential source of moral decline of Japanese society (Debroux, 1989). However, while the companies were opposed to a welfare state, the larger companies were ready to develop, in collaboration with the unions, a more comprehensive corporate welfare system.

The Development of a Multifaceted Strategy

Globalization and economic stagnation have left Japanese unions with little room to manoeuvre or to pursue the twin objectives of job security and wage increases. The rise in unemployment and the stagnation of disposable income affected a growing part of the Japanese population. As such, the concept of global liberalization moved from an international economic process to a serious domestic socio-political problem. Rengo's acceptance, out of necessity, of the globalization process provided a legitimization of it. Nevertheless, in the Rengo declarations concerning the quality of life in the 1990s can be found elements that are similar to those used in the failed 1970s attempt to reorientate the *Shunto*.

That trade unions will now not be able protect all workers' jobs will require a fundamental shift in the perception of union members and the type of strategies the union will need to adopt. Nevertheless, trade unions will need to defend their present conditions, especially those such as employees' pension schemes and health insurance. These aspects of an employee's remuneration are under attack not only from the economic efficiency forces of globalization but also from the economics of an ageing population. It is argued that these schemes must be overhauled as they currently stand in the way of the development of a more appropriate employment and wage system (Nikkeiren, 1995). Increasingly, companies are asking for a restructuring of their welfare provisions as part of the overall review of their personnel and labour management. For example, housing and family allowances, employees' saving schemes and other social benefits that were seen as necessary to retain good employees, and were implemented with lifetime employment and seniority wages, are now believed to have outlived their usefulness.

Employees' demands for enterprise welfare arrangements remain strong (Narikawa, 1996). Unions have, however, acknowledged that many companies cannot cope with the growing financial burden that such provisions entail (Matsui, 1997). Therefore, reminiscent of the attempt to develop a welfare state in the 1970s, Rengo has urged that such social problems must be resolved through the expansion of the public social insurance system. This strategy is aimed at the shortcomings of the social safety net and, in particular, the high cost of medical and living expenses for those in retirement. At the same time the gap in welfare benefits is widening between enterprises. So Rengo has also argued for the creation of regional joint welfare projects, not confined to the corporate sector, and a strengthening of the public housing support scheme. This would, if successful, narrow the gap in intercompany welfare benefits.

The union movement has thus launched a two-pronged strategy. On the one hand, unions will attempt to defend the wages, job security and working conditions of their members through enterprise mechanisms. This will be particularly the case with the lifetime employment system (Narikawa, 1997). On the other hand, unions through Rengo are attempting to involve the wider society in their welfare initiatives. This policy calls for an extension of union activities to workers and employees beyond the enterprise. In addition, unions are trying to organize the increasing number of non-regular employees in their firms, more middle management employees and workers in subsidiary and subcontracting companies. This represents a departure from the traditional union policy of limiting their membership to regular, full-time workers below a certain level of management.

Another trend that can be directly attributed to globalization is that a number of large companies are disengaging from their long-term relations with their primary subcontractors. In place of these arrangements, more market-orientated and contract-related relationships have been instituted. This has exerted enormous pressure on smaller subcontracting companies to maintain their competitiveness and has caused a growing number of industrial disputes with their employees. Some trade unions have started to organize these workers to retain their influence over management. According to Inagami (1995), 10.6 per cent of unions are now attempting to organize part-time workers and 12.1 per cent of unions have started to organize managers. In the 1996 *Shunto*, the Japanese Federation of Electrical Machine Workers' Union (*Denki Rosen*) argued that affiliated unions should be able to organize middle management employees who have suffered from the restructuring policy. This request was acceded to by management (*Shakai Keizai Seisansei Shimbun*, 6 March 1996: 2).

A further outcome of the globalization process is a proposal to revise the Labour Standards Law to provide improved flexibility by basing wages on performance rather than the number of hours worked. Under the proposal, overtime rates and penalty rates for work performed on weekends and holidays would be abolished. This system, which already applies to 11 employee categories, including researchers, designers and public accountants, would be conditional upon the consent of individual employees (Kajima, 1997: 9–10). Refusal to accept such a payment system could not be used to deny promotion. Nevertheless, Rengo is concerned as it will involve primarily workers employed in small companies who will have difficulty refusing the new system for fear of losing their jobs. In reality, the new legislation would simply force employees to work overtime without payment if they wished to maintain their employment (*Asahi Shimbun*, 12 May 1999: 3).

GLOBALIZATION AND A UNITED LABOUR MOVEMENT?

Unification of the Labour Movement: The Birth of Rengo?

With the introduction of *Shunto* most enterprise unions were able to satisfy member's demands by trading increased productivity for wage increases and improved welfare programmes. This bargaining took place on the understanding that employment security was guaranteed. Bargaining occurred at the enterprise level, so most agreements did not create universal norms that applied to a particular industry or occupation. As a consequence, the major shortcoming of this system was its lack of social and political influence on national labour policy. Four peak union bodies existed and any influence they may have had on national labour policy was minimized by the ideological divisions that existed between these bodies and their support for different political parties.

The internationalization of the Japanese economy and the rationalization of key industries in the 1970s led to the divisions within the labour movement being seen as a key impediment to the advancement of the labour cause. The worldwide move towards privatization of state enterprises in the 1970s and 1980s flowed inevitably to Japan. This led to a change in the power balance within the Japanese labour movement. The most militant unions that supported the socialist and communist parties were concentrated in the public sector. The weakening of the public sector through privatization enabled the large private company unions to take the initiative towards unification of the labour movement. By 1987, the Japanese Private Sector Trade Union Confederation (*Private Rengo*) was established as the new national centre for private sector enterprise unions. Soon afterwards, the public sector unions accepted the conditions demanded by Private Rengo to join a unified body.

From the beginning, Rengo's policy was to distance itself from actual political parties and to be involved in policy changes and institutional reforms at the national level. Rengo accepted the need for unions to engage in political activities, not in the normal sense of ideological politics, but in terms of interest politics. This strategy is a recognition of the limitations of an industrial relations system based on enterprise unionism. Private sector unions have become increasingly aware of the profound impact of government policies on the jobs and living standards of their members. That awareness grew out of the first oil shock in 1973–74 and has consolidated with the increasing level of globalization.

By the mid-1970s labour and management collaboration had developed to the stage where governmental advisory committees included labour representatives, and direct communication channels with the LDP and the bureaucracy were opened. Such practices were, however, mainly limited to the public sector unions. The effects of globalization have forced Rengo to expand such an approach and is now trying to reach a consensus with the bureaucracy on various issues in the same way as they do with the private sector (Shinoda, 1997). This relationship with the government has consolidated with the introduction of the tripartite Round Table Discussion Meetings (*Sanrokon*) modelled after the German experience. As a result, Rengo succeeded in 1992 in achieving a reduction of the legal working hours and a standard five-day working week for civil servants. The government also introduced a Rengo-backed five-year plan for 'Advancing the Quality of Life' and reached agreement with Rengo on the revision of the Equal Employment Opportunity Act in 1997.

It remains uncertain, however, whether these developments will allow the union movement to proactively cope with the negative affects of globalization. In addition, it is not clear that the divisions within the labour movement will not resurface. In the 1970s, the call for a 'People's Spring Offensive' caught the imagination of many workers and the wider community. The demands went beyond wage increases and called for a major policy shift that would have meant that many of the welfare provisions now provided by the enterprise would be provided by the government. It was dismissed by the LDP as a call from the left for political unionism. Will the same fate be bestowed on the current request for improved national welfare?

One difference lies with the changing political landscape. A new political party, *Minshuto*, may, if it survives, support such a platform. Nevertheless, Minshuto will find it difficult to develop united policies supporting Rengo initiatives as the party is made up of a coalition of trade unionists, socialists and former members of the LDP. Similarly, divisions exist within Rengo for support of one political party (*Nikkei Weekly*, 1997). Certainly, Rengo has shed the remnants of the leftist ideology of some of its constituents and now publicly supports a market-based economy. Its strategy is to work within the current socio-political structure to achieve gradual reform. This has lessened the worries of conservative politicians and, as a result, conservative parties such as the LDP are seeking ways to cooperate and gain the support of Rengo-affiliated political elements.

The Management of Interest Conflicts

What then will be Rengo's response to the many issues that are now arising from globalization? There appears to be substantial disagreement between the private and public sector constituents of Rengo. For example, from the early 1980s the private sector unions had actively supported administrative reforms such as those contained in the Maekawa Report (1986). In this case they supported the goals of reconstructing public finance without tax increases, controlling social security costs, and the privatization of NTT, Japan Tobacco and Japan Railways. This neoliberal tendency was inherited by Rengo (Inagami, 1992), but has become a source of discontent with the public sector unions.

Whatever the willingness of Rengo to address wider issues, enterprise unions will remain the key union organizations in Japan for the foreseeable future. Rengo does not intend, nor could it achieve, centralized control over its members. It reflects the autonomy of the affiliated unions in its managerial structure. There is, however, a growing source of disagreement between constituent industrial federations that is leading to a decline in the common front during *Shunto*. Unions in export-led industries place the responsibility for the recent low wage increases on the opposition of some unions to the deregulation process. They also criticize industries with low productivity for free-riding on those industries that have achieved wage increases based on improved productivity.

The division on the key issue of deregulation is representative of the problems facing Japanese trade unions in a period of globalization, low economic growth and increasing unemployment. One example, which illustrates these divisions, is the deregulation of public utility prices. The private sector unions, particularly those in large companies in export-orientated industries, believe it is in the interest of the Japanese economy to deregulate utilities' fees as soon as possible. Moreover, they argue that wage rises in these utilities should only be granted if corresponding productivity improvements are realized. Only by doing so will higher growth and improved competitiveness be achieved. On the other hand, unions in sectors bound to suffer from the deregulation, for example unions in the public sector, transport and medium-sized enterprises, are opposed to it. This is clearly a fundamental issue, but is one for which Rengo has been unable to develop a common policy (Egami, 1994). If left unresolved, such divisions will lead to a widening of the wage differential and have the potential to cause a structural split at the peak level of labour.

For some commentators, the labour unification movement has strengthened Japanese labour and has allowed a corporatist arrangement to evolve in Japan. Some balance has been provided between the extreme of central corporatism and the decentralizing forces that would lead ultimately to the destruction of corporatism (Inagami, 1992). Thus, in a period of globalization in which most issues have macroeconomic and political dimensions, Rengo now has the potential to overcome the inherent weaknesses of enterprise unions and the capacity to exert a strong influence on government policy.

Not all unions are happy with this state of affairs. Unions from smaller companies are concerned that their views are being neglected in favour of the large private company unions. They also want to avoid being caught up in the private and public sector union division. This has led many of these unions to express the need to organize themselves into a 'third front' (Sato, 1997). In short, they want to break away from the enterprise union concept and to develop organizations that can recruit members on a wider basis. These unions also want to expand union membership beyond the permanent employees. At present, some of these unions are competing with enterprise unions and are promoting industrial level campaigns. In addition, they have developed joint action with non-unionized workers (Ohki, 1998).

Rengo also faces a challenge from *Zenroren*, a smaller but more militant peak labour organization. Zenroren was formed in 1989 with the aim of opposing the 'collaborationist' line advocated by the unions that were instrumental in the formation of Rengo. Zenroren has formed 'Spring Struggle Committees' throughout Japan and is also attempting to organize workers in small enterprises and farmers. In addition, Zenroren believes that the management strategy of Japanese multinational corporations is to take advantage of low wages in other countries. This, coupled with concern that the current restructuring occurring in Japan may spread to the whole of the Asian region, has led them to argue that the employment and living standards of workers are now under serious threat. As a consequence, Zenroren has began to develop more formal relations with labour unions in East Asia (Ohki, 1998).

The attempts by Rengo to provide a united front for all workers and to link its actions to issues concerning the wider society are taking place in a period of decline of the union movement. Trade unions in Japan have been losing influence not only in society at large but also within the enterprise. Since 1990 trade union density has fallen to 22.8 per cent: a fall of 13.5 per cent in union coverage in seven years (JIL, 1998: 48). Part of the reason for this decline has been the sectoral shifts taking place in Japan. Another part of the reason relates to the inability of unions to organize new workplaces and the members' perceptions of the value of unionism (Freeman and Rebick, 1989: 603; Tsuru, 1995: 15–16). In addition, unions do not appear to have increased monthly wages or annual earnings above those of non-union firms, nor has union membership increased job satisfaction or reduced turnover propensity (Tsuru, 1995). While union voice may have improved communications between workers and management, unions remain susceptible to management interference and their bargaining power has become weak in this period of growing unemployment.

The weakness of unions is demonstrated by their acceptance of performance related pay and the individualization of the personnel appraisal system. Over time these practices will lead to increased wage differentials. Unions will have to respond to a multitude of different individual grievances concerning pay and appraisals and this may force firms to undertake radical organizational changes such as a division by job category. Recent examples show that the unions are not equipped to cope with such problems (*Nikkei Business*, 1998). Finally, the strengthening of unions by the recruitment of non-regular workers is fraught with difficulty, as the example of Takashimaya demonstrates. In this case, the union decided to accept part-time workers as members. Given their lower wage, they paid a substantially reduced membership fee to the union. These workers, however, requested the same benefits and conditions as regular members, such as union contributions to their hospitalization costs and insurance policies. The regular workers rejected those demands and publicly questioned the benefits of union membership (ibid.).

CONCLUSION

By the end of the decade the union movement in Japan was faced with a number of serious problems. In attempting to represent unions with a conflicting range of interests, Rengo was having difficulty making coherent and consistent demands for policy changes and institutional reform. At the enterprise level, workers were becoming increasingly sceptical that their unions can defend their jobs against either global economic forces or managerial ineptitude. At the same time, without the prospect of a lifetime career in one company, workers will not be as patient as they have been in the past in waiting for promotions and opportunities for advancement. Many of the new schemes only apply to a limited number of employees. Therefore, those workers excluded from these schemes are beginning to feel that the cost of their 'investment' in one company is too high. Talented employees, in particular, may see a benefit in changing firms before being trapped with hard to sell company-specific skills. While this state of mind has emerged with managers, it is also becoming more the norm among workers with intellectual and technical skills.

These issues are placing increased pressure on enterprise unions to develop more avenues for direct influence in the management of the enterprise. This new function will be more than institutionalizing the role they play now. In large firms, for example, about 70 per cent of union officers are now university graduates. They are more sophisticated than the previous generation of union officials and want greater formal involvement of the union in management (Kumazawa, 1997). The growing share of foreign capital in the shareholding structure is also placing pressure on the corporate governance system. Rengo officials argue there is a need for outside directors and shareholders to be placed on the enterprise board to provide a countervailing influence to management. According to some commentators, a multiple stakeholder system will require a union presence in the body legally in charge of controlling and monitoring management (Nakamura, 1997).

At the enterprise level there is a movement from collective bargaining to joint consultation, and now most issues are settled at this level before reaching the collective bargaining stage (Araki, 1996: 18). A 1990 survey explored the practices of joint consultation in 15 large firms (JPC, 1990). In 14 of these firms a wide range of business issues were discussed between unions and management at joint consultation committees. There was, however, no requirement for the firm to reach agreement with the union. In some of the respondent companies, for instance Ajinomoto, Fujitsu and Honda, the unions had a special department or committee analysing and monitoring business policies and making suggestions to management. Moreover, a recent survey of senior managers in listed companies agreed with this approach. The survey found no departure from a multiple stakeholder corporate governance system in which the role of trade unions was reinforced as an internal control mechanism. These managers wanted to institutionalize the joint labour–management consultation system and to downgrade the collective bargaining system that had developed since the 1970s (*Shakai Keizai Seisansei Shimbun*, 25 August 1998: 2).

The role of unions in Japan is becoming an important issue for debate and it is possible that a 'new deal' between unions and companies will be formed. This may allow a more participative and collaborative system to develop between management and labour; a system that management claim is necessary if they are to meet the economic imperatives of globalization. It is too early to predict the final form of any new labour–management arrangements, but it could possibly lead to the formal integration of the enterprise union into the firm's corporate governance system. In this event, the impact of globalization on trade union structure and activity at the enterprise would be extensive. The integration of trade unions in such a manner would fundamentally change the nature of unionism. In turn, such a change would make it extremely difficult for Rengo to maintain even a semblance of unity. Contradictions in role and the traditional private–public union conflict would be replaced by a more fundamental division that could lead to the demise of an already shaky national labour movement.

NOTE

1. Authors are listed alphabetically and contributed equally to the research and writing.

REFERENCES

Araki, Takashi (1996) 'Developing Employment Relations Law in Japan', Part 12: 'Collective Bargaining and Collective Agreements', *Labour Issues Quarterly*, Summer, No. 31, pp. 19–24.

Asahi Shimbun (The), 12 May 1999.

Benson, John (1988) 'Labour Management during Recessions: Japanese Manufacturing Enterprises during the 1990s', *Industrial Relations Journal*, Vol. 29, No. 3, pp. 1–15.

Debroux, Philippe (1989) 'L'Etat et le Monde des Affairs' (Relations between the State and the Business World), *Civilizations*, Vol. 34, No. 1/2, pp. 445–67.

Dertouzos, Michael, Lester, Robert and Solow, Robert (1989) *Made in America: Regaining the Productive Edge*. New York: Harper Perennial.

Economist (The), 5 December 1998.

Egami, Sumio (1994) 'The Trade Unions Challenge a High Yen and Corporate Restructuring', *Labour Issues Quarterly*, Autumn, No. 25, pp. 15–16.

Freeman, Richard. and Rebick, Marcus (1989) 'Crumbling Pillar? Declining Union Density in Japan', *Journal of the Japanese and International Economies*, Vol. 3, No. 4, December, pp. 578–605.

Inagami, Takeshi (1992) 'On Japanese-style Neo-corporatism: Era of a Tripartite Honeymoon', *International Journal of Japanese Sociology*, Vol. 1, No. 1, pp. 61–77.

Inagami, Takeshi (1995) *Seijuku Shakai no Nakano Kigyobetsu Kumiai* (Enterprise Unions in a Mature Society). Tokyo: Japan Institute of Labour.

Inohara, Hideo (1990) *Human Resource Management in Japanese Companies*. Tokyo: Asian Productivity Organization.

Iwase, Takashi (1997a) 'Changing Japanese Labour and Employment System', *Journal of Japanese Trade and Industry*, Vol. 16, No. 4, pp. 20–4.

Iwase, Takashi (1997b) 'Data Reveal Changes in Labour and Employment Patterns', *Journal of Japanese Trade and Industry*, Vol. 16, No. 4, pp. 26–9.

JIL (1998) *Japanese Working Life Profile, 1997–1998*. Tokyo: Japan Institute of Labour.

JPC (1990) *Roshi Kyogizei no Jujitsu o Motomete-Kigyo, Sangyo, Chiiki no Genjo to Seika* (Towards Enrichment of Joint-Consultation Schemes: The Present Condition and the Result of Enterprise-based, Industry-wide, and Regional Joint Consultation Schemes). Tokyo: Japan Productivity Center.

Kojima, Noriaki (1997) 'Japanese Employment and Labour Laws in Transition', *Journal of Japanese Trade and Industry*, Vol. 16, No. 4, pp. 8–11.

Kumazawa, Makoto (1997) *Noryokushugi to Kigyo Shakai* (Meritocratism and Company's Society). Tokyo: Iwanami Shinsho.

Legewie, Jochen (1997) 'The Hollowing Out of Japanese Industry and its Effects on Employment in Japan', in *The Japanese Employment System in Transition*. Working paper 97/3, Economic Section, German Institute for Japanese Studies, Tokyo, pp. 19–34.

Maekawa, Haruo (1986) *Report to Research Council for Economic Structural Adjustment to Aid International Cooperation*. Tokyo: Ministry for International Trade and Industry .

Matsui, Hiroyuki (1997) 'Management Stance toward Employment of Aged', *Labour Issues Quarterly*, No. 37, Autumn, pp. 9–10.

MITI (1995) *Tsusho Sangyosho Hakusho* (White Paper). Tokyo: Ministry for International Trade and Industry.

MITI (1996) *Wagakuni Kigyo no Kaigai Jigyo Katsudo* (Basic Survey of Overseas Business Activities of Domestic Firms), Vol. 25. Tokyo: Ministry for International Trade and Industry.

MITI (1997a) *Wagakuni Kigyo no Kaigai Jigyo Katsudo* (Basic Survey of Overseas Business Activities of Domestic Firms), Vol. 26. Tokyo: Ministry for International Trade and Industry.

MITI (1997b) *Tsusho Sangyosho Hakusho* (White Paper). Tokyo: Ministry for International Trade and Industry.

MITI (1998) 'White Paper on International Trade 1998: A Summary', *Journal of Japanese Trade and Industry*, Vol. 17, No. 5, pp. 8–19.

MOF (1998) *Chusho Kigyo Hakusho* (White Book on Small Enterprises). Tokyo: Small and Medium Enterprise Agency, Ministry of Finance.

Mouer, Ross (1989) 'Japanese Model of Industrial Relations: Warnings or Opportunities', *Hitotsubashi Journal of Social Studies*, Vol. 21, pp. 105–24.

Nakamura, Takao (1981) *The Postwar Japanese Economy*. Tokyo: University of Tokyo Press.

Nakamura, Keisuke (1997) 'Worker Participation: Collective Bargaining and Joint Consultation', in Mari Sako and Hiroki Sato (eds), *Japanese Labour and Management in Transition*. London: Routledge, pp. 280–95.

Narikawa, Hideaki (1996) 'Present Status of Enterprise-based Welfare Arrangements and Targets of Approach by Trade Unions', *Labour Issues Quarterly*, Autumn, No. 33, pp. 4–5.

Narikawa, Hideaki (1997) 'Present Japanese Labour System and Problems for the Future', *Journal of Japanese Trade and Industry*, Vol. 16, No. 4, pp. 12–15.

Naruse, Takeo (1997) 'Toward a New Japanese-style Employment System', *Journal of Japanese Trade and Industry*, Vol. 16, No. 4, pp. 16–19.

Nikkei Business (The), 27 April 1998 pp. 14–23.

Nikkei Weekly (The), 5 April 1997 p.17.

Nikkeiren (1995) *Shin Jidai no Nihonteki Keiei* (Japanese Style Management for a New Age). Tokyo: Nikkeiren.

Ohki, Kazunori (1998) 'New Trends in Enterprise Unions and the Labour Movement', in H. Hasegawa and G. Hook (eds), *Japanese Business Management – Restructuring for Low Growth and Globalization*. London: Routledge, pp. 217–40.

Petrella, Riccardo (1996) 'Globalization and Internationalization: The Dynamics of the Emerging World Order', in R. Boyer and D. Drache (eds), *States against Markets: The Limits of Globalization*. London: Routledge.

Sato, Koichi (1997) 'Activities of Citizen-Rengo Volunteer Network Related to Volunteer Activities', *Labour Issues Quarterly*, Summer 1995, No. 28, pp. 8–9.

Seki, Mitsuhiro (1997) *Kudoka o Koete-Gijutsu to Chiiki no Saikochiku* (Overcoming Hollowing Out: The Reorganization of Technique and Regions). Tokyo: Nihon Keizai Shimposha.

Shakai Keizai Seisansei Shimbun, various editions.

Shinoda, Toru (1997) '*Rengo* and Policy Participation: Japanese-style Neo-corporatism', in Mari Sako and Hiroki Sato (eds), *Japanese Labour and Management in Transition*. London: Routledge, pp. 187–214.

Tsuru, Tsuyoshi (1995) 'The Determinant of Union Decline in Japan', *Labour Issues Quarterly*, No. 26, Winter, pp. 14–16.

8

Globalization and Labour Rights: The Case of Korea

DONG-ONE KIM, JOHNGSEOK BAE and CHANGWON LEE

Since 1994 the linkage of labour and trade, frequently referred as the 'social clause', has been a major issue in Asia and Europe. The International Labour Organization (ILO) uses the term 'social dimension of the liberalization of trade', and its concerns on the issue have recently focused on the social dimension of 'globalization'. Globalization includes not only the liberalization of trade but also the free flows of international investment. Nevertheless, social clause discussions have paid more attention to the linkage of trade and labour, while relatively downplaying the linkage between investment and labour. As the capital flows have been rapid and basically transnational, capital investments between countries have increasingly shaped the economic development of countries.

The industrial relations (IR) implications of globalization are many and varied. Some examples include the impact on employment, wages, union density, bargaining power of IR actors, labour rights, working conditions, and skill formation. Globalization does not necessarily create positive conditions for IR outcomes. The reverse could be also true. One hypothesis attributes the current Asian economic crisis to the 'globalized' nature of the Asian economies (Erickson and Kuruvilla, 1998). With the outbreak of the Asian financial crisis, the globalization of the economy, including both trade and investment, has frequently been regarded as one of the fundamental factors affecting basic labour rights. In some countries, unionization rates have rapidly fallen and the bargaining power of trade unions has contracted.

This chapter aims to examine the linkage between globalization and labour rights focusing on the case of Korea.[1] To tackle this issue, one must take the fundamental change of the global economy into account as well as understand the process that certain national policies and institutions have evolved under the constraints basically determined by the impact of globalization. The moral commitment of international societies to protecting basic labour rights plays an important role in this regard.

The purpose of the present contribution is to provide an account that draws attention to the tradition of Korean IR and recent challenges under the global financial and economic system. It focuses especially on the experience of Korean IR after the International Monetary Fund (IMF) rescue package of November 1997. First, we delineate the globalization of the Korean economy, followed by the general background of IR in Korea. Some current IR issues under globalization trends are then discussed.

GLOBALIZATION OF THE KOREAN ECONOMY

The economic success of Korea during the past few decades can be attributed to its export-orientated development. The export-orientated strategy, combined with the gradual import liberalization process, has been accompanied by a steady increase in trade flows (see Figures 1 and 2). Since 1970, the volume of trade has been multiplied by a factor of five, with exports increasing much faster than imports. The ratio of trade to gross domestic product (GDP) soared from below 20 per cent in the 1960s to over 60 per cent in the early 1980s, and has broadly stabilized since then. Korea's presence in world markets has risen substantially.

FIGURE 1

EVOLUTION OF TRADE FLOWS (PER CENT OF GDP)

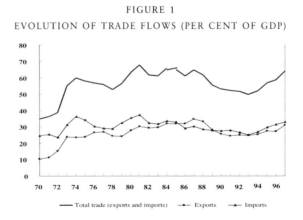

Sources: Bank of Korea and IMF, *International Financial Statistics Yearbook* (1996).

However, foreign direct investment (FDI) flows had been small until the mid-1980s, as shown in Figure 2. Following a somewhat more liberal attitude towards foreign investment, both inflows and outflows have increased since then. Thus, in 1997, there were 636 projects of FDI in Korea, representing a record high of US$7 billion, while the 1,561 projects of outward investment amounted to US$5.8 billion. Even so, FDI continued to perform a less significant role compared with other countries. However, the Korean government and firms realized that the Korean economy needed more FDI after the severe dollar liquidity problems. Koreans have realized that it could now be difficult to separate one country's economy from another.

FIGURE 2

TRENDS OF FDI INFLOWS AND OUTFLOWS (US$ MILLION)

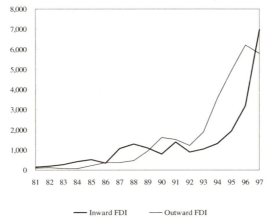

Note: The figures indicate the amount of officially-accepted FDI flows.

Source: Ministry of Finance and Economy, *Trends in International Investment and Technology Inducement* (1998).

OVERVIEW OF KOREAN INDUSTRIAL RELATIONS

The Economy and Labour Market in Korea

Korea, with a population of approximately 47 million, has shown the most remarkable economic growth among newly developed countries. Growth rates, in terms of real GDP, of the Korean economy have averaged nearly eight per cent per year since the 1970s (see Table 1).

TABLE 1

ECONOMIC INDICATORS AND LABOUR STATISTICS IN KOREA

Years	Growth rates of real GDP[a]	Per capita GNP[b]	Trade balances[c]	Unemployment rates[a]	Hourly labour costs[b, d]	Unionization rates[a]	Number of labour disputes
1970	7.6	252	−623	4.4	−	12.6	4
1975	6.6	594	−1,887	4.1	0.32	15.8	52
1980	2.7	1,592	−5,321	5.2	0.96	14.7	206
1985	6.5	2,242	−887	4.0	1.23	12.4	265
1986	11.6	2,568	4,617	3.8	1.31	12.3	276
1987	11.5	3,218	9,854	3.1	1.59	13.8	3,749
1988	11.3	4,295	14,161	2.5	2.20	17.8	1,873
1989	6.4	5,210	5,055	2.6	3.17	17.2	322
1990	9.5	5,883	−2,179	2.4	3.71	17.2	322
1991	9.1	6,757	−8,728	2.3	4.61	15.9	234
1992	5.1	7,007	−4,529	2.4	5.22	15.0	235
1993	5.8	7,513	385	2.8	5.64	14.2	144
1994	8.6	8,508	−4,531	2.4	6.40	13.5	121
1995	9.0	10,076	−8,948	2.0	7.40	12.7	88
1996	7.1	1,0543	−23,005	2.0	8.22	12.2	85
1997	5.5	9,511	−8,618	2.6	−	11.2	78

a Per cent.
b US dollars.
c Millions of US dollars.
d Production workers in the manufacturing sector.

Source: Korea Labor Institute (1994, 1996, 1997, 1998).

Real wages, defined as nominal wages deflated by consumer price increases, grew at an annual rate of 9.3 per cent during the period 1985–94, which exceeded even wage increases in Japan in the 1960s and 1970s (Park and Lee, 1995). Real wage growth was most outstanding during the second half of the 1970s and for the whole period of the 1980s, recording an average annual growth rate of 10.3 per cent and 8.3 per cent, respectively. Despite its slowdown, even during the first half of the 1990s, the real wage growth rate of Korea was much higher than those observed in most industrialized countries and higher than in any other newly industrialized economy (NIE) in Asia, such as Taiwan, Singapore and Hong Kong. The current economic crisis in Korea, however, brought about much lower real wage growth rates (see Table 5).

The remarkable economic growth has been associated with rapid urbanization and growth of the manufacturing workforce. The number of workers in the manufacturing sector increased from 601,000 in 1963 to 4,475,000 in 1997. In the 1990s the labour force participation rate has been approximately 62 per cent (Korea

Labor Institute, 1994, 1996). The unemployment rate dropped from 8.2 per cent in 1963 to 4.4 per cent in 1970, and since 1980 it has remained under 3 per cent (see Table 1). In the early stages of industrialization, the Korean economy faced the challenge of creating enough jobs to reduce a relatively high unemployment rate (of some 7 per cent in the mid-1960s) and, more importantly, to absorb large cohorts of new labour market entrants. Since then, the high growth process had translated into the creation of over ten million jobs. This achievement allowed absorption of not only the overall rise in the labour force, but also the expanding labour force participation of female workers. Since 1970 the participation rate of women had been raised by ten percentage points to 49.5 per cent in 1997. Taken together, the total unemployment rate for both males and females declined to around 4 per cent in the 1970s and 2–3 per cent between the early 1980s and 1997.

One feature captured in the growth process of the Korean economy lies in its growth-cum-equity development path that held true until the mid-1990s. During the 1975–95 period, the Gini coefficient of concentration declined from 0.39 to 0.28, which was at the low end of the scale compared with other Asian countries. Such improvement in income distribution, achieved through the sustained economic growth process, is primarily ascribed to human capital accumulation (Jung, 1992).

Despite the remarkable economic growth, long working hours and the high incidence of industrial accidents showed the 'darker side' of the Korean labour market. Although working hours in Korea have decreased substantially since the mid-1980s (Kim, 1993), they are still longer (46.7 hours per week in the non-agricultural sector in 1997) than in most countries for which relevant data are reported in the *ILO Yearbook*. In addition, the injury rate in Korea's manufacturing sector (4,283 workdays lost per 1,000 employees due to occupational injuries in 1994) is also higher than that of any other major economy (Korea Labor Institute, 1996, 1998; Park and Lee, 1995).

Since the early 1990s, the labour market has responded to the slowdown of the economy. Mid-career employees, even in large corporations, have been forced to accept 'honorary' early retirement, and private firms and public employers have reduced substantially the number of job openings for new college graduates. After the 1997 IMF rescue package, several economic indexes changed rapidly. For example, the foreign exchange rate (Won/US$) rose from 921.85 in October 1997 through 1,706.8 in January 1998 to 1,213.65 in December 1998. In just a month after 19 November 1997, when Korea decided to approach the IMF, the value of the Korean Won fell by about 50 per cent against the US dollar, and the stock market followed by dropping some 60 per cent (for more details on the Korean crisis, see, *inter alia*, Cathie, 1998; Rowley and Bae, 1998a). The unemployment rate, although it declined a little for three consecutive months (from August to October 1998), increased to reach 8.5 per cent in January 1999, equalling some 1,762,000 people (see Table 2). Among the unemployed, 1,263,000 had lost their jobs within a year of being hired. In fact, the world's 11th largest economy suddenly became an economy surviving on overnight loans from international financial institutions (Park, 1998).

TABLE 2

LABOUR AND ECONOMIC STATISTICS, LATE 1997 AND 1998

Year	Month	Stock price index	Average exchange rate (won/US$)	No. unemployment (1,000)	Unemployment rate (%)	Growth rate of real GDP
1997	10	584.1	921.85	452	2.1	3.9
	11	494.1	1,025.58	574	2.6	
	12	390.3	1,484.08	658	3.1	
1998	1	475.2	1,706.80	934	4.5	−3.6
	2	525.2	1,623.06	1,235	5.9	
	3	523.0	1,505.28	1,378	6.5	
	4	444.2	1,391.97	1,434	6.7	−7.2
	5	356.3	1,394.62	1,492	6.9	
	6	313.3	1,397.18	1,529	7.0	
	7	327.8	1,300.77	1,651	7.6	−7.5
	8	312.8	1,303.22	1,578	7.4	
	9	312.2	1,370.80	1,572	7.3	
	10	358.8	1,336.72	1,536	7.1	−5.3
	11	429.2	1,294.13	1,557	7.3	
	12	524.7	1,213.65	1,665	7.9	

Government Policy on Employment and IR

Throughout the period of rapid economic growth, the Korean government exercised a dominant role in determining employment and IR practices. In the early stages of industrial development, Korea, being a country with few natural resources, achieved economic competitiveness in the international market through abundant and cheap labour. The major goal of employment policy was to provide labour market and labour relations conditions which best promoted rapid economic growth (Kim, 1993; Rodgers, 1990).

Korean economic growth was accompanied by extensive investment in human resources, and the ratio of government expenditure on education to the total government budget reached 14.8 per cent in 1992. The ratio was higher than those of most major countries except Japan (for example, 12.3 per cent in the USA, 8.6 per cent in Germany, 14.1 per cent in Australia, 11.5 per cent in Singapore and 16.5 per cent in Japan) (Korea Labor Institute, 1996). The cultural value placed on education, influenced by Confucianism, was also instrumental in building a relatively high-quality labour force during the early period of economic growth. In the 1970s, emphasis shifted to developing vocational and technical skills for the newly emerging heavy and chemical industries. In the early 1980s, government efforts were increasingly directed at improving the quality of technical education at both the vocational and the college levels to create a labour force with more sophisticated skills (Park and Lee, 1995).[2] Hence, 'lack of natural resources has been turned into a blessing' (L. Kim, 1997: 60) in building capable human capital.

During the period of rapid economic growth, the Korean government acted as a 'benevolent dictator' through comprehensive and detailed legal frameworks and direct state intervention in the labour market. The rights of Korean workers were protected by detailed legislative measures. Korean laws and regulations covering individual workers' rights were more extensive in some respects than those of Western countries (S. Kim, 1995). For example, establishments with five or more employees could not lay off workers without just cause, and the court recognized layoffs only if there was no other way of solving business problems. Furthermore, 'fair criteria' would have to be used for selecting the workers to be laid off.

On the other hand, the government suppressed any independent labour movement. While American-style labour laws were enacted in 1953 and guaranteed trade union rights, throughout the 1960s and 1970s labour law was frequently revised to place substantial restrictions on union activities. For example, labour legislation was amended in 1972 to suppress unions, and strikes were prohibited until 1980. Since the late 1980s, there have been revisions of labour laws to provide freedom for the labour movement. However, the current labour law, revised in March 1997, still contains some restrictions on the labour movement, such as a prohibition of union activities by public employees and teachers, and emergency adjustment of labour disputes in some industries by the Ministry of Labour.

The process of political democratization since the late 1980s has been accompanied by a surge of workforce militancy and violent labour disputes. Since the labour movement was suppressed by successive governments during the post-war period, political democratization was perceived by workers as an opportunity to remove the vestiges of past labour suppression. Workers' demands did not stop with improved wages and working conditions. They sought political liberalization, the right to form and control their own unions, and intervention in certain management prerogatives (Kim, 1993). Confronting unprecedented workforce militancy, the state has increasingly lost control over the labour market as well as trade unions since the late 1980s.

Employers and Employment Practices

Economic growth in Korea was led by large indigenous private organizations and chaebols, with close guidance and various supports (such as low-interest, long-term bank loans) from the state. Unlike Singapore and Taiwan, FDI did not play the central role in economic development. The Korean economy had been heavily dependent upon chaebols, such as Hyundai, Samsung, LG, Daewoo, Sk and Ssangyong. In 1997, the top 30 chaebols accounted for 13.5 per cent of gross national product (GNP) and 45.9 per cent of sales in the entire Korean economy (Choi, 1998).

Most private companies in Korea are still dominated by the founding father or his family members. The style of management is generally considered authoritarian or paternalistic. Tayloristic management systems have been the dominant method of production, especially in manufacturing facilities, although a few progressive employers (for example, Samsung, LG, Ssangyong) have experimented with teams, flexible production, employee involvement, multi-skills training and job rotation (T. Kim, 1995; Park and Lee, 1995). The responses of employers to the newly emerging militant unionism have been varied. The main response since 1987 has been, however, the adoption of hard-line methods (such as dismissal of union activists and blacklisting), rather than the use of more accommodative means (Wilkinson, 1994).

It is well known that the essence of Japanese IR is summarized by the term 'three pillars' – seniority-based wages, lifetime employment and enterprise unions. A less known fact is that the Japanese system of IR bequeathed similar characteristics to Korea.[3] Under the lifetime employment system both in Korea and Japan, a company usually hired recent school graduates. After being hired, workers receive training within the company and perform various jobs through rotation and transfers. Once hired, employees usually complete their careers at the same company. Their employment is, in principle, 'guaranteed' until a certain age. Although this age varies between companies and industries, it is generally between 50 and 60.

Traditionally, there is no formal layoff system in Korea comparable to that of the USA or European countries, and companies generally do not dismiss permanent employees. Even when certain departments are overstaffed (because of business downturns), companies try not to dismiss affected workers against their will. Employers try to retain employees as long as possible through their reallocation, reduction in overtime, and paid off-the-job training sessions. Although lifetime employment systems are limited mainly to regular, particularly male, workers in large companies, there is little doubt that they are the norm in Korean management practices. Furthermore, the normative influence of these practices extends to smaller companies and even to peripheral groups such as part-time workers.

Since the 1997 economic crisis in Korea, the lifetime employment principle has been more frequently violated in Korea than in Japan. Despite the recent economic difficulties, Japanese employers have been more conservative than their Korean counterparts in conducting massive layoffs by utilizing various substitutes. This is one of the reasons why the unemployment rate in Japan is still under five per cent, although the rate has steadily increased from about three per cent in 1997. However, Korean employers were more eager to adopt alternative employment principles during the economic crisis. Korean government officials believed that securing labour market flexibility is one promising approach to improving the economic competitiveness of Korean firms, and encouraged private firms to implement bold restructuring programmes, including massive layoffs. When there were business downturns, there have been many incidents of dismissals of workers against their will, through the use of honorary retirement plans. Since a condition of the IMF bailout programme in 1997 was the passing of laws to break down lifetime employment immediately,[4] downsizing has become a major social issue. Consequently, the number of permanent workers in establishments with ten or more employees has been decreasing, reflecting the slowdown of the economy and firms' efforts to reduce the number of permanent workers by relying more on part-time or temporary workers (Park and Lee, 1995). The unemployment rate in Korea has sharply increased from 2.1 per cent in October 1997 to almost nine per cent in the early part of 1999 (see Table 2).

While the seniority-based pay system is still a dominant form of remuneration in Korea, a wage system emphasizing individual ability (called 'annual pay', a type of merit-pay system) has gained in popularity in recent years (Kim and Park, 1997). Studies surveying the pay practices in Korean firms showed that about 15–20 per cent of Korean firms had already implemented an annual pay system, and more than 30 per cent of them were considering its implementation within the next two to three years (Yu and Park, 1999).

Trade Unionism in Korea

After the breakdown by force of the Communist labour movement in 1949, the government recognized the Federation of Korean Trade Unions (FKTU) as the only legal national-level union federation. The FKTU, established in 1960, has received financial support from the government, and its policies and activities have been generally subordinated to the government. Economic success, substantial wage increases, and the military threat from North Korea justified the state's authoritarian IR policy. However, fast industrial growth, the emergence of a middle-class population, and the rising level of education, contributed to strengthening the potential political basis of workers.

Since the late 1970s, a strong labour movement has emerged separate from the formal union organization. This movement was characterized by a proliferation of wildcat strikes in the late 1970s and early 1980s, and disputes over management-controlled company unions. The late 1980s witnessed a turning point. Initiated by the 'Democratization Declaration' in June 1987, the union movement underwent an unprecedented expansion. Union membership almost doubled during 1985–89, with union density rising from 12.4 to 18.6 per cent. This, however, led to labour turmoil and indeed there were nearly 4,000 disputes for the single year 1987 (see Table 1). In 1990, a militant and illegal national federation, the Korea Trade Union Congress (KTUC) was organized. After the biggest general strike in Korean history in early 1997 (see Bae *et al.*, 1997; Bae, 1997), the Trade Union Law was revised to allow the KTUC to become a legitimate union federation.

The labour law amendment in 1987 took a step forward to guarantee workers' collective rights. Workers could exercise their basic rights more freely, to organize, to bargain collectively, and to strike. Nevertheless, there remained some restrictions on freedom of association and collective bargaining, inclusive of the prohibition of multiple unions, and political activities of trade unions.

Most Korean unions are organized at the level of the individual enterprise. Members of enterprise unions include only full-time, blue-collar, and some white-collar workers (excluding temporary or part-time employees). While collective bargaining was circumscribed severely by the government until the late 1980s, it has become an increasingly important method of wage determination since the 'Great Labour Struggle' in 1987. In the unionized sector, wages and working hours are determined by collective bargaining between enterprise unions and individual employers, while multi-employer bargaining practices exist in transportation, mining and textile industries. As in Japan, each enterprise union negotiates with its own management on wages and working conditions every spring.

GLOBALIZATION AND LABOUR RIGHTS

Globalization has two contrasting effects on labour rights. There is the positive side of globalization in terms of worker rights, but also a negative side in terms of working conditions and employment practices.

The Positive Impact of Globalization on Labour Rights

Basic labour rights in Korea expanded as the economy grew. Although there was an imbalance in speed between this economic growth and the expansion of workers' rights, the gap reduced after the late 1980s. It is a common understanding that full employment or labour shortage (the unemployment rate was lower than three per cent until December 1997) since the mid-1980s played an important role in inducing the improvement in workers' rights.

Economic- and labour-related international organizations also have influenced Korean worker rights. Korea joined the ILO in December 1991. Since 1992, Korea has ratified seven ILO Conventions. In addition, Korea made a commitment to 'reform existing laws and regulations on industrial relations in line with internationally accepted standards, including those concerning basic human rights, such as freedom of association and collective bargaining', when it became the 29th member of Organization for Economic Cooperation and Development (OECD) in December 1996.

Another example is the report of the 'Overseas Private Investment Corporation' (OPIC). All the actors in the IR system in Korea paid attention to the OPIC report on 'Iinternationally Recognized Worker Rights in Korea'. In July 1991, OPIC, an independent US government agency that sells investment services to assist US companies investing in some 140 emerging economies around the world, suspended its programmes in Korea as it had failed to take steps to adopt and implement internationally recognized worker rights. In June 1998, OPIC determined that Korea now met the worker rights eligibility criteria applicable to its programmes. The major steps taken by Korea since 1991 are shown in Table 3. All these international organizations have prompted Korea to take actions to confirm global standardization of labour rights.

TABLE 3

MAJOR STEPS TAKEN BY KOREA SINCE 1991

- Joining the ILO and ratification of some ILO conventions
- Legalization and *de facto* recognition of multiple unions at the national and industrial levels
- Elimination of the prohibition on third party intervention in industrial disputes and its replacement with a notification provision for non-affiliated third parties
- Establishment of Works Consultative Committees for government workers as a prelude to full unionization
- Progressive reduction in the list of 'essential' public services ineligible to strike
- Temporary removal of the prohibition on union involvement in political activity
- Full extension of worker rights to workers in Export Processing Zones
- Amnesty for workers previously convicted or arrested for legitimate union activity
- Reduction in the legal maximum weekly working hours

Source: From OPIC (1998).

In early 1996, the key actors in the IR system began to arrange a new institutional arena in which most labour issues could be discussed in a formal way. The Presidential Commission on IR Reform was launched. One purpose of the Commission was to improve Korean labour standards up to the level required by international organizations, such as the ILO and the OECD. The Commission, comprising the representatives of labour, management and public, held a series of public hearings and panels of experts for six months in order to reach a consensus on the labour issues in question. In 1997, after experiencing some conflicts among the tripartite actors, the labour law revision was completed. Among the major contents of this revision, there was a significant development in basic labour rights, as shown in Table 4.

TABLE 4

RECENT LABOUR LAW CHANGES IN BASIC WORKER RIGHTS

Freedom of association

1. Enhanced right to organize
    • By granting union pluralism, multiple trade unions at the national and industrial level are immediately permitted.
    • At the enterprise level, multiple trade unions will be allowed starting in the year 2002 to prepare for complementary measures in collective bargaining, such as single representation system.

2. Expanded Assistance from Third Parties
    • Eliminating the provision prohibiting intervention of third parties allows a broadened range of professional assistance in collective bargaining.
    • Enhanced autonomy in financial management of trade unions
    • By removing the upper limit (2%) on union membership dues, and autonomous fiscal operation and financial self-reliance of trade unions are founded.

Strengthened right to bargain collectively

1. The scope of parties entrusted with the right to bargain collectively is extended.

2. By authorizing representatives of labour and management to conclude a collective agreement, the new laws guarantee that collective bargaining is carried out under the autonomy and responsibility of the representatives concerned.

3. Should the representatives agree, the terms of validity of wage agreement may be extended in order to heighten autonomy of employees and employers in determining working conditions, including wages.

4. Punishment of employers committing unfair labour practices is enforced.

The 1997 revision of labour laws aimed at improving workers' well-being by strengthening basic labour rights, while at the same time strengthening firm competitiveness by enhancing labour market flexibility. In return for the legalization of multiple unions, the legalization of layoffs (with a two-year reservation for implementation) and flexible working hours systems have also been adopted.

The Negative Impact of Globalization on Labour Rights

However, the favourable progress in labour rights has encountered the challenge of globalization in 1990s. While some labour rights have additionally been legalized as a result of national efforts to meet global labour standards, labour markets and other conditions for workers and trade unions have seriously eroded under intense global competition. As the Korean economy has entered the advanced world economy, IR in Korea also became exposed to the worldwide changes in IR. In particular, because of the globalization-orientated economic policy of the government in the 1990s, both labour and management have experienced direct pressures from the world economy.

What are the driving forces behind the global standards? With the growing necessity of labour market flexibility, employment instability stemming from collective dismissals, layoffs, outsourcing, part-time work and the like has been evident (Bae *et al.*, 1997; Bridges, 1994; Frank and Cook, 1995; Heckscher, 1995; ILO, 1996). This trend has weakened the position of unions as a collective force for employment security. Moreover, union members have often been in the minority within the company because of the increasing use of non-standard labour. As a result, workers' interests have been less represented through union activities than before, while broader representative bodies, such as worker councils, play a similar but more cooperative role within companies. This trend jeopardizes enterprise unions as well as industry unions, because the diversified characteristics of workers within a company may prevent them from organizing their interests. With rapid technological innovations and shortened cycles of technological applications to production, massive unemployment due to industrial changes based on technological innovations has occurred in advanced countries (Craver, 1993).

Downsizing has been common in almost all sectors of the Korean economy. As a consequence, collective bargaining aiming at wage increases has been displaced by negotiations focusing more on employment security. Accordingly, wage levels for most workers have stagnated or deteriorated in recent years. As shown in Table 5,

TABLE 5

MAJOR INDICATORS IN WAGE CHANGES

Items	1995	1996	1997	1998	1997 1/4	2/4	3/4	4/4	1998 1/4	2/4	3/4	4/4	1999 1/4
Nominal wage increase rate (%)[a]	11.2	11.9	7.0	–2.5	11.6	9.8	6.8	0.9	0.1	–1.2	–8.1	–0.4	5.6
Consumer price change (%)	4.5	4.9	4.5	7.5	4.7	4.0	4.0	5.1	8.9	8.2	7.0	6.0	0.7
Real wage increase rate (%)[a]	6.4	6.7	2.4	–9.3	6.7	0.8	2.7	–4.0	–8.1	–8.6	–14.2	–6.0	4.9

a All industries.

Source: Korea Ministry of Labor, *Monthly Labor Statistics* (various issues).

both nominal and real wage rates have decreased recently. The real wage decrease for 1998 was 9.3 per cent.

With the financial crisis in 1997, a great number of workers in Korea lost their basis for keeping basic labour rights. Korea had increased people's welfare by enlarging the size of employment and raising income level and corporate welfare. However, with the sudden economic crisis, the existing socio-economic safety net has been found to be inadequate. The decline in employment has been dramatic since the outbreak of the crisis. The unemployment rate was 8.5 per cent as of January 1999, a four per cent increase from the previous year (see Table 2).

The sudden decline in employment was attributed mostly to the bankruptcy of small and medium-sized firms which suffered more from the credit squeeze arising from a tightened control of loans among highly scrutinized banking sectors, where most banks have been struggling to meet the standard set by the Bank for International Settlements (BIS). Moreover, as large firms begin to start their employment adjustment programmes, the unemployment rate is forecast to remain high for some time.

More drastic changes in Korean IR have resulted from restructuring programmes. As a result, IR has become unstable, and struggles and conflicts around the issue of comprehensive economic reform have increased. Economic adjustment programmes (such as downsizing, restructuring, so-called 'big deals' among *chaebols*, mergers and acquisitions, and intra- and inter-firm ventures) have been pursued by firms under the initiative of the new government prompted by IMF monitoring. These have been painful for unions and workers.

On 20 January 1998, all parties of the Tripartite Commission announced the first Tripartite Joint Statement identifying the goal of economic reform and the principle of fair burden-sharing. On 9 February 1998, the Tripartite Commission agreed upon some major agenda items and declared its Social Agreement to the public. The major agreed-upon issues of the Social Agreement were enormous in terms of their impacts on society and their relation to other fields. In particular, in return for accepting the immediate implementation of legal redundancy dismissals, unions and workers gained additional legalization of basic labour rights. This point has been regarded as the main content of the Social Agreement. Tripartite representatives, with regard to basic labour rights, have agreed to:

- allow the establishment of workplace association for government officials from January 1999;

- guarantee the right to organize trade unions of teachers from July 1999 (to revise the related laws at the regular session of the National Assembly in 1998);

- guarantee political activities of trade unions by revising the Elections Act and the Political Funds Act during the first half of 1998;

- recognize unemployed workers' rights to join trade unions organized on a trans-enterprise level from 1999 (to revise the related laws in February 1998);

- mandatory advance notice given of six months before the unilateral termination of collective agreements (to revise the related laws in February 1998);

- devise measures to provide tax benefits for trade unions at the earliest moment possible to facilitate their financial independence.

Despite these nominal enhancements in labour rights, it needs to be remembered that unions and workers in Korea have experienced substantial setbacks since the beginning of the financial crisis. Unions in Korea lost about 50,000, or three per cent, of their members during the first nine months after the IMF intervention. The pattern of concession bargaining is evident in 1998. A decline in real wages was common among the large establishments. Thus, the power basis of unions has rapidly eroded (apart from their formally expanded labour rights). Thus, in sum, the social impact for workers of globalization in Korea has been both positive and negative, yet with much more weight on the latter.

DISCUSSION

In this contribution we reviewed the backgrounds of Korean IR and examined recent changes with a special focus on globalization issues. We argued that globalization has both negative and positive effects on labour rights in Korea. However, the relationship between globalization and IR outcomes can be moderated by the IR actors. Although there are some benefits of globalization, the benefits are not always fully realized in every country. These are dependent upon the dynamic reciprocal interactions among IR actors. The Korean case clearly shows that global environments affect labour rights and conditions, but also that there is room for strategic choice among the IR actors.

First of all, the government may need to take a more progressive, rather than retrospective, economic policy (Kim, 1997; Rowley and Bae, 1998b). The progressive approach includes such policy options as a radical upgrading of the economic structure by enhancing productivity through greater investment in human resources, improving the flexibility of human resource utilization, and developing advanced technology and high value-added products; while the retrospective strategy is to undertake a series of measures that would maintain the advantages of the previous stages and includes such policies as wage controls and subordination and/or suppression of unions and collective bargaining. The latter strategy may be attractive to the state and employers in the short run, but may be untenable in the long run. However, recent Korean government policy seems to be mixed, containing both progressive and retrospective approaches by emphasizing higher value-added production and, at the same time, an export-orientated policy with lower prices (Cho, 1999). Verma (1998) argued that IR systems could play an important mediating role between foreign investment and desirable outcomes (such as sustainable growth). More specifically, he argued that more effective skill formation and greater 'voice' would be necessary conditions in converting FDI flow into sustainable growth. This implies that the government needs to make progressive policies to achieve the 'virtuous circle'.

The employers also have, at the risk of oversimplification, two strategies: cost minimization and value maximization. It would be easier to take the first route to competition, but it is almost impossible for Korean firms to gain competitive advantage through such an approach. Although globalization requires Korean firms to enhance organizational and international management capability by investing more in R&D, training and education, many firms have unfortunately reduced, postponed or cancelled their investments (Park, 1998; Rowley and Bae, 1998b).

Labour can also take either a traditional militant confrontation strategy or a more cooperative and participative approach under a new order (that is, changing environmental forces). Labour union leaders are currently facing this dilemma. They have both the tough elements and the moderate advocates. The former want to go out on strike by opposing the restructuring programmes and layoff policies. Some union leaders take this position because they regard the hard line as the best strategy for the survival of unions. However, it is hard to take this strategy without heavy burdens. First of all, labour and social unrest will prevent further FDI. In addition, they cannot defy public opinion, which wishes for industrial peace.

The IR actors may need to formulate policies that can enhance national economic competitiveness, and at the same time that can also protect worker rights, which seems to be a very difficult task under the current economic conditions in Asia. Therefore, there are some inherent dilemmas (Rowley and Bae, 1998b). When the IR actors take their own approaches without considering other parties, the Korean economy can be easily locked into a vicious circle. This problem can be partly resolved through institutions such as the Tripartite Commission, although its longer-term viability is uncertain (Erickson and Kuruvilla, 1998).

CONCLUSION

In the 1990s, the Korean economy faced a new social environment basically determined by the globalization of the world economy. Workers' basic rights have been improved by both internal and external pressures. However, Koreans also have witnessed the negative influences of the integrated world in terms of finance and information. Major changes in capital gains and the well-being of workers in a certain country may be determined by financial flows and information gaps, as well as by trade with other countries.

The critical role during the economic development process of Korea brought 'the political subordination of workers' and labour suppression (Deyo, 1989). Now the critical role of the global economic system could bring 'the global subordination of workers' and labour suppression. Since many firms have already been bankrupted,[5] and many firms plan to lay off more and more unionized employees, unions and workers have gradually lost their bargaining power. Economic globalization provides great possibilities and opportunities but also produces substantial threats, risks and challenges for all the IR actors. To achieve their goals, all IR actors may need some consistent and integrated approaches with a longer-term perspective. Since Korean labour issues are basically country-specific, labour policies should be driven by national conditions. At the same time, it would be desirable to pursue international cooperation and to make moral efforts to enhance some common concerns (such as labour rights) imposed by globalized economic and financial systems.

NOTES

1. From now on, 'Korea' is used as shorthand for South Korea.
2. The most significant state-financed training organization is the Korean Manpower Agency (KMA), which operates 37 vocational training centres around the country (Park and Lee, 1995).
3. Korea and Japan have been members of the same cultural area as Taiwan and China, an area characterized by Confucianism. Also significant here is the fact that Japan occupied the Korean peninsula by force from 1910 to 1945, during the dawn of Korea's industrialization. In addition, Japan exerted great influence on the industrialization of Korea, including the initial formation of an industrial relations system (Castley, 1998; Kim, 1993).
4. The clause on 'layoffs upon business dissolution' was first introduced in the Labor Standard Law of 26 December 1996. This brought about a general strike, and as a result on 13 March 1997 parliament approved a more lenient version of the labour law. The implementation of the clause was postponed for two years. However, the IMF bailout required a further revision of the labour laws, so the law was again revised on 20 February 1998.
5. During the period between December 1997 and December 1998, an average of about 2,000 firms per month went bankrupt .

REFERENCES

Bae, Johngseok (1997) 'Beyond Seniority-Based Systems: A Paradigm Shift in Korean HRM?', *Asia Pacific Business Review*, Vol. 3, No. 4, pp. 82–110.

Bae, Johngseok, Rowley, Chris, Kim, Dong-Heon and Lawler, John (1997) 'Korean Industrial Relations at the Crossroads: The Recent Labour Troubles', *Asia Pacific Business Review*, Vol. 3, No. 3, pp. 148–60.

Bank of Korea (various years) *Statistics DB*. Seoul: BOK.

Bridges, William (1994) *Job Shift: How to Prosper in a Workplace without Jobs*. Reading, MA: Addison-Wesley.

Castley, Robert J. (1998) 'The Korean Electronics Industry: The Japanese Role in Its Growth', *Asia Pacific Business Review*, Vol. 4, Nos. 2/3, pp. 29–47.

Cathie, John (1998) 'Financial Contagion in East Asia and the Origins of the Economic and Financial Crisis in Korea', *Asia Pacific Business Review*, Vol. 4, Nos. 2/3, pp. 18–28.

Cho, Dong-Sung (1999) 'The Causes of Korea Economic Crisis and the Future Tasks for Firm Restructuring', in *Proceedings of the Korean Academic Society of Business Administration*. Seoul: KASBA, pp. 29–56.

Choi, Seung No (1998) *Large Conglomerates in Korea*. Seoul: The Center for Free Enterprise (in Korean).

Craver, Charles B. (1993) *Can Unions Survive?* New York: New York University Press.

Deyo, Frederic C. (1989) *Beneath the Miracle: Labor Subordination in the New Asian Industrialism*. Berkeley, CA: University of California Press.

Erickson, Christopher L. and Kuruvilla, Sarosh (1998) 'Industrial Relations Implications of the Asian Economic Crisis', *Perspectives on Work: The Magazine of the IRRA*, Vol. 2, No. 2, pp. 42–7.

Frank, Robert and Cook, Phillip (1995) *The Winner-Take-All Society*. New York: Free Press.

Heckscher, Charles (1995) *White-Collar Blues: Management Loyalties in an Age of Corporate Restructuring*. New York: Basic Books.

ILO (1996) *World Employment 1996/97*. Geneva: ILO.

International Monetary Fund (1996) *International Financial Statistics Yearbook*. Washington, DC: IMF.

Jung, Jin Hwa (1992) 'Personal Income Distribution in Korea, 1963–1986: A Human Capital Approach', *Journal of Asian Economics*, Vol. 3, No. 1, pp. 57–72.

Kim, Dong-One (1993) 'An Analysis of Labour Disputes in Korea and Japan: The Search for an Alternative Model', *European Sociological Review*, Vol. 9, No. 2, pp. 139–54.

Kim, Dong-One (1997) 'Employment and Industrial Relations in East and Southeast Asia: Focusing on Japan, South Korea, Taiwan, and Singapore'. Paper presented at the International Meeting on Employment and Labor Relations, São Paulo, Brazil, 7–8 April.

Kim, Dong-One and Park, Sungsoo (1997) 'Changing Patterns of Pay Systems in Japan and Korea: From Seniority to Performance', *International Journal of Employment Studies*, Vol. 5, No. 2, pp. 117–34.

Kim, Linsu (1997) *Imitation to Innovation: The Dynamics of Korea's Technological Learning*. Boston: Harvard Business School Press.

Kim, Sookon (1995) 'Labor Standards in Korea'. Paper presented at the Ministerial Meeting of the OECD, March.

Kim, Taigi (1995) 'Human Resource Management for Production Workers in Large Korean Manufacturing Firms', in S. Frenkel and J. Harrod (eds), *Industrialization and Labor Relations: Contemporary Research in Seven Countries*. Ithaca, New York: ILR Press, pp. 216–35.

Korea Labor Institute (1994) *Overseas Labor Statistics*. Seoul: Korea Labor Institute.

Korea Labor Institute (1996) *Overseas Labor Statistics*. Seoul: Korea Labor Institute.

Korea Labor Institute (1997) *Overseas Labor Statistics*. Seoul: Korea Labor Institute.

Korea Labor Institute (1998) *KLI Labor Statistics*. Seoul: Korea Labor Institute.

Ministry of Finance and Economy (1998) *Trends in International Investment and Technology Inducement*. Seoul: Korea Ministry of Finance and Economy.

OPIC (1998) *OPIC Report on 'Internationally Recognized Worker Rights in Korea'*, 5 June. Overseas Private Investment Corporation.

Park, Young-Bum (1998) 'The Financial Crisis in Korea: The Industrial Relations

Connection', *Perspectives on Work: The Magazine of the IRRA*, Vol. 2, No. 2, pp. 37–41.

Park, Young-Bum and Lee, Michael B. (1995) 'Economic Development, Globalization, and Practices in Industrial Relations and Human Resource Management in Korea', in A. Verma, T.A. Kochan and R.D. Lansbury (eds), *Employment Relations in the Growing Asian Economies*, New York: Routledge, pp. 27–61.

Rodgers, Ronald A. (1990) 'An Exclusive Labor Regime under Pressure: The Changes in Labor Relations in the Republic of Korea since Mid-1987', *UCLA Pacific Basin Law Journal*, Vol. 8, pp. 91–161.

Rowley, Chris and Bae, Johngseok (1998a) 'Introduction: The Icarus Paradox in Korean Business and Management', *Asia Pacific Business Review*, Vol. 4, Nos. 2/3, pp. 1–17.

Rowley, Chris and Bae, Johngseok (1998b) 'Conclusion: Korean Business and Management – The End of the Model?', *Asia Pacific Business Review*, Vol. 4, Nos. 2/3, pp. 130–9.

Verma, Anil (1998) 'When Foreign Investment Does Not Necessary Create Sustainable Growth: Lessons in Skill Formation from the Asian Crisis', *Perspectives on Work: The Magazine of the IRRA*, Vol. 2, No. 2, pp. 48–51.

Wilkinson, Barry (1994) *Labour and Industry in the Asia-Pacific: Lessons from the Newly-Industrialized Countries*. New York: Walter de Gruyter.

Yu, Gyu-Chang and Park, Woo-Sung (1999) 'Theoretical Considerations on the Implementation and Effects of Annual Pay System'. Unpublished manuscript (in Korean).

9

Globalization, Labour Market Deregulation and Trade Unions in Singapore

YUEN CHI CHING and LIM GHEE SOON

The post-independence period in Singapore was generally marked by employment security and regulated employment relations, as well as institutionalized means of dispute resolution. However, the internationalization of production and capital in the past couple of decades has brought about labour market deregulation with ramifications for employment and trade unions. While the challenges posed by globalization are similar for most developing countries, the responses to globalization are varied, reflecting differences in culture, political structure and ideology, as well as institutional arrangements of labour–management relations. In this chapter we examine how Singapore's system of tripartite industrial relations has responded to the challenges of globalization, and how trade unions and workers have fared in the process. The relative advantages and disadvantages of such a system are also discussed.

In discussing globalization and its effects on trade unions and labour market deregulation, two features distinguish Singapore's case: first, the vulnerability of a small, yet highly internationalized economy; and second, the symbiotic relationship between the trade union movement and the ruling People's Action Party (PAP).

The Internationalized Singapore Economy

Singapore took its first step in internationalization in 1965 when it was separated from Malaysia. With independence, the government faced a myriad of economic and social problems which it tried to resolve by embarking on the course of industrialization. Without many natural resources, the state turned to foreign investors whom it managed to attract by providing good infrastructure support, tax and other incentives. The type of investment the nation attracted at this stage was invariably in low-skilled, labour intensive industries.

Nonetheless, by pursuing the course of dependent development, Singapore managed to attain, in just 14 years, the basic industrial and social structure for further economic development. By 1979, the nation had achieved full employment, managed to house its population in public housing estates, and established a basic education system and basic medical services. It set up the Central Providence Fund (CPF) to provide for the retirement of its citizenry, as well as the Skills Development Fund (SDF) for the training of its workforce. Through the local subsidiaries of multinational corporations (MNCs), the nation also managed to gain access to international markets and solved the problem of having a small domestic market.

Having attained the foundation for further development, the government decided in 1979 to shift to high-technology, higher value-added industries. To force low-skilled, labour intensive industries out of the country, the government adopted a high-wage policy. Between 1979 and 1981, the National Wage Council (NWC) recommended a cumulative wage increase of around 36 per cent. Wages went up another 17.6 per cent between 1982 and 1984 due partly to the tight labour market (Yuen, 1997). At the same time, the government used tax and other incentives to attract high-technology, capital intensive investment. To support its push for higher technology, the government invested in the education, training and development of its workforce. However, it should be noted that the course the government pursued remained one of 'dependent development', as Singapore needed MNCs not only for their capital but critically also for technological transfer and market access.

Between 1985 and 1988, Singapore went through a recession as its high business and labour costs drove away foreign investors. The government introduced policy changes to restore Singapore's competitiveness. By the early 1990s, the economy recovered and the city-state achieved growth rates of eight to ten per cent between 1991 and 1997. With renewed economic growth, the government spearheaded the 'go regional' drive in 1992. It urged local businesses to invest in developing economies in the region in order to ride on their growth momentum and to gain access to their markets.

As the result of the government's economic development policies, the Singapore economy is highly internationalized. As of

1993, MNCs accounted for 12.1 per cent of the companies in Singapore, and employed 34.7 per cent of its labour force (Economic Development Board, 1993). However, given the extent of internationalization and the size of the Singapore economy, it is highly vulnerable to the vicissitudes of global political and economic changes. Invariably, such changes affect not only the local labour market, but employment relations as well.

Symbiotic Relationship between the Government and the Trade Union Movement

Labour organizations played an important role in the struggle against the Japanese occupation during World War II, and in the immediate post-war period, labour leaders joined a group of English-educated intellectuals to form the PAP and overthrew British colonial rule. However, differences in political ideology led to a split within the party, resulting in the left-wing fraction breaking away to form the *Barisan Sosialis* party and the Singapore Association of Trade Unions (SATU), while the moderates in the PAP formed the National Trade Union Congress (NTUC). When the PAP won control of the parliament in the 1968 election, all the trade unions were reorganized under the NTUC. This sequence of events accounted for the symbiotic relationship between the labour movement and the ruling PAP.

To help attract foreign investors, the government delivered for investors a disciplined, hardworking workforce by placing the trade unions under heavy legislative control. Strict legislation governing the registration of trade unions depoliticized the unions. While the Employment Act (1968) set down basic legislation regarding working hours, leave entitlements, contracts and their termination, retrenchment benefits and so on, the Industrial Relations Act of the same year excluded specific issues, such as promotion, internal transfer, retirement, retrenchment and work assignment from collective bargaining, making decisions on these issues management prerogatives. The Trade Dispute Act of 1960 and 1981 further rendered industrial actions illegal by making arbitration of industrial disputes by the Industrial Arbitration Court compulsory, and the Court's decisions final. As a result, in the 17 years between 1978 and 1994, only 122 worker-days were lost due to strikes. In 1972, the government established the tripartite NWC, which was responsible for setting wage guidelines for application across all sectors of the economy. The above legislation not only subjected labour to heavy regulation, but also rendered many traditional roles played by trade unions *vis-à-vis* their members redundant.

The industrial relations system in Singapore has often been described as a tripartite system with the government playing the key coordinating/balancing role in labour–management relations. While the government wanted the state and its citizenry to benefit as much as possible from economic development, given the state's dependency on foreign investors it had to meet their demands as well.

While Singapore's highly internationalized economy exposes the small city-state to the uncertainties of the global economy, its tripartite industrial relations system enables it to respond to globalization in a manner different from other Asian countries. In the subsequent sections, we discuss recent trends in globalization and how such developments have affected the labour market and trade unions in Singapore.

RECENT TRENDS IN GLOBALIZATION

Internationalization is not a new phenomenon. However, over the past few decades, it has taken on a drastic shift along three dimensions: the internationalization of consumer markets, production systems and financial markets. Since these developments are relevant to the case of Singapore, each will be dealt with briefly.

The Internationalization of Consumer Markets

Harvey (1989) identified time/space compression as the single most important cause of recent changes. Simply stated, recent developments in transportation and communication have greatly reduced the time needed to traverse or communicate across geographical distances. Giddens (1990) noted that 'time-space distantiation' has the effect of intensifying international relations, such that local happenings can be shaped by events occurring thousands of miles away (see also Rowley and Bae, 1998b).

Not only has travel/communication time been reduced, advancement in container shipping has made it economically viable to mass transport products (not just spice, silk and gold, but trucks, machines and heavy equipment as well) over long distances.

Manufacturers can now target their products at major markets in the world. With container shipping, mass production can now be matched by distribution *en masse*. As a result, manufacturers compete internationally for markets, and nations include negotiation on trade and market access as part of their foreign diplomacy.

MNCs and International Production Systems

In the 1970s, 'offshore production' was considered a novelty adopted by a small number of innovative companies. By the 1990s, it had become a necessary survival strategy for organizations. Over the last couple of decades, technological advancement has made integrated international production systems a common practice. First, the use of computers and new communication technologies in businesses has enabled companies to develop sophisticated logistic management systems that make the coordination of international production activities viable. Second, with the advancement in transportation mentioned earlier, companies are now able to manufacture different parts of a product at locations that offer the best cost-advantage. As a result, capital moves relentlessly across national boundaries in search of the lowest production cost.

There are recent indications that international production systems are giving way to international subcontracting of production capacity. Citing Jaikumar and Upton (1994) and the United Nations *World Investment Report* (1994), Hoogvelt (1997) described how companies like Nike used an Intranet (restricted communication network within an organization) to make loosely linked providers of flexible production capacities bid competitively for subcontracting orders. With the popularization of the Internet, bidding has gone international. Nowadays, bidding notices appear on the Internet inviting producers with quality assurance certificates to bid for orders. With this development, organizations will no longer be the same. For example, the computer retail industry in the USA is composed of many small companies that assemble personal computers to meet customers' needs. These companies use parts sourced from all over the world and are mainly marketing outfits with limited assembly capacity.

The Deepening of International Financial Markets

In terms of transaction value, international financial transactions have overshadowed international trade. According to Helleiner

(1996), as a result of states' decisions to abolish capital control, the volume of trading in financial markets has reached US$ one trillion per day, making it 40 times the amount of daily international trade. Because of their sheer volume, footloose investment funds have brought havoc to many economies (such as the euro dollar crisis, the Mexican and Asian financial crises, and the recent assault on the Russian currency), reducing states to responding to situations rather than managing them. States are sometimes afraid to exercise policy control over funds for fear of triggering fund movement to markets that are less restrictive and/or provide more profitable short-term gains. In a market dominated by huge, mobile international investment funds, companies tend to focus on short-term tangible results. Social capital, which does not show up in the short term, tends to be neglected (Reich, 1997; Leana, 1996).

The internationalization of consumer markets, production systems and financial markets has brought about profound changes in organizations, work and employment relations in developed countries. (For the situation in France see the *New York Times*, 19 March 1998; in Britain MacDonald, 1997; in America *New York Times*, 1996; and in Canada Betcherman, 1996.) With production shifting to developing countries to take advantage of the cheap labour there, developed countries have been 'losing jobs' to developing ones. To remain competitive, companies in developed nations have become 'leaner' by downsizing to the core, and 'meaner' by replacing regular employees (who enjoy employment security, medical and retirement benefits) with contractual workers paid at competitive market rates. Unemployment has risen, with a sizeable proportion of the workforce on short-term contracts and/or in part-time employment, while underemployment is also on the increase (Hutton, 1995). In the USA, wages at the bottom have declined while professional and knowledge workers have managed to maintain their wage levels or have seen them increase (Leana and Van Buren, 1998). The divergent trends have resulted in a widening gap between the top and the bottom in the workforce. Furthermore, with the deregulation of labour, union membership has been on the decline, and organized labour seems impotent amidst unemployment and job insecurity. Even in the USA, where the economy has recovered and the stock market has been hitting record highs, the working mass has accepted the loss of employment security as a fact of life.

While researchers do not disagree about the changes going on, there are considerable disagreements regarding whether recent changes represent a new phenomenon – globalization – that is different from internationalization in the past. Hirst and Thompson (1996) reviewed historical data in relation to three economic indicators of internationalization: the ratio of world trade to world output, foreign direct investment (FDI) through MNCs, and capital flows in relation to degrees of financial and monetary integration. They came to the conclusion that the level of integration, interdependence and openness of national economies in the present era is not unprecedented, and therefore that recent developments do not depart significantly from past internationalization. Hoogvelt (1997) concurred that in terms of economic data on world trade, capital and investment flows, recent developments are not unprecedented. However, he suggested that in a sociological sense, time-space compression has changed the very nature of how economic activities are conceptualized and organized. In this sense, recent developments do represent a process *qualitatively* different from internationalization in the past.

EFFECTS OF GLOBALIZATION ON THE LOCAL LABOUR MARKET

Corporate Relocation and Retrenchment

Among the nations in the region, Singapore had an early start in industrialization. As the other Asian countries resolved their political problems and embarked on industrialization, they entered the competition for FDI. With the competition for FDI heating up, what started off as a government initiative in 1979 – that of driving low-skilled, low-technology, labour intensive foreign investment out of the country – soon became a process with a life of its own. The relocation of production operations out of Singapore gathered momentum in the 1980s as labour costs in Singapore outstripped those of other developing nations in the region. For example, in the late 1970s, AT&T moved the production of standard telephones from Louisiana to Singapore where the same products could be produced at a far lower cost. By the late 1980s, production was moved again, this time to Thailand (Reich, 1991).

A number of local managers observed a pattern emerging among MNCs relocating their production operations to the region. MNCs often choose Singapore as the first stop when they decide to relocate their operations. With good infrastructure support, political stability, and a well-trained, hardworking labour force in Singapore, the chance of a successful overseas relocation is high. Thus, once the logistics and operational arrangements are established and tested, the operation is then relocated to a nearby country where labour and operational costs are cheaper. The exceptions to this practice are firms that engage in more sophisticated technologies. Thus, to retain its share of FDI, Singapore has no alternative but to move up on the skills ladder (see also Bae *et al.*, 1997).

With MNCs relocating out of Singapore, retrenchment, economic restructuring, and retraining are inevitable. Official statistics on retrenchment shows that between 1995 and 1996, the number of retrenching establishments rose by 13.7 per cent (from 351 to 399), while the number of retrenched workers increased by 84 per cent (from 5,950 to 10,956) in the four years between 1992 and 1996. Although the overall trend is towards more retrenchment, year-to-year figures suggest volatility, reflecting an unstable environment. Until 1997, the effects of retrenchment were moderated by the tight labour market. In 1996, only two per cent of the workforce was unemployed, and the 10,956 retrenched workers represented a mere 0.6 per cent of the workforce. Furthermore, with a median duration of unemployment of 4.9 weeks, retrenched workers did not seem to have much trouble obtaining other jobs. However, with the Asian economic crisis, the number of retrenched workers shot up by an unprecedented 289 per cent, to 28,300 in 1998 (Table 1).

Economic Restructuring and Older Workers

A concurrent change in the labour market is the continuing shift towards higher skills requirements as the result of economic restructuring. In comparing vacancies available in 1992 and 1998, it was noted that nearly three in ten of the jobs available in 1998 were for professionals, managers and technicians, almost double the number available in 1992. In contrast, the share of job openings for plant and machine operators fell to 12.9 per cent, roughly half of what it was in 1992 (*Straits Times*, 1999). With the ongoing

TABLE 1

NUMBER OF RETRENCHED WORKERS, 1992–98

Year	No. of retrenched workers	Year-to-year change (%)
1992	5,950	21.4
1993	6,487	9.0
1994	9,444	45.6
1995	8,788	– 6.9
1996	10,956	24.7
1997	9,784	–10.7
1998	28,300	289.2

Source: Singapore Yearbook of Labour Statistics (various issues).

restructuring towards higher value-added and knowledge-based activities, older workers became particularly vulnerable.

With many of the older workers born during the war years or before independence, when education was a luxury for the mass, Singapore faces the problem that a sizeable proportion of its older workers are poorly educated. Even during the early years of Singapore's nationhood, government policy focused more on 'the basics' – basic housing, healthcare, education, etc. Consequently, a figure as high as 39 per cent of its workforce in 1996 had 'below primary' or 'primary/lower secondary' education. The concentration of the poorly educated among older workers became evident when the government raised the national retirement age from 55 to 60 years in 1995. Workers who were born between 1936 and 1941 remained in the workforce instead of retiring. As a result, the percentage of the workforce with 'below primary' education shot up from 11.3 in 1995 to 15.5 in 1996 (Table 2).

Training of older workers has proved to be a difficult task. First, without basic education, it is difficult for them to acquire new skills. This is especially so when the nation is shifting towards more sophisticated technologies. Second, many older workers cannot see the threat of industrial restructuring. They typically decline to go for basic education and skills training because of such immediate concerns as reduced overtime earnings, family commitments, lack of time, unsuitable work hours and/or work location. With reduced job security, older workers have also become more disadvantaged in terms of employability. For example, it is not uncommon for employers to specify age limits for applicants in their employment advertisements. Thus, older workers face a double handicap of structural unemployment and discriminatory practices.

TABLE 2

EDUCATIONAL PROFILE OF THE LABOUR FORCE

Educational level	1995 (%)	1996 (%)
Below Primary	11.3	15.5
Primary/Lower Secondary	24.9	23.5
Secondary	30.4	30.5
Post Secondary/Diploma	20.0	18.9
Degree	13.3	11.6

Source: Singapore Yearbook of Labour Statistics (1995,1996).

Income Disparity and Social Inequality

In Singapore, unskilled and semi-skilled workers have to compete with the abundant supply of cheap labourers in the region. Wages for these workers are unlikely to increase significantly over time. At the top end of the skills range, as the government strives to position Singapore as the service (financial, medical and informational services), research and high-technology production hub of the region, private and public sector organizations are prepared to pay high salaries to attract qualified workers. In an effort to compete with the private sector for talent, the government tabled a White Paper, *Competitive Salaries for Competent and Honest Government*, in October 1994. The Paper laid down a formula to peg the entry-level ministerial salary at two-thirds of the income of the highest paid professionals in the nation. According to one estimate, the move could double the salaries of ministers from the average of $600,000 (S$1.48 = US$1) at the end of 1994 (Kwok, 1995). Under such a competitive environment for knowledge and skills, income disparity is inevitable.

GOVERNMENT AND TRADE UNION RESPONSES TO GLOBALIZATION

Labour Market Deregulation

Until the mid-1980s, labour–management relations in Singapore remained highly regulated and institutionalized. Between 1985 and 1988, Singapore went through a recession. With hindsight, the recession was inevitable and reflected the increasing competitiveness of the global economy. As wages in Singapore escalated and developing nations in the region entered the competition for foreign investment, Singapore lost out in terms of competitiveness. The recession signalled the need not only for wage moderation, but also for a more flexible system in an increasingly turbulent environment. Based on the recommendation of a tripartite committee looking into the cause of the recession, the government adopted a less rigid wage system. First, NWC wage recommendations would in the future be given in ranges rather than exact dollars and percentages. Second, the individual remuneration package would comprise, in addition to basic pay, three variable components reflecting respectively the state of the national economy, the performance of the firm, and individual performance. This change effectively allowed different industries/firms to pay different wages. Third, the standard 25 per cent employer contribution to the CPF of employees would also become variable depending on the state of the economy. At the height of the recession in 1987, the government slashed employer CPF contributions to ten per cent, and as the economy improved it climbed back to 20 per cent. In addition to CPF contributions, corporate contributions to the SDF, as well as other business taxes, were to be reviewed and adjusted as required. The range of payments subject to adjustment provides considerable flexibility for the system.

The trend towards labour market deregulation is likely to continue as the region becomes more integrated into the world economy (see Rowley and Lewis, 1996; Rowley, 1997; Rowley and Bae, 1998a, on such 'flexibilities'). However, instead of adopting a free labour market strategy, Singapore is more likely to adopt a strategy of *managed flexibility*.

Training and Human Resource Development

The response of the government and trade union responses to intense competition brought about by globalization is human resource development (HRD). While the government has, since the 1980s, emphasized HRD, global changes in the 1990s have made the government pursue HRD with greater determination and urgency. Multi-pronged programmes targeted at different levels/segments of the society are under way.

As noted earlier, in the early years of Singapore's nationhood, attention to education focused heavily on basic aspects (primary, secondary and technical training). It was not until the early 1980s that more attention was given to higher education. Since the early 1990s, education has been given the top priority in government policies. The upgrading of school buildings and facilities has been going on for some time, as have school curriculum changes. As is often the case in developed countries, the teaching profession in Singapore had not been able to attract or retain good quality people due to the economic boom and attractive private sector salaries. To reverse the trend, the government decided in 1996 to substantially improve the salary and promotional prospects of school teachers, a move which greatly boosted the morale of the teaching profession. At the tertiary level, reviews and restructuring are already in progress with the objectives of improving the quality of programmes and placing great emphasis on research and development.

Mindful that with a population of only three million, the nation's development may be constrained by a shortage of talent, the government views the inflow of talent as a source of long-term supply of the required skills and market competitiveness. To this end, it launched a recruitment initiative in 1997 for selected categories of people, such as 'entrepreneurs, industrialists, bankers, scientists, engineers, academics, artists, artisans and even sportsmen' (*The Straits Times*, 15 February 1999). On the educational front, the government offers scholarships in secondary schools, junior colleges and universities to attract bright scholars from the region to Singapore. It has also significantly increased the number of research scholarships in universities to attract more postgraduate students from the region. In fact, the government has been so active in recruiting foreign talent that there is some uneasiness among existing Singaporeans who fear that foreigners may take away the good jobs and promotional opportunities from them, dilute national cohesiveness, and upset racial composition.

In the provision of training for the workforce, the government works closely with the labour movement. Since the early 1980s, the NTUC has provided a variety of training programmes for workers with little education. In particular, the NTUC has been directly involved in providing Basic Education and Skills Training (BEST) to workers who had less than Primary 6 education.[1] BEST aimed to teach workers in basic Mathematics and English up to the Primary 6 level. Workers aspiring to receive education up to the Secondary and Pre-university level could opt for the Worker Improvement through Secondary Education (Wise) and the Continuation Education (Secondary and Pre-University) programmes. These basic education qualifications are essential for workers who want to receive specialized skills training in, for example, robotics and machine operations in a high-tech environment.

Even with the regional economic crisis, the government has not slackened in its training efforts. To steer the rising number of unemployed engineering graduates from taking on non-engineering jobs, and hence wasting their professional training, the government has devised a scheme whereby MNCs are paid to recruit engineering graduates and send them overseas for training. Through the scheme, such MNCs are able to equip the engineering graduates with company-specific skills so that when the business climate improves, their operations will not be constrained by the shortage of qualified manpower. Should a company decide to retain a trainee upon the completion of training, it will have to repay the government 30 per cent of the employee's salary while he/she was under training. Thus far, 500 engineers have received overseas training and a new batch of engineers will start their overseas training soon.

Helping Workers Cope with Retrenchment

In 1995, when signals surfaced that the numbers of retrenching establishments and unemployed workers were on the increase, the trade union movement organized a conference on globalization and invited representatives from government departments, employer organizations and academics to discuss the issue. The Singapore Institute of Labour Studies (the research and training arm of the NTUC) and individual unions had been conducting research and briefing sessions to help workers better understand the impact of globalization. The labour movement has also been an active promoter of multi-skill training as it believes that multi-skilling will enable workers to be more versatile and improve their employability. For workers affected by industrial restructuring, multi-skilling can make the transition more expeditious and less painful.

In 1996, the Ministry of Labour, the Singapore Productivity and Standards Board, the Singapore National Employers' Federation and the NTUC launched the 'Back to Work' scheme, under which participants who had been matched with a job would attend a core skills programme that included confidence building, personal effectiveness, and computer and communication skills. Besides training, trade unions have been effective in securing fairly favourable retrenchment compensation (between two weeks and one month of pay per year of service) for the laid-off workers. In addition, retrenched workers are provided with outplacement services such as alternative employment opportunities, résumé writing, interview skills, tips on starting a new business, and so on.

Policies to Address Income Disparity and Social Inequality

To address the disparity between Singaporeans who live in highly expensive private properties and those who dwell in public housing, the government introduced two programmes in 1996. The first was a programme to help low-income families acquire their own home (in any case, 91 per cent of the population owned the home they lived in, in 1996). A second programme, to use state funds to subsidize the upgrading of all public housing by stages, was also introduced. The objective of the programme was to upgrade public housing to a standard close to that of private apartments, and in so doing to narrow the status gap between public and private apartment dwellers. Property owners still have to come up with a portion of the upgrading costs, but will see the value of their property appreciate after upgrading.

In other areas, the government has also tried to redistribute wealth in the nation. For example, car owners in Singapore are taxed heavily, while the government used state funds to construct a comprehensive public transport system, the Mass Rail Transit (MRT), and upon its completion transferred the system at a nominal one dollar to the MRT Corporation which operates the transportation network (Chua and Tan, 1995).

LABOUR MARKET DEREGULATION AND EFFECTS ON TRADE UNIONS

One effect of globalization was labour market deregulation. The common perception of labour–management relations in Singapore is that it was highly regulated. A major piece of legislation that contributed to this perception was the Trade Dispute Act of 1960 and 1981. The Act, which made arbitration of industrial disputes by the Industrial Arbitration Court (IAC) compulsory and the Court's decisions final, effectively rendered industrial action by workers and trade unions illegal. In addition, the NWC had, in the past, provided specific guidelines for wage increments and bonuses. Most employers observed the guidelines, as the IAC, in settling disputes, invariably followed NWC wage guidelines. However, in spite of the web of industrial legislation, labour–management relations in Singapore remained fairly unregulated from an employer's perspective. Since the 1985 recession, the government has relaxed wage regulation. With the Asian economic crisis, employers' contributions to the workers' CPF have also been subject to adjustment. With the trend towards more fierce international competition, the already pro-business industrial relations system has become even more flexible.

In the midst of globalization and labour market deregulation, what is the reaction of the labour movement in Singapore? Overall, the reaction has been positive and this could be due to the unique structure/position of the labour movement in Singapore. Firstly, the relationship between NTUC and its affiliated unions has enabled it to meet the challenges of a globalized economy well. Trade unions in Singapore are a mixture of craft, industry, general, house and staff unions. There is, therefore, no clear boundary demarcation. Furthermore, with the close association between the NTUC and the ruling political party, the NTUC has undisputed control over individual unions. Therefore, individual unions are not in a position to set up boundaries and demarcations. The structure, thus, allows flexibility and helps facilitate the movement of workers across industry, skill and job categories. Such flexibility is desirable, as mobility across sectors and job categories becomes all the more important with corporate relocations, redundancy, and career changes.

The structure of the trade union movement has another advantage. Instead of each union catering to and defending the interests of a segment of the labour force, hanging onto redundant skills, and impeding the introduction of new technologies, the NTUC tends to adopt a broader perspective. As an umbrella organization, NTUC caters to the long-term interests of all the workers – that is, their ability to remain employable under the challenges of an internationalized economy. As such, it is more progressive and less myopic than a craft-, company- or industry-based system would have been.

Turning to the future role of the labour movement in Singapore, the prospect of local trade unions seems promising in comparison to those of their counterparts in many developed nations. In the West, trade unions have been threatened by internationalization. In America, as corporations resorted to non-unionized, part-time and other contingent workers, trade unions have seen their membership decline over the years. The bargaining power of trade unions has also diminished. Unemployment and retrenchment during the past decade and a half have created a deep sense of job insecurity among the workers, making some of them reluctant to join trade unions for fear of being discriminated against in employment. MNCs also have the alternative of shifting their operations elsewhere. To the extent that MNCs have become less dependent on specific labour pools, workers and their unions have less bargaining power *vis-à-vis* the MNCs. While corporations are reporting record profits and the stock market keeps breaking new records, wages have remained stagnant, except for the professionals and the highly educated 'knowledge' workers whose skills are in high demand (Leana, 1998).

In comparison, the labour movement in Singapore is likely to emerge from recent developments stronger and more influential. In the past, the labour–management relationship in Singapore was highly institutionalized and the role of trade unions much diminished. Workers found little incentive for joining trade unions other than enjoying discounts at NTUC supermarkets. As a result, union membership among non-managerial and non-professional employees had been in steady decline since 1979 (when the NWC-enforced high wage policy was adopted), until it reached a low of 192,394 members (18.9 per cent of the non-managerial and non-professional employees) in 1984, a 29.8 per cent reduction from the 249,710 members (26.6 per cent) in 1979.

In recent years, globalization and labour market deregulation have allowed the trade unions to play a more active role in wage negotiation. Union membership started to pick up in 1985, the year Singapore experienced its first recession, and continued through the introduction of qualitative, flexible wage guidelines, which permit a certain degree of bargaining. With economic restructuring and the recent regional financial crisis, the trade union movement has been actively involved in negotiation of retrenchment terms, training and development, and the provision of assistance for the retrenched workers. In a recent incident in which a sizeable number of workers were retrenched by a large electronics MNC, the company worked with the labour movement to retrain the workers and match them with new jobs months ahead of the actual retrenchment. On the day of the retrenchment, the parties concerned scored well in terms of public relations by having buses ready early in the morning to take the laid-off workers to the NTUC for job search and other assistance.

With recession and hard times for workers, the public came to appreciate the labour movement's roles as a reasonably priced service provider (in child care, dental care, insurance and care of the aged), and a moderator of consumer prices through its extensive network of supermarkets and taxis. As a result, union membership among non-managerial and non-professional employees climbed to 255,020 (22.1 per cent) in 1996 and reached 283,500 (25.2 per cent) in December 1998.

With the increasingly important role trade unions play in society, there has been a shift in the relationship between the PAP and the labour movement. In the past, the labour movement was apparently the subservient party in the symbiotic relationship. With globalization and the regional economic crisis, trade unions have reached out to the public and grown closer to the population. Recognizing the unions' increasing influence, the government has worked closely with the labour movement in communicating and marshalling support for tough economic policies. In the process, the NTUC has become more of a partner.

The peculiar circumstances facing Singapore (including lack of natural resources, land, and technology, and a small domestic market) have perhaps resulted in the adoption of a peculiar industrial relations system to ensure its long-term viability and success. Thus, on the one hand, legislation has been kept to a minimum to allow employers a great deal of leeway in managing their businesses and bringing in technology. This calculated move has enhanced the attractiveness of the investment environment and generated more jobs and income sources for workers. The absence of such legal constraints in regard of minimum wages, discrimination of employees (based on sex, age, race, handicapped status and others), attests to the government's commitment to provide a 'no hassle' business environment for foreign investors. At the same time, statutory laws, when enacted, are targeted at ensuring that employers have sufficient control over labour demands, and that workers receive a reasonable share of the returns from economic activities.

At the onset, the nature and role of the labour movement in Singapore were defined quite differently from those of its counterparts in the West. In Singapore, the management of the bulk of the population's concerns (that is, housing, education and medical care) was assumed by the founding government. Consequently, the labour movement championed a smaller portfolio of issues compared with labour movements in Western countries. Thus, instead of a 'fully fledged' labour movement charged with championing a plethora of complex labour demands (substantive, procedural and emotional), what we see in Singapore is a more focused labour movement confined to dealing with a relatively smaller subset of issues and problems. A fair comparison between the labour movement in Singapore and its counterparts in other countries should therefore not be based on the size of the portfolio of issues handled by the labour movement, but on outcomes such as employment and standard of living achieved by the working mass.

CONCLUSION

Singapore has responded to the challenges of globalization with a strategy of 'managed flexibility'. Through tax and wage adjustments, it has managed to provide sufficient incentives to attract foreign investment, and at the same time has provided workers with some protection against ruthless international capital. Various measures were also introduced to help workers affected by globalization. For example, during the recent economic crisis, the Housing Development Board reduced rental and service charges for lower income families. Special arrangements were also made to help families that have trouble with mortgage payments. Through the NTUC, workers also had access to training and job matching programmes, and price reductions on basic food/daily items in its chain of supermarkets.

With the above measures, Singaporeans have managed to pull through the economic crisis relatively unscathed. Singapore is officially out of recession. The state achieved a 5.4 per cent growth in 1999, and while the first quarter 2000 growth hit 9.1 per cent, projections for 2000 ranged from 5.5 per cent to 7.5 per cent. In spite of the projected recovery, the government has announced that employers' CPF contributions will remain at the reduced rate of ten per cent of basic wage for another one and a half years to ensure the nation's full recovery. To support the government's decision, NTUC cooperatives also announced that price cuts throughout its supermarket chain would continue until the end of 1999. At the same time, the government continued aggressively to upgrade educational and training programmes to support the shift to a knowledge-based economy.

The recent economic recession has reinforced and refined an emerging policy in labour–management relations, that of 'managed flexibility'. With the new policy, the NTUC has emerged as the government's partner in managing the challenges associated with globalization. In doing so, the trade union movement has gained in membership, stature and influence in society. The approach does have its merits. However, for such a system to work, one needs a centralized government that is able to make long-term policies without having to face challenges from interested parties.

NOTE

1. In Singapore, children start formal education with entry to Primary 1 at the age of six. They complete six years of primary education (Primary 6) before commencing secondary education at the age of 12.

REFERENCES

Bae, J., Rowley, C., Kim, D.H. and Lawler, J. (1997) 'Korean Industrial Relations at the Crossroads: The Recent Labour Troubles', *Asia Pacific Business Review*, Vol. 3, No. 3, pp. 148–60.

Betcherman, G. (1996) 'Globalization, Labour Markets and Public Policy', in R. Boyer and D. Drache (eds), *States against Markets*. London: Routledge, pp. 250–69.

Boyer, R. (1996) 'State and market', in R. Boyer and D. Drache (eds), *States against Markets*. London: Routledge, pp. 84–110.

Chua, B. H. and Tan, J.E. (1995) 'Singapore: new configurationn of a socially stratified culture', Working paper series, Department of Sociology, National University of Singapore

Giddens, A. (1990) *The Consequences of Modernity*. Cambridge: Polity Press.

Harvey, D. (1989) *The Condition of Postmodernity*. Oxford: Basil Blackwell.

Helleiner, E. (1996) 'Post-globalization: Is the Financial Liberalization Trend Likely to be Reversed?', in R. Boyer and D. Drache (eds), *States against Markets*. London: Routledge, pp. 193–210.

Hirst, P. and Thompson, G. (1996) *Globalization in Question*. Cambridge: Polity Press.

Hoogvelt, A. (1997) *Globalization and the Postcolonial World*. Baltimore, MD: Johns Hopkins University Press.

Hutton, W. (1995) *The State We're In*. London: Jonathan Cape.

Jaikumar, R. and Upton, D.M. (1994) 'The Co-ordination of Global Manufacturing', in S.A. Bradley, J. Hausman and A. Nolan (eds), *Globalization, Technology and Competition: The Fusion of Computers and Telecommunication in the 1990s*. Cambridge, MA: Harvard Business School Press.

Kwok, K.W. (1995) 'Singapore: Consolidating the New Political Economy', in *Southeast Asian Affairs*. Singapore: Institute of Southeast Asian Studies.

Leana, C.R. (1996) 'Why Downsizing Won't Work', *Chicago Tribune Magazine*, 14 April.

Leana, C. R. and Van Buren, H. J. (1998) 'Organizational Social Capital: The case for stability', Working paper series, The Joseph M. Katz Graduate School of Business, University of Pittsburgh.

MacDonald, R. (1997) 'Informal Working, Survival Strategies and the Idea of an "Underclass"', in R.K. Brown (ed.), *The Changing Shape of Work*. London: Macmillan Press.

Ministry of Labour, *Singapore Yearbook of Labour Statistics*. Singapore: Ministry of Labour, various issues.

Reich, R. (1991) *The Work of Nations*. London: Simon and Schuster.

Reich, R. (1997) Keynote Address at the 21st Century Employment Conference, University of Pittsburgh/Carnegie Mellow University, 23 October.

Rowley, C. (1997) 'Reassessing HRM's Convergence', *Asia Pacific Business Review*, Vol. 3, No. 4, pp. 198–211.

Rowley, C. and Bae, J. (1998a) 'Korean Business and Management: The End of the Model', *Asia Pacific Business Review*, Vol. 4, No. 3, pp. 130–9.

Rowley, C. and Bae, J. (1998b) *Korean Business: Internal and External Industrialization*. London: Cass.

Rowley, C. and Lewis, M. (1996) 'Greater China at the Crossroads? Convergence, Culture and Competitiveness', *Asia Pacific Business Review*, Vol. 2, No. 3, pp. 1–22.

New York Times (1996) *The Downsizing of America*. New York: Times Books.

New York Times, 19 March 1998.

Straits Times, 15 February and 2 June 1999. Singapore: Singapore Press Holdings.

United Nations (1994) *United Nations World Investment Report*.

Vobejda, B. and Chandler, C. (1997) 'Income in US up, but Not for the Poor', *Washington Post*, 29 September.

Yuen, C. (1997) 'Human Resource Management under Guided Economic Development: The Singapore Experience', *Asia Pacific Business Review*, Vol. 3, No. 4.

10

Globalization and Hong Kong's Labour Market: The Deregulation Paradox

NG SEK HONG and CHRIS ROWLEY

The globalization of business and economic activities has affected Hong Kong in recent years, giving rise to important changes in its labour market (Ng, 1995: 197–203) and with impacts on workers and labour organizations. This has been felt in the migration of manufacturing plants to China in combination with labour market deregulation via the government's guest worker policy.

While globalization may not be new nor its meaning agreed (see Hirst and Thompson, 1996), its effects and impacts are manifold and can be both direct and indirect. Hong Kong provides an interesting example of this. In this contribution we examine the institutional implications of liberalizing the previous ban on the admission of lower-skilled 'guest' ('foreign', 'alien', 'migrant') workers (except as domestic helpers) in the early 1990s. This seeming reversal was tantamount to partially deregulating a policy which was lukewarm about, or even apathetic towards, guest workers. However, it unwittingly produced regulation via a new body of norms and rules governing guest labour which were, paradoxically, restrictive and disabling for the affected parties.

This contribution provides an analysis of the impact of globalization in terms of the migration of business and labour and the effects on workers and trade unions in Hong Kong. We examine regulation in a system that is supposed to be deregulatory and the way in which labour importation has been affected by globalization of the Hong Kong economy and its businesses. The implications of the deregulation of guest working for Hong Kong employment norms, practices and institutions are then outlined. The irony of having to regulate in order to deregulate in this domain of guest labour helps strengthen scepticism about the nominal appearance of labour market freedoms in Hong Kong. It also displays the problems for organized labour with the dilemma of protecting and championing both local and guest workers simultaneously.

Most countries that attempt to deregulate the labour market are really replacing one set of regulations with another. In some ways this represents an irony, although one could argue that it is simply moving the constraints away from management and placing them on labour.[1] The UK's Thatcherite reforms of the 1980s were seen as such and labelled the 'free economy and the strong state' by some (see Gamble, 1988).

LABOUR MARKET FREEDOMS?

Global competition has induced many enterprises to consolidate and rationalize costs. One way of achieving this is via labour costs, often disguised as 'flexibility'. In order to hold labour costs down, workplaces have instituted various devices for enhancing flexibility which rest upon weakening 'restrictive' regulations. This development has given rise to a deregulation agenda in human resource and labour market practices (Dicken, 1998: 436–43).

The global trend of labour market deregulation (see Felstead and Jewson, 1999) has not made such a salient and problematic impact in Hong Kong as in Western advanced economies. First, the pressure on businesses to cut costs arrived much later. Economic problems came in the early 1990s in the wake of soaring prices due to sharply escalating pressures of land and labour shortages. Second, institutional regulation of economic activities has always been loose for both business transactions and employment (Ng, 1996: 295–8). Hong Kong was taken as a bastion of 'freewheeling' capitalism. By international standards, its economy has been able to conserve a comparatively free and permissive wage and labour market, hardly constrained by law, public administrative controls or trade unions' collective actions and bargaining activities.

Such perspectives have been criticized. First, a state of institutional openness actually betrays the paucity of rules prescribing regulatory standards in the labour market. It is a vacuum reflecting the underdeveloped state of Hong Kong as an industrial society because of its newness and immaturity. Second, such an image is simply a stereotypical overgeneralization. Turner *et al.* (1980: 43–8) challenged this conventional wisdom of Hong Kong's labour market as highly efficient and responsive, as three clusters of institutional and cultural constraints handicapped workers in their mobility and labour market freedom. First, there was a type of geographically based parochialism, producing a narrow and localized horizon and low preparedness to travel very far from homes in search of jobs or to commute. Second, there was a type of socially rooted localism cherished at the workplace, as enmeshed in the traditional Chinese web of kinship networks and other forms of particularistic ties. Hence, local employers conserved strong preferences for workers from particular families, clans or regional associations in China. Third, there was a hybrid mix of modern and traditional employers' strategies to enhance labour commitment and retention. Employers established a spectrum of benefits, backed by manipulation of piece rates, incentives, bonuses and the like, the hoarding of labour through seasonal or trade recessions (aided by worker willingness to share work on a reduced time basis). In some cases potentially bidding employers developed tacit, yet collusive, understandings not to poach labour from each other.

Ten years later the same authors reported that many of these customary barriers against poaching had largely eroded due to acute labour shortages (Turner *et al.*, 1991). However, some industries continued coordinating pay policies, but in a subtle and non-coercive way. This was achieved largely through a network of 'persuasive understandings' (and often via organized collective decisions), by keeping wage rises ahead of inflation and roughly in line with profitability (ibid.). Thus, what actually existed in the labour market was far more complex and structured than it appeared.

LABOUR IMPORTATION AND LABOUR MARKET STABILIZATION: TOWARDS DEREGULATION OR REGULATION?

What has beset Hong Kong's labour market since the late 1980s is the highly contested agenda of admitting large numbers of guest workers (ibid.). The government justified this by pledging these arrangements were temporary, stop-gap devices to address labour shortages and production bottlenecks (Lethbridge and Ng, 1995: 65–6, 71–3). Paradoxically, this led an otherwise passive administration to drift unwittingly towards building a new control regime of regulating the workplace and the labour market. Such developments impaired deregulation aimed at giving greater flexibility to employers. They produced a dualism of both deregulation and regulation with control policy implications. Also, organized labour's anxiety to regulate to constrain guest worker numbers nurtured, in the pluralistic and permissive context of cosmopolitan Hong Kong, a local ethos of protectionist and hostile sentiments (Ng and Lee, 1997).

Chinese Immigration and Business Globalization

By default, Hong Kong coped with rapid growth and labour demands during the 1970s with a hidden reliance upon illegal immigrants from China. This so-called 'Touch Base' policy was a benevolent compromise by the government, based largely upon humanitarian considerations of not enforcing a strict ban on illegal entrants. Formally, such an embargo constituted the core of an immigration policy mutually upheld by both the Chinese and Hong Kong authorities to help stabilize the latter's population. In practice, Touch Base granted a *de facto* right of tolerated residence to arrivals able to make for urban areas and secure shelter. This norm furnished a consistent, albeit masked, source of low skill/wage labour (Ng, 1997a: 173). However, this stance was rescinded in 1980 with demographic pressures emanating from an influx of illegal arrivals encouraged by this informally relaxed norm (ibid.). Enhanced regulation of immigration followed and all those apprehended were returned to China. Along with trade prosperity and materialistic affluence, an upward spiral of escalating wages and prices ensued.

The labour market drama of the late 1980s and early 1990s needs contextualization. A principal stimulation of economic activity was the potent 'China factor', and the opening-up of its economy and modernization reforms. This helped convert Hong Kong into a 'post-industrial' city (see Aarnio and Rowley, 1996, on service growth), to become a business-financial centre, yet leaning heavily upon its Mainland hinterland. In a spontaneous market-led process practically void of any state sponsorship, Hong Kong was launched, by default, into restructuring into a reputedly high value-adding commercial centre. However, escalating labour and land costs quickly produced a high-inflation syndrome and high-cost impasse. By the early 1990s, labour market reforms were seen as imperative if industrial activities were to remain viable. The fear was that both labour and capital would soon price themselves out of the market in Asian and global business arenas alike (Enright *et al.*, 1997; Berger and Lester, 1997; Chen, 1995: 13–22).

Ironically, and again by default, Hong Kong was passively launched into its labour market changes by the 'China factor'. Wide cost differentials with the Mainland had always existed, but their appropriation was not tenable until China's reforms. These included the free movement of overseas capital, and cross-border economic linkages. These were particularly conspicuous and well developed with Hong Kong, a situation partly encouraged by approaching reunification (Ng and Poon, 1997: 37–8).

Cheap land and abundant labour in China were powerful inducements to Hong Kong factories to migrate. This was labour market deregulation for Hong Kong industrial capital, which explored and assumed a new logic in the division of labour by reconfiguring and fractionalizing production. For the bulk of plants, shopfloor production activities (largely assembly line in nature) were detached from head offices and relocated. This left Hong Kong core establishments to consolidate and concentrate upon back-up roles, such as those of an administrative coordinating nerve centre; design, marketing and distribution; and warehousing (Tang, 1995: 119–25). This had implications for the management of work and the labour process. The workforce became dichotomized, each segment belonging to the two physical locations. Most of the Hong Kong based manufacturing businesses continued to rely upon the home labour market for sourcing key staff, who were either office white-collar workers deployed at the headquarters (in Hong Kong) or professional-managerial personnel assigned to organize and supervise production activities (in China). Simultaneously, almost entirely Chinese shopfloor labour was recruited for Mainland plants. According to estimates, Hong Kong capital was responsible for employing three million Chinese workers in the early 1990s, reaching about five million by 1998 (Ng, 1998). However, such capital mobility can be part of the 'race to the bottom' and drive for ever-lower labour standards with implications for home labour markets (see Mehmet *et al.*, 1999; Lui and Chiu, 1999).

Supplementing the Labour Supply Locally
Simultaneously, industry responded to the pressures of escalating labour costs and bottlenecks caused by skill shortages by attempting

to pressurize and persuade the government to augment local labour supply via deregulatory measures (Ng, 1995: 199–201). The solution, albeit packaged nominally as a stop-gap measure in order not to prejudice the employment chances of locals, was to introduce large scale admission of guest workers (Ng, 1997b: 662–4). Capital's argument for such liberalization – to help fill labour gaps – emulated the same logic behind the parallel drama of the exodus of factories to escape high labour costs. The latter process had already precipitated rising apprehension about redundancies (ibid.). However, industry made it clear that unless the government adopted definite steps, labour shortages and rising wage costs would lead to a drain of manufacturing activities and jobs at an even faster pace. The administration, albeit hesitantly and reluctantly, removed the labour importation ban for want of alternative options on a pilot basis in 1989, consolidated in the 1991 General Labour Importation Scheme.

Such a policy move on guest workers posed a dilemma for the government inasmuch as deregulation almost implied simultaneous discretionary intervention rather than leaving the labour market in a unregulated state to conform to the free play of supply and demand. An inherent paradox arose, since the government was compelled to begin formulating and codifying an increasingly sophisticated body of etiquette and rules in order to regulate the organization of labour importation. Such a control regime of rules by the authorities to steer, monitor and police guest workers is discussed later.

The liberalization of guest working was not an isolated case of official policy on the deregulation of business and workplace activities. The decision coincided with a growth, since the mid-1980s, of the deregulation ethos emulative of some practices in Western industrialized nations.[2] The classic agenda of such a deregulatory strategy was witnessed in Hong Kong telecommunications, where the previously protective shelter of a state monopoly granted to Cable and Wireless (C&W, which dominated the sector) was steadily rescinded from the late 1980s. The proliferation of new entrants produced such a competitive arena that the internal labour market of C&W was heavily eroded and in 1991 touched off large-scale retrenchment following merger with Hong Kong Telephone (Lethbridge and Ng, 1995).

PROTECTION AND CONTROL:
REGULATION TO DEREGULATE ENTRY

It was declared unequivocally by the government at the policy inception that the intake of guest workers needed to be strictly policed and controlled in size, subject to stipulated, centrally administered quotas. From the onset, the entire exercise was hence heavily rule-bound. However, the deregulatory device did appear to give organizations latitude in numerical and functional flexibility within the framework of the web of importation regulatory rules.[3] The cornerstone instrument was a fixed term standard contract (of two years, renewable twice at most). While such contracts had the intrinsic appeal of delimiting the parties' commitments, the provisions (including a normative assumption that any premature contractual breach or dissolution was not likely) also helped to enhance the parties' certainty during contract duration. A crucial benefit to organizations appeared to be the ability of management to better control production as labour shortages were remedied.

The irony of the decision to deregulate the hiring of guest workers has been, concomitantly, a meticulous concern by the authorities to restrict strenuously the freedom of employing units to redeploy recruits from posts specified in the contract. This control served a multiple purpose. First, it assisted the government to better administer quotas, which allocated intake by industry within a highly regulated control regime. Second, it appeased and reassured hostile locals and organized labour that guest workers should not take precedence over locals. Third, it built in a disincentive factor to discourage employers from drifting into indiscriminately using guest labour.

Yet, these secondary policy actions worked paradoxically. First, they perverted the basic rationale of importing labour to augment flexibilities. Second, they created dualism in employment conditions with local workers (Ng, 1995: 220–1). For instance, employers were coerced by the official rules of labour importation to deny access to promotion and career advancement by virtue of the 'fixed station' rule, encouraging discriminatory practices against guest workers.

The labour importation policy was hence contradicted by a paradox due to the ambivalence clouding over both the government and organized labour because of their dualistic, yet conflicting, agenda. On the one hand this attempted to contain the competitive marketplace threats poised by guest workers to locals, while on the other it sought to present an image of a benevolent 'host' protecting guest workers against exploitation. In this context, some of the rules regulating guest workers were double-edged. We will return to this later.

A REFRACTORY LABOUR MOVEMENT AND HIATUS OF PROTECTIONISM

What has evolved from the experience of institutionalizing the use of guest workers is an increasingly sophisticated web of formalized rules whose design caters, in an equivocal rhetorical language, both to safeguard guest workers' rights and to contain threats to locals. Local unions have consistently harboured a defensive hostility towards guest workers, with their lower wage price undercutting local workers.

Trade unions in Hong Kong have been hitherto feeble and docile industrially. However, their political role as representative organizations of the labouring class has been nurtured, both purposively and by default, by the hectic process of reforms to erect a system of popularly elected democracy prior to reversion back to China in 1997 (Ng, 1997b: 667–8). As a sequel, a politicized labour movement soon became enshrined as a key player or vanguard stakeholder in the new 'game' of electoral contests. Articulating itself as the custodian of the labouring mass's interests, and anxious to appeal for electoral support at the grass roots level, the labour movement steadfastly insisted that guest workers were responsible for pre-empting local hiring (ibid.). By implication, guest workers were presented as the 'culprits' of rising unemployment. In essence, organized labour upheld a basically protectionist perspective, which castigated guest workers as unwelcome intruders impoverishing local job security and living standards. For this reason the labour movement demonstrated its hostility with public protests punctuated by militant calls for a general strike.

The irony accompanying this defensive posture and actions of organized labour has been an anxiety, articulated simultaneously, to act as the 'fraternal' agent on behalf of vulnerable guest workers. Such a mix of antagonism and care was amply betrayed by construction guest worker wage abuses in the mid-1990s. The manner by which these workers were brought into Hong Kong featured a variety of devious practices whereby wages were deducted and extorted by both the intermediary agencies responsible for recruitment and the employing subcontractors. The press publicized such abuses, inducing the labour movement to intervene as the champion of guest workers toiling in conditions reminiscent of Hong Kong's 'sweat shops' of the 1950s and 1960s (see England and Rear, 1975: 64–8). Protest actions by guest workers, largely orchestrated by local unions, were instrumental in forcing the authorities in the workers' home countries and Hong Kong to investigate and introduce policing to halt them.

The event helped unmask the dilemma of organized labour's stance towards guest workers. This arose as the labour movement had been trapped in a political impasse because of the 1997 dateline and China's economic reforms. However, what compounded the whole issue were the democratic reforms in anticipation of 1997's handover. It was an ingrained political drama that actually pulled Hong Kong's unions from docility and enshrined them as a new 'estate of the realm' and key political force, appearing like a quasi-labour party. Their anxiety to propagate and consolidate their popular appeal to the electorate at the grass roots level coincided with growing local apprehension about unemployment. The labour movement, as the political *nouveau riche* purporting to be the authentic and representative voice of the impoverished labouring mass on the 'fringe', was practically devoid of any alternative platform except to target guest workers and to vociferously demand their withdrawal. Such a cause was emotively and fiercely canvassed by a nominally divided and pluralistic labour movement as its mission in defending the unemployed (Ng and Rowley, 1997).

At the height of this industrial drama, guest workers were widely ostracized by local unions for pre-empting the transfer of locals into the new services. The labour movement's split consciousness was betrayed by a lukewarm attitude about recruiting guest workers into membership, let alone helping their self-organization into unions. Obviously, for political prudence, local worker combinations opted to retain a basically localized horizon in their organizational ambits (Ng, 1997b: 670–2; Ng and Rowley, 1997: 94).

The dialectics of labour market deregulation are elucidated by this case of opening up access to guest workers. This demonstrated a syndrome by which a new set of regulatory norms had to be conceived and enforced with coercive rigour in order to help ensure 'fair' competition and preclude detrimental acts. The irony of having to face a trade-off between the benefits of liberalizing admission controls and the price of having to regulate the deregulated arena of market activities presents a potent dilemma to policy makers. This is not only an issue of labour importation alone as deregulation was extended to sectors like telecommunications and public utilities. The codification of new rules to regulate guest workers has proved, ironically, to be discriminatory in levying formidable restrictions upon their job freedom and career advancement.

STATE CONTROL IN LABOUR MARKET DEREGULATION

One set of new rules emanating from the guest worker drama centred upon the argument that what was imported was a 'cargo' of 'alien labour' which hence had to be taxed on a retributory and compensatory basis. The inspiration behind placing a levy on per capita entry (largely in emulation of Singaporian practice) was economistic. It was intended to help regulate numbers by serving as a rationing device. Such a tax would also dissuade employers from drifting into this type of hiring at the expense of locals. Interestingly, this tax went into a fund to help finance retraining of the unemployed, although the government maintained its equivocal attitude in not publicizing the rationale. Whether this was a tacit acknowledgement that there existed an association between labour importation and unemployment of locals (a perspective canvassed relentlessly by unions but formally denied by the authorities) was left unclear because of official silence (Ng and Lee, 1997: 12).

A number of other regulations governing the hiring of guest workers suggest a highly prescriptive system of state-sponsored control to achieve a plurality of what could prove to be mutually conflicting aims. These objectives and expectations perverted the primary and original intention of giving businesses flexibility by allowing an intake of supplementary labour. An example was the standard fixed-term hiring contract. This served to introduce, yet also to limit, the parties' commitment to the prescribed period.

Such a contract design helped assure apprehensive locals of the temporary nature of guest workers. Guest workers were also guaranteed an almost two-year secure job, and for many such a limited stability was an attractive incentive (Ng and Lee, 1998: 183–4).

Job Assignment

However, the corollary to these advantages of certainty was a formidable rigidity due to the rules against lateral or vertical transfer across designated jobs. Under this highly regulated scheme, guest workers' 'life chances' were frozen with assignments as given in the contract's job title. These provisions were intended to be protective but in practice had the effect of demarcating and enveloping guest workers as an 'enclave' segregated and detached from the wider labour market or even company based internal labour markets.

Given such a tacit divide drawn between guest and local workers, a dualism in human resource practices arose in many organizations. Discrimination was levied upon guest workers as the disadvantaged group in the secondary layer of internal labour markets. Guest workers were cut off from mainstream career ladders and access to promotion. As noted earlier, such a blockage was largely due to the rule of non-negotiable job posting. This regulation helped limit the movement within organizations of guest workers and prevented them usurping locals. It could also assist guest workers by shielding them from the whim of employer dictates by specifying in advance relevant duties and task portfolios. Yet, such restrictive regulation against redeployment after entry tended to erode functional flexibility (see Rowley and Lewis, 1996; Rowley, 1997; Rowley and Bae, 1998), as well as freedom to make maximum use in covering spatially and occupationally scattered labour gaps. Such single-job engagement precluded versatile application of workers across different jobs within host enterprises.

Concomitantly, there were hardly any incentives for either employers or guest workers to invest in skill upgrading and human resource development due to the limited horizon of mutual commitment. Thus, training of guest workers at workplace level has been problematic. Instead, what prevailed was a 'commodity' perspective in interpreting the role of guest workers. This has induced both parties to maximize their immediate and 'marketplace' gains and benefits – namely, the exchange between cash wages and labour services. In this context, the government's desire to regulate and restrict the job freedom of guest workers contributed to their segregation into a subclass of peripheral labour within the labour pool of the firm (Ng, 1995: 200–1).

Dormitory Rules and Social Integration Problems

Other important regulations governing guest workers included employer obligations to provide board and lodging and repatriation upon contract expiry.[4] These rules are based primarily upon humanitarian considerations of the moral duty of the host (at both national and company levels). However, the practical implications of these hospitality rules have been to restrict the freedom of guest workers and place them in the custody of employers. Such roles were consistent with a paternalistic imagery of employers (Fox, 1974: Chapter 7). Yet, it was also a practice liable to place guest workers totally dependent upon, and at the mercy of, employers, which could breed servile labour (as alleged in complaints by guest domestic helpers).

Socially, these rules were also prone to segregate workers into isolated pockets of ethnically and occupationally narrow communities which were detached or poorly integrated into the wider society, in spite of Hong Kong's cosmopolitanism and pluralistic character (Ng and Lee, 1998: 184–5). This policy unwittingly created a subclass of a relatively deprived and alienated labouring mass, which guest workers replenished and perpetuated, at least partly. Alongside other disadvantaged groups (the middle-aged and elderly displaced from plant relocations; recent legal Chinese immigrants; housewives looking for part-time work), these workers constituted the bulk of the new industrial proletarians trapped in the secondary labour market, susceptible to long hours and poor pay, conditions and tenure (Ng, 1995: 203-5).

Surveys on the work (and non-work) life patterns of guest workers indicate that they associate among their own ethnic peers, and have little propensity to acclimatize themselves to the wider community and life-style (Ng and Lee, 1998: 184). Such inclusivity worked to perpetuate and reinforce further their isolation and 'alienness', transient mentalities and ambivalence.[5] These guest workers were largely pulled by attractive pay compared to relatively meagre earnings at home. Yet, their aspirations to work in Hong Kong were for limited periods and essentially instrumental –

to save for use back home either to improve family living standards or as capital to start a business (Ng and Lee, 1998: 184–5).[6] Therefore, it was natural that guest workers were lukewarm about investing socially in any effective interpersonal ties or contact networks, apart from those serving their instrumental needs (ibid.). The scope of their association and sociability was correspondingly narrow and confined, largely based upon ethnicity as the solidaristic anchor upon which pockets of occupational community were built. Basically perceiving Hong Kong as a transient place for work and wages, workers were psychologically aloof or even apathetic about the host society, preferring to associate among their ethnic peers. The mutual detachment between visitors and host community could breed a hostile, albeit hidden and latent, sentiment of emotive alienation harboured by guest workers.

Guest workers were also viewed with apprehension by locals as cheap labour liable to displace them. This contribution has argued that such a defensive psychology of working people helps explain the relatively bureaucratic procedures which evolved to govern and control guest workers. Such a body of rules, intended to protect simultaneously the interests of both host and guest workers, became unsurprisingly restrictive and even discriminatory, encroaching arbitrarily upon the employment freedom and life chances of guest workers.

Wage Intervention

Deregulating guest worker employment has also compromised the unregulated, basically free wage policy norm taken as a hallmark of Hong Kong's free enterprise ethos. The government has been compelled to extend its interventionist lever of a standard wage floor (since the 1970s) for guest domestic household helpers to all guest workers. The government made it mandatory for employers not to pay less than the median wage in the relevant industry to guest workers. Such an official prescription on the wage level 'floor' was tantamount to declaring a sectoral minimum wage, although its application was explicitly limited to guest workers (Ng, 1997a: 270). Official acts of intervention into wages were to protect not only against low pay and sweatshop conditions, but also the interests of locals fearful about cheap labour. The irony is that by liberalizing its guest worker ban, the government has inadvertently stepped into an area of minimum wage regulation which represents a radical departure from its celebrated free and self-adjusting market left at the private sector's own choice and self-regulation. Again, such intervention can be seen as an erosion of Hong Kong's institutional permissiveness.

THE PARADOX OF THE LABOUR–CAPITAL DIVIDE AND CLASS DIALECTICS

The syndrome by which the case of guest workers has become politicized as one of the core public policy controversies betrays a class issue compounded by the transnational (cross-border) movement of labour. The polemics of the policy debate has to be appreciated in the relativity context of the 'we–they' dichotomy of the parties' class consciousness, solidarity and actions (Hyman, 1971; Mann, 1973). Such a contested phenomenon helps explain the dialectics and cross-cutting interests confronting Hong Kong's labour and their collective combinations, especially as these conflicts became crystallized and sharpened prior to the economy's return to China.

Labour market deregulation and the opening-up of access to guest workers have, inadvertently, accentuated the intensity of the class divide and interest conflict between labour and capital, the employed and the employer (see also Hyman, 1999; Vilrokx, 1999). As pointed out in classic writings (Commons, 1909, 1924; Perlman, 1928), the former are always pessimistic and subscribe basically to a 'scarcity' (of opportunities) consciousness. By contrast, the latter are always optimistic, embracing, conversely, an 'abundance' psychology. For this reason, organized labour as workers' combinations are inclined towards a defensive mentality, while business and capital are liable to become indulged in an expansionist mood. (ibid.: 237–53).

The above perspective on the political-industrial implications of the class dichotomy for workplace relations helps explain the conflicting and polarized interpretations attached by business and organized labour to the letter and spirit of the labour importation policy. Confident about continuous economic prosperity at the beginning of the 1990s, the business lobby was apprehensive about constraints posed by labour shortages. They were anxious and vociferous about enlarging the labour supply from outside sources by transient and *ad hoc* measures so that business would not be handicapped by labour deficiencies (Ng, 1998: 120–1). Conversely, the class interests of the labouring class, purportedly represented by an industrially docile labour movement, were perceived to be in peril with growing concern with employment security. The admission of guest workers coinciding with the relocating and downsizing of manufacturing naturally provoked a defensive apprehension among the working class that the newcomers, albeit transient, would further drain away their job opportunities (Ng, 1997: 669–70).

Evidently, a 'we–they' divide in class interests was largely at issue in polarizing the orientation between business and labour in their approach to guest workers. In the wake of prosperity in the early 1990s, capital was optimistic and anxious to exploit business opportunities while labour was pessimistic and defensive about conserving job opportunities. The antagonism emanating from such class interest contradictions was further compounded by the politicization of labour affairs due to the hasty introduction of elections and democratic reforms before Hong Kong's return to China in 1997.

The officially sponsored reform package was basically designed to convert the legislature (Legislative Council) into an elected organ returned by a hybrid electorate. This combined both geographically denominated universal suffrage and a host of designated functional constituencies (either demarcated along occupational lines, or more broadly, sectarian based and segmentalized by criteria like religious affiliation or the capital–labour 'watershed'). As a sequel, organized labour has been designated in this electoral arena as the largest functional constituency, returning three Council seats. Trade union leaders, also keen on consolidating their grass roots appeal by direct election on the geographically based common suffrage, rose quickly to be a new 'estate of the realm' by acquiring a fresh institutionalized base of political power. Defensive rhetoric emotively castigating guest workers and the importation policy was freely articulated by these labour politicians in canvassing for the abrogation of admissions (Ng and Rowley, 1997: 92–5).

Furthermore, such a parochial consciousness, albeit 'organic' and 'native' in the language of Perlman's (1928) classic exposition on the genesis of the labour movement, has paradoxically also given rise to intra-class antagonism and ambivalence. This has crystallized along cleavages between 'insiders' and 'aliens' within the labouring class in the political-industrial drama of the pre-1997 transition. The local labour movement was, at the beginning of the new importation policy, ideologically and economistically hostile towards liberalizing the ban. In the media, guest workers became widely castigated as the poachers of locals' job opportunities. Such an inhospitable reception for guest workers later escalated to a new height with economic problems and continuingly high unemployment in the mid-1990s. Parochial sentiments were precipitated among local labour at the grass roots level, representing a working class fear about scarcity of jobs. The ironical implications of such a protectionist mentality were, however, their ambivalent position and antagonism towards their imported counterparts. Clearly, intra-class competition for jobs and conflict of economistic interests worked to divide and neutralize whatever transnational working class solidarity could have been nurtured during this crisis. In an unwitting way, the local and narrow horizon of a sectarian labour movement, insensitive to or even discriminatory against guest workers, has been exposed by this crusade to conserve the employment interests of locals (Ng and Rowley, 1997: 93–5).

The labour movement was actually later drawn into a self-contradicting position when it began to extend solidaristic support to guest workers. As employer exploitation unfolded in the media, labour union centres began to assist guest workers to organize collective protests at the workplace, as well as public demonstrations to lobby the government and the Chinese mission in Hong Kong. These sympathetic actions, however, contrasted sharply with the earlier and high-profile 'street corner' protests and demonstrations staged by local unions castigating guest workers and demanding their withdrawal when labour importation began. The solidaristic involvement of the labour movement, in spite of its apparent reluctance, in the collective grievances of guest workers has unwittingly blurred the strength of its previous unequivocal position of opposition against the labour importation policy. This episode of guest worker deregulation helps demonstrate that, in the post-industrial context of Hong Kong society, the dialectics of a 'we–they' class divide, when compounded by narrower sectarian 'intra-class' conflicts, can inflate, distort and emasculate working class consciousness and solidarity as espoused by its politically sensitized labour movement.

CONCLUSION

Globalization has impacted on workers and labour organizations via a two-way migration flow: of businesses to the Mainland and of labour to Hong Kong. The appearance of government deregulation of control over guest workers was more nominal than real. The paradox has been an emergent need to formulate and codify a new regulatory body of rules and policing devices to ensure that the policy was applied fairly without discrimination. In addition, a new set of governing protocols was also essential to define the boundaries and safeguard the interests of affected parties. Thus, a liberalized policy of labour intake required a regime of protective rules so as to conserve the employment interests of local workers as well as to shield guest workers from abuses.

There are two essential attributes in the background leading to the deregulatory intake of guest workers. First, there was the freer movement of people and workers across national borders in East Asia. These flows of labour have been largely sustained by the attraction of better wages and employment opportunities. Second, there was the specific factor of Hong Kong's socio-political situation prior to reversion back to China in 1997. The impact of this episode upon labour and society has been complex. As the latter part of this contribution has argued, the bitter tussle between capital and organized labour on this issue of labour importation deregulation has added to, and epitomized, the politicization of labour and employment affairs.

In short, we have examined one aspect of globalization – its role in the migration of business and labour. This in turn has had a number of effects on workers and trade unions in Hong Kong. The long term impacts on the labour movement of these – such as the difficult and ambiguous position of trade unions on business relocations and also as 'protectors' of locals versus 'fraternal' hosts – are pertinent to other labour movements at the dawn of the new century.

NOTES

1. We would like to thank John Benson for reminding us of this.
2. These were attested by the popularization of 'Reaganomics' and 'Thatcherism' as the 'doctrinal' prescriptions to answer the challenge of austerity in the wake of the stagnation syndrome plaguing industrially advanced societies in the 1980s.
3. On the parallel UK experience of restructuring workplaces for flexibility, see Millward *et al.* (1992: Chapter 9).

4. Both rules were actually enshrined by the International Labour Organization in its conventions protecting migrant workers (International Labour Convention, 1949).
5. These transient mentalities and ambivalence were analogous to the 'home bound' and 'visitor' consciousness masking the occupational orientation of guest workers, and were strongly reminiscent of the labouring psychology of Chinese labour shipped abroad in successive waves from the Mainland (mostly from the coastal provinces and pushed largely by rural poverty) at the beginning of the twentieth century. This was in the age of the 'human cargo', which suggested a degrading state of 'servile' labour, 'balkanized' as 'second class' aliens outside the mainstream Western culture of the host society (Lasker, 1945) The assimilation of migrant workers into the host society was always trivialized as an issue for the latter, partly because of this transient mentality predominating among guest workers. As a result, deprivations and discriminatory practices towards visiting labour were simply tolerated, more or less as given.
6. A similar 'myth of return' has been identified in some ethnic groups working in the UK.

REFERENCES

Aarnio, O. and Rowley, C. (1996) 'Skall Servicebranshen Var Reddning? Sysselsathning Tillvaxtoch Tjanstesekton', *Ekonomiska Samfundets Tidskvivt*, Vol. 40, No. 22, pp. 63–81.

Berger, Suzanne and Lester, Richard K. (eds) (1997) *Made by Hong Kong*. Hong Kong: Oxford University Press.

Chen, Edward K.Y. (1995) 'The Economic Setting', in Ng Sek Hong and David G. Lethbridge (eds), *The Business Environment in Hong Kong*, 3rd edn. Hong Kong: Oxford University Press, pp. 1–43.

Commons, John R. (1909) 'American Shoemakers, 1628–1895: A Sketch of Industrial Evolution', *Quarterly Journal of Economics*, Nov., pp. 39–84.

Commons, John R. (1924) *The Legal Foundation of Capitalism*. New York: Macmillan.

Dicken, Peter (1998)) *Global Shift: Transforming the World Economy*, 3rd edn. London: Paul Chapman.

England, Joe and Rear, John (1975) *Chinese Labour under British Rule*. Hong Kong: Oxford University Press.

Enright, Michael J., Scott, Edith E. and Dodwell, David (1997) *The Hong Kong Advantage*. Hong Kong: Oxford University Press.

Felstead, A. and Jewson, N. (eds) (1999) *Global Trends in Flexible Labour*. London: Macmillan.

Fox, Alan (1974) *Beyond Contract: Work, Power and Trust Relations*. London: Faber and Faber.

Gamble, A. (1988) *The Free Economy and the Strong State*. London: Macmillan.

Hong Kong Labour Department (1994) *The International Labour Organization and the Application of International Labour Conventions in Hong Kong*. Hong Kong: Government Printer.

Hirst, P. and Thompson, G. (eds) (1996) *Globalization in Question*. Cambridge: Polity.

Hyman, Richard (1971) *Marxism and the Sociology of Trade Unionism*. London: Pluto Press.

Hyman, Richard (1999) 'Imagined Solidarities: Can Trade Unions Resist Globalization?', in P. Leisink (ed.), *Globalization and Labour Relations*. Cheltenham: Edward Elgar, pp. 94–115.

International Labour Convention (1949) *Migration for Employment Convention*, revised edn, No. 97.

Lasker, B. (1945) *Asia on the Move*. New York: Henry Holt.

Lethbridge, David G. and Ng Sek Hong (1995), 'Labour and Employment', in Ng Sek Hong and David G. Lethbridge (eds), *The Business Environment in Hong Kong*, 3rd edn. Hong Kong: Oxford University Press, pp. 64–88.

Lui, Tai-Lok and Chiu, Tony Man-Yui (1999) 'Global Restructuring and Non-standard Work in Newly Industrialized Economies: The Organization of Flexible Production in Hong Kong and Taiwan', in A. Felstead and N. Jewson (eds), *Global Trends in Flexible Labour*. London: Macmillan, pp. 166–80.

Mann, Michael (1973) *Consciousness and Action Among the Western Working Class*. London: Macmillan Press.

Mehmet, O., Mendes, E. and Sinding, R. (1999) *Towards a Fair Global Labour Market*. London: Routledge.

Millward, Neil, Stevens, Mark, Smart, David and Hawes, W.R. (1992) *Workplace Industrial Relations in Transition: The ED/ESRC/PSI/ACAS Surveys*. Aldershot: Dartmouth.

Ng, Sek Hong (1995) 'Labour and Employment', in Joseph Y.S. Cheng and Sonny S.H. Lo (eds), *From Colony to SAR: Hong Kong's Challenges Ahead*. Hong Kong: The Chinese University Press, pp. 197–225.

Ng, Sek Hong (1996) 'The Development of Labour Relations in Hong Kong and Some Implications for the Future', in Ian Nish, Gordon Redding and Ng Sek Hong (eds), *Work and Society: Labour and Human Resources in East Asia*. Hong Kong: Hong Kong University Press, pp. 289–300.

Ng, Sek Hong (1997a) 'Hong Kong: A Country Monograph', in Rodger Blanpain (ed.), *International Encyclopaedia of Laws*. The Hague, Netherlands: Kluwer Law International, ELL-Supplement 190, February.

Ng, Sek Hong (1997b) 'Reversion to China: Implications for Labour in Hong Kong', *International Journal of Human Resource Management*, Vol. 8, No. 5, pp. 660–76.

Ng, Sek-Hong (1998) 'Hong Kong Labour and Manpower Policies', in Siu-lun Wong and Toyojiro Maruya (eds), *Hong Kong Economy and Society: Challenges in the New Era*, Hong Kong: Centre of Asian Studies, University of Hong Kong, pp. 101–33.

Ng, Sek Hong and Ip, Olivia (1999) 'Manpower', in Larry Chuen-ho Chow and Yiu-kwan Fan (eds), *The Other Hong Kong Report*. Hong Kong: The Chinese University Press, pp. 247–64.

Ng, Sek Hong and Lee, Grace (1997) 'The Hong Kong Labour Market at the Close of British Rule', *International Journal of Employment Studies*, Vol. 5, No. 2, pp. 1–16.

Ng, Sek Hong and Lee, Grace O.M. (1998) ' Hong Kong Labour Market in the Aftermath of the Crisis: Implications for Foreign Workers', *Asian and Pacific Migration Journal*, Vol. 7, Nos 2–3, pp. 171–86.

Ng, Sek Hong and Lethbridge, David (1995) 'Concluding Remarks', in Ng Sek Hong and David G. Lethbridge (eds), *The Business Environment in Hong Kong*, 3rd edn. Hong Kong: Oxford University Press, pp. 212–14.

Ng, Sek Hong and Poon, Carolyn (1997) 'Economic Restructuring and HRM in Hong Kong', *Asia Pacific Business Review*, Vol. 3, No. 4, pp. 34–61.

Ng, Sek Hong and Rowley, Chris (1997) 'At the Break of Dawn? Hong Kong Industrial Relations and Prospects under its Political Transition', *Asia Pacific Business Review*, Vol. 4, No. 1, pp. 83–96.

Perlman, Selig (1928) *A Theory of the Labour Movement*. New York: Macmillan.

Rowley, C. (1997) 'Reassessing HRM's Convergence', *Asia Pacific Business Review*, Vol. 3, No. 4, pp. 198–211.

Rowley, C. and Lewis, M. (1996) 'Greater China at the Crossroads? Convergence, Culture and Competitiveness', *Asia Pacific Business Review*, Vol. 2, No. 3, pp. 1–22.

Rowley, C. and Bae, J. (1998) 'Korean Business and Management: The End of the Model', *Asia Pacific Business Review*, Vol. 4, No. 3, pp. 130–9.

Storey, John and Sisson, Keith (1993) *Managing Human Resources and Industrial Relations*, Buckingham: Open University Press.

Tang, Shu-Hung (1995) 'The Economy', in Joseph Y. S. Cheng and Sonny S. H. Lo (eds), *From Colony to SAR: Hong Kong's Challenges Ahead*, Hong Kong: The Chinese University Press, pp. 117–50.

Turner H.A., Fosh, Patricia, Gardner, Margaret, Hart, Keith, Morris, Richard, Ng, Sek Hong, Quinlan, Michael and Yerbury, Dianne (1980) *The Last Colony: But Whose?* Cambridge: Cambridge University Press.

Turner, H. A., Fosh, Patricia and Ng, Sek Hong (1991) *Between Two Societies: Hong Kong Labour in Transition*, Hong Kong: Centre of Asian Studies, University of Hong Kong.

Vilrokx, Jacques (1999) 'Towards the Denaturing of Class Relations? The Political Economy of the Firm in Global Capitalism', in P. Leisink (ed.), *Globalization and Labour Relations*. Cheltenham: Edward Elgar, pp. 57–77.

11

Multinational Corporations and Trade Union Development in Malaysia

MHINDER BHOPAL and PATRICIA TODD

One strand of the globalization debate urges that companies should be free to locate and compete unimpeded by borders and institutional rigidities, and that the state's role should be to ensure market impediments are removed to create a 'frictionless world' (Ohmae, 1994, 1996). In labour markets, the state is urged to create conditions for enterprise-based management control in a context of labour flexibility, and this may involve reconfiguring the institutional framework of industrial relations. Such debate is not new; since the colonial period, organized labour in Malaysia has been restricted in its activities to ensure that it does not pose a major challenge to capital's interests (Jomo and Todd, 1994). This contribution explores multinational corporations' (MNCs') responses to, and effects upon, Malaysian trade unions in a context where the post-colonial 'developmentalist' state has attempted to maintain and increase control over organized labour, as part of a package to attract foreign direct investment (FDI).[1] It is argued that there are distinct differences in the manner that Australian, Japanese and US MNCs have adapted and responded to Malaysian labour, despite the general weakness of the labour movement.

THE MALAYSIAN CONTEXT

Within the two decades following 1976 the Malaysian economy transformed from an agricultural to a predominantly manufacturing one. By 1996, manufacturing accounted for 80.6 per cent of commodity exports, contributed 34.3 per cent of gross domestic product (GDP) and employed 25.5 per cent of the workforce. However, development has occurred on a narrow, primarily electronics, base; in 1996 electrical and electronic goods and electrical machinery, appliance and parts accounted for 48.0 per cent and 19.6 per cent respectively of manufactured exports (Malaysia, Department of Statistics, 1998). The proportion of Malays, Chinese and Indians in the labour movement has reflected the changing political economy of Malaysia. This economic development has expanded the Malay waged class such that Malays comprise the majority of trade union members (Jomo and Todd, 1994). While the ethnic basis of political organization and identity has historically enabled the state to marginalize organized labour and curtail its activities, the growth of a Malay urban workforce heightened government sensitivity to labour issues and in-house unions became the favoured model (Wad, 1988; Kuruvilla, 1995). Despite a general right of workers to form unions and be accorded recognition by employers, in the event of a failure to agree the matter is passed to the Minister of Labour for adjudication within the parameters of existing labour law. Even where the poorly resourced unions gain recognition, they have to contend with tight government restrictions placed on their ability to take industrial action. This includes use of the Internal Security Act, the military and the police to intimidate activists who attempt to challenge state set boundaries (Jomo and Todd, 1994).

METHODOLOGY

In investigating the impact of MNCs' nationality on unions and unionization in Malaysia, two factors were considered: the amount of foreign investment and the home pattern of labour-management relations. Japan and the USA, two of the largest and most powerful investors, were selected together with a less substantial investor, Australia.

There has been little reported research on Australian MNCs in Malaysia, and this section, drawing from broader research in 20 companies,[2] adds such literature. Interviews were conducted between 1993 and 1995 and six companies were studied in depth. Australian investments, while relatively small, are not insignificant; Australia was the ninth largest foreign investor between 1990 and 1995 (MIDA, 1995). Unlike Japanese or American investments, the sample reflects the distribution of Australian investments across industrial sectors. US companies were the largest investors in 1997 with cumulative private investment exceeding $10 billion, of which

60 per cent was in the oil and gas sector; the rest was mainly accounted for by manufacturing (American Malaysian Chamber of Commerce, 1997). Eighteen US electronics companies represented the largest American industrial grouping and accounted for almost ten per cent of Malaysia's gross manufactured exports and employed 65,000 people (Malaysian American Electronics Industry, 1998). The macro and micro union strategies of the American electronics group is explored through primary research conducted in 1993 and secondary material derived from academic research and press reports. The primary research involved interviews with trade union officials in the Malaysian Trade Unions Congress (MTUC), Malaysian Labour Organization (MLO) and Harris Solid State Workers' Union (HSSWU) and an extensive study of the documentation held by these organizations and their representatives. Analysis of Japanese MNCs is based on the relatively abundant secondary sources. This reflects the difficulty of access, but the necessity of inclusion given their large presence and symbolic importance as organizational innovators and representatives of the discourse of 'Asian' management, which itself draws from, and contributes to, the notion of 'Asian industrial values'. The electronics and electrical sectors reflects the 'lion's share' of Japanese companies (Anazawa, 1994) and unlike the American concentration, Japanese investments are broader and they are represented in consumer and electrical industries as well as component electronics and other industrial sectors (such as textiles).

The three investing countries have a history and approach to labour–management relations that are different from each other and from Malaysia's. This enables an exploration of the transferability or adaptation of the recognition component of home-based industrial management styles and strategies to an environment with weak trade unions and a strong state, which is pro-MNC capital. Kochan et al. (1994) argue that the mind-set of most American top managers is to avoid trade unionism, and companies that voluntarily recognize unions are viewed as mavericks. Such views, they argue, have spread since the 1960s when capital started to relocate to the Southern States' anti-union social and political climates and lower labour costs. Much has been written about the 'three pillars', and in particular the nature and significance of enterprise unionism, in large Japanese firms. Enterprise unionism, as an integral part of the core Japanese system, has been argued to have been sustained by common interest in enhancing productivity and efficiency (Kawamura, 1994) in a system that recognizes differing and shared interests. A system of collective bargaining and consultation exists within a welfare corporatist framework, which seeks to incorporate the union as a legitimate workers' 'voice' in the context of the enterprise as community (Dore, 1990). Australian industrial relations have not been held up as an exemplar, but unions have been an integral part of a centralized system with a less developed workplace structure or enterprise focus. During the past decade the position of unions has been challenged by restructuring and unemployment, and by legislative reforms which have created an enterprise-based system and placed greater restrictions on the movement (see Davis and Lansbury, 1998).

Access and sensitivity had a major influence upon the means by which the material was gathered for this study. Nonetheless, the methodology enabled exploration of behaviours occurring at different levels. Given the sectoral concentration of different MNC capital, there is a case for utilizing a 'matching sample' approach. Such research designs, however, are problematic owing to the combination of finding matching samples, gaining entry (Cray and Mallory, 1998), and because MNCs from different countries may have international competitive advantage in different sectors (Sorge, 1991). Our contribution is, therefore, intended to be indicative rather than definitive, but nonetheless timely given the current debates over globalization and the failure of public policy to reflect the potential differential impact of MNCs on trade union and representation structures.

MNCs AND TRADE UNIONS

While globalization is argued to be uneven and poorly specified, most authors accept that there has been significant change in global financial markets assisted by financial liberalization and deregulation (Hoogvelt, 1997). Financial markets are seen to act as a disciplining force on macroeconomic management as well as a source of potential system stability driven by the degree and direction of the flow of funds (see Jomo, 1998). However, manufacturing needs to be distinguished from financial globalization, not least because of the lower mobility, longer-term focus and direct impact on employment of manufacturing capital. Due to the growth, or recognition, of MNCs and their significance for domestic economies, it has been argued that companies should no longer be viewed in 'national interest' terms but as beneficial corporate players, and as such they should be accorded equal treatment (Reich, 1992; Ohmae, 1996). Despite these different strands of the debate, advocates of the 'borderless world' argue both finance and manufacturing capital should be able to flow freely from one economic area to another without the friction of different institutional formations. The potential benefits of convergence between national economies are argued to be the levelling of wages and productivity differentials and the creation of aggregate wealth and jobs through 'mutual enrichment'. States unwilling to restructure will be directed and disciplined by MNC locational strategies and international financial markets and, through such 'market' mechanisms, jobs that might otherwise be lost may be maintained. Labour relations are not marginal to this in so far as non-domestic firms would produce more in environments with 'good' labour relations, while labour flexibility would help firms increase efficiency and boost productivity (Ohmae, 1994; *The Economist*, 1997).

Some critics, while accepting the forward march of free market laissez-faire practices, argue that 'regime shopping' by MNCs and 'regime competition' amongst states would drive socially useful regulatory frameworks down to the lowest common denominator (Streeck, 1992). In so far it is argued that governments are increasingly powerless to resist globalizing trends, and labour's ability to stand up to the dictates of capital is diminished (see Harman, 1996), stronger and coordinated action by supranational institutions is urged (see Hirst and Thompson, 1996). Dependency theorists argued that MNC investment in dependent states result in the suppression of trade unionism. MNCs in their quest for lower labour costs and weak labour, in the context of competition between dependent countries for MNC investment, results in state led labour repression as part of the package of investment inducements (see Southall, 1988). Both globalization and dependency positions, by virtue of their level of analysis, underplay the interrelated and complex impact of national development strategies, types of capital investment, the nature of MNCs and the internal dynamics within societies. These limitations are discussed below.

National Development Strategies

Harrod (1988) proposes a greater propensity to union recognition and collective bargaining in advanced, as opposed to simple, export-orientated industrialization. The characteristics of capital intensity, high value-added industries with high skill and wage development human resource strategies enable a unionization strategy as a means of incorporating labour and minimizing the risk of disruption of the accumulation process (see Rowley and Lewis, 1996; Rowley, 1997; Rowley and Bae, 1998, for 'high–low' routes to competition). In simple export-orientated industrialization there are greater labour restrictions because labour intensive, low value-added, low skill and low wage characteristics provide greater potential for challenge owing to the difficulty of incorporation in a context of labour cost reduction and control (Bjorkman *et al.*, 1988; Deyo, 1989).

Types of Capital Investment

While these approaches have utility, they privilege export-orientation and assume MNC homogeneity and state captivity. Market-seeking investments can make MNCs 'captive' to the state and the latter can exact conformity as a 'cost of entry' (Aldaeaj *et al.*, 1991). While 'production base seeking' strategies are assumed to give greater power to MNCs, 'safe' or known practices may be preferred to potentially 'alien' ones for fear of disruption of internationally integrated production (Campbell, 1994), this does not necessarily imply anti-unionism. Approaches to unions *may depend upon* MNC perceptions, experience and knowledge of unions in their home base, felt competence in managing with a union presence, and the nature of the political formation in the host environment.

Nature of MNCs

Perlmutter (1969) classified MNCs that transfer their home practices as ethnocentric, and those that localize decision making as polycentric. Within the globalization debate, MNCs are assumed to be global, adopting (perceived) 'best practices' from all locations, and disassociated from any particular national configuration. MNCs may be best conceptualized as national companies with international operations (Hu, 1992) because their main boards tend to be from the home base and the majority of sales and revenues generated from home markets (Ruigrok and van Tudler, 1995; Hirst and Thompson, 1996). In so far as they build upon competitive advantage gained or learned at home (Sorge, 1991), MNCs may be ethnocentric because they believe their home recipe is superior or provides a competitive advantage (Perlmutter, 1969). The implication is that MNCs' home learning and knowledge base should be expected to affect their organizational cognitive framework (see Cray and Mallory, 1998),[3] not least in their perception of what is (or is not) controllable, risky, necessary or desirable. It is normally argued that labour market issues are decentralized because the socio-cultural and economic environment of the host countries cannot be easily ignored (Evans and Lorange, 1989; Rosenweig and Nohria, 1994). However, not all MNCs adapt to local socio-cultural logics in the management of labour due, in part, to a 'country of origin' effect. Japanese and American companies have been argued to be more ethnocentric than European ones (Marginson and Sisson, 1994).

Internal Dynamics

Institutional approaches also raise the issue over the practical difficulty involved in any external homogenizing tendency because of societal embeddedness arising from a view of society as an organizational, not merely an economic, unit (see Whitley, 1998). However, some national business systems can be relatively embedded and inflexible; others can be permissive and flexible. While this implies that MNCs can effect potentially significant and frictionful structural changes in the former (less so in the latter), the state itself needs to be viewed as an arena for interest group and class-coalitional conflict (Smith, 1993). Ferner (1994) argues that ethnocentric companies are likely to be 'innovators' in their host countries in so far as they bring novel or new approaches but if the state does not, or ceases to, view MNCs as desirable innovators (see Elger and Smith, 1994), MNC behaviours that create adverse effects for the state are likely to be resisted. This may be particularly so if MNCs undermine the basis upon which regime legitimacy is constructed and the economy directed. Where a conflict ensues, the nature and extent of such conflict will reflect the degree and intensity of their respective divergent and mutual goals while the outcome will depend on the balance of respective power resources (see Aldaeaj *et al.*, 1991).

US, JAPANESE AND AUSTRALIAN MNCS IN MALAYSIA

The discussion below assesses the impact of MNCs from the USA, Japan and Australia on Malaysian trade unions. The analysis is undertaken under three broad, though not mutually exclusive, areas of management–employee relations strategy – non-unionism, anti-unionism and unionism. Non-unionism aims to negate the 'felt need' for unionization through such human resource management methods as communication, welfare, relatively high pay and benefits, open door policies etc. In contrast, unionism strategies recognize the legitimacy, or inevitability, of labour representation. Such a strategy encompasses a broad spectrum of practices that can range from incorporation through business unionism to an acceptance of power bargaining in a relationship that is, nonetheless, seen as functional to management control. Anti-unionism, however, is a more direct, power-based strategy. Such a strategy may be aimed at either maintaining union-free status through various anti-union strategies to counter-organizing efforts, or confronting organized labour in an antagonistic labour–management relationship. Anti-unionism, therefore, may not simply be an alternative to non-unionism or unionism; it can underpin both.

Non-Unionism

Human relations approaches as a justification for non-unionism have been promoted in the media and in some HRM textbooks (for example, Foulkes, 1980). *Electronics Business Asia* (1990: 46) featured Texas Instruments (Malaysia) and stated that 'an axiom of modern management theory is that when companies treat employees well and listen to their concerns, employees usually have little interest in forming unions'. In support, the Managing Director of Texas Instruments, and Chairman of the Malaysian American Electronics Industry (MAEI),[4] stated that 'it's not [about] union busting, or total anti-unionization. It's taking care of people and forming a working relationship so that you don't need unions.'

US electronics MNCs argue that their personnel policies negate the need, and desire, for union representation amongst their workforces. For instance, Abdullah's (1992) 'US Tom' utilized a proclaimed 'people centered' non-union approach that involved an open door policy, direct communication and above average compensation.[5] However, confidence in such an approach appeared to be mitigated in so far as assessment of 'cultural fit' included 'fit' with the non-union policy, and applicants were checked against a list of union organizers held by the company. There is also evidence of Japanese and Australian companies taking proactive measures to remain non-union. Abdullah (1992) reports that 'Jap Tim', an electronics company, used its pioneer status, and other strategies, including checking for pro-union sympathies and ensuring that new recruits were not 'potentially controversial', to keep unions out. The motto of 'Jap Tim' included harmony, serenity and goodwill (*Wa*), and sincerity and faithfulness (*Makoto*), while it offered free meals, annual dinners, picnics and had a budget to nurture good 'human relations'. Many of the Japanese MNCs utilize aspects of their corporate philosophy to encourage employee identification with the employer, including singing the company song, reference to the organization as 'family' and encouragement to work hard and 'develop with the company'.

In some instances, Australian managements have also adopted a paternalistic approach to the workforce. One general manager stated that 'the company is small enough that they can air grievances without going through a union',[6] whilst in another company the 'one big family' ethos was being cultivated with birthday celebrations, family outings, and the production supervisor playing a very prominent counselling role by assisting employees with their personal problems.[7] Australian managers in two non-unionized factories surveyed established formal consultative procedures to minimize the possibility of employees seeking union representation for negotiations and grievances.[8] Three of the four Australian managers in non-unionized worksites commented that wages and conditions comparable to, or above, unionized factories ought to be enough to 'keep the union out'.[9]

Anti-Unionism

Despite these strategies, labour–management conflict has been documented in MNCs in Malaysia. Academic reporting on the conflict between the Malaysian labour movement and the government, arising from the Malaysian state's accommodation of the wishes of MNCs, is well documented (Wad, 1988; Wangel, 1988; Grace, 1990; Jomo and Todd, 1994; Kuruvilla, 1995). While few of these studies fail to mention the issue of freedom of association in the electronics industry and the ongoing International Labour Organization (ILO) case, these more readily accessible analyses inevitably tend to privilege macro coverage at the expense of detailed workplace data. Nonetheless, there are a number of studies that provide insights to workplace processes arising from potential, or actual, union formation attempts. Abdullah (1992) reports that industrial conflict and harsh discipline in 'US Tom' possibly resulted in an expressed preference for unionization emerging in a company-organized attitude survey. In response, the company increased salaries, introduced job rotation, provided additional human relations training for supervisors and improved communications channels and rest pauses. Similarly, in response to a unionization drive Abdullah's 'Jap Tim' formed a joint consultative committee and enhanced benefits, while union activists were transferred or pressurized to resign. Japanese managers have also complained that unions are too strong (Smith, 1994; Hirokazu, 1989), indicating that union–management relations are neither necessarily one-sided nor unproblematic.

One Australian factory manager claimed that the workers staged unofficial go-slows when they were dissatisfied.[10] Other acts of unorganized action in Australian factories include acts of vandalism, theft and – possibly as a result of the labour shortage – 'exit'. Some of these actions did result in management reconsideration of the remuneration package, but often after the individual(s) had been dismissed or had resigned. Three of the Malaysian managers in Australian non-unionized factories openly declared their hostility towards the unions; one of the managers described unionists as 'troublemakers' and 'ignorant',[11] while another claimed that he could detect any moves to unionize the factory and would quickly 'remove' any such activists.[12] In an Australian plant that had one brief overtime ban during the collective agreement negotiations at one site,[13] workers taking 'unofficial' action, including a work stoppage, were dismissed 'as an example to others'.[14] Hirokazu's (1989) study of the Pen textile group also documents labour militancy and a management response involving dismissals, intimidation and harassment of union activists. Hitachi also dismissed 1,000 workers who went on strike in support of their in-house union affiliating to an industry union (*Straits Times*, 1990).[15] However, it is US electronics MNCs that have been the most collective, vociferous and consistent in their anti-unionism.

In the early 1970s when the Electrical Industry Workers' Union (EIWU) attempted to recruit in a Monsanto plant, a member of the American electronics grouping (MTUC, 1974–76), the state decreed that the electronics industry was outside the EIWU's legitimate domain. Applications to form a National Union for Electronics Workers (NUEW)[16] were ignored until a combination of recession, political instability, opening of the domestic political regime, and international pressure[17] led the government to concede unionization in 1988 (Bhopal, 1997). Shortly after, Motorola awarded a pay rise and informed employees that it was against unions and their formation while pro-union workers were warned of the 'difficulties of joblessness' and the most outspoken transferred to 'less desirable' positions (Grace, 1990; Hamilton, 1991). Two large electronics MNCs in Penang threatened the dismissal of pro-union workers and a number of US managing directors threatened relocation (*Business Times*, 1988; Rajah, quoted in Grace, 1990). In the meantime, US MNCs, after an industry meeting, argued employees should be free to choose 'between an industry, in-house or no union' (Bhopal, 1997). Although some Japanese companies were reported as making representations against the formation of a national electronics union (*Business Times*, 1992), some, such as Hitachi and Mitsumi, have recognized in-house unions. Nonetheless, despite the chairman of MAEI stating 'we will not use or tolerate any form of harassment to sway the workers' decision' (*Business Times*, 1988), the government 'ticked off' 'several' American owned electronics companies for 'not respecting the struggle for workers' rights' (*New Straits Times*, 1988a; *New Straits Times*, 1989). In the Kuala Lumpur area, another US electronics company, Harris, started a union avoidance programme which involved supervisors and managers as the front line of surveillance to ensure workers did not engage in discussion of union formation[18] (*New Straits Times*, 1988b). Immediately before a meeting of MAEI and the Minister of Labour to discuss the policy change, in which the Malaysian government acceded to 'freedom of choice', Advanced Micro Devices announced 900 illegal redundancies (*New Straits Times*, 1988a). In response to a subsequent MTUC announcement of its intention to ballot workers in support of a national union, the state announced that an industry union would not be allowed irrespective of the outcome; only in-house unions would be permitted (*New Straits Times*, 1988c).

In contrast to the 20-year struggle for the unionization of electronics workers, and three months after the industry union issue, an in-house union was accorded state registration in Harris[19] within just eight days of its application,[20] and the Deputy Labour Minister agreed to open the first Annual General Meeting.[21] Despite state support, and assurance by management, that the union would be recognized, management mobilized against the union.[22] Tactics deployed included a company name change while the application was being validated,[23] transfer of employee contracts to a sister company,[24] and eventual termination of unions' contracts prior to the expiry of state imposed deadlines for recognition.[25] Between these 'context manipulation' strategies, intense pressure, supervision and surveillance on union activists and their activities was applied. Workers were warned that company surveillance was mobilized, while attempts were made to disorganize on religious, gender and ethnic grounds (see Bhopal, 1997).

Unionism

In contrast to the above, Smith (1994) reports attempts by many Japanese companies in Malaysia to establish enterprise unions, prior to the 1980s change of government policy. At that stage, these companies were required to conform to government policy on union formation and allow their employees to join industry unions (ibid.: 168). Nonetheless, there is evidence that Japanese and Australian managers in Malaysia are influenced by their home experience and actively wish to operate within a familiar managerial style, if not a similar structure (Wolfe and Arnold, 1994; Smith, 1994; Abdullah and Keenoy, 1995). For instance, Abdullah and Keenoy (1995: 752), in their second case, report that management had been uncomfortable operating on a non-union basis and that the factory manager insisted: 'The non-union way is not the way to manage people, you must recognize that people work in groups (and) allow them to organize themselves in groups'. Abdullah (1992) reports that in response to a unionization drive, and after a company survey indicated dissatisfaction with supervision, wages and work pressure, a company successfully achieved reclassification as an electrical, as opposed to electronics, firm to enable it to recognize the EIWU. However, this occurred in parallel with a 'family' ideology, welfare benefits, and social activities indicating that unionism was supplementary to, rather than a replacement for, such activities. Hiramoto (1995) also reports a Japanese television transplant willing to accept the EIWU in its Malaysian operation, despite its reputation as a 'hard negotiator'. In Poon *et al.*'s (1990) sample, 43 per cent of Japanese companies were unionized. However, Thong and Jain (1988) suggest that Japanese firms modify their labour–management practices in Malaysia and while all five companies studied were unionized in Japan, two were non-union in Malaysia, though the remainder recognized industry-wide unions – a finding that concurs with other research reporting the recognition of industry unions in Malaysia (Smith, 1994; Hirokazu, 1989).

Of the eight Australian Malaysian factories managed by local managers, only two were unionized compared with seven of the 11 managed by Australian managers. The Malaysian managers found the prospect of a unionized workplace more threatening to their costs and managerial prerogative than Australian managers,[26] the latter having generally gained their managerial experience in unionized workplaces where unions potentially have substantially more power than their Malaysian counterparts. All nine unionized factories recognized industry-based unions, although each operated virtually as a conglomerate of on-site unions, enabling management to negotiate and communicate with little-experienced workplace delegates. In eight of the nine unionized factories, management regarded the union as unable to threaten managerial control of the workplace. In this context, general managers were comfortable with according a role to the workplace delegates.[27] The role, mainly that of 'communicator' between management and workers, whilst providing the union representatives with a degree of power over members, served to advance the interests of management in so far as once an accord was struck, union leaders legitimated and often enforced changes on the workforce. There was little evidence of union delegates having input into the decision making process other than on peripheral matters, such as social club events, minor disciplinary issues and the design of staff lockers. Within Australian unionized workplaces, shopfloor delegates appeared to accept their restricted role. Members' expectations were generally limited to wage increases and assistance with disciplinary measures in a context of an acceptance of management prerogative over matters such as the allocation of work, work process and training and promotion. Members had no expectations of participation beyond good communication.

Despite the *de facto* trade union structure akin to a federation of company-based unions with on-site union committees, and the institutional constraints on the scope of bargaining and ability to take industrial action, non-union approaches have been reported in non-electronics US companies. A study of a US pharmaceutical company shows that the corporate policy was pragmatic, aiming to 'continue to maintain union free status where it currently existed and to ensure cordial relations in plants that are unionized' (Frenkel, 1995: 204). Abdullah (1992) reports that 'US Meg', an American MNC in the electrical sector, had an avowedly non-union aim, while General Electric (USA) Television threatened relocation if unionization was imposed.[28] However, after state intervention, in-house unions have been reluctantly accepted in these cases, although the US electronics companies remain non-union.

DISCUSSION

While there are examples of Australian and Japanese MNCs utilizing the legislative framework to firmly quash official and unofficial actions deemed to be against their interests, they, in contrast to the Americans, are more likely to provide a window of opportunity for unionism. In this sense there are differences in the degree of anti-unionism. However, while Japanese companies appear to be less ideologically opposed to organized labour and have accepted industry unions, they show a preference for in-house unions. Australian companies, without exception, have recognized industry unions where the Registrar of Trade Unions has accorded recognition. Nonetheless, it is clear that both Australian and Japanese MNCs want minimal union power, and a union recognition strategy is acceptable in so far as unions can be coopted to serve managerial ends or are insignificant to issues of management control. Japanese and Australian approaches, however, need to be viewed in the context of the nature of the Malaysian labour movements' uneven response to MNCs. There is a general acceptance of a very unequal position within the workplace and little evidence of class ideology and consciousness and commitment to struggle. This may indicate that local context, together with companies' economic goals, may have greater influence on labour-management practices, at least in the Malaysian subsidiaries of Japanese and Australian MNCs, than government policy *per se*.[29] The comparatively greater polycentric approach to the union issue amongst Australian and Japanese MNCs indicates a larger repertoire of management strategies towards organized labour, possibly due to their expectations, experience and perceived competence of managing through unions at home and in Malaysia.

Unlike the Australian companies, US MNCs, owing to the size and significance of their investments, have greater power to advance their 'interests', but this power has been used differently from the equally powerful Japanese, not least because of a difference in perception of 'interests'. Their respective approaches have, in different ways, contributed to the macro context of Malaysian trade union development. The Malaysian union structure has allowed Japanese MNCs to accommodate industry unions and to feel comfortable with an in-house union policy. This has not only avoided conflict with the developing state's strategy towards the growing Malay urban workforce, but has actually, perhaps unwittingly, supported it. The state's strategy has not been to eliminate trade unions *per se* but to incorporate and accommodate labour and ensure regime legitimacy as embodied in its 'Look East' policy and promotion of in-house unions (Wad, 1988). Such a union structure is seen as representing a model for the advancement of national and enterprise interest, while an anti-Western and, in particular, pro-Japan, rhetoric has been used to try and mask labour exploitation and ensure control at the level of the factory and nation.

The approach of the Japanese and Australian MNCs contrasts with the ability and willingness of US companies to pursue anti-unionism, even where this has involved conflict with the state. The electronics industry union issue, and therefore American capital, has had a direct impact on the unionization of electronics workers and an indirect effect on the Malaysian labour movement. The MTUCs attempt to advance independent unionism in the electronics sector has exposed state dependency and its degree of captivity to MNCs. Caught between international and national pressure for unionization and vociferous opposition by US MNCs, the state was confronted with a 'no-win' situation. As a result, the state went on an offensive against the MTUC. Critics of government industrial relations policy, particularly as it relates to the electronics sector, have, ironically, been accused of being 'mouthpieces' of US labour and of supporting the aims of 'first world' labour to reduce the attractiveness of overseas locations (Deputy Prime Minister Ghafar Baba, reported in *New Straits Times*, 1993). The state also began to bypass the MTUC in tripartite bodies, in favour of the breakaway, pro-government labour centre, the MLO. Overseas visits by MTUC officials were also obstructed and leading labour radicals charged with criminal offences (US Department of State, 1997), in a general environment of marginalization and intimidation.

CONCLUSION

US, Japanese and Australian MNCs have the same goal of maximizing their control of the workplace but there are differences in the way this is conceived and operationalized. There are examples of all MNCs deploying similar non-union human relations type paternalistic strategies, involving welfare, communication and approachable management styles coupled with the payment of a non-union mark-up (or at least avoiding the opportunity of 'a mark-down'). However, while these MNCs expect a supportive industrial relations environment, they differ in their perceptions and expectations of what that supportive environment is, particularly in relation to trade unions. Unlike the Americans, the Australian and Japanese MNCs, including those in the electronics sector, are willing to work through unions. This indicates that management philosophy, rather than inevitable production logic in itself, drives the union issue.

While MNCs do not have a homogeneous approach to trade unions, some approaches, like those of US MNCs, can have a significant impact, even where unions as a whole do not represent a fundamental threat to management control. MNC preferences in relation to trade unions in 'host' environments may be affected by 'home' knowledge and competence of managing with unions, as well as their experience of managing with and through unions in the host environment. The way in which the gap between home knowledge and host context is bridged will depend upon their degree of divergence, as well as the willingness and ability to impose home preferences. The ability to impose home practices may be affected by the balance of power between MNCs and the dependent state, the prevailing host policy and the trade union response relating to the regulation of trade union recognition. While these configurations are open to change and reversal, they determine the scope of the 'zone of maneouvre' in which 'choice' may be exercised at any particular time. The terrain of industrial relations, even in a dependent state, is open to contestation at macro and micro levels. National and local industrial relations configurations in host states reflect a changing combination of, and interaction between, MNC home and host contexts. These configurations cannot be predicted nor wished away, at least until or unless a hegemonic global order gives rise to the end of diversity.

NOTES

1. The dominance of US investments was superseded by Japanese investments, due to the mid-1980s high Yen. Other major investor countries have been Singapore, Taiwan, Australia, UK and France (MIDA, 1996).
2. One company withdrew access, leaving a total of 19.
3. The 'organizational cognitive framework ... helps to clarify ... shared cognitions through which groups negotiate and maintain common perceptions of their environments' (Cray and Mallory, 1998: 105).
4. MAEI is an advocate, pressure group and PR body of American electronics companies in Malaysia.
5. US and other large MNCs are reported to pay more than local or Taiwanese companies (personal communication with MTUC).
6. Interview: General Manager, Company A, 7 July 1994. During the second round of interviews a new General Manager had arrived. The workers complained that the new person had not seen them, suggesting smallness does not necessarily guarantee good communication.
7. Interviews: Company B, General Manager, Production Supervisor, employees, 26–7 June 1995.
8. Interviews: Company B, 26–7 June 1995; Company D, 7 July 1995.
9. Interviews: Managing Director, Company D, 7 July 1995; the Manager of Company G, 1 Oct. 1993.
10. Interview: 24 Nov. 1995.
11. Interview: Business Development Manager, Company S, 5 Oct. 1993.
12. Interview: Factory Foreman, Company C, 23 Nov. 1995.
13. Interviews: Company E, Human Resources Manager, Union President and employees, 29–30 Nov. 1995.
14. Interview: Company C, General Manager, 27 Sept. 1993.
15. All the strikers, except union activists, were reinstated.
16. Penang has amongst the most concentrated US and other electronics investments in South East Asia (Henderson, 1989).
17. American labour interests in human rights possibly reflects concern over the relocation of US MNCs to developing countries (Benider, 1987; Hecker, 1993). The electronics industry union issue is ongoing.
18. Interview: Harris Solid State Workers' Union, 11–16 Aug. 1993.
19. Harris acquired RCA from General Electric in December 1988 and it has some unionized plants in the USA (*Electronic Business Asia*, 1990).
20. This is a prerequisite before recognition can be sought.
21. Interview: Harris Solid State Workers' Union, 11–16 Aug. 1993.

22. Ibid.
23. The employer has a right to seek validation of recognition claims through the Industrial Relations Department.
24. The main company employed 2,500, the sister company approximately 100; the 24 union activists were not transferred.
25. The company relocated to new premises but the unionists were left in the old factory; a building that accommodated many hundreds now accommodated 22, although they were divided by shift working.
26. Interviews: General Manager, Company I, 4 July 1994; General Manager, Company A, 28 Nov. 1995; General Manager and Factory Foreman, 27 Sept. 1993 and 23 Nov. 1995.
27. Interviews: Company F, General Manager and Personnel Manager, 24 Sept. 1993, 10–11 July 1995; Company E, Managing Director, 30 Sept. 1993 and 29 Nov. 1995.
28. Interview: MTUC, 10 Aug. 1993; MLO, 13 Aug. 1993.
29. Japanese MNCs – like others in Malaysia – are much more likely to employ a local personnel manager (Smith, 1994; Sim, 1977: 48), indicating their expectation of conforming to local practice.

REFERENCES

Abdullah, Syed R.S. (1992) 'Management Strategies and Employee Responses in Malaysia: A Study of Management Industrial Relations Styles of US and Japanese Multinational Companies in the Malaysian Electronics Industry'. Ph.D. Thesis. Cardiff: University of Wales

Abdullah, Syed R.S. and Keenoy, Tom (1995) 'Japanese Managerial Practices in the Malaysian Electronics Industry: Two Case Studies', *Journal of Management Studies*, Vol. 32, No. 6, pp. 719–30.

Aldaeaj, Hamad, Thibodeaux, Mary and Nasif, Ercan (1991) 'A Power Model of Corporation-Nation-State Relationships', *SAM Advanced Management Journal*, Summer, pp. 11–17.

American Malaysian Chamber of Commerce (1997) *Corporate Survey* (online), Kuala Lumpur: AMCC. Available from: http://www.jaring.my/amcham/businessinfo.htm

Anazawa, Makoto (1994) 'Japanese Manufacturing Investment in Malaysia', in K.S. Jomo (ed.), *Japan and Malaysian Development*. London: Routledge, pp.75–101.

Benider, Burton (1987) *International Labour Affairs: The World Trade Union and Multinational Companies*. Oxford: Clarendon Press.

Bhopal, Mhinder (1997) 'Industrial Relations in Malaysia – Multinational Preferences and State Concessions in Dependent Development: A Case Study of the Electronics Industry', *Economic and Industrial Democracy*, Vol. 18, No. 4, pp. 567–97.

Bjorkman, Maja, Lauridsen, Laurids S. and Secher Marcussen, Henrik (1988) 'Types of Industrialization and the Capital–Labour Relation in the Third World', in Roger Southall (ed.), *Trade Unions and the New Industrialization of the Third World*. London: Zed Books, pp. 59–80.

Business Times (1992) 4 Sept.

Business Times (1988) 6 Oct.

Campbell, Duncan (1994) 'Foreign Investment, Labour Immobility and the Quality of Employment', *International Labour Review*, Vol. 133, No. 2, pp. 185–204.

Cray, David and Mallory, Geoffrey (1998) *Making Sense of Managing Culture*. London: International Thomson Business Press.

Deyo, Frederick (1989) 'Labour Systems, Production Structures and Export-manufacturing: The East Asian NICs', *South East Asian Journal of Social Sciences*, Vol. 17, No. 2, pp. 8–24.

Davis, Edward and Lansbury, Russell (1998) 'Employment Relations in Australia', in Greg Bamber and Russel Lansbury (eds), *International and Comparative Employment Relations*. London: Sage, pp. 110–43.

Dore, Ronald (1990) *British Factory – Japanese Factory*. Berkeley: University of California Press.

Economist, The (1997), 18–24 Jan., pp. 15–16, 65–6.

Electronics Business Asia (1990), Sept., pp. 45–53.

Elger, Tony and Smith, Chris (1994) 'Global Japanization? Convergence and Competition in the Organization of the Labour Process', in Tony Elger and Chris Smith (eds), *Global Japanization: The Transnational Transformation of the Labour Process*. London: Routledge.

Evans, Paul and Lorange, Peter (1989) 'The Two Logics behind Human Resource Management', in P. Evans, Y. Doz and A. Laurent (eds), *Human Resource Management in International Firms: Change, Globalization and Innovation*. London: Macmillan.

Ferner, Anthony (1994) 'Multinational Companies and Human Resource Management: An Overview of Research Issues', *Human Resource Management Journal*, Vol. 4, No. 2. pp. 79–102.

Foulkes, F. (1980) *Personnel Policies in Large Nonunion Companies*. New Jersey: Prentice Hall.

Frenkel, Stephen (1995) 'Workplace Relations in the Global Corporation: A Comparative Analysis of Subsidiaries in Malaysia and Taiwan', in Stephen Frenkel and Jeffrey Harrod (eds), *Industrialization and Labour Relations: Contemporary Research in Seven Countries*. New York: ILR Press, pp. 179–215.

Grace, Elizabeth (1990) *Shortcircuiting Labour: Unionising Electronics Workers in Malaysia*. Kuala Lumpur: INSAN.

Hamilton, Florence (1991) 'Organising at Motorola', in Women Working Worldwide (eds), *Women Organising in Global Electronics*. London: Women Working Worldwide.

Harman, Chris (1996) 'Globalization: A Critique of a New Orthodoxy', *International Socialism*, Winter, pp. 3–33.

Harrod, J. (1988) 'Social Relations of Production, Systems of Labour Control and Third World Trade Unions', in Roger Southall (ed.), *Trade Unions and the New Industrialization of the Third World*. London: Zed Books, pp. 41–58.

Hecker, Steven (1993) 'US Unions, Trade and International Solidarity: Emerging Issues and Tactics', *Economic and Industrial Democracy*, Vol. 14, No. 3, pp. 355–67.

Henderson, Jeffrey (1989) *The Globalization of High Technology Production: Society, Space and Semiconductors in the Restructuring of the Modern World*. London: Routledge.

Hiramoto, Atsushi (1995) 'Overseas Japanese Plants under Global Strategies: TV Transplants in Asia', in Stephen Frenkel and Jeffrey Harrod (eds), *Industrialization and Labour Relations: Contemporary Research in Seven Countries*. ILR Press: New York, pp. 236–62.

Hirst, Paul and Thompson, Graham (1996) *Globalization in Question*. London: Polity Press.

Hirokazu, Shiode (1989) *Japanese Investment in South East Asia: Three Malaysian Case Studies*. Hong Kong: The Centre for the Progress of Peoples Ltd.

Hoogvelt, Ankie (1997) *Globalization and the Postcolonial World*. Basingstoke: Macmillan Press.

Hu, Yao-Su (1992) 'Global or Stateless Corporations', *California Management Review*, Vol. 34, No. 2, pp. 107–26.

Jomo, K.S. (1998) 'Malaysian Debacle: Whose Fault?', *Cambridge Journal of Economics*, Vol. 22, No. 6, pp. 707–22.

Jomo, K.S. and Todd, Patricia (1994) *Trade Unions and the State in Peninsular Malaysia*. Kuala Lumpur: Oxford University Press.

Kawamura, Nozomu (1994) *Sociology and Society of Japan*. London: Kegan-Paul International.

Kochan, Thomas, Katz, Harry and McKersie, Robert (1994) *The Transformation of American Industrial Relations*. New York: ILR Press.

Kuruvilla, Sarosh (1995) 'Industrialization Strategy and Industrial Relations Policy in Malaysia', in Stephen Frenkel and Jeffrey Harrod (eds), *Industrialization and Labour Relations: Contemporary Research in Seven Countries*. ILR Press: New York, pp. 37–63.

Malaysia, Department of Statistics (1998) 'Composition of Manufactured Exports, 1996–97', online. Kuala Lumpur: Malaysian Government. Available from http://miti.gov.my/trdind/app3htm

Malaysian American Electronics Industry (1998) *Annual Survey 1997*. Kuala Lumpur: MAEI.

Marginson, Paul and Sisson, Keith (1994) 'The Structure of Transnational Capital in Europe:

The Emerging Euro-company and its Implications for Industrial Relations', in Richard Hyman and Anthony Ferner (eds), *New Frontiers in European Industrial Relations*. London: Blackwell, pp. 15–51.

MIDA (Malaysian Industrial Development Authority) (1996) *Investment in the Manufacturing Sector*. Kuala Lumpur: Malaysian Government.

MTUC (1974–1976) 23rd Biennial General Council Report, 1974–1976.

New Straits Times (1988a) 4 Oct.

New Straits Times (1988b) 5 Oct.

New Straits Times (1988c) 20 Oct.

New Straits Times (1989) 20 Jan.

New Straits Times (1993) 15 Jan.

Ohmae, Kenichi (1994) *The Borderless World: Power and Strategy in the Global Marketplace*. London: Harper-Collins.

Ohmae, Kenichi (1996) *The End of the Nation State: The Rise of Regional Economies*. London: Harper-Collins.

Perlmutter, Howard V. (1969) 'The Tortuous Evolution of the Multinational Corporation', *Columbia Journal of World Business*, Vol. 4, No. 1, pp. 9–18.

Poon, June M.L., Ainuddin, Raja and Affrin, Hamdan (1990) 'Management Policies and Practices of American, British, European, and Japanese Subsidiaries in Malaysia: A Comparative Study', in *International Journal of Management*, Vol. 7, No. 4, pp. 467–74.

Reich, Robert (1992) *The Work of Nations*. New York: Vintage Books.

Rowley, Chris (1997) 'Reassessing HRM's Convergence', *Asia Pacific Business Review*, Vol. 3, No. 4, pp. 198–211.

Rowley, Chris and Bae, Johngseok (1998) 'Korean Business and Management: The End of the Model', *Asia Pacific Business Review*, Vol. 4, No. 3, pp. 130–9.

Rowley, Chris and Lewis, M. (1996) 'Greater China at the Crossroads? Convergence, Culture and Competitiveness', *Asia Pacific Business Review*, Vol. 3, No. 3, pp. 1–22.

Rosenweig, Philip and Nohria, Nitin (1994) 'Influences on Human Resource Management Practices in Multinational Corporations', *Journal of International Business*, Vol. 25, No. 2, pp. 229–51.

Ruigrok, Winfried and van Tulder, Rob (1995) *The Logic of International Restructuring*. London: Routledge.

Sim, A.B. (1977) 'Decentralized Management of Subsidiaries and their Performance – A Comparative Study of American, British and Japanese Subsidiaries in Malaysia', *Management International Review*, Vol. 19, No. 2, pp. 39–52.

Smith, Rand W. (1993) 'International Economy and State Strategies', *Comparative Politics*, April, pp. 351–72.

Smith, Wendy (1994) 'A Japanese Factory in Malaysia: Ethnicity as a Management Ideology' in K.S. Jomo (ed.), *Japan and Malaysian Development*. London: Routledge.

Sorge, Arndt (1991) 'Strategic Fit and the Societal Effect: Interpreting Cross-National Comparisons of Technology, Organization and Human Resources', *Organization Studies*, Vol. 12, No. 2, pp. 161–90.

Southall, Roger (ed.) (1988) *Trade Unions and the New Industrialization of the Third World*. London: Zed Books.

Straits Times (1990), 24 June.

Streeck, Wolfgang (1992) 'National Diversity, Regime Competition and Institutional Deadlock: Problems in Forming a European Industrial Relations System', *Journal of Public Policy*, Vol. 12, No. 4, pp. 301–30.

Thong, Gregory Tin Sin and Jain, Hem C. (1988) 'Human Resource Management Practices of Japanese and Malaysian Companies: A Comparative Study', *Malaysian Management Review*, Vol. 23, No. 2, pp. 28–49.

Upham, Martin (1995) *Trade Unions and Employers' Organizations of the World*. London: Cartermill Publishing.

US Department of State (1997) *Malaysia Report on Human Rights Practices for 1996*, online. Department of State, Bureau of Democracy, Human Rights, and Labour. Available from: http:///www.state.gov/www/global/human_rights/1996_hrp_report/malaysia.html

Valuenzela, Jaime (1992) 'Labour Movements and Political Systems: Some Variations', in M. Regini (ed.), *The Future of Labour Movements*. London: Sage.

Wad, Peter (1988) 'The Japanization of the Malaysian Trade Union Movement', in Roger Southall (ed.), *Trade Unions and the New Industrialization of the Third World*. London: Zed Books, pp. 210–29.

Wangel, Arne (1988) 'The ILO and Protection of Trade Union Rights: The Electronics Industry in Malaysia', in Roger Southall (ed.), *Trade Unions and the New Industrialization of the Third World*. London: Zed Books, pp. 287–305.

Whitley, Richard (1998) 'Internationalization and Varieties of Capitalism: The Limited Effects of Cross-National Coordination of Economic Activities on the Nature of Business Systems', *Review of International Political Economy*, Vol. 5, No. 3, pp. 445–81.

Wolfe, Doug and Arnold, Brad (1994) 'Human Resource Management in Malaysia: A Comparison between American and Japanese Approaches', *Journal of Asian Business*, Vol. 10, No. 4, pp. 80–103.

12

Labour Unions, Globalization and Deregulation in Thailand

JOHN J. LAWLER and CHOKECHAI SUTTAWET

Profound economic change rooted in the phenomenon of globalization has been a fundamental force in Asia for more than two decades. Thailand, a later arrival in this process, initially enjoyed great success and, for some of this period, laid claim to having the fastest growing economy in the world. All of that ended rather abruptly with the country's effective bankruptcy and currency devaluation in mid-1997, necessitating the first of several International Monetary Fund (IMF) bailouts in the region.

Globalization has affected nations in many ways, although the primary impact seems to have been increasing competitive pressures. As countries seek greater flexibility in order to be competitive internationally, government deregulation of both labour and product markets is another important force that many believe to be responsible, in part, for the worldwide decline of organized labour. This contribution explores the twin issues of globalization and deregulation as seen in the Thai context, examining their effect on Thailand's labour market and the viability of its fledgling labour movement.

Thailand and the Global Economy

As one of Asia's 'little tiger' economies, Thailand experienced nothing short of dramatic economic development from the late 1980s through 1997, with real growth rates in the range of eight to nine per cent during most of this period (*Thailand in Figures*, 1997: 268). In the early 1980s, agriculture accounted for about 25 per cent of gross domestic product (GDP), with the manufacturing sector accounting for about 20 per cent of GDP (ibid.: 269); by 1995, agriculture had shrunk to only about ten per cent of GDP, while manufacturing had risen to 28 per cent (ibid.: 269).

Thailand's growth in this period was very much rooted in the phenomenon of globalization and had been driven by foreign direct investment. For example, between January 1995 and June 1997, nearly 1,200 projects were begun under sponsorship of the government's Board of Investment. Seventeen per cent of these projects were wholly owned by foreign investors while another 41 per cent were joint ventures involving Thai and foreign partners (ibid.: 518). About 40 per cent of the total capital invested in these projects came from foreign sources. Yet, despite rapid and extensive growth, the pattern of development in Thailand has been quite unbalanced, favouring metropolitan areas, especially Bangkok. In 1995, 50 per cent of the labour force was still employed in the agricultural sector, despite the fact that this sector only accounts for ten per cent of GDP.

Although warning signs abounded long before the economic crisis of mid-1997, these were largely ignored, at least within Thailand. Sensing potential problems, many foreign investors began shifting investments out of Thailand and declines in certain export industries reduced the inflow of foreign currency. Huge loans secured from foreign banks were invested in projects with dubious potential returns, particularly in the real estate sector where overbuilding in Bangkok seems to have been an important precipitator of the crisis. With a burgeoning current account deficit and debt payments to foreign creditors looming that exceeded foreign reserves, foreign exchange speculators began selling short on Thai currency in anticipation of a major devaluation. In defending the baht, the Bank of Thailand exhausted almost all of its foreign reserves and the country risked defaulting on pending loan payments. A weakened financial sector could not supply funds to businesses that might have generated inflows of currency. As its currency collapsed, the country was forced to request assistance from the IMF and to submit to a series of conditions that were seen by many Thais as nothing less than a surrender of national sovereignty. Thailand was the first of a series of highly successful Asian countries that experienced economic collapse in 1997–98. While many saw the Thai crash as precipitating the Asian economic crisis, its problems were probably more a symptom than a cause of a more general problem.

INDUSTRIAL RELATIONS AND EMPLOYMENT SYSTEMS
IN THAILAND

The pattern of economic development adopted by the various military-dominated regimes that governed Thailand from the mid-1930s up until the early 1990s strongly influenced the country's industrial relations system. The use of cheap, largely uneducated labour as a key element of comparative advantage, particularly for foreign investors, necessitated the promotion and maintenance of an unorganized workforce, weak trade unions and dominant employer authority. Although Thailand is very much of a collectivist culture (Hofstede, 1980), there generally seems to be a lack of class consciousness among workers, resulting at least in part from reliance on rural labour to fill the increasing number of jobs in the industrial sector. Such workers have, at least to this point, not formed a strong sense of class identity and are thus more difficult to organize. And the centrality of Theravada Buddhism to Thai culture certainly contributes to the industrial relations framework (Suttawet, 1994). Thai society is hierarchical in character, with those in the lower rungs of society tending to defer to their social superiors, which is often reflected in the processes by which Thai organizations are managed (Lawler *et al.*, 1997). Such ordering of society is supported by Buddhist doctrine, which encourages individuals to accept their current station in life (seen as a consequence of one's past life) and to work for a good 'next life'. Theravada Buddhism tends to be personal and introspective and is not as prone to social activism as is the Mahayana Buddhism dominant in East Asia as well in as neighbouring countries such as Vietnam (as reflected, for example, in the actions taken by Buddhist monks there during the Vietnam War). Apart from recurring, rapid and normally bloodless military coups, social unrest and political turmoil in Thailand is relatively infrequent and, in recent times, has been driven largely by the actions of the middle classes and students, as during the upheavals of the 1970s and 1992.

Industrial relations policies and programmes in Thailand vary widely by firm type. In general, the employment relationship is less formal and less overtly structured within Thailand's numerous family owned enterprises (Lawler *et al.*, 1997; Isarangkhun na Ayuthaya and Taira, 1977). Employment practices tend to be more sophisticated in publicly owned corporations, as well as in firms owned by Western or Japanese multinational corporations (MNCs) (Lawler *et al.*, 1997). Larger-scale Thai-owned firms tend towards Western business practices rather than the stereotypical Japanese approach, though Thai culture is still a dominant influence, even within the largest and most internationally active of firms. The country's state-owned enterprises (SOEs), where unions have been especially active, vary considerably with respect to industrial relations and human resource management (HRM) systems, with some managed very much like family-owned enterprises and others utilizing highly sophisticated systems.

The urban labour force, once composed essentially of alien Chinese, has become predominantly ethnic Thai as a result of extensive migration from rural areas to population centres (particularly Bangkok). In general, ethnic Thai workers generally accept the imbalance of power with authority figures and tend to be deferential to their superiors, as befits a culture that scores high on Hofstede's (1980) 'power distance' cultural dimension. Certainly, as industrialization continues and as democratic reforms under the new Thai constitution that was adopted in 1997 'empower' people and encourage political involvement, the traditional Thai attitude towards superior–subordinate relationships, shaped by a feudal heritage that ended only in this century, may change.

Employment, if not for life, normally entails a long-term commitment of the firm to the master–servant relationship. This commitment is reinforced by legislation imposing high separation costs upon employers for releasing long-service employees (Chantaravitoon and Vause, 1994). Hence, most firms divide their labour force into two components, a permanent element and a temporary element. The permanent element will consist of employees whose skills are more specific to the firm and who require a period of on-the-job training. Temporary employees serve for less than six months, are typically unskilled, and are put in jobs requiring little training. Many are raw recruits from rural areas, perhaps supplied by a labour contractor. In recent years, many such workers have come from poorer neighbouring countries, especially Myanmar (Burma), as the number of Thais willing to accept the lowest level occupations has dwindled. The 1997 economic crisis caused a backlash against immigrant workers, many of whom are in the country illegally.

Given the nature of Thai culture and the employment system, it is not surprising that employers tend to resist unions and that the labour movement, certainly in the private sector, lacks much power. The legal status of trade unions has shifted several times since the 1950s (Brown and Frenkel, 1993). Although many limitations exist, unions have enjoyed certain legal guarantees continuously since the 1970s and strikes have been legal since 1981. Yet, the trade union movement is weak both in terms of breadth of coverage and in workplace industrial relations. In 1988, there were an estimated 500 unions (most being enterprise-level organizations), representing around 300,000 workers, or a little over three per cent of the country's total non-agricultural workforce (US Department of Labour, 1988), which is quite small even by regional standards. The core strength of the labour movement was to be found in the country's numerous commercial SOEs. For political reasons and perhaps because of the general lack of competitive pressures in this sector, trade union organization had progressed much further in SOEs than in the private sector. In the late 1980s, there were 123 recognized unions in the country's 69 public enterprises, with a union density rate of around 60 per cent (Brown and Frenkel, 1993).

The unionization rate changed little over the course of the country's rapid economic growth in the 1990s. However, following a military coup in 1991, the rights of the SOE unions were severely curtailed, so that unions with rights fully protected under the law accounted for only about 1.7 per cent of the non-agricultural labour force. Brown and Frenkel (1993) note, however, that such a gross union density rate (that is, union members relative to total non-agricultural labour force) understates the true strength of the labour movement. Adjusting for the various groups excluded from the possibility of unionization (such as employers, household workers, civil servants), the effective or net union density is more than six per cent (if SOE employees are included). At present, the official estimate of union strength indicated that a total of 562 unions represented about 296,000, or less than three per cent of the country's non-agricultural workforce (from unpublished information provided by the Department of Welfare and Labour Protection, Thai Ministry of Interior).

Although unions negotiate contracts with employers over a wide range of issues, contracts do not exist in all facilities with unions. Overall, the bargaining power and influence of unions over management appears fairly weak, certainly in the private sector.

This is partly due to the extensive system of laws and regulations that provide at least basic rights to employees, including significant restrictions on the ability of employers to discharge workers without appropriate cause (Vause, 1992). The national labour court system serves as an alternative means by which Thai workers can redress mistreatment at the hands of employers.

Even though Thai unions may work to increase wages as a principal goal (Brown and Frenkel, 1993), their ability to do this via collective bargaining is quite limited. Given an almost endless supply of labour to urban centres from rural areas, most operative-level employees were paid at, or near, the minimum wage (about US$6 per day prior to currency depreciation that occurred as a result of the economic crisis of 1997). Thus, the only effective way of raising wages for these workers is through increases in the minimum wage (which varies somewhat by region, being highest in the Bangkok area). To this end, unions are politically and culturally active, especially through participation in the country's various tripartite commissions, in endeavouring to increase minimum wages. At the workplace level, union activities are now concerned more with issues such as health and safety concerns. Even though the new Labour Protection Act (1998) is in force, workers in Thai plants can still be exposed to dangerous conditions through weak enforcement of health and safety laws. In one case several years ago, workers became ill after employers spiked drinking water with amphetamines. The most egregious violation of such standards was the Kader Toy Company fire in 1993 in which some 200 workers, mostly women, were killed in a factory fire because they could not escape through fire exits that had been locked to discourage employees from taking unauthorized breaks. Such cases are compelling ammunition in efforts to organize workers. Some of the most intense labour disputes have involved these types of issues, as in a protracted strike several years ago against Seagate Technologies, an American computer components manufacturer. All of these problems have caused the Thai labour movement to demand establishment of occupational health and safety standards backed by legislation. Subsequent to the onset of the 1997 economic crisis, another important union initiative has been helping to absorb the effects of economic decline.

THAI LABOUR LAW

The legal status of unions has varied in the period following the abolition of the absolute monarchy in 1932. At times unions have been tolerated, while at other times they have been prohibited (Mabry, 1977; Brown and Frenkel, 1993). The operative legislation currently is the Labour Relations Act, passed in 1975 but significantly amended in 1991. The major provisions of the law, as summarized by Chantaravitoon and Vause (1994), include the following: a process for recognizing and registering unions; procedures for establishing labour union and employer associations; unfair labour practices; and procedures for conducting collective bargaining and labour disputes.

The Thai Labour Relations Act is patterned, to some extent, on the American National Labour Relations Act. For example, employers are, in principle, prohibited from interfering in union affairs or discriminating against union members. An administrative agency (the Labour Relations Committee) is responsible for overseeing and enforcing the Act. Methods are in place for registering unions. Litigation regarding disputes under the law is an administrative matter before the Labour Relations Committee, which resolves differences by establishing remedies rather than imposing sanctions.

There are, however, important differences between Thai and US practice. There are fewer restrictions on employer conduct and virtually none on union conduct. Perhaps most significant is the absence of what is known in the USA as exclusive representation: only one union may be recognized as a worker representative in a given workplace and this organization must be supported by the majority of employees in that unit. In Thailand, as in most other countries, different groups of workers in a particular workplace may establish their own separate unions. Thai law allows any group of ten or more workers to establish and register a union. Another feature of the law, again different from American labour law, is that it provides for the establishment of worker committees that can act, at least in principle, rather like European works councils. Although workers can establish such committees on their own, most are established by and under the control of unions.

Trade unions can be organized as enterprise (that is, company-specific) unions, on an industrial basis, or nationally. However, two important restrictions apply: (1) the Union Registrar, a government agency, has the power to register and dissolve unions, and (2) individuals who are not employees of the company or companies the union represents cannot become union members. In practice, this means that unions are generally organized as enterprise unions (that is, as unions with membership restricted to employees in the same firm). For example, of approximately 600 recognized unions that existed in 1989, about 400 were enterprise unions (Brown and Frenkel, 1993). Very few industrial unions exist. The Act also permits the establishment of peak labour federations and congresses.

A significant feature of the law is its limitations as to coverage. As with the US Act, the Thai law exempts agricultural workers. While agricultural workers are a small component of workers in the USA and other industrialized countries, this provision precludes around 50 per cent of the labour force in Thailand from protection. More significantly, as a consequence of the last military coup in February 1991, the Labour Relations Act was amended in April of that year to exclude employees of Thai SOEs. SOE workers had, to that point, represented the single largest concentration of union members in Thailand and were the most powerful of labour groups in the country. This move, then, had significant implications for the vitality of the Thai labour movement. Although the SOE unions were not disbanded, they were changed from 'unions' to 'associations', and their power was substantially curtailed under the State Enterprise Labour Act (Vause, 1992). As we shall see later, this action is directly related to pressures on the Thai economy linked to globalization and the opening of markets, including processes of deregulation. Despite the restoration democracy in 1992, constitutional reforms in 1997, and assistance from external bodies such as the American AFL-CIO, many limitations on SOE unions remain in effect. The SOE unions are objects of especially hostile views from many members of the Thai Senate, so it is not possible to pass legislation expanding SOE union rights.

LABOUR IN THAILAND: AN HISTORICAL PERSPECTIVE

An understanding of trade unionism in Thailand and its relationship to forces such as globalization and deregulation requires knowledge of the historical evolution of the Thai working class. Indeed, forces related to global, or at least regional, market forces have had a surprisingly long history in Thailand. The first labour organizations in the country can be traced to the arrival of Chinese immigrant labour in the nineteenth century, which itself was the consequence of the country's expanding foreign trade that led to shortages of skilled, urban-based workers. Labour market regulation also has a long history in Thailand, as the country operated under what was essentially a feudal system until the early twentieth century (Watana, 1982).

Feudalism

The contemporary Thai worker has his origins in two different groups, the first being the *prais* (common people) or serfs and the second being immigrant Chinese labour. The *prais* originated during the Sukhothai Period (*c.* AD 1200–1300). At that time, workers were independent in choosing their occupations. They were not controlled by any group nor were they taxed, although they were obliged to fight in the army in time of war. Monarchial institutions strengthened during the Ayuthaya Period (*c.* 1300–1767). The *prais* were decreed to serve the king and the aristocracy, both during times of war and peace. The necessity of having the *prais* declined after the defeat of Ayuthaya by Burma in 1767, and the new capital Ratanakosin (Bangkok) was built in 1782. When the frequency of war with neighbouring countries declined, Thailand became more engaged in trade with China and Europe. The state then gradually relaxed the labouring service obligation of the *prais*. Those who were still controlled by the aristocracy continued their struggles to be independent and succeeded in so doing when King Chulalongkorn (also known as Rama V) abolished serfdom in 1903.

Chinese Immigrants

Chinese labour has played a role in the Thai economy since the early 1800s, when the monarchy began the large-scale cultivation of sugar cane and sugar refining. Chinese labour was imported because of shortages in the number of available the *prais*. Chinese labour continued to increase in numbers and expanded into various occupations. Ethnic Thai workers, on the other hand, were much less involved in early trade and industry than the Chinese, who came to control the Bangkok economy. Thus, the urban labour force in Thailand was, until relatively recently, mainly composed of ethnic Chinese and Chinese intermarried with Thais (Sino-Thais).

The earliest labour organizations in Thailand can, in fact, be traced to the Chinese. As Thailand's trade expanded in the late 1800s and early 1900s, Chinese labourers working in the same plant formed workers' associations. These were secret associations, as Chinese workers had a patron–client relationship with the Chinese owners. At first, the state attempted to suppress the associations, but without success. However, legislation in 1897 allowed the establishment of worker associations. Although this measure could not control the operation of secret Chinese associations, labourers in various industries were encouraged to establish organizations. The first of these to be established was the Tramway Workers' Association. As with many of the early unions in the USA and Europe, this association had mutual aid as its objective and did not have the goal of creating economic and political bargaining power.

The First Modern Unions

A revolution conducted by military officers and civilian government officials ended the absolute monarchy in 1932, resulting in the establishment of a constitutional monarchy. Trade unions appeared on the scene in Thailand, mainly after World War II, although a few had existed in earlier periods. In 1950, there were 150 unions; by 1956, they had achieved the passage of a national labour law, including labour protection clauses, registration of unions and rules for settling industrial conflicts. This Act was abolished by the Sarit government after the 1958 military coup and a legal framework for trade unions and negotiation of industrial disputes was not re-established until 1965.

As the union movement developed and became more militant, deficiencies in HRM practices became more glaring. A survey in 1974 of 81 large firms by the American Chamber of Commerce in Bangkok revealed that 85 per cent had published work rules. The larger the firm and the more Western its orientation, the more likely it was that it had formalized company rules, orientated employees to them, and sought to enforce them. Similarly, well developed industrial relations departments existed only in the larger establishments. The same survey revealed in 1974 that only 60 per cent of the surveyed companies employed a personnel manager. Recognition of the need for modern human resource management techniques developed only as the number of large employers increased, as labour legislation was extended and enforced, and as the labour union movement expanded, gained experience and flexed its muscles.

The major obstacle to the development of Thai unions in the direction seen in Western countries was that, just as industrialization was accelerating in the 1970s, the Thai government went only part-way towards freedom of association. It decreed that workers should not join unions with workers from other provinces or from establishments having different working conditions. This policy served to promote enterprise unionism as the dominant form in Thailand. Also, by discouraging the formation of larger union bodies, the labour movement, though tolerated, was kept relatively weak. Rather than a single, strong peak organization, there were and remain multiple competing labour congresses (at least 14 in 1974).

Organized labour was, however, able to make certain inroads during the period of political liberalization that took place in the early to mid-1970s. The number of strikes increased from 34 in 1972 to 100 in 1973 and continued in the hundreds for the next several years, fuelled by the oil crisis and inflation, along with the looser political climate prior to 1977. The Thai military acted in October 1976 to ban strikes and lock-outs, and arrested union leaders, but found that in the interests of efficient production they had to moderate these policies and allow trade union growth to continue. Finally, in January 1981, remaining bans were lifted and at the end of 1982 some 377 unions were registered with a membership of 250,000.

Unionism and Economic Take-off

Perhaps one of the most significant impacts of globalization on labour unions in Thailand has been the importation of newer and highly effective methods of union avoidance to Thailand by MNCs, particularly those from the USA. Despite some movement forward for unions, the 1980s saw a real increase in these more sophisticated and subtler forms of union resistance on the part of employers. To the extend employers actively opposed unions, Thai employers had mainly relied on *union suppression* strategies: discharging union supporters, using armed force, and colluding with government officials to foster state opposition to unions (by banning unions outright or by restricting union activities such as strikes). These firms often use a wide range of methods to endeavour to placate workers and defuse union organizing effort before they get out of hand (Lawler, 1990). The growth of the HRM function in Thai firms can be linked, to some extent, to efforts to avoid unionization through behavioural and managerial initiatives. For example, token wage increases or changes in working conditions might be instituted, potential employees might be screened based on possible union proneness, or supervisors and others on the shop floor may carefully monitor employee actions to provide helpful information to upper management regarding a union's likely moves. Failing in an effort to dissuade workers from organizing, employers might then use legal or quasi-legal initiatives to keep unions at bay. There is reason to believe that the emergence of more sophisticated HRM systems in Thai-owned companies, as in the USA, has been to some extent motivated by efforts to undercut current unions or deflect potential unionization efforts.

A study commissioned by the International Labour Organization (ILO) notes the use of various union avoidance tactics by companies, including tactics that were illegal or that exploited legal loopholes to maintain non-union status, and temporary companies (Samakkitam, 1989). Brown and Frenkel (1993) highlight a number of successful anti-union campaigns in Thai companies, using both traditional union suppression techniques and more modern approaches. Management is thus often more effective in its efforts to contain unionism at the enterprise level than at the industrial and national levels (Suttawet, 1994).

The election of the Choonhavan government in 1988, after a long period of relative stagnation and quiescence by unions, opened up new prospects. Not only were wage increases promised and conditions in the public sector improved for workers, but a new tolerance of 'responsible' unionism emerged. This reflected the decline of the older families and of alliances based on feudal-military interests. They were replaced by a coalition of new and more dynamic business sectors with important wings of the intelligentsia and the 'technocracy'.

TRADE UNIONISM IN AN ERA OF GLOBALIZATION:
THE 1990s

Although it represented a restoration of democracy, charges of corruption plagued the Choonhavan administration. Vote buying, particularly in rural constituencies, was apparently endemic in the 1988 election. Corrupt practices at the highest levels of the government were also seemingly commonplace. This, along with other political disputes, led to a confrontation between the military and the civilian government. The Thai military staged numerous coups in the period after the 1932 revolution and, in many ways, sees itself as a kind of 'fourth estate', serving as a protector of the people from oppressive and dishonest government (though military leaders doubtlessly also have other, less public-spirited, motives). Rumours of a possible coup were commonplace for quite some time when the military high command overthrew the government in early 1991. The military high command established the National Peace Keeping Council (NPKC), consisting of the principal leaders involved in staging the coup. However, the NPKC did not exercise direct rule, in large part because of the reaction of the USA and the European Union (EU) countries to the suppression of democracy in Thailand. Indeed, it was Thailand's visibility as a significant player in the world economy that certainly engendered the strong response of major democracies. A caretaker government of 'technocrats' was appointed as a new constitution was drafted to restore the electoral process and avoid various sanctions by the USA and EU. An investigation was also launched into the sources of wealth of 'unusually rich' politicians.

The NPKC also took direct action against segments of organized labour that was motivated in part by the global economic forces felt in Thailand and concomitant pressures for limited government involvement in commercial activities. It removed the unions representing workers in the SOEs from coverage under the Labour Relations Act and established new laws regulating and significantly reducing the power of these unions (Chantaravitoon and Vause, 1994). Indeed, the action against the unions was one of the most significant measures taken by the NPKC.

SOEs operate in a variety of industries, ranging from tobacco production and distribution to utilities to the railways and national airline. To understand the reasons for the NPKC move against the unions, it is necessary to consider the origins of the SOE. An important cadre of civilians involved in the 1932 revolution, led by law professor Pridi Bhanomyong (who served as one of the architects of the revolution), had a clear socialist agenda (SarDesai, 1997). In this way, the actions taken by the Thai government paralleled other states in the region, most notably post-independence India. However, the military, which was certainly not leftist, also favoured the creation of SOEs, but this was for nationalistic reasons: SOEs were seen as a means of weakening the influence of the Chinese merchant class, which then controlled most segments of the Thai economy (Phongpaichit and Baker, 1998). In the end, both objectives failed. The socialists were marginalized and many, including Pridi, were ultimately forced into exile. On the other hand, financial performance in the SOEs was initially poor, necessitating the appointment of large numbers of Chinese managers to salvage the companies. Later on, the leading Chinese merchants effectively coopted the military by regularly appointing important military and ex-military officers to their companies' boards of directors and then handsomely compensating them (Phongpaichit and Baker, 1998).

The military, then, came to have a vested interest in the functioning of the economy (and indeed the military continues to own companies, including television stations and a leading bank), but also generally supported the continuation of the SOEs. Yet over the years, a number of the SOEs had been sold off, largely at the behest of the US government, which exercised influence over a succession of Thai governments and saw state-owned businesses as anti-competitive. With the economic take-off of the late 1980s, pressures to privatize many of the remaining SOEs grew. A number had become quite profitable, such as the Thai Airways, the 'jewel in the crown' of Thai SOEs. Being so profitable, these firms were seen as potential cash cows for private investors. Major opposition to privatization was centred in the powerful SOE unions. These organizations naturally felt that privatization would create competitive pressures that would undercut their power.

Brown and Frenkel (1993) argue that the SOE unions really overplayed their hand in their strong opposition to privatization throughout the 1980s, when they staged various strikes and other disruptive actions to pressure the government to back off from its commitment to further privatization. Thus, by the time the coup took place, union actions were seen as threatening continued economic growth. Indeed, the action taken against the SOE unions, though anti-democratic, did not seem to be particularly unpopular, even with staunch opponents of the NPKC. The Thai middle class, which played a prominent role in ending the NPKC and restoring democracy in 1992, perhaps saw these unions as only promoting their vested interests and not especially concerned with the condition of Thai workers in general. After all, SOE union leaders had had close relationships with elements of the military in the past and some union leaders were themselves implicated in at least one failed attempted coup in the 1980s. Phongpaichit and Baker (1997: 204) describe the traditional relationship between the SOE unions and the military as 'corporatist'. Interestingly, the restoration of democracy saw only modest progress in re-establishing the full rights of the state-enterprise unions, despite continuing agitation for this on the part of the unions. The government finally took some action in 1996 to extend greater rights to these unions (Nontarit, 1996).

By eclipsing the power of the SOE unions, the NPKC also seriously weakened the private sector unions, even though they imposed no legal restrictions on these unions. The private sector unions derived power and resources from the stronger state-enterprise unions, so the emasculation of those unions naturally carried over to private sector, where the labour movement was already highly fragmented. Although it did not prohibit private sector unions, the NPKC did enact legislation allowing a labour congress to be established by as few as ten plant-level labour unions. This resulting in the formation of several new congresses, which spawned further disunity within the ranks of organized labour (Nontarit, 1996).

Perhaps the most intriguing event of this episode was the mysterious disappearance of Thanong Po-Arn, president of largest of the private sector labour congresses, in June 1991 (US Department of Labour, 1992). Thanong had been a vocal critic of the government and its treatment of workers. He had been slated to be a member of Thailand's delegation to an ILO convention in Geneva, but was removed by the government, presumably because of his staunch opposition. He has neither reappeared subsequently nor has his body turned up, so his fate remains unclear. His widow has campaigned often for greater police attention to the matter.

The police counter that without a body there is little evidence that Thanong met with an untimely end. They also note that there was a lengthy list of individuals besides opponents of the labour movement who may have wished Thanong ill, including labour union rivals, gangsters to whom he may have owed gambling debts, and several former mistresses. They speculate that he may have staged his own disappearance to avoid his many enemies. The general belief of supporters of organized labour, however, is that Thanong was removed from the scene by unknown parties seizing advantage of the post-coup environment in order to further weaken organized labour.

Opposition to the NPKC came to a head in May 1992. NPKC leader General Suchinda Kraprayoon became prime minister after an election that was widely seen as orchestrated. Constitutional changes pushed through by the NPKC extended great influence to military-allied groups in the process of establishing a government following any parliamentary elections. The principal opposition to Suchinda came from a populist candidate generally backed by students and the middle class, especially in Bangkok and other urban areas. Massive street demonstrations followed General Suchinda's appointment and were met with repressive measures by army units. Hundreds were killed during the demonstrations. Intervention by the king ultimately restored order, with Suchinda forced to step down. To date, the restoration of democracy has been successful and the military appears to have returned more or less permanently to the barracks.

The widespread popular reaction to the Suchinda matter was clearly quite sobering to the military. Just as importantly, the 1992 uprising demonstrated that a significant middle class, largely dominated by private-sector managers, professionals and entrepreneurs, had emerged as an effective counter-force to the military. It was not just students, as in the 1970s, but significant numbers individuals from this middle class who took to the streets in opposition to the military usurpation of power.

Prior to the economic surge that began in the 1980s, relatively few ethnic Thais were involved in the private sector in these roles, as such occupations were primarily the domain of the Chinese community. Educated ethnic Thais typically gravitated to the secure and prestigious, if not highly compensated, civil service. The opportunity to make fortunes in the private sector after the economic take-off drew large numbers of middle class ethnic Thais into the private sector, and the proliferation of MBA and other business-orientated academic programmes made the private sector, rather than the civil service, the object of their children's career ambitions.

The country's involvement in the global economy had created this new centre of power and the military seemed to recognize that its own prosperity depended on this group. The new middle class also saw itself as the architect of national prosperity and was no longer willing to submit to a military elite now seen as an anachronism. As one bumper sticker, prominently displayed on a Mercedes, put it: 'No Democracy, No Money!', a reflection of middle class sentiments regarding its ultimate source of power. At the same time, the commercially orientated middle class would not be naturally sympathetic to unions and probably shared the generals' belief that the state-enterprise unions, for example, exercised too much power, which explains the slowness in restoring full rights to these unions. Although legislation has now been passed in this matter, the state-enterprise unions are still prohibited from striking. Thus globalization has exercised indirect effects on union welfare in Thailand as well, through the advent of a strong middle class with a pro-commerce and pro-free trade bent. Labour unions, particularly the state-enterprise unions, enjoyed a certain level of political influence under the old regime; they have now been displaced in part by this ascending middle class.

Organized labour's record in the period since the restoration of democracy is something of a mix. On the one hand, there was progress made at re-establishing certain rights for the once powerful SOE unions. In 1994, Thailand established a full-fledged labour ministry. Prior to that time, the Labour Relations Act had been administered by the Ministry of the Interior, which, among other its responsibilities, controls the national police force. Establishment of an independent labour ministry had been a long-standing labour objective. Rudimentary social security legislation was passed. Following the economic collapse in 1997, the Labour Protection Act was adopted in 1998; this law provided greater regulation of overtime and higher severance payments for redundant workers. However, this was also controversial in that it placed restrictions on the working hours of pregnant women, leading many to believe that employers would be much more likely to discriminate against women, at least of child-bearing age, to avoid interruption in work schedules.

Despite these gains, the consensus of Thai observers is that, notwithstanding the promise of enhanced union power and influence afforded by the new era of democracy in the country, the labour movement continues to be highly fragmented and weak. Indeed, the labour movement's apex of power and influence may have been during a decade of student-led uprisings, the early 1970s to the early 1980s. As Nikhom Chantaravitoon (1998), a distinguished authority on Thai labour law and the labour movement and former Director-general of Department of Labour (which preceded the Ministry of Labour) has observed: '[D]uring the past five years ... the democratic atmosphere was so conducive to improvement. Labour leaders, unfortunately, have not been able to benefit fully from this.' Labour leaders certainly concur in this assessment. Panich Charoenpao, head of one of Thailand's labour congresses, observed 'The Government is not seriously promoting labour organizations. On the contrary, it appears to have joined hands with employers, causing a wider gap between classes of people' (from Nontarit, 1994). Suvit Hathong, a successor to the ill-fated Thanong Po-Arn as president of the Labour Congress of Thailand, adds: 'Employers are still taking advantage of workers and oppressing them. When employers know a labour union is being formed in their establishments, they simply fire founders of the union' (ibid.).

Thus, despite legal protection under the provisions of the Labour Relations Act, successive Thai administrations, both before and after the 1992 uprising, have generally ignored union rights, especially in the private sector that is so critical to the long-term performance of the economy. If not outright hostile to these unions, governments have pursued a policy of 'divide and conquer' through the encouragement of multiple centres of power within the labour movement, as well as through benign neglect (Phongpaichit and Baker, 1998).

Much of this is due to the impact of globalization and the need for Thailand to maintain a competitive posture in the face of growing economic pressure. Indeed, these pressures pre-date the 1997 economic crisis. As Lawler *et al.* (1997) noted, Thailand's rising wages mean that other countries with lower wages, both in Asia (such as China, Vietnam, Indonesia, India) and in other parts of the world (such as Mexico), have presented significant competitive challenges to Thai-based firms in the world marketplace (see also Rowley and Lewis, 1996; Rowley, 1997; Rowley and Bae, 1998). Thailand has done little to upgrade the skill base of lower-level workers through training and education. Although the literacy rate is high in Thailand, the vast majority of workers have, at best, only six or seven years of schooling, and the level of educational attainment in Thailand is relatively low in comparison to other countries in the region that experienced rapid growth in the 1990s. Thus, although the real wages of urban workers increased substantially during this decade, productivity increases have not kept pace. Therefore, labour costs in Thailand are often higher than in the newly emerging economies (such as Vietnam, India, China) for low skill work and the educational deficit makes introduction of more sophisticated technologies, those that would support higher wages, difficult.

Although Thailand has been a quite vibrant liberal democracy since the demise of the NPKC in 1992, successive governments have typically been more concerned with issues of international trade and finance than labour problems, certainly those of labour unions. As Nikom Chantaravitoon has also observed 'The Government is still reluctant to give workers full support for fear that if workers are backed to set up unions and have full power to negotiate in labour disputes there will be problems concerning investment. The Government gives higher priority to investment and exports' (Nontarit, 1994).

Subsequent to the 1997 financial crisis, a government led by Chuan Leekpai was established. The Leekpai government, and the prime minister in particular, have been given high praise for the professional manner in which the country's financial difficulties have been handled. Prime Minister Chuan and his followers take great pride in the fact that he is, in what often is a millionaires' club, the 'poorest member of parliament' and really does seem to be a man of modest means who is dedicated to bringing transparency and openness to Thai government. His style is in marked contrast to previous elected governments that were generally headed by wealthy and powerful individuals who secured office via heavy spending to buy votes and who used political office primarily as a vehicle for personal enrichment. In addition to implementing political and economic reforms mandated by the

IMF relief package, the Leekpai government has also so far avoided the political turmoil that gripped first Indonesia and more recently Malaysia.

The actions of the Leekpai government have, at least to date, generated significant reforms and led to a degree of stabilization in the Thai economy (though economic recovery efforts continue to be hampered by regional difficulties). Prime Minister Chuan seems to be a liberal pragmatist in the Bill Clinton or Tony Blair mould and his efforts have been praised by both leaders. However, his pragmatism and concern for political reform and economic recovery do not bode especially well for the Thai labour movement. The Leekpai government has been faulted for insensitivity to the plight of the poor and its inclination to place economic recovery ahead of worker welfare. And his support is centred largely in the urban middle class, among the 'Thuppies' (Thai urban professionals) of Bangkok, a group that views unions, and especially union leaders, in the same pejorative manner as its counterparts in much of the rest of the world. As a consequence of their linkages to old-order politicians and, to some extent, the military, labour leaders are not infrequently viewed by this group as part of the past rather than the future.

Despite continuing setbacks on the political front, the economic difficulties Thailand now experiences may, in certain ways, actually bolster the labour movement to the extent that it is seen as a protector of a working class that has experienced immense deprivation as a result of these problems. Even before the onset of the economic crisis, globalization may have been a mixed blessing for Thailand. Unlike Malaysia, where economic growth has been fairly balanced and its benefits widely shared by the population, Thailand's more hectic approach has generated significant increases in income inequality, with one report suggesting that Thailand has one of the highest income disparities in the world, a condition that has evolved only over the past decade (Assavanonda, 1998). Unemployment apparently increased threefold or fourfold within a year of the 1997 currency devaluation, with the actual impact probably being much greater as many urban workers have simply withdrawn from the labour force and returned to their villages. The presence of large numbers of foreign workers who compete with Thais for lower-level jobs is a festering sore as well. There is, then, plenty of grist for labour's mill in the country's economic woes.

Unions have often been at the forefront of employee–management conflict engendered by the economic crisis, such as plant closings and large-scale layoffs. There is continuing opposition by state-enterprise unions to privatization. Foreign companies often seem to be targeted and one strike against Sanyo, over the company's cutting of bonuses because of poor economic performance, resulted in a part of the company's plant being burned to the ground by angry workers (Phongpaichit and Baker, 1998). Although this incident took place in 1996 and thus preceded the 1997 crisis, it was prompted by the growing economic problems that ultimately precipitated the currency devaluation and IMF bailout. Labour-sponsored rallies at government offices to protest against worker mistreatment are commonplace, though generally peaceful.

A significant fear in Thailand, and one that pervades all classes, is that the economic crisis and devalued currency will serve as an opportunity for foreign interests to acquire substantial control of Thai businesses. This is certainly prompted in part by nationalistic sentiments and a general scepticism regarding the motives of foreigners, one that is deeply rooted in Thai experiences during the colonial era. Although Thailand, unlike all of its neighbours, was never colonized, it was forced to relinquish significant territory both to France and Britain and spent much of the nineteenth century and first part of the twentieth century placating foreign powers. Massive acquisitions of Thai assets by foreigner companies evoke a fear of neocolonial domination (as this does elsewhere in the region).

Beyond concerns with sovereignty, Thais fear that foreign influences may undermine treasured cultural practices. Thailand, with its highly assimilated Chinese population, is culturally quite homogeneous, and the ethnic rivalries so characteristic of Indonesia and Malaysia are, for the most part, non-existent (except in the few Moslem-dominated southern provinces). Thus, there is a well defined sense of 'Thainess'. Kindness and gentleness, especially toward one's inferiors, are considered desirable traits and are not taken as signs of weakness on the part of a leader. There is concern, then, that takeovers by foreign companies will undermine 'Thai ways' in the workplace, where managers may be authoritarian but are still empathetic. These concerns are perhaps best articulated by reference again to the observations of Nikom Chantaravitoon (1998), who states:

Under the conditions (imposed by) the International Monetary Fund loan and general world trend, the Thai economy will open up more and more. ... Multinational companies and corporations will have a role to play and will control Thai businesses. Work regulations and rules and the relationship between management and employees will become more international in character, making administration more complex and basing it on a structure introduced from overseas. *Such changes will affect relations between employees and employers that in the past have been Thai or Asian in character. Compromise and sympathy will decrease and everything will be tied up by rules and regulations that are international.* (emphasis added)

Nikhom sees these changes, the direct consequence of globalization, as serving to weaken organized labour in Thailand. Yet, foreign companies have often been the targets of organizing efforts in the private sector, perhaps for the very reasons Nikhom cites: the erosion of compromise and sympathy in the work relationship. Cultural conflict may thus serve as a catalyst to union expansion, assuming the absence of repressive interference on the part of the government. This could turn another way, however, if foreign management could offer an approach to worker participation involving unions that would enhance firm effectiveness. What happens will in all likelihood depend, in the end, on the extent to which the new constitution facilitates meaningful democratic reforms.

CONCLUSION

The strength of a national labour movement might be attributable to a multiplicity of influences. Industrial relations scholars point to such factors as the structure of the economy, the nature of management organizations, the supportiveness of the legal system, the political system, and labour force demographics (Lawler, 1990; Dunlop, 1958). In the context of a developing country, such as Thailand, other factors are also quite significant, including unionism as an instrument of nationalism (Sharma, 1996). The Thai labour movement is extremely weak, even by regional standards. Part of this might, in fact, have to do with the role unions often played in neighbouring countries in the struggle against colonialism. For Thailand, free of colonial domination, nationalism was not a major force supporting the emergence of unionism. Nationalism was a force in Thailand, particularly in the era following the 1932 revolution against the monarchy, but workers were not a major element in the elite, largely composed of civil servants and military officers, that was the major force. In so traditional and hierarchical a society as Thailand, workers were loath to challenge a social elite composed of Thais, not foreign colonialists.

With these limitations in mind there is, of course, a fledgling labour movement in Thailand. It is rooted to a large extent in the unions that formed in the country's SOEs. But because these unions were in the public sector, they really acted historically more as lobbyists for SOE workers than as conventional unions with an economic or political agenda challenging the status quo. Thai unions engaged in militant action and came into conflict with the government, but this has not been a pervasive mode of action as it has in some other Asian countries.

The historical context is important for understanding the current situation confronting Thai unions. The forces of globalization, so pervasive over the past decade or more, have clearly reduced an already weakened labour movement. Most significant has been the conflict over privatization of the SOEs, the stronghold of Thai unions. The privatization effort is clearly linked to globalization pressures and efforts by economic planners to make the Thai economy as open and free as possible. Of course, the profit potential of many of the SOEs is an inducement, as are the conditions imposed more recently by the IMF. Fearing the consequences of privatization, the SOE unions have staunchly opposed such moves. The military government of the early 1990s responded by effectively disbanding those unions. The restoration of democracy in 1992 did little to provide a reinvigoration of SOE unions. The elected government, closely aligned with the middle class responsible for Thailand's rapid development, has not been inclined to strengthen the unions, although the government has often claimed support for unionism. Also, SOE workers have traditionally been viewed as privileged, enjoying protected, relatively high paying jobs and facing limited demands for work performance. Indeed, in many people's minds, the SOE unions were an integral part of the corporatist complex, along with the military, that long curtailed democracy (Phongpaichit and Baker, 1997). Thus, the general public, including perhaps lower-level workers in the private sector who might benefit from trade union activity, has not been overly sympathetic to the plight of the SOE unions.

Ironically, however, the consensus of observers of organized labour in Thailand seems to be that the fate of the private sector unions is really linked to the SOE unions. Although private sector unions were not greatly restricted by the laws enacted by the NPKC, they would really require the resources of the SOE unions in order to gain any meaningful power. This is not unrecognized by the government, which is unwilling to undertake actions that would undercut the economy's competitiveness.

It seems fair to conclude then that globalization and deregulation (as manifested in Thailand largely through SOE privatization) have severely undercut the viability of the Thai labour movement. The country's continuing democratization seems unlikely to result in policies in the near future that will reinvigorate trade unions. However, the diminished strength of the unions does not seem to have had much impact on the typical worker, partly because unions have been generally weak in the private sector and partly because the SOE unions seemed to create a privileged elite within the workforce rather than extend effective representation to a large number of workers.

REFERENCES

Assavanonda, Anjira (1998) 'Study Details Effects of Globalization Here', *Bangkok Post*, 28 March.
Brown, Andrew, and Frenkel, Stephen (1993) 'Union Unevenness and Insecurity in Thailand', in Stephen Frenkel (ed.), *Organized Labour in the Asia-Pacific Region: A Comparative Study of Trade Unionism in Nine Countries*. Ithaca, NY: ILIR Press, pp. 82–107.
Chantaravitoon, Nikhom (1998) 'Labour in Dire Need of Guidance', *Bangkok Post*, 1 May.
Chantaravitoon, Nikhom and Vause, W. Gary (1994) *Thailand's Labour and Employment Law: A Practical Guide*. Bangkok: Manager Publishing.
Dunlop, John (1958) *Industrial Relations Systems*. New York: Henry Holt.
Hofstede, G. (1980) *Culture's Consequences: International Differences in Work-Related Values*. Beverly Hills: Sage.
Isarangkhun na Ayuthaya, Chirayu, and Taira, Koji (1977) 'The Organization and Behaviour of the Factory Work Force in Thailand', *The Developing Economies*, Vol. 15, No. 1, pp. 16–36.

Lawler, John J. (1990) *Unionization and Deunionization: Strategy, Tactics, and Outcomes*. Columbia: University of South Carolina Press.

Lawler, John J., Siengthai, Sununta and Atmiyananana, Vinita (1997) 'HRM in Thailand: Eroding Traditions', *Asia Pacific Business Review*, Vol. 3, No. 4, pp. 170–96.

Mabry, D.B. (1977) 'The Thai Labour Movement', *Asian Survey*, Vol. 17, No. 10, pp. 931–61.

Mabry, D.B. (1987) 'The Labour Movement and the Practice of Professional Management in Thailand', *Journal of Southeast Asian Studies*, Vol. 18, Sept., pp. 303–26.

Nontarit, Wut (1994) 'Leadership Problem Mars Labour Movement', *Bangkok Post*, 1 May.

Nontarit, Wut (1996) 'Labour Glimpses Light at End of the Tunnel', *Bangkok Post*, 1 May.

Phongpaichit, Pasuk and Baker, Chris (1997) *Thailand: Economy and Politics*. Oxford: Oxford University Press.

Phongpaichit, Pasuk and Baker, Chris (1998) *Thailand's Boom and Bust*. Bangkok: Silkworm Books.

Rowley, C. (1997) 'Reassessing HRM's Convergence', *Asia Pacific Business Review*, Vol. 3, No. 4, pp. 198–211.

Rowley, C. and Bae, J. (1998) 'Korean Business and Management: The End of the Model', *Asia Pacific Business Review*, Vol. 2, No. 3, pp. 130–9.

Rowley, C. and Lewis, M. (1996) 'Greater China at the Crossroads? Convergence, Culture, and Competitiveness', *Asia Pacific Business Review*, Vol. 2, No. 3, pp. 1–22.

Samakkitam, Somsak (1989) 'Short-Term Employment: The Analysis of Labour Movement in 1989', *Labour's Overview (Raeng-nagarn Paritat)*, Vol. 4, No. 3, pp. 4–7.

SarDesai, D.R. (1997) *Southeast Asia: Past and Present*. Boulder, CO: Westview Press.

Suttawet, Chokchai (1994) 'Industrial Relations Practices and Strategies: A Theoretical Construction for Thailand'. Doctoral Dissertation, Bielefeld University, Germany.

US Department of Labour (1988) *Foreign Labour Trends (Thailand) – 1988*. Washington: US Government Printing Office.

US Department of Labour (1992) *Foreign Labour Trends (Thailand) – 1991–92*. Washington: US Government Printing Office.

US Department of Labour (1995) *Foreign Labour Trends (Thailand) – 1994–95*. Washington: US Government Printing Office.

Vause, Gary (1992) 'Labour Relations in Thailand', *East Asian Executive* Reports, Vol. 14, No. 11, pp. 9–17.

Watana, Somkiet (1982) *The Evolution of the Thai Working Class: The Historical Structure of Labour for 200 Years*. Bangkok: Thai Khadi Suksa.

13

Globalization, Labour and the State: The Case of Indonesia

VEDI R. HADIZ

WORKERS AS A SOCIAL FORCE

The international development literature has lately emphasized the consequences of the growing internationalization of economic activity. In fact, it seems no longer possible to discuss developments within national politico-economic entities without reference to that ubiquitous term, 'globalization'. Often used as shorthand for a variety of complex developments in the economic, political and cultural spheres over the last few decades, it is most commonly associated with the growing internationalization of the processes of production and of finance. A central proposition has usually been the concomitant rapidly diminishing status and importance of national politico-economic entities.

Globalization, however, is a rather nebulous term about which there are some serious disagreements. Hirst and Thompson (1996: Chapter 1), for example, remain sceptical about the scope and novelty of economic globalization and the extent to which it has left national economies and states completely at the mercy of uncontrollable global market forces. Weiss (1997) argues that rather than being completely subordinated by these forces, some states actually have the capacity to effectively exploit opportunities presented by the process of economic globalization, pointing in particular to the case of East Asian states (before the current economic debacle). Petrella (1996: 28), on the other hand, argues that economic globalization is a new phenomenon, 'putting an end to the *national* economy and national capitalism as the most pertinent and effective basis for the organization and management and production of wealth'. He also contrasts globalization to internationalization, suggesting that the latter is an older process, merely referring to the 'ensemble of flows of exchanges' of raw materials, products, services and the like between nation-states. But it is Strange (1996) who perhaps most strongly argues that the process of economic globalization has caused the dramatic 'retreat of the state' in presiding over national economies and societies, in favour of non-state actors like international cartels.

Notwithstanding such debates, the consequences of globalization have clearly been profound for the state and, it is argued, for labour. It is not necessary to adopt the views of the most extreme proponents of the globalization thesis to recognize that the terrain on which established labour movements operate in advanced industrial countries, as well in as struggling ones in late industrializing countries like Indonesia, has been quite irrevocably reshaped. The enhanced mobility of capital greatly increases its power relative to more immobile labour forces and states. This has allowed international capital to successfully 'demand' favourable investment climates, thereby increasing pressure on states world wide to restrict the activities of organized labour (Beeson and Hadiz, 1997). In the advanced industrial countries, such developments have added pressure towards the unravelling of the welfare state, the great historical compromise between state, capital and labour, as labour increasingly becomes marginalized as a social and political force.

Offering a structural explanation for the decline in the global bargaining position of labour that focuses on the impact of capital mobility, Winters (1996: 195) argues that this decline will vary according to the mobility options of investors and employers:

> Hence, unions facing employers that can cross national jurisdictions with relative ease will feel the full force of devastation of capital's structural power. Those confronting investors that can relocate mainly across subnational lines will also be greatly weakened, though the prospect still exists of organizing out to the limits of the national boundary and pressuring employers with the strike option. Strongest of all are workers who confront highly immobile employers that have very little structural power at their disposal. They would include university employees, those working in city and state bureaucracies, transportation workers, and so on.

Commencing a reflective article on the plight of workers in the new global economy, Kapstein (1996: 16) writes that:

> The global economy is leaving millions of disaffected workers in its train. Inequality, unemployment, and endemic poverty have become its handmaidens. Rapid technological change and heightening international competition are fraying the job markets of the major industrialized countries. At the same time systemic pressures are curtailing every government's ability to respond with new spending. Just when working people most need the nation-state as a buffer from the world economy, it is abandoning them.
>
> This is not how things were supposed to work ... despite a continuing boom in international trade and finance, productivity has faltered, and inequality in the United States and unemployment in Europe have worsened.

Even Moody (1997: 13), who emphasizes the capacity of workers to strike back even in the most dire of circumstances, observes of recent decades that:

> Driven by its own intensified international competition, capital was demanding and winning more. Working class incomes were slumping almost everywhere. Life on the job was more dangerous and unhealthy than it had been for decades. Holding a job was more precarious. This last fact underlay the apparent passivity of the workers and their unions in most of the developed industrial nations that set in around the late 1970s and early 1980s.

We are not, however, concerned here to develop yet another thesis about the essential and irrevocable powerlessness of labour. Our analysis is informed by the recognition that workers and their organizations – in the advanced industrial countries, as well as late industrializing ones like Indonesia – are operating within an international context increasingly unfavourable to both, and that they have not found effective national or cross-national strategies to deal with this.

The effects of globalization on labour are clearly reflected in Indonesia, a country struggling to find a niche within the international division of labour as a production site for labour-intensive manufactures. In Indonesia, the development of an export-orientated manufacturing sector – driven for about a decade by huge inflows of foreign capital – has been the most crucial element of a broader effort to reduce the country's reliance on oil revenues. Notably, these foreign investors are amongst the most globally mobile, thereby rendering Indonesian manufacturing workers amongst the most globally vulnerable, according to Winters' scheme of things.

The enhanced bargaining position of capital has certainly served to further compromise the bargaining position of workers in labour-surplus economies like Indonesia, who already face great difficulties in developing effective labour movements. Although the relationship between the emergence of effective labour movements and the tightening of labour markets is more complex than often conceded by neoclassical economists, a chronic labour surplus condition commonly acts as a constraint on the potential power of organized labour.[1] In such a situation, someone less troublesome from the long unemployment line all too easily substitutes for the worker with an inclination to organize, thereby constraining the development of strong workers' organizations. It is not surprising that international investors operating in Indonesia are keen to reiterate that the country's attractiveness as a production site in part lies in the presence of a cheap (and generally unorganized) labour force.[2] Changes in these conditions, they suggest, could facilitate relocation decisions to such countries as Vietnam or China, and many others offering a cheap labour force and some measure of political stability.

Interestingly, globalization or the internationalization of economic activity was not always viewed as exerting a negative influence on the global bargaining position of labour. At one time, Levinson (1974) and others (for example, Labour Research Association, 1984) confidently asserted that it would usher in the objective conditions for greater international working class solidarity. A material base would be more or less created to strengthen labour's position *vis-à-vis* global capital. However, as Jenkins (1984) and Southall (1988: 18–20, 24–6) argue, the process has actually produced conditions equally conducive to greater rivalry between individual, national, working class movements. They point to the employment of protectionist strategies by unions in the advanced industrial countries to halt the relocation of jobs overseas, where labour is cheaper. This has in some ways reinforced the division of the global working class along national and even ethnic lines (see also Olle and Schoeller, 1987: 42–3).

There are, however, clearly some simultaneously contradictory tendencies at work, as employers and state in Indonesia have been confronted by increasing labour strife since the early 1990s. To their great consternation, workers – apparently oblivious to global developments – have strongly begun to demand higher pay, better work conditions and the recognition of the freedom to organize, as well as other labour rights.

The main contradiction lies in the fact that Indonesia's greater integration with the world economy through the export of light manufactures has spurred the steady growth of a larger, 'maturing' industrial workforce with a greater propensity to organize. Such a propensity has developed in spite of long established state mechanisms of labour control, usually legitimized in official discourse by reference to supposedly authentic Indonesian values. The latter is embodied in the state ideology *Pancasila*, that – according to this discourse – eschews any form of conflict in favour of harmony and cooperation in all areas of life. Although it is legally recognized, the exercise of the right to strike is thus frowned upon in official circles.[3] While labour remains severely constrained as an effective social force, the development of a slowly maturing working class as industrialization proceeded created some pressure for limited reforms, especially with regards to the officially stipulated minimum wage. Notably, much of the frustration of workers has been directed toward the ineffective FSPSI (*Federasi Serikat Pekerja Seluruh Indonesia*; Federation of All-Indonesia Workers' Union), the state-backed labour federation.

In spite of its now rather long standing nature, state policy makers have not yet offered an effective response to this growing labour unrest, thereby creating some anxiety about the longer-term affects on Indonesia's status as a prime investment site for light manufacturing industry. However, there remain few real indications that Indonesia's status as an attractive investment location for low wage manufactures is being eroded solely because of growing labour unrest or because of the resultant rise in wages (for example, Dhanani, 1992). Indonesian manufacturing labour is, for example, still amongst the cheapest in Asia, in spite of recent wage rises. Notably, the growth of labour productivity in the Indonesian manufacturing sector not only exceeded the real levels of income growth of workers over the period 1970–90, but also far outstripped that of other ASEAN countries.[4]

In the wider context, it is rather Indonesia's 'high-cost economy', stemming from inefficiencies and widespread corruption, that seems to pose a greater threat, as demonstrated in the loss of investor confidence following the Asian currency crisis beginning in 1997. There are signs, however, that limited reforms begun earlier in the decade to placate workers have not done much to significantly curb labour unrest. This contravenes the Indonesian government's obsession with stability and control and, thus, state officials have reverted to a strategy emphasizing repressive measures to keep workers in line.

A model of accommodation between state, capital and labour that would make possible Western-style trade unionism in Indonesia is not a result that can be realistically expected at present. Workers remain constrained as a social force, so there is little real incentive for the state, as well as employers, to replace strategies of repression and stringent control with those of negotiation or co-optation. The latter would necessitate fundamental concessions – for example, in the enforcement of the right to organize.

INDONESIA AND THE WORLD ECONOMY

Indonesia's greater integration with the world economy was spurred by the fall of international oil prices in the 1980s. This gave rise to more export-orientated economic development strategies that contrast sharply with earlier, import-substitution strategies made possible by abundant oil revenues. Thus, in spite of the continuing influence in the state bureaucracy of economic nationalist ideas of developing an autonomous national industrial base, the international neoliberal development orthodoxy became dominant in Indonesia because of pressures to adjust to the exigencies of the world economy (Chalmers and Hadiz, 1997: 139–41). Until recently, the *economic* benefits of taking part in the international economy were being almost universally lauded in Indonesia. It was only the shock of the recent Asian crisis, which saw a host of currencies suddenly tumble in value (including the rupiah), that gave rise to a growing sense that the fruits of globalization may be considerably less sweet than they have usually been presented.[5]

It was the fall of international oil prices in the 1980s that initially robbed the state of its most important source of revenue. In 1982, international oil prices fell from US$38 to $29 per barrel before collapsing to just $12 in 1986 (Robison, 1988: 66). Indeed, the oil sector's contribution to overall state revenue fell from a high of 62 per cent in 1981–82 to just 20 per cent in 1990 (Winters, 1996: 100). This made it impossible for the state to act any longer as a 'development engine' capable of insulating Indonesia from the demands of the world economy.

As mentioned earlier, a new, more outward looking approach was then adopted, an important part of which has been the drive to increase Indonesia's manufactured exports. The emphasis has been on labour-intensive industries such as textiles, garments and footwear. This strategy was quite successful. The value of Indonesia's non-oil exports increased from about US$6.5 billion in 1986 to almost $36.3 billion in 1996 (World Bank, 1997: 160). Significantly, Indonesia's perceived comparative advantage in low wage industries – flowing from the presence of a cheap and abundant labour force – helped to provide renewed legitimacy for Indonesia's stringent system of controls over organized labour, though its existence clearly pre-dates the export drive.

At the same time, the cultivation of Indonesia's attractiveness to foreign investors acquired greater importance. This offered a starkly different situation to that which existed during much of the oil boom period, when state officials seemed somewhat uninterested in creating incentives for foreign investment (Winters, 1996: 123–4). It is notable that much of the surge in foreign investment in the all-important light manufacturing sector over the last decade has been driven by the relocation of production facilities from the East Asian Newly industrialized economies (NIEs) because of the rise in labour costs in those countries (Thee, 1993: 434–60). Cumulative Korean foreign direct investment (FDI) in Indonesia between 1988 and 1993, for example, constituted 83 per cent of its total investment for the period 1967–93 (Shin and Lee, 1995: 188).

Overall, approved foreign investment increased from just US$2.9 billion in 1983 to nearly $40 billion in 1995. In particular, its value in the increasingly outward-looking manufacturing sector grew from

US$2.6 billion to almost $30.5 billion in the same period (World Bank, 1997: 189), again demonstrating the success of the strategy of integrating Indonesia more closely with the world economy.

In this context, growing labour unrest has been criticized by state officials for its potential to deter foreign direct investment. In reality, the investment decisions of internationally mobile capital are influenced by a number of considerations. In spite of past successes, one of the greatest disincentives to investing in Indonesia has been the country's reputation for high levels of bureaucratic red-tape, besides the presence of only weak infrastructural support in such areas as electricity and communications (see, for example, *Prospek*, 1991: 10, 34). It is also significant that the costs incurred while dealing with an inefficient, and often corrupt, bureaucracy have been presented by businesses, both foreign and domestic, as a justification for maintaining low wages. This has given rise to the idea that a trade-off is involved between welfare and corruption levels as workers in reality are subsidizing corrupt bureaucrats. Notably, in April 1997 (just before the Asian currency crisis), the Hong Kong based group Political and Economic Risk Consultancy (PERC) named Indonesia the most corrupt country in Asia (*Jakarta Post*, 22 September 1997).

SHAPING LABOUR RELATIONS

The framework of industrial relations in Indonesia is in many ways the product of political upheavals taking place after September 1965, essentially the culmination of a protracted struggle between the Indonesian Communist Party (PKI) and the military leadership for political dominance. It is thus inextricably related to the establishment of the New Order, representing the victory of a coalition of anti-PKI social forces (such as petty traders, the urban salaried, and rural landed interests) led by an army leadership under General Soeharto. These forces were opposed to the radical redistribution of economic and social power. SOBSI *(Sentral Organisasi Buruh Seluruh Indonesia*, the All-Indonesia Central Workers' Organization) – linked to the PKI – was destroyed along with the party during these upheavals. It was the largest union organization in Indonesia. General Soeharto himself eventually replaced the increasingly left-leaning President Soekarno at the helm of the country in 1968.

Relations between SOBSI and the military had become increasingly tense after 1957, when the army took control over the management of newly nationalized foreign companies. The army was also taking up major political and administrative positions in regions all over Indonesia, in the context of the martial law promulgated in response to emerging regional rebellions (Kahin, 1994: 207–8). SOBSI's interests, as the most radical of the trade union federations then in existence, grew to be diametrically opposed to that of an army leadership that had found a new vested interest in maintaining industrial peace as managers of state firms.[6] An informal alliance between the army and an array of non-communist trade unions gradually developed to try to curb SOBSI's influence over rank-and-file workers. The army also spawned its own self-styled labour organization, SOKSI (*Sentral Organisasi Karyawan Sosialis Indonesia*; the Central Organization of Socialist *Karyawan* of Indonesia) (Hawkins, 1963: 269).

The early years of the New Order were characterized in the labour field by state-initiated attempts to amalgamate the existing non-communist labour federations into one easily controllable, state-sanctioned organization. Although these labour organizations had assisted the army in its struggle against the communists, they found that they were too weak to bargain with the powerful military, which soon became the unchallenged centre of power. In 1973, an organization called the FBSI (*Federasi Buruh Seluruh Indonesia*; the All-Indonesia Labour Federation) was finally established to play this role after a couple of earlier experiments had faltered. In late 1974, the doctrine of Pancasila Labour Relations (later Pancasila Industrial Relations) was promulgated, which dismissed conflict between employer and employee as culturally unsuitable to Indonesia (Moertopo, 1975: 20), being the product of 'alien' liberal and/or Marxist philosophies. State initiatives to contain organized labour must be viewed in the wider context of its strategy of demobilizing and controlling society-based movements and groups for the purposes of ensuring political stability, especially given the PKI's past success in mobilizing workers and peasants.

Nevertheless, in the context of currency devaluations and recessionary economic trends in the late 1970s and early 1980s, a considerable amount of labour unrest somehow still took place in spite of the absence of an effective, independent trade union movement. The government's response was to transform the FBSI in 1985 into the even more centralized and hierarchical SPSI (*Serikat Pekerja Seluruh Indonesia*; the All-Indonesia Workers' Union), largely through the efforts of Minister of Manpower and former security chief, retired Admiral Sudomo. Throughout most of this time FBSI/SPSI officials actively took part in military-led security teams (also a Sudomo initiative) whose purpose was to prevent, discourage and repress strike action by workers (see Tanter, 1990). These teams seem to have undertaken their task quite successfully as labour unrest reached almost negligible levels by the late 1980s. Notably, Sudomo had taken up the reins of the Department of Manpower in 1983, as Indonesia was about to embark on a more outward-looking development strategy.

The later outbreak of labour unrest in the 1990s, however, encouraged Sudomo's successors as Minister, Cosmas Batubara (1988–93) and Abdul Latief (1993–98),[7] to undertake limited reforms in the labour area. They seemed to recognize that the employment of a strategy of sheer coercion was lately becoming counterproductive – as it frequently tended to radicalize workers. Importantly, these civilian ministers also had no influence with the state's security apparatus, so it was in their interests to try to enhance the role of such institutions as the Department of Manpower, over which they did have direct jurisdiction and control.

Under the direction of Batubara and then Latief, the SPSI, for example, was transformed yet again into the FSPSI, geared, on paper at least, to be more accommodating to the aspirations of the rank-and-file worker. The organization received a face-lift by the re-establishment of industrial-sector unions that would theoretically enjoy some measure of autonomy from its central body. This effectively nullified a previous Sudomo innovation: the establishment of the SPSI in 1985 under his direction had eliminated industrial-sector unions because they were seen by the former security chief to be less directly controllable.

The FSPSI, however, has merely taken over the role that was played by its 'predecessors', though its officials are keener to downplay any complicity with the activities of security-orientated institutions. The FSPSI (as did the SPSI and FBSI) 'represents' workers in a number of 'legal-formal' institutions, organized on a tripartite basis, which comprise Indonesia's formal industrial relations framework. For example, together with APINDO (*Asosiasi Pengusaha Indonesia*), the employers' association, it sits on such bodies as the Central and Regional Labour Disputes Resolution Committees (respectively called P4P and P4D) as well as in other tripartite bodies headed by a representative of the government.

While these bodies have formal jurisdiction over the labour area, in reality they have often had to take a back seat to local and national-level security/military organizations, especially in areas pertaining to conflict between workers and management. Especially in cases of labour disputes, the formal industrial relations institutions have often been superseded by a security/military apparatus with a tradition of involvement in labour affairs going back to the 1950s.

INDUSTRIALIZATION AND LABOUR UNREST

In recent years, the legitimacy of Indonesia's industrial relations framework has been challenged by the proliferation of independent, local community-based organizing vehicles. Many of these have operated in conjunction with labour-orientated non-government organizations (NGOs). The presence of such organizing vehicles directly challenges the idea of a sole state-sanctioned union federation, an instrument that has helped the state to exercise control over labour organizing down to the local level.

In 1990, efforts to establish an independent trade union organization were pioneered by the establishment of the now defunct SBM *Setiakawan* (*Serikat Buruh Merdeka Setiakawan*; the Solidarity Independent Workers' Union). Such efforts gained impetus with the establishment of the SBSI (*Serikat Buruh Sejahtera Indonesia*; the Indonesian Prosperous Workers' Union) formed in 1992 under the leadership of lawyer and activist Muchtar Pakpahan. The later establishment of a third union, the PPBI (*Pusat Perjuangan Buruh Indonesia*; Centre for Indonesian Working Class Struggle), demonstrated the existence of links between student and worker groups that suggested parallels with those that existed in South Korea (see, for example, AMRC, 1987; Ogle, 1990). In addition to these organizations, there remains a wide array of NGOs that have assisted in the development of local organizing vehicles by carrying out activities as diverse as promoting workers' education, cooperatives, and the establishment of training programmes and discussion groups.

In a recent book (Hadiz, 1997a), I argue that the contemporary upsurge of labour unrest in Indonesia is inextricably related to a process of sustained industrialization that has transformed the country's social and economic landscape and changed the way that increasingly large numbers of Indonesians experience everyday life. A new urban-based industrial working class has been developing, whose social and political sensibilities are being conditioned by the experience of life in the city and work in the factory.[8] Unlike their predecessors of two or three decades ago, the current generation of industrial workers regard their status as urban residents as more or less permanent, given the lack of availability of land, particularly in Java, which makes relocating permanently to the village both improbable and unattractive.[9] Thus, the contemporary urban worker – who is also typically younger and better educated – has been more inclined to be directly involved in the struggle to ensure better life and work conditions, now and for the future. For many, this has logically meant involvement in independent locally based organizing activities unrecognized by the state and viewed as troublesome by employers.

A large part of the growth of manufacturing employment in Indonesia over the last decade has been concentrated in only a few industrial centres, thus giving rise to new cramped urban *kampung* – essentially expansive slum areas around factories – where the majority of workers live. In 1990, according to White (1993: 131), 'the two regions of Jabotabek (Jakarta–Bogor–Tangerang–Bekasi) in West Java, together with Surabaya–Malang–Mojokerto–Gresik in East Java' were the sites of virtually two-fifths of manufacturing employment in Indonesia and over half of it in Java. Not surprisingly, a large proportion of industrial unrest in the 1990s took place in the industrial areas of Jabotabek, the location of the greatest concentration of export-orientated factories as well as the proliferation of new, more distinctly working class *kampung*. Nevertheless, labour unrest has also rocked industrial areas in East Java and North Sumatra. East Java was the site of the brutal kidnapping, torture and murder of a female labour leader, Marsinah, a case that did much to focus national and international attention on the abuse of labour rights in Indonesia (YLBHI,

1994a). Labour struggles in North Sumatra became especially prominent because of riots in the city of Medan in April 1994, which involved unprecedented mass action by an estimated 20,000–30,000 workers, and the clampdown on labour activists that followed, including the arrest and imprisonment of independent union leader Muchtar Pakpahan (YLBHI, 1994b).

The largest proportion of industrial unrest has involved cases having to do with demands for higher wages and better working conditions. Cases of unrest have also been triggered by worker demands for the establishment of workplace-level FSPSI units free from employer or government intervention, though often linked to the demand for an alternative union altogether. Still other cases have involved actions of solidarity for unfairly dismissed or maltreated colleagues. (See Table 1.)

TABLE 1

INDUSTRIAL ACTION

Year	1989	1991	1993	1996
Number of strikes	19	114	180	350

Sources: Various, including Manning (1993: 81), who quotes preceding official reports, and *Pulahta Setditjen Binawas*, Indonesian Department of Manpower (1996). The figures presented in such reports constitute very conservative estimates, as many strikes go unreported. Therefore, estimates have varied widely. One labour activist puts the number of strikes from 1989 to 1994 at 3,000 (Razif, 1994).

Although workers have made significant progress in organizing independently under difficult circumstances, the present economic crisis in Indonesia has the potential to make things even more arduous. The crisis, which threatens to wipe out many of the economic gains attained over the last three decades, has caused numerous factories to shut down due to dramatically rising production costs resulting from ever more expensive (in rupiah terms) imports of raw material and equipment. Workers are thus being dismissed in massive waves. Indeed, according to the Indonesian government 17 million workers were unemployed at the beginning of 1999, thus providing little incentive for those who still have full-time jobs to struggle for better wages and conditions or freedom to organize.

INTERNATIONAL PRESSURE AND LABOUR POLICY

If the rise of industrial action in the 1990s created domestic pressure for labour reform, the Indonesian government has also been forced to contend, from time to time, with increasing international criticism of its labour (and human rights) policies. It is important not to overstate the influence of such criticism in changing Indonesian government labour policy up to now. At times, however, international pressure has played an important role in winning, albeit temporarily, greater room for manoeuvre for independent labour activists. A good example of this was seen in 1993–94, when the threat emerged that Indonesia would be taken off the US list of countries receiving GSP (General System of Preferences) privileges.[10] The programme, enacted in 1974, provides duty-free entry to the US market of eligible products from beneficiary developing countries. The law governing it requires that such countries have taken or are taking steps to ensure internationally recognized labour rights.

It was especially the AFL-CIO, the American labour federation, that took the lead in applying pressure on the Indonesian government. In the late 1980s, it lodged petitions with the US Trade Representative's Office to have Indonesia removed from the list of countries receiving GSP facilities, alleging the infringement of international labour standards (American Embassy, 1994: 43). Though the GSP helped to raise Indonesian exports to the USA (despite not covering the import of garments or textiles), its real importance was more indirect. US investment levels could have been affected by the removal of the GSP facilities because American firms would no longer be covered under the so-called OPIC (Overseas Private Investment Corporation) scheme, whereby their operations in Indonesia are insured by the US government.

The AFL-CIO's actions were followed up in 1992, as two American NGOs filed separate petitions to the US Trade Representative for the elimination of Indonesia's GSP privileges.[11] In response, the USTR did order that Indonesia's GSP status be reviewed for non-compliance with international labour standards (*Far Eastern Economic Review*, 13 May 1993: 13).

It is important to emphasize that the criticism that has often emanated from such organizations as the AFL-CIO is not exclusively premised on 'lofty' ideas about international working class solidarity. Instead, it grew as much from domestic concern in the USA about employment security in the face of job relocation overseas, especially in the area of manufacturing. Nevertheless, this is what constitutes the 'material base' for international working class solidarity – linked to the internationalization of the process of production – however much more modest than that envisaged by such former sages as Levinson (1974).

In the end, however, the GSP threat did not even materialize, demonstrating the fickleness with which major world governments pursue human rights when economic or political interests are at stake. That virtually nothing came out of the extended period of threats probably demonstrated as well some of the limits to American organized labour's ability to influence the national agenda, even in a Democratic Party led USA.[12]

The most important policy reform that the Indonesian government has undertaken in response to growing labour unrest and international criticism has involved the periodic increase of the minimum wage. Between 1990 and 1997 the minimum wage in the Jakarta area, for example, virtually tripled (though in June 1997 – just before the Asian currency crisis – it still stood at less than US$2.50 per day). Significantly, these reforms were carried out in spite of business protests about the purported threat that rising wages pose to Indonesia's export competitiveness. Not surprisingly, the current economic crisis resulted in the temporary abandonment of this policy.

The issue of rising minimum wages has been linked to the highly charged issue of 'invisible costs' – unofficial funds which enterprises have to allocate to state officials at various levels to ensure the unhindered operations of business. Their prevalence significantly adds to the total cost of doing business in Indonesia, and indirectly serves to repress wages. Minister of Manpower Abdul Latief (1993–98) maintained that labour costs in the most labour-intensive of firms account for less than ten per cent of total production expenditure. Another 30 per cent, he said, are accounted for by bureaucracy-related costs (see *Forum Keadilan*, 25 March 1996: 95–9, 107).

Latief thus opted for the strategy of conceding some of the demands of workers that relate to pay, while largely ignoring those that relate to more politically problematic things like the freedom to organize. He was adamant that the policy of raising wages would not significantly increase production costs and affect Indonesia's global competitiveness in low wage manufacturing. The fact that labour unrest continued at levels that clearly troubled the government, however, is a good indication that the policy did not placate workers sufficiently.

Latief, himself a major industrialist, was not the first official to recognize the necessity of conceding some worker demands. Noting how Indonesia's 'image must be upheld in the world forum' (*Jakarta Post*, 31 August 1992), his immediate predecessor Cosmas Batubara (1988–93) argued that:

> If [Indonesia] wants to take part in globalization, we have to respect international labour standards, such as the right to organize, the right to bargain. If we do not follow international labour standards, our commodities will be blocked. We are often criticised by American workers, and then we tell them that the Indonesian government has taken action against businesses that do not pay the minimum wage (*Prisma*, 1992: 67).

In spite of this spirit of limited reformism and the concessions made by both Batubara and Latief, it is clear that a more repressive approach to handling labour problems was never completely abandoned. In fact, it may be ascendant again, after first making a comeback following the Medan riots, when security forces targeted the SBSI and local NGOs. Later, PPBI leaders were imprisoned as well.

A new Manpower Law sponsored by Latief in 1997 furnished more evidence that an approach veering once more towards the repressive was becoming ascendant. The law places severe restrictions on the exercise of the right to strike. On the basis of this law, workers are only permitted to protest within their own company compound, and 'sympathy strikes are thereby ruled out, leaving little room for trade union muscle-flexing at the national or industry level'. Moreover, under the new legislation, if workers fail to give written notice of a strike a week beforehand, they face such sanctions as six months' imprisonment or a fine of rupiah 50 million (*Far Eastern Economic Review*, 25 September 1997: 21). Even this, however, was an improvement over the heavily criticized originally proposed bill, stipulating that an individual could not incite colleagues to go on strike. That would have made the organizing of any legal strike action completely impossible, although the right to strike was nominally recognized (Hadiz, 1997b).

CONCLUSION:
GLOBALIZATION AND HISTORICAL TRAJECTORIES

Globalization and Indonesia's increased integration with the world economy have had contradictory effects on Indonesian labour. On the one hand, the declining bargaining position of labour, internationally, helps to ensure that the options available to Indonesian workers are considerably limited in terms of struggling for a favourable accommodation with capital and state. The fact that such existing accommodations, the product of struggles beginning in the nineteenth century, are themselves now being undermined makes the task of labour activists in Indonesia considerably more daunting. One only needs to note the numerous references to the breaking of post-Second World War deals with workers in the West (see, for example, Kapstein, 1996).

On the other hand, rapid industrialization and greater integration with the world economy ensured the slow development of a substantial urban-based industrial working class, whose aspirations now seem to be outgrowing the confines of the framework of state–capital–labour relations ushered in by the New Order. There is no other better explanation for the dramatic upsurge of labour unrest in Indonesia in the 1990s in spite of the absence of effective trade unions.

Labour unrest certainly sits very uncomfortably with the overriding concern with political stability and control that the New Order has displayed since its inception. It has arguably provided the starkest challenge to the state-propagated ideology that places so much emphasis on social harmony and rejects conflict as a matter of principle. At the same time, further labour reform is a process contingent on and deeply interrelated with any unravelling of the New Order's broader institutional framework. The idea that there is a relationship between changes in the labour field and broader social, political and institutional change is not an artificial one, given the political considerations that initially gave rise to and continue to underpin strict labour controls.

Even though the institutional framework is unravelling during the post-Soeharto period (with new unions being formed, for example), it is clear that Indonesian workers are on a different historical trajectory from their counterparts in the advanced industrial countries. The imminent flourishing of Western-type social democratic trade unionism is highly unlikely – in spite of notions currently in vogue about the automatic relationship between globalization and the diffusion of social and political freedoms, worldwide. A possible scenario, if Indonesia rebounds from the current economic crisis, is one of prolonged tension, in which workers fail to make rapid progress in such areas as enforcing labour rights, but in which the state is also incapable of stamping out independent organizing altogether.

On the other hand, if trade unions continue their steep decline in some parts of Europe, North America and Australia, their workers could well see privileges hard-won in previous struggles eliminated. Clearly, the process of globalization is intricately related to this decline. Indeed, if trade unions become as redundant as envisaged by some prophets of 'post-industrial' society, workers in such countries may see a part of their future reflected in the conditions prevailing in industrializing countries like Indonesia – where organized labour has traditionally been weak – rather than the other way around.

Workers have certainly not stood still throughout all of this. Moody (1997), for example, argues that the 1990s have witnessed an upsurge of worker unrest, globally. He points to successful strike action in France, South Korea and other countries. In these episodes, he sees great hope for the future. While we should not be dismissive of worker attempts, anywhere, to actively respond to their restrictive environments, the evidence offered is somewhat too patchy to be convincing or genuinely encouraging. There is much more for workers of the world to do in forging an effective strategy to ensure that labour remains a vital force in the context of a globalizing world.

NOTES

1. Nevertheless, it must be remembered that Luddism and Chartism developed in nineteenth century Britain in the context of acute unemployment. Also, that economic insecurity provided 'the mainstay of support for the German Communist Party (KPD) between the wars' (Geary, 1981: 16), and that fairly strong and influential labour movements emerged in the first half of this century in some Latin American countries in the context of unfavourable labour market conditions.
2. Nike CEO Phil Night is quoted as remarking that: 'there were thousands of Indonesians

lined up outside the factory gates, waiting for jobs', in answer to questions about subsistence wages paid to Nike production workers (*Nike in Indonesia*, 1995).

3. I have heard at least two representatives of business interests in Australia speak approvingly of so-called Pancasila Industrial Relations, going as far to suggest that much of it should be adopted by Australia. As in many advanced industrial countries, trade unions (as well as the welfare state) have been under siege in Australia. Pancasila, the Five Principles, refers to Belief in One God, Humanitarianism, Indonesian Unity, Consultative Democracy, and Social Justice.

4. Indonesian manufacturing workers were paid US$0.28 per hour in 1993, compared to $0.71 in Thailand, $1.80 in Malaysia, $0.68 in the Philippines and $0.54 dollars in China (*Kompas*, 1994, citing Morgan Stanley Research). Productivity growth in manufacturing in Indonesia also outstripped that of Thailand and the Philippines, where similar data are available for the same period (World Bank, 1993: 251–2). Indonesian workers are now paid a fraction of the 1993 amount given the currency's (rupiah) recent free-fall.

5. The rupiah's value fell 30 to 40 per cent against the US dollar within several months of the crisis that began in July 1997, initiated by fall of the Thai baht. It was only after an emergency aid package led by the International Monetary Fund was arranged that the rupiah began to stabilize (*Jakarta Post*, 6 November 1997). But this was only short lived. The rupiah plummeted badly again and had lost 70 to 80 per cent of its former value by early 1998.

6. SOBSI claimed a membership of more than 2.7 million workers in 1958. Total trade union *claimed* membership was then just under 5.7 million (Hawkins, 1963: 260).

7. Latief was replaced as Minister by a professional politician, Theo Sambuaga, in 1998, while he moved to another cabinet post.

8. At the beginning of the New Order, manufacturing accounted for a mere eight per cent of Indonesia's GDP (Hill, 1994: 57). However, this changed quite dramatically after the fall of international oil prices. Although manufacturing only contributed 12.2 per cent of GDP in 1981, it had contributed 24 per cent by 1995 (World Bank, 1996: 139). In 1993, the export of manufactured products already accounted for over half of total exports (World Bank, 1995: 190). Manufacturing employment gradually expanded at the same time. In 1971 there were only 2.7 million employed in the manufacturing sector, representing 6.5 per cent of the labour force. In 1995, there were 10.1 million people employed in this sector, representing 12.6 per cent of the workforce (World Bank, 1997: 153). In 1991, three million of them worked in firms classified as large and medium scale (BPS, 1993: 307).

9. See Hanagan's (1986) discussion of the importance of workers' perception of the permanence of their urban situation to the rise of labour protest in a European context.

10. This is the elaboration provided by the GSP Information Center (1993: 1).

11. These were Asiawatch and the International Labour Rights Education and Research Fund.

12. Indonesia was due to host an APEC summit meeting in November 1994. Indicative of Indonesian government confidence in the importance of APEC's success to the USA and other countries (such as Australia) is the fact that SBSI leader Pakpahan received his original gaol sentencing in the same month that world leaders, including US President Clinton, were present in Indonesia.

REFERENCES

American Embassy (1994) 'Labour Trends in Indonesia'. Unpublished report, Jakarta.

Asia Monitor Research Center (1987) Minju No-Jo, *South Korea's New Trade Unions: The Struggle for Free Trade Unions*. Hong Kong.

Beeson, Mark and Hadiz, Vedi (1997) 'Globalisation and Labour: The Politics of Structural Adjustment in Australia and Indonesia', in G. Crowder, H. Manning, D.S. Mathieson, A. Parkin and L. Seabrooke (eds), *Australasian Political Studies 1997*. Proceedings of the 1997 APSA Conference, Vol. 1. Department of Politics, Flinders University of South Australia, pp. 43–63.

BPS (Biro Pusat Statistik) (1993) *Statistik Indonesia*. Jakarta.

Chalmers, Ian and Hadiz, Vedi R. (eds) (1997) *The Politics of Economic Development in Indonesia: Contending Perspectives*. London: Routledge.

Dhanani, Shafiq (1992) 'Estimating Informal Sector Employment and Incomes in Indonesia', Bappenas/RMPT, Technical Report No. 1. Jakarta.

Far Eastern Economic Review, 13 May 1993, 13 May 1996 and 25 Sept. 1997.

Forum Keadilan (1996) 25 March.

Geary, Dick (1981) *European Labour Protest, 1848–1939*. New York: St Martin's Press.

GSP Information Center (1993) *GSP Subcommittee of the Trade Policy Staff Committee 1992 GSP Annual Review: Worker Rights Review Summary, Case 007-CP-92, Indonesia*. Washington, July.

Hadiz, Vedi R. (1997a) *Workers and the State in New Order Indonesia*. London: Routledge.

Hadiz, Vedi R. (1997b) 'RUU Ketenagakerjaan: Pantas Meresahkan Buruh', in Komisi Pembaharuan Hukum Perburuhan, *RUU Ketenagakerjaan: Pantas Meresahkan Buruh*, Jakarta.

Hanagan, Michael (1986) 'Agriculture and Industry in the Nineteenth Century Stephanois: Household Employment Patterns and the Rise of a Permanent Proletariat', in Michael Hanagan and Charles Stephenson (eds), *Proletarians and Protest: The Roots of Class Formation in an Industrializing World*. New York: Greenwood Press.

Hawkins, Everett D. (1963) 'Labour in Transition', in Ruth McVey (ed.), *Indonesia*. New Haven, CT: Yale University Press.

Hill, Hal (1994) 'The Economy', in Hal Hill (ed.), *Indonesia's New Order: The Dynamics of Socio-Economic Transformation*. St Leonards: Allen and Unwin.

Hirst, Paul and Thompson, Grahame (1996) *Globalization in Question: The International Economy and the Possibilities of Governance*. Cambridge: Polity Press.

Indonesian Documentation and Information Center (1981) *Indonesian Workers and their Right to Organize*. Leiden.

Jakarta Post 31 August 1992, 4 February 1994, 19 February 1995, 22 September 1997 and 6 November 1997.

Jenkins, Rhys (1984) 'Divisions over the International Division of Labour', *Capital and Class*, Vol. 22 pp. 28–57.

Kahin, Audrey (1994) 'Regionalism and Decentralisation', in David Bourchier and John Legge (eds), *Democracy in Indonesia, 1950s and 1990s*, Monash Papers on Southeast Asia, No. 31. Clayton: Center for Southeast Asian Studies, Monash University.

Kapstein, Ethan B. (1996) 'Workers and the World Economy', *Foreign Affairs*, May–June pp. 16–37.

Kompas (1994) 23 June.

Labour Research Association (1984) *Labour Confronts the Transnationals*. New York: International Publishers.

Levinson, Charles (1974) *International Trade Unionism*. London: Allen and Unwin.

Manning, Chris (1993) 'Structural Change and Industrial Relations during the Soeharto Period: An Approaching Crisis', *Bulletin of Indonesian Economic Studies*, Vol. 29, No. 2, pp. 59–95.

Moertopo, Ali (1975) *Buruh dan Tani Dalam Pembangunan*. Jakarta: Center for Strategic and International Studies.

Moody, Kim (1997) *Workers in a Lean World: Unions in the International Economy*. London: Verso.

Nike in Indonesia (1995), Vol. 1, No. 2, Feb.

Ogle, George E. (1990) *South Korea: Dissent within the Economic Miracle*. London: Zed Books.

Olle, Werner and Schoeller, Wolfgang (1987) 'World Market Competition and Restrictions upon International Trade Policies', in Rosalind E. Boyd, Robin Cohen and Peter C.W. Gutkind (eds)', *International Labour and the Third World*. Aldershot: Avebury.

Petrella, Riccardo (1996) 'Globalization and Internationalization: The Dynamics of the Emerging World Order', in Robert Boyer and Daniel Drache (eds), *States against Markets: The Limits of Globalization*. London: Routledge.

Prisma (1992) Interview with Cosmas Batubara, No. 3.

Prospek (1991) 21 Sept.

Pulahta Setditjen Binawas, Indonesian Department of Manpower (1996) 'Data Perkembangan Pemogokan/Unjuk Rasa 1996'. Jakarta, Dec.

Razif (1994) 'Sejarah Pemikiran Serikat Buruh Indonesia'. Unpublished paper.

Robison, Richard (1988) 'Authoritarian States, Capital-Owning Classes and the Politics of Newly Industrializing Countries: The Case of Indonesia', *World Politics*, Vol. 41, Oct., pp. 52–74.

Shin, Yoon-Hwan and You-il Lee (1995) 'Korean Direct Investment in Southeast Asia', *Journal of Contemporary Asia*, Vol. 25, No. 2, pp. 179–96.

Southall, Roger (1988) 'Introduction', in Roger Southall (ed.), *Trade Unions and the New Industrialization of the Third World*. London: Zed Books.

Strange, Susan (1996) *The Retreat of the State*. Cambridge: Cambridge University Press.

Tanter, Richard (1990) 'The Totalitarian Ambition: Intelligence and Security Agencies in Indonesia', in Arief Budiman (ed.), *State and Civil Society in Indonesia*, Monash Papers on Southeast Asia, No. 22. Clayton: Center of Southeast Asian Studies, Monash University.

Thee, Kian Wie (1993) 'Foreign Investment and the ASEAN Economies with Special Reference to Indonesia', *Indonesian Quarterly*, Vol. 21, No. 4, pp. 434–60.

Weiss, Linda (1997) 'The Myth of the Powerless State', *New Left Review*, 225, pp. 3–27.

White, Benjamin (1993) 'Industrial Workers in West Java's Urban Fringe', in Chris Manning and Joan Hardjono (eds), *Labour: Sharing in the Benefits of Growth?* Canberra: Department of Political and Social Change, Research School of Pacific Studies, Australian National University.

Winters, Jeffrey (1996) *Power in Motion: Capital Mobility and the Indonesian State*. Ithaca: Cornell University Press.

World Bank (1993) *World Development Report 1993: Investing in Health*. New York: Oxford University Press.

World Bank (1995) *World Development Report 1995: Workers in an Integrating World*. New York: Oxford University Press.

World Bank (1996) Indonesia: Dimensions of Growth, Report no. 15383–ND, 7 May.

World Bank (1997) *Indonesia: Sustaining High Growth with Equity*, Report no. 16433-IND, Country Department III, East Asia and Pacific Region, 30 May.

YLBHI (Yayasan Lembaga Bantuan Hukum Indonesia) (1994a) *Laporan Pendahuluan Kasus Pembunuhan Marsinah*, Fact-finding Team, March.

YLBHI (Yayasan Lembaga Bantuan Hukum Indonesia) (1994b) *Indonesian Labour News: Repression and Violence against Labour Continues*. Jakarta.

14

Globalization, China's Free (Read Bonded) Labour Market, and the Chinese Trade Unions

ANITA CHAN

Once largely cut off in the days of Mao from the world's capitalist economy, in the two decades since the 1970s China has out-competed all of its Asian neighbours in attracting foreign direct investment (FDI), becoming the world's second largest recipient of FDI after the United States. Formerly largely self-reliant, China has become a huge exporter of labour-intensive consumer goods. Many reasons account for the scale and speed at which China has obtained investment capital and penetrated international export markets. One that is frequently cited is that Chinese labour is cheap compared to most of its East and South-East Asian neighbours.[1] From an almost complete absence of a labour market two decades ago – when factory jobs were strictly allocated by the authorities – China now has a relatively flexible labour market. It also has a geographically mobile labour force, an estimated 'floating population' of at least 70 million rural people on the move all over the country in search of urban jobs (Beja, 1996). This abundant supply of cheap labour will help ensure that China remains internationally competitive for some years to come.

Manufacturers from elsewhere in Asia who have established factories in Southern China repeatedly assert that if labour costs and work conditions cannot be kept strictly in line, they will move their facilities to Vietnam or Indonesia (Chan, 1998a). Their joint venture partners in China normally are local government bodies, who find it in their own interests to try to sustain a profitable environment for the firms. They have become willing participants in an effort to keep a lid on the wages and conditions of labour of the migrant workers who have flooded into Southern China from poorer inland provinces in search of work. This part of the new labour market has been placed at the service of the forces of globalization. The local authorities' capacity to provide this has been enhanced by decentral-ization of the political system, level by level – to the province, city, county, township, village and down to the workplace (Zweig, 1995).

Despite this decentralization, the central government has attempted to keep pace with China's rapid economic transformation by issuing Party *fiats* and by enacting a large number of laws over the past decade. However, these high-level efforts have often been given a local twist or ignored. As far as labour–management relations are concerned, as will be seen in the following pages, a deregulated situation has often led to abusive management practices, deteriorating labour standards and violations of labour laws. These malpractices first appeared in the foreign-funded sector, predominantly in the firms established by investors from Hong Kong, Taiwan and Korea. These are concentrated in the coastal provinces, and in a ripple effect, their management techniques have spread to the inland regions and into the state sector.

Various scholars have described how China's economic reforms have affected Chinese enterprises and, in turn, workers (O'Leary, 1992; Ng and Ip, 1994; Warner, 1996; Zhu and Campbell, 1996; Leung, 1997). This contribution will focus on how globalization and a deregulated economic situation affect China's 'free' labour market and conditions of work. It will also examine the Chinese unions' attempts to adjust to the new developments in this 'free' labour market.

'Free' is deliberately put in inverted commas because the thrust of my argument is that the Chinese labour market introduced by the economic reforms is 'free' only in a superficial way. To be sure, most workers are no longer constrained by the Maoist system of allocating people to jobs under a planned command economy. Yet, large numbers of people today are constrained instead in the sense that they have become bonded labour. As shall be observed, two separate types of bonded labour have emerged in China: one in the non-state sector (especially in many of the labour-intensive foreign-funded joint ventures) and another in the state-owned industries.

THE 'FREE' LABOUR MARKET AND BONDED LABOUR

Bonded Labour in the Non-State Sector

Very large numbers of peasant migrants from China's poorer

interior provinces fill most of the production-line positions in the factories that have sprouted in the coastal regions. For example, in the industrially booming delta region of Guangdong in Southern China, about 90 per cent of production line workers are migrants.[2] In the less developed regions where locals are still willing to work at very low wages they work alongside such migrants on production lines.[3] But China's household registration (*hukou*) system ensures that the large numbers of migrant workers do not enjoy the same status as the local residents (Mallee, 1995: 1–29). For social control purposes, the central government during the Maoist period curtailed geographic mobility through this system, in particular controlling rural–urban migration. Even today, the household registration system acts as a 'sluice gate' regulating the rural–urban flow. It allows more workers into the economic zones and economically booming areas when they are needed and drives them out when infrastructure becomes stretched to the limit or when economic recessions strike. Their residential status is similar to that of foreign 'guest workers' subject to tight 'immigration' controls. To leave their villages peasants are required to apply for a permit from their local government. To stay in any other district they have to apply to the local police station for a temporary residential permit. When they are offered employment they need to secure a contract with an employer, and their application to work then has to be approved by the local labour bureau, which issues a work permit. Periodically, the police carry out raids to round up those who do not possess the temporary residential and work permits (Zhao, 1996: 42–6). Those caught are harassed, humiliated and mistreated, thrown into detention centres and then deported from the cities.

Most of those who are allowed to stay live in crowded dormitories provided by the factories, or in shanties. They are not entitled to any of the benefits enjoyed by local residents, such as social welfare, nor may they bring their spouses or children with them.[4] Once their labour is no longer required they are supposed to go back to their place of origin.[5] Socially, they are discriminated against by local residents (Chan *et al.*, 1992: 299–308). In the face of all of these impediments, their work experience is precarious and exploitative (see, for example, Gao, 1994; Solinger, 1998).

The household registration system provides fertile conditions for the creation of a system of forced and bonded labour. For a start, workers are required to buy their temporary work permit in one lump sum. In places where the cost of the permit is too high for the migrants to afford, the factory often pays for it on behalf of the worker as an advance, thereby immediately trapping the worker in a bonded relationship.[6] In a buyers' labour market, the factories dictate the terms of employment. They often charge a 'deposit' (*yajin*) that normally varies from a week's to a fortnight's wages, further bonding the workers (Wang, 1998: 474). Workers forfeit the deposit if they are fired or if they quit without management permission before the contract expires. So even if the working conditions at some particular plant are poor and physically abusive, migrant workers who cannot afford to lose this money feel a need to continue to work there until their contract expires.

The above findings are based not only upon official documentation from China, but also five years of documentary research and fieldwork visits to factories in a large variety of industries. To supplement interviewing, in 1996 a detailed questionnaire survey was carried out in one industry – footwear. Questionnaires were filled out by a total of 1,531 workers and staff in 54 footwear factories in five cities spread across China. Because the foreign-funded part of the footwear industry is heavily dominated by Asian investors, predominantly Taiwanese, Hong Kong and Korean firms, all 30 of the foreign-invested factories in the survey involve Asian partners. Of these, 13 are largely owned and managed by Taiwanese, seven by Hong Kong Chinese, and one by a Vietnamese of Chinese ethnic origin. This reflects the overall pattern of foreign direct investment in labour-intensive industries in China. Indeed, 50 per cent of all of the FDI in China derives from Hong Kong and Taiwan (*Zhongguo laodong tongji nianjian 1997*: 353). The percentage of Taiwanese enterprises is higher in this sample because Taiwanese firms are the biggest suppliers of footwear in the world. The foreign-invested footwear joint ventures were divided into two categories: those that are actually managed by mainland Chinese managers and those that are directly managed on-site by 'foreigners'; that is, by overseas Chinese from Taiwan and Hong Kong. (There are no Korean factories in the sample because these factories denied access to the survey.)[7]

Based on the survey, 58.6 per cent of the migrants among the production line workers were obliged to pay deposits, as opposed to 20.4 per cent of the non-migrant workers. As seen, too, in Figure

1, a far higher percentage of the production-line workers in the foreign joint-venture firms and private Chinese firms than in the state and collective sectors, needed to pay such bonds.

FIGURE 1

PERCENTAGE OF PRODUCTION-LINE WORKERS WHO PAID DEPOSITS, BY OWNERSHIP/MANAGEMENT TYPE

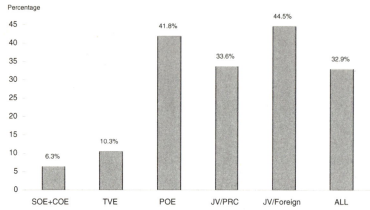

Key: SOE + COE : State-owned enterprises and collective-owned urban enterprises;
TVE: Collective township and village enterprises;
POE: Privately-owned enterprises;
JV/PRC: Joint ventures, with managers from the People's Republic of China;
JV/Foreign: Joint ventures, with foreign managers

Interviews and documentation reveal that very often the joint-venture factories pay workers irregularly, or systematically withhold a portion of each pay period as a further means to bond labour (Asia Monitor Resource Centre, 1995a: 14).[8] In some cases, when management is short of operating funds, workers do not get paid for some months. Under such circumstances, workers still have to continue to work in the hope that they will get back the money owed to them. In some cases, too, the factory management collects the workers' residential permits and identity papers for 'safekeeping', a practice that is illegal. Without the permit, workers cannot go onto the streets without becoming vulnerable to a police identity check, still less quit to go back to their home village or to find another job. Once workers are bonded by any of the methods described above, the factories can be assured of a low turnover in their workforce, even when workers are physically abused (Chan, 1998c).[9]

The system stacks all of the odds against the workers. Taking advantage of this, a common practice is to pay them illegally low wages. In the early 1990s, the government established a minimum wage system that required local governments to compute a local minimum wage standard based on the cost of living for the area under their jurisdiction (*China News Analysis*, 1995: 1–4). Yet, many Asian-invested enterprises and Chinese domestic private enterprises pay workers below the local monthly minimum legal wage, or pay them just up to the minimum monthly wage by including in the figures a large amount of overtime work (*Laodong daobao*, 19 August 1995). Table 1 shows that workers at the foreign joint-venture footwear firms normally work 11 hours a day, whereas workers in the state and collective-run footwear factories keep to the legal eight-hour workday. Working two or three hours of overtime on a normal workday, with only one or two days off every month, is commonplace at the Asian foreign-funded firms. In 1996, in the shoe manufacturing city of Putian in Fujian province, local trade union officials were proud that they finally had been able to get the foreign-funded factories (mainly Taiwanese) to agree to grant workers at least two days off a month.[10] This local trade union effort in fact breaches China's Labour Law, which stipulates not more than 36 hours of overtime a month and at least one day off a week.

TABLE 1

AVERAGE NORMAL WORKING HOURS OF PRODUCTION LINE WORKERS AT FOOTWEAR FACTORIES, BY *DE FACTO* OWNERSHIP/MANAGEMENT TYPE
(N=56)

	SOV+COE	TVE	POE	JV/PRC	JV/Foreign
Maximum	12	8	16	16	16
Minimum	7	8	7	6	6
Mean	8	8	10	9	11

To top it all, the wage system is usually constructed around a structure of rigid penalties, deductions and fines. Factories devise their own sets of arbitrary rules and regulations in open breach of national Labour Law. Workers caught in violation of such rules will be fined. Fines are meted out for being late, or for not turning up because of illness, or for negligence at work. The penalties can also be for behaviour not related to production: fines for talking and laughing at work, for littering, for forgetting to turn off lights in factory dormitory rooms, for untidy dormitories, and so on. (*Zhuhai laodong bao*, 19 May 1995).[11] That is to say, some of the labour that a worker has performed during the month can be left unpaid, because of a multitude of deductions. This system of monetary penalties induces great anxiety and uncertainty among workers.

As a further mechanism for controlling workers, the use of private security guards in factory and dormitory compounds is very common. Companies that supply private security guards are often connected to the local police and employ off-duty officers. Guards normally carry electric batons and handcuffs, which are freely available on China's domestic arms market. The internal security system set up behind factory walls is extremely effective in intimidating and controlling workers, especially since it can be augmented by off-duty police through a simple switch of uniforms. Even the official government public relations magazine for foreigners, *Beijing Review*, admits to an excessive use of police force: 'The problem is that the public security police, for their own reasons, the moment there is an incident, send policemen in to intervene in labour disputes, thus aggravating industrial relations.'[12]

In this atmosphere of intimidation, some factories can get away with meting out physical punishment. In several years of sifting through Chinese documentation no report was found of any serious abuses of workers in the factories operated by direct investors from Japan or Western countries.[13] Overall, the Chinese documentation gives an impression that, in contrast, the Taiwanese and Korean management styles are often harsh. Hitting workers for being slow or for making defective products is relatively commonplace at some of these factories (Hsing, 1998:104). To cite just one case among many, several Chinese newspaper reporters posing as migrants went to work in a Taiwanese-managed footwear factory in Guangzhou. The Taiwanese manager routinely, on a daily basis, meted out physical punishment to the 'bonded' workers and production-line team leaders (*Yangcheng wanbao*, 30 August 1997; for an English translation see Chan, 2000).

In my survey, 24 per cent of the production-line footwear workers report that physical punishment exists in their factories, and of these, the percentage is highest for foreign joint ventures: 27 per cent of the joint ventures run by foreign managers and 26 per cent of those run by mainland Chinese managers (Figure 2). The survey also shows unexpected results – that physical punishment also exists in state and collectively owned factories. There were very few such reports from the early days of the reforms. Even in the state sector, the low-skill footwear industry has begun to employ migrant workers, and this new evidence appears to reflect a transfer of the harsh labour regime of the foreign Asian managers to the mainland state and collective sectors.

FIGURE 2

EXISTENCE OF PHYSICAL PUNISHMENT AS REPORTED BY WORKERS, BY OWNERSHIP/MANAGEMENT TYPE

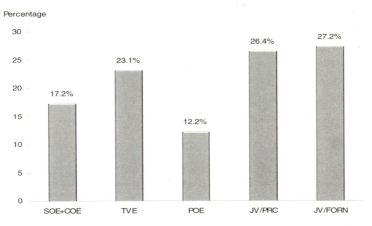

FIGURE 3

RESTRICTIONS ON TOILET-GOING BY OWNERSHIP/MANAGEMENT TYPE

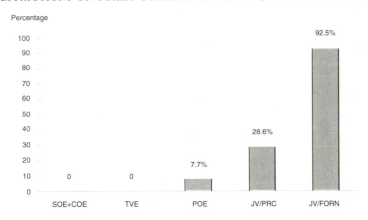

In this atmosphere of intimidation, some joint ventures can even get away with imposing strict rules to control workers' bodily functions by drastically restricting the frequency and length of time

allowed for going to the toilet (in an extreme case, workers at one factory who go to the toilet more than twice in a day are fined Y60, more than two days' wages). As seen in Figure 3, a full 92 per cent of the production-line workers in the foreign joint ventures under foreign management report that there are restrictions against relieving themselves, compared with no such restrictions at all for workers at the state and collective factories.

Of all labour rights violations, the worst involve occupational health and safety (*China Labour Bulletin*, 1995; Shuman, 1996: 50–4; *Exchange*, 1997).[14] The footwear industry, for example, commonly uses toxic glues in poorly ventilated workplaces (Chen and Chan, forthcoming). In the 20-plus footwear factories personally visited, none provided the workers who handle toxic adhesives with effective protective gloves and masks.[15]

The Emergence of 'Bonded' Labour in the State Sector

To supporters of China's economic reforms, the freeing of the labour market since the Maoist era is a cause for celebration. The absence of a labour market in China under the centralized, rigid Maoist planned economy had been an obstacle to the efficient use of human resources and adversely affected economic development. Nationwide, all state-factory employees were paid on an eight-scale seniority-based wage system, thus stifling work incentives. The industrial labour force also was not free in the sense that urban jobs were allocated under the Ministry of Labour, mostly on the basis of political credentials and perceived loyalty to the Chinese Communist Party rather than for professional or technical merit. Work units did not have much say in recruiting the most appropriately qualified employees, and individuals had almost no choice as to where they worked. Once assigned to a work unit, one basically had lifetime employment. Job mobility was extremely low. From the perspective of the work unit and the individual there was no free choice.

The Dengist reforms enormously affected the conditions of urban workers. The macroeconomic and enterprise reform programmes involved entering the global economy; raising productivity in the state sector by reforming management practices; forcing state-owned enterprises to be responsible for their own profits and losses; reducing excess labour in the state-owned enterprises; gradually instituting a contract system in place of lifetime employment; reductions in state workers' benefits; a widening of the wage gap; and separation of a factory's Party organ from administration by vesting the enterprise manager with greater power. On the shop floor, work discipline has been tightened, and welfare socialism can no longer be taken for granted by the workers. At the same time, termination of the lifetime employment system has ushered in a labour market in which state-sector industrial wages increasingly are set by free-market mechanisms. Workplaces can freely recruit employees, and people can seek jobs by themselves. However, this shift has been occurring at a time of narrowing opportunities for state-sector workers. In order to compete with the non-state sector, the state sector progressively has been laying off its bloated workforce to maintain economic viability (*Zhongguo laodong bao*, 3 July 1996; *Gongren ribao*, 11 August 1997).

However, the Chinese government could only implement this downsizing cautiously for fear of social instability. During the 1989 Tiananmen protest movement, the workers' message to the government was clear: they should not be sacrificed to the economic reforms (Walder and Gong, 1993). Nevertheless, in the 1990s the government renewed its attempt to rid state enterprises of excess workers. The government was determined to press for growing numbers of bankruptcies, especially since the proportion of money-losing state enterprises continued to climb from about 30 per cent in the 1980s to 41 per cent by 1995 and 75 per cent in 1996 (*Japan Economic Newswire*, 27 October 1994; *Zhongguo tongji*, No. 1, 1996; *Nanfang gongbao*, 29 April 1997). By 1995 the number of officially registered unemployed reached five million, and workers who had been instructed to stay at home on partial or no pay had reached another 20 million. This latter figure amounted to about 18 per cent of the 109 million state-sector employees (out of a total of 148 million urban employees) (*Gongren ribao*, 30 November 1995). In addition, the pensions of 30 million urban retirees have not kept up with inflation, and some have not been receiving any of their pensions at all (*Gongren ribao*, 7 March 1996). According to a 1996 report in the *Workers' Daily,* the number of staff and employees in financial difficulties reached more than 15 million, or ten per cent of the total urban workforce. Of these, about nine million employees and their dependents lived below the Chinese poverty line: 'The number of people affected is large and their situation is deteriorating' (*Gongren ribao*, 13 March 1996). The dissatisfaction of state-enterprise workers and retirees worries the political leadership as potential sources of social instability.

Still, without sufficient funds in the state coffers to prop up loss-making state enterprises, the Party declared at the 15th Party Congress in October 1997 that the reforms would be 'deepened', which is to say ownership restructuring, privatization and bankruptcies in the state sector will throw even larger numbers of workers onto the streets. For example, in the first half of 1998, 400,000 textile workers were laid off (*China Daily*, 22 July 1998).

In these circumstances, the inexhaustible buyers' market of cheap migrant labour is exacerbating the difficulties faced by the core labour force in China's state-owned factories. For several decades, workers have enjoyed a steady monthly income and fringe benefits such as subsidized flats and health care, and that makes them more expensive to employ than the young unmarried workers flooding in from the poorest rural regions of China. Even with the household registration system, decentralization of decision-making powers to enterprise management has led to unregulated labour practices. Faced with stiff competition from the non-state sector, state and collective factories have been bypassing regulations or taking advantage of loopholes to replace part of their permanent workforce with these migrant workers (Solinger, 1995, 1998; *Zhongguo laodong bao*, 3 July 1996), who not only are paid less, but enjoy far fewer, or no, benefits.[16] Local governments, which own the factories and gain from this constant supply of cheap migrant labour, often ignore such irregularities.

In line with this, the workplace labour regime in some of the publicly owned factories has undergone a drastic change, sometimes becoming as harsh as is found in many of the Asian foreign-funded enterprises in China. A study of several large state-owned cotton mills in 1993 and 1994 in an inland province revealed 'a work system that includes quota increases and speed-ups; longer working hours; ... new draconian controls over labour attendance; and the use of monetary sanctions and penalties to control labour' (Zhao and Nichols, 1996: 1). This entailed a large amount of overtime work and physical exhaustion, and a penalty system that severely docked workers' pay. The wage system was calculated on a workpoints system down to three decimal points –

85.631 points being worth 39.98 yuan (ibid.: 16). It is 'scientific management' in its most refined form. Pressured by the competition of the free-market economy, these practices are spreading within state-owned industries.

A second consequence has become evident. With urban unemployment rising, both laid-off workers and recent school graduates in the cities are faced with a new form of 'bonded' labour when seeking work. It is becoming increasingly common for urban recruits to pay a bond or 'deposit' (this, too, in Chinese is called *yajin*) in order to secure a public-sector job. This type of payment is different from those required of the migrant workers, in that the purpose is not so much to tie the worker to the employers. Rather, for these urban job seekers there is now a price to be paid for a job: put another way, a job seeker has to buy his or her way into the state and collective sector labour market. The jobs in financially healthy enterprises are still desirable because they are perceived, correctly or not, to provide at least some job security and benefits. Jobs in the state-owned commercial, service and financial sectors are particularly pricey (*Gongren ribao*, 2 December 1995; *Shaanxi gongren bao*, 1 November 1997). Of course, paying for a job also inhibits labour mobility.

This phenomenon began emerging in China in the early 1990s and is becoming more and more common. Take, as one example, a county in Sichuan Province whose 276 state and publicly owned collective enterprises recruited 12,343 people between 1993 and mid-1995. Of these, 80 per cent had to 'enter the factory with capital' (*dai zi ru chang*), an expression coined for the new phenomenon. These entry fees amounted to an average of 5,977 yuan per recruit (*Sichuan gongren bao*, 30 August 1995; see also *Zhongguo laodong bao*, 24 August 1995 and 29 July 1997). In 1995, the average per capita annual income in Sichuan Province for state employees was 4,897 yuan and for collective employees 3,251 yuan (*Zhongguo laodong tongji nianjian 1996*), so the bond was a truly hefty sum, well over a year's salary. Job seekers, many of whom are laid-off workers in imminent financial straits, either have to use their life-savings or borrow heavily from relatives and friends to get employment (*Gongren ribao*, 9 September 1995).[17]

Other cases involve enterprises in financial trouble that are in the process of changing their ownership structure into shareholding companies. Lacking capital, they demand that their workers sink capital into the factory by buying shares or by providing loans to the factory. For example, in a survey of 640 shareholding enterprises carried out by the Chinese Social Research Office in four provinces in April 1998, it was found that 63 per cent of these enterprises had forced workers to buy shares if they wanted to keep their jobs. These tended to be enterprises that were not making much profit or running at a loss (*Liaoning gongren bao,* 30 July 1998). Often, the managers try to obfuscate, or later redefine, the nature of the monies demanded, which variously come under the guise of 'bonds', 'deposits', 'buying shares', 'risk security funds', 'capital injection', and so on. Some of these supposedly are 'returnable', sometimes with interest, but some are not. Sometimes those who cannot afford to pay up lose their jobs, which gives rise to a new form of industrial conflict. On top of this variety of payments, it has become customary to charge new recruits a 'training fee', which is not refundable. The kind of 'training' that is provided sometimes is no more than several military drills to instil discipline before recruits are assigned to jobs.

In 1994 the Ministry of Labour issued two documents, one forbidding the collection of bonds by foreign-funded enterprises, and one specifying that state and collective enterprises had to abide by the same regulations laid down for the foreign-funded enterprises (*Zhongguo laodong bao,* 24 August 1995). Even so, as layoffs and unemployment continue to rise, the use of bonds in the public industrial sector is spreading and arouses increasing resentment. For example, in Luoyang, the capital of Henan Province, by 1995 disputes over recruitment fees constituted 15 per cent of all industrial disputes (ibid.). In Baoji City in Shaanxi Province, the average bond jumped from 5,000 yuan in 1993 to 15,000 yuan in 1997, again leading to angry complaints (*Shaanxi gongren bao,* 1 November 1997). Another Chinese report focused on Zhengzhou, the capital of Henan Province, and Jilin City in Jilin Province, where state enterprises, which had been losing money for years, forced employees to purchase enterprise stocks. Otherwise all those under 40 years old were to be dismissed *en masse* and those over 40 would be forced into early retirement (Luo, 1998). Media reports indicate that such demands are spreading, especially in inland cities, where unemployment is higher than along the coast. In Anhua in inland Hunan Province some poorly performing enterprises were forcing employees to retire if they could not each buy 4000 yuan of shares, meanwhile asking for bonds from newly hired recruits (*Inside China Mainland*, 1998).

The green light that the 15th Party Congress in October 1997 signalled for the massive conversion of the country's small and medium-size state enterprises into shareholding corporations exacerbated all of these trends: at once threatening to throw a large new wave of workers out of work, and at the same time giving extra leverage to managements' demands that workers pay for 'shares' in order to retain their jobs. Complaints mounted, and so in July 1998, the powerful State Economic and Trade Commission issued a document calling 'for an end to across-the-board sales of small state firms to avoid social unrest' and specifically criticizing the officials in charge of the conversions for forcing employees to become shareholders (Asia Intelligence Wire China Business Network, 1998). Yet, it will not be easy to stop the deluge of conversions (Kazer, 1998; Hillis, 1998), and the asking price for jobs is likely to soar in the coming years.

THE ROLE OF THE CHINESE TRADE UNION

Under the command economy, the only Chinese trade union, the All China Federation of Trade Unions (ACFTU), like the trade unions in other socialist states, had only a minor bureaucratic role. The unions in the Communist states have been labelled 'transmission belts' (Pravda and Ruble, 1986), a term that conjures up an image of a government bureaucracy, an impotent institution, and a third rate one at that. Its two major functions in China were to help management spur workers to fulfil production quotas handed down from the state, and to help in allocating housing and welfare assistance to the workforce. As part of this second function, the union officials were to help workers to resolve personal and financial distress. Any concept of collective bargaining or of unions as protectors of workers' rights barely existed.

Now that the Chinese labour market has been deregulated and management autonomy has provided managers and employers in all sectors of the economy with an increasingly free hand to deal with labour, what has become the function of the Chinese trade union? Western scholars have divided opinions on the extent to which the ACFTU today is a docile tool of the party-state. Some dismiss it, arguing it has not attempted to change its role from the days of the command economy (Leung, 1997). Some others are less begrudging and present empirical findings showing that the ACFTU has tried to assume a new role (White *et al.*, 1996; Howell, 1997; Warner and Ng, 1998). I am inclined to the latter position, believing that the trade union, particularly at the national level, has tried to act on behalf of workers' interests, albeit sometimes half-heartedly, inconsistently and not particularly effectively. But whatever the Chinese trade union does or does not attempt, it is motivated above all by its bureaucratic mission to carry out the role assigned to it by the party-state to officially look after workers' interests (this is to be carried out in conjunction with the contradictory mission of simultaneously working for the state's interests). At levels below the province, however, union branches are marginalized and under-resourced, making it all but impossible for them to defend workers against abuses.

The foreign-funded enterprises and domestic private enterprises that have sprung up in the past two decades were not established with workplace union branches. The central government and national trade union were aware of the rising incidences of abuse and exploitation, and in the early 1990s began a programme of planting workplace unions in these enterprises (Chan 1998a; Warner and Ng, 1998). However, many of the local governments (which, we should recall, often are co-investors in joint ventures) have worked hand-in-glove with foreign investors to prevent any genuine workers' representation at the workplace. Impressive unionization rates in foreign-funded factories in some of the new industrial zones, reaching 90 per cent or even higher only one or two years after the implementation of the new Labour Law of 1995, are in fact a sham. The chairs of the new workplace union branches are usually none other than the enterprise managers, or are ranking members of the managerial staff (Chan, 1998a).

Thus, impressive unionization coverage, as of early 1998 reaching three-quarters of the eligible 56,000 joint-venture firms (*Xinhua News Agency*, 1998), has done little to alleviate the plight of the migrant workers. The harsh labour regimes and the bonding of migrant workers in South China continue. In fact, under increasing competition from cheap labour in other Asian countries, overproduction and the overall thrust of globalization, migrant workers' wages have not kept up with inflation. Even the legal minimum wages set by local governments do not always keep up with inflation. For example, at a time of substantial inflation, the legal minimum wage for Dongguan City in Guangdong was 350 yuan in 1995, and was the same in 1997 (Asia Monitor Resource Centre, 1995; Hong Kong Christian Industrial Committee *et al.*, 1997); while Zhuhai City's minimum wage of 380 yuan similarly remained unchanged between 1995 and 1997 (*Laodong daobao*, 19 August 1995; *Zhongguo laodong bao*, 28 July 1997).

Aware that the local governments are on side and that even the enterprise unions are under their own control, when Asian investors lose money or lack operating capital they find it feasible, in turn, to squeeze the bonded migrant workers. Owing workers many months' back pay has become a particularly serious issue (*Ming Pao*, 4 November 1997; *Zhongguo laodong bao*, 11 November 1995). Unable to lodge complaints at the workplace, migrant workers in some cases have been staging spontaneous strikes, and taking their problems beyond the factory to local labour bureaus and local governments, and occasionally to the local district trade unions. These local bureaucracies act like firefighters, seeking to put out the spontaneous conflagrations within their areas of jurisdiction.

In the state and collective sectors, the government and trade union are pushing a programme of signing workplace-level collective contracts (Warner, 1997). In these sectors, where labour is better organized and educated and more aware of their rights, preconditions exist for some form of collective bargaining, or at least some kind of consultation in future years, provided the trade unions and workers become more assertive. Yet, this can only take place in those enterprises that are financially healthy, and not in those that are already in dire financial straits, in particular those on the verge of bankruptcy. Financially troubled enterprises today constitute more than half of the state-owned and collectively owned firms. When several millions of state workers are not even getting their regular pay (Forney, 1997), collective bargaining and the signing of collective contracts in such enterprises has scant meaning. Workers can in reality only bring their grievances to the local government or central authorities.

The Chinese trade union is at a crossroads in these dire circumstances. To survive as a bureaucracy it needs to define a role for itself and to gain greater trust from its assigned constituency, the workers. During the past two decades since the economic reforms began, it has not been a totally docile bureaucracy (Jiang, 1996). It has initiated pro-labour programmes (Chang, 1997), has argued with other bureaucracies over drafts of labour legislation, and has in other ways confronted bureaucracies whose functions by their very nature are anti-labour, such as those entrusted to develop the economy. No matter how weak and ineffectual the ACFTU has been, it is the only bureaucracy in China today that holds a pro-worker stance.

Yet, the Party is careful to ensure that the trade union comes under tighter surveillance than other bureaucracies. A second obstacle facing the union is that the ACFTU's basic structure is enterprise unionism, which prevents cohesiveness within the union bureaucracy. Under Mao, the 'transmission belt' vertical command structure held the union bureaucracy together; economic decentralization weakens this command structure, allowing local Party authorities who are antagonistic to the union to dominate some of the union branches. Marketization and privatization exacerbate the fragmentation. In some of the state-owned enterprises today, the trade union is being sidelined; in the newly transformed shareholding enterprises, managers are trying hard to rid themselves of workplace unions; in the Asian foreign-funded enterprises, as described above, the new workplace union branches are predominantly chaired by factory managers. At a time of increasing marketization and privatization of the Chinese economy and increasing penetration of China by the tide of globalization, represented most directly in China by these Asian subcontractors for Western multinationals, the Chinese union's on-site influence almost everywhere is in retreat.

CONCLUSION

These pages have traced the revolutionary changes that have occurred in China's labour market within a period of less than two decades, shifting from a rigid planned command economy to a decentralized market economy. Important parts of the Chinese economy have been globalized, and labour practices all but deregulated. As each province, each city and locality competes for capital, especially foreign capital, labour standards have declined and human rights violations, including a form of forced labour, have become commonplace in factories managed by overseas Chinese from Taiwan and Hong Kong, and by Koreans.

These Asian investors are the brokers and producers of labour-intensive products for the developed world's transnational corporations, operating in the world's most rapidly industrializing region. Their presence has exerted enormous competitive wage pressures in China, and their management techniques are spreading to China's inland provinces and to the non-foreign-funded sector. Harsh labour regimes are beginning to surface even in China's state-owned enterprises, though not yet to the extent of 'bonding' workers in the same way as is possible with migrant workers. However, another kind of 'bonding' has appeared in the state sector that undermines a free labour market. Desirable jobs, especially those that promise job security, increasingly now have to be bought. Decentralization of power to the regions and enterprises has made it nigh impossible for the central government to arrest such a trend. With Asia now in recession, and in the midst of the Chinese government's reform programme to downsize bureaucracies and to divest itself of state and collective enterprises, the conditions of state-sector workers and migrant workers are likely to deteriorate further.

The central state lacks the will and the administrative capacity to enforce compliance to the national labour law. Its half-hearted measures to defend workers from being taken advantage of is motivated by a fear of social instability. When this threat becomes imminent, the central party-state will have two options: to resort to violent suppression or allow the ACFTU genuine autonomy in the hope of releasing some of the pressure. Predicting which scenario is more likely is beyond the capability of this author.

NOTES

1. According to the *Asian Food Worker* (1995), a news bulletin published by the Allied Workers' Association in Asia and the Pacific, the legal minimum wage set for Shenzhen, one of the highest-cost cities in China, was lower in 1995 than in Hong Kong, Indonesia, South Korea, the Philippines and Thailand. Only Vietnam was lower, but only slightly. The legal minimum wage set for Beijing was lower than in Vietnam.
2. This estimate is based on my fieldwork in factories in that region in 1995, 1996 and 1997. For example, in Dongguan City in Guangdong Province in 1986, 22.4% of the labour force was made up of migrants; in 1996 it had risen to 87.4%. The percentage of migrants in the blue-collar workforce there was even higher. On this phenomenon, also see Li, 1996.
3. This observation is based on my fieldwork in Putian City, Fujian, in 1996. See also *Zhongguo laodong bao* (3 July 1996) and Solinger (1995).
4. These rules and regulations vary slightly from place to place in accordance with local government policies. In some places, an urban registration can be bought for several thousand to more than ten thousand yuan, several times a peasant's annual income.

5. The 'International Convention on the Protection of the Rights of All Migrant Workers' refers only to cross-national labour migrants, but it could be applied equally well here, as these people are trapped in analogous circumstances. See United Nations (1995: 383–402).

6. The cost of the work permit varies from place to place, from as low as 20 yuan in some places to several hundred yuan in the Shenzhen region. See Zhao (1996: 35).

7. Although Korean factories are not represented in the survey, Korean management will be included in the general discussion that follows of exploitative management practices in Asian-invested Chinese factories. There is now ample evidence from within China that Korean managers have been among the most hard-driving and abusive on the shop floor. Reports from other developing countries similarly point a finger at Korean managers as particularly prone to malpractices in their treatment of workers (Sun, 1993; Paisley and Kiernan, 1994; Biers *et al.*, 1996, Slaughter, 1995; Vietnam Labor Watch, 1997). The hitting of workers by line managers was also quite common in factories within South Korea in the 1960s and 1970s (Christian Conference of Asia, Urban Rural Mission, 1982).

8. My own field study in April 1997 in a township in Guangdong where most manufacturing enterprises are small, private and locally owned revealed that the payment of wages was even more irregular there than at the foreign-funded enterprises.

9. For an excellent example of how this system was able to bond workers under horrific conditions, see *Workers' Daily* (*Gongren ribao*), 17 April 1994. In the notorious Zhili Toy Factory fire of 1993, 84 workers lost their lives in a factory dormitory, trapped by barred windows and locked exits; a letter retrieved from the wreckage, written by a victim and never handed over to management, revealed that the victim had repeatedly asked permission to resign from her job but without success.

10. Based on June 1996 field interviews in Putian.

11. Monetary penalties have also become prevalent in state enterprises in recent years. See *Gongren ribao*, 20 June 1995, p. 5.

12. Shocking examples of police violence inflicted on workers can be found in *Zhuhai laodong bao* (24 October 1994), *South China Morning Post* (6 December 1995), and *Fujian tongxun* (No. 2, 1994: 21–3).

13. For an elaboration of how these abuses are found almost exclusively in Asian-invested firms, see Chan (1995).

14. A very serious case of atmospheric and workplace mass poisoning in the footwear industry was carried in a three-part investigative report in *Zhongguo Funu* (15, 16 and 17 January 1996). A translation of this report is available in Chan (1998b: 35–48).

15. In the footwear industry, glues account for less than one per cent of the cost of production. In China, carcinogenic benzene-based glues, which cause leukemia, are 30 per cent cheaper than the less toxic toluene-based glues. Taiwanese-funded footwear factories in China often use the former (Chen and Chan, forthcoming).

16. I came across this in my fieldwork in Beijing in 1995 and in Shanghai in 1996.

17. The newspaper devoted half a page to letters to the editor from workers complaining about being forced to pay such bonds.

REFERENCES

Asia Intelligence Wire China Business Information Network (1998) 'China to Curb Prevalence of Selling Small State-owned Enterprises', 13 July.

Asia Monitor Resource Centre (1995a) *Zhujiang sanjiaozhou gongren quanyi zhuangkuang* (The Situation of Workers' Rights in the Pearl River Delta Region). Hong Kong: Asia Monitor Resource Centre.

Asia Monitor Resource Centre (1995b) *Conditions of Workers in the Shoe Industry of China.*

Asian Food Worker (1995) 'Vietnam: Asia's Newest Member of the Global Economy', Vol. 25, No. 2, pp. 8–9.

Beja, Jean-Philippe (1996) 'Migrant Workers: An Asset for China?', *Chinese Perspectives*, No. 7, pp. 58–9.

Biers, Dan, Rose, Matthew, Schuman, Michael and Namju Cho (1996) 'Korea Exporting

Tough Labour Practices: Some of the Country's Overseas Plants Abuse Their Workers, Critics Say', *Asian Wall Street Journal*, 18 July, p. 1.

Chan, Anita (1995) 'The Emerging Patterns of Industrial Relations in China and the Rise of Two New Labour Movements', *China Information*, Vol. 9, No. 4, pp. 36–59.

Chan, Anita (1998a) 'Labour Relations in Foreign-funded Ventures', in Greg O'Leary (ed.), *Adjusting to Capitalism: Chinese Workers and Their State*. Armonk, NY: M.E. Sharpe, pp. 122–49.

Chan, Anita (ed.) (1998b) Special issue on 'The Conditions of Chinese Workers in East Asian-funded Enterprises', *Chinese Sociology and Anthropology*, Vol. 30, No. 4, pp. 3–101.

Chan, Anita (1998c) 'Labour Standards and Human Rights: The Case of Chinese Workers under Market Socialism', *Human Rights Quarterly*, Vol. 20, No 4, pp. 886–904.

Chan, Anita (ed.) (2000) *China's Workers Under Assault*. Armonk, NY: M.E. Sharpe.

Chan, Anita, Madsen, Richard and Unger, Jonathan(1992) *Chen Village under Mao and Deng*. Berkeley: University of California Press.

Child, John (1994) *Management in China during the Age of Reform*. Cambridge: Cambridge University Press.

Chang, Kai (1997) 'A Survey and Investigation of Unemployment and Reemployment of Female Employees in State-Owned Enterprises', *Chinese Sociology and Anthropology*, Vol. 30, No. 2, pp. 17–27.

Chen, Mei-shia and Anita Chan (2000) 'China's "Market Economics in Command": Footwear Workers' Health in Jeopardy', *International Journal of Health Services*.

China Labour Bulletin (1995) Special issue on environment and health *vs* survival. Nos. 16 and 17.

China Daily (Beijing).

China News Analysis (1995) 'The Minimum Wage Policy', No. 1544, pp. 1–4.

Christian Conference of Asia, Urban Rural Mission (1982), *From the Womb of Han: Stories of Korean Women Workers*. Hong Kong: Christian Conference of Asia, Urban Rural Mission.

Development Research Centre of the State Council, PRC (1994) 'How We Should View Labour Problems in Three-Capital Enterprises', *Research Report*, No. 27.

Exchange (1997) Special issue on 'China's Labour Safety and Health Standards', June.

Fan, Chengze Simon (1998) 'Why China Has Been Successful in Attracting Foreign Direct Investment: A Transaction Cost Approach', *Journal of Contemporary China*, Vol. 7, No. 7, pp. 21–32.

Forney, Matt (1997) 'We Want to Eat', *Far Eastern Economic Review*, 26 June, pp. 14–16.

Fujian tongxun (Fujian Province Bulletin) (1994), No. 2, pp. 21–3.

Gao, Mobo (1994) 'Migrant Workers from Rural China: Their Conditions and Some Implications for Economic Development in South China', in David Schak (ed.), *Entrepreneurship, Economic Growth and Social Change: The Transformation of Southern China*. Brisbane: Centre for the Study of Australia–Asia Relations, Griffith University, pp. 21–38.

Gongren ribao (Workers' Daily).

Greenfield, Gerard and Apo Leong (1997) 'China's Communist Capitalism: The Real World of Market Socialism', in Leo Panitch (ed.), *Ruthless Criticism of All That Exists*. Special issue of *Socialist Register*. Suffolk: Merlin Press, pp. 96–122.

Hillis, Scott (1998) 'China Eases State Firm Reform, Pushes Finances', *Reuters News Service*, 12 July.

Hong Kong Christian Industrial Committee and Asia Monitor Resource Center (1997) *Working Conditions in the Sports Shoe Industry in China*.

Howell, Jude (1997) 'The Chinese Economic Miracle and Urban Workers', *The European Journal of Development Research*, Vol. 9, No. 2, pp. 149–75.

Hsing You-tien (1998) *Making Capitalism in China: The Taiwan Connexion*. New York: Oxford University Press.

Inside China Mainland (1998) 'Employees Ordered to Invest Large Sums in Company or Face Dismissal' (translated from Chinese, excerpted from *Dongxiang* (Trend), Nov. 1997, p. 81), Vol. 20, No. 1, p. 51.

Jiang, Kaiwen (1996) 'Gonghui yu dang-guojia de chongtu: bashi niandai yilai de Zhongguo gonghui gaige' (The Conflicts between the Trade Union and the Party-State: The Reform of the Chinese Trade Union in the Eighties), *Xianggang shehui kexue jikan* (Hong Kong Journal of Social Science), No. 8, pp. 121–6.

Kazer, William (1998) 'China Calls Retreat on State Sector Reform', *Reuters News Service*, 11 July.

Laodong daobao (Labour News).

Lee, Ching Kwan (1995) 'Engendering the Worlds of Labour: Women Workers, Labour Markets, and Production Politics in the South China Economic Miracle', *American Sociological Review*, Vol. 60, pp. 378–97.

Leung, Trini Wing-yue (1988) *Smashing the Iron Rice Pot: Workers and Unions in China's Market Socialism*. Hong Kong: Asia Monitor Resource Centre.

Leung, Trini Wing-yue (1997) 'Trade Unions and Labour Relations under Market Socialism in China', in Gerd Schienstock, Paul Thompson and Franz Traxler (eds), *Industrial Relations between Command and Market: A Comparative Analysis of Eastern Europe and China*. New York: Nova Science, pp. 239–90.

Li, Cheng (1996) 'Surplus Rural Labourers and Internal Migration in China', *Asian Survey*, Vol. 31, No. 11, p. 1132.

Liaoning gongren bao (Liaoning Workers' News).

Luo, Bing (1998) 'A Major Test for State Enterprise Reform', *Inside China Mainland*, Vol. 20, No. 1, pp. 41–7 (translated and excerpted from *Dongxiang* (Trend), November, pp. 25–6.

Mallee, Hein (1995) 'China's Household Registration System under Reform', *Employment and Change*, Vol. 26, No. 1, pp. 1–29.

Ming Pao (Bright News).

Nanfang gongbao (Southern Workers' News).

Ng, Sek Hong and Olivia K.M. Ip (1994) 'The Public Domain and Labour Oragnizations', in *China Review 1994*. Hong Kong: Chinese University of Hong Kong Press, pp. 14.1–14.33.

Ng, Sek Hong and Warner, Malcolm (1998) *China's Trade Unions and Management*. London: Macmillan.

O'Leary, Greg (1992) 'Redefining Workers' Interests – Reform and the Trade Unions', in Andrew Watson (ed.), *Economic Reform and Social Change in China*. London and New York: Routledge, pp. 39–62.

Paisley, Ed and Kiernan, Terrence (1994) 'South Korea: Trade and Investment Focus – Reforms Boost Capital', *Far Eastern Economic Review*, Vol. 157, No. 21, pp. 53–7.

Pearson, Margaret M. (1991) *Joint Ventures in the People's Republic of China: The Control of Foreign Direct Investment under Socialism*. Princeton: Princeton University Press.

Pravda, Alex and Ruble, Blair A. (1986) 'Communist Trade Unions: Varieties of Dualism', in A. Pravda and B.A. Ruble (eds), *Trade Unions in Communist States*. Boston: Allen and Unwin, pp. 1–22.

Shaanxi gongren bao (Shaanxi Workers' News).

Shuman, Mark (1996) 'Will China's Economic Growth Compromise Safety?', *Safety and Health*, December, pp. 50–4.

Sichuan gongren bao (Sichuan Workers' Daily).

Slaughter, Jane (1995) 'Inside Guatemala's Maquiladoras: $3 per Day, and You Fit the Boss with Condom', *Labour Notes*, Dec., pp. 8–9.

Solinger, Dorothy (1995) 'The Chinese Work Unit and Transient Labour in the Transition from Socialism', *Modern China*, Vol. 21, No. 2, pp. 155–83.

Solinger, Dorothy (1998) 'Employment Channels and Job Categories among the Floating Population', in Gregory O'Leary (ed.), *Adjusting to Capitalism: Chinese Workers and the State*. Armonk, NY: M.E. Sharpe, pp. 3–47.

Sun, Lena (1993) 'Capitalism Puts China's Workers on Their Knees', *Guardian Weekly*, 28 Nov., p. 17.

Teargarden, Mary B. and Von Glinow, Mary Ann (1991) 'Sino-Foreign Strategic Alliance Types and Related Operating Characteristics: Implications for Research and Practice', in Oded Shenkar (ed.), *Organization and Management in China 1979–1990*. Armonk, NY: M.E. Sharpe, pp. 99–108.

United Nations (1995) *The United Nations and Human Rights 1945–1995*. New York:

Department of Public Information.

Vietnam Labour Watch (1997) 'Nike Labour Practices in Vietnam'. Unpublished report.

Walder, Andrew G. and Gong Xiaoxia (1993) 'Workers in the Tiananmen Protests: The Politics of the Beijing Workers' Autonomous Federation', *Australian Journal of Chinese Affairs*, No. 29, pp. 1–29.

Wang Fei-ling (1998) 'Floaters, Moonlighters, and the Underemployed: A National Labour Market with Chinese Characteristics', *Journal of Contemporary China*, Vol. 7, No. 19, pp. 459–75.

Warner, Malcolm (1996) 'Human Resources in the People's Republic of China: The "Three Systems" Reform', *Human Resource Management Journal*, Vol. 6, No. 2, pp. 30–9.

Warner, Malcolm (1997) 'China's HRM in Transition: Towards Relative Convergence?', *Asia Pacific Business Review*, Vol. 3, No. 4, pp. 19–33.

Warner, Malcolm and Ng, Sek Hong (1998) 'The Ongoing Evolution of Chinese Industrial Relations: The Negotiation of "Collective Contracts" in the Shenzhen Special Economic Zone', *China Information*, Vol. 12, No. 4, pp. 1–20.

White, Gordon, Howell, Jude and Shang Xiaoyuan (1996) *In Search of Civil Society: Market Reform and Social Change in Contemporary China*. Oxford: Oxford University Press, pp. 39–68

Xinhua News Agency News Bulletin (1998) 'More Trade Unions To Be Set Up in Foreign-Funded Firms', 17 July.

Yangcheng wanbao (Canton Evening News).

Zhao, Minghua and Nichols, Theo (1996) 'Management Control of Labour in State-owned Enterprises: Cases from the Textile Industry', *The China Journal*, No. 36, pp. 1–21.

Zhao, Shukai (1996) *Nongmin liudong de jizhi yu zuzhi* (A Research Report on the Mechanisms and Organization of the [Labour] Migration of Peasants). Beijing: Village Section, State Council Development Research Centre.

Zhongguo funu (Chinese Women).

Zhongguo laodong bao (China Labour News).

Zhongguo laodong tongji nianjian 1996 (China Labour Statistical Yearbook 1996). Beijing: Zhongguo tongji chubanshe.

Zhongguo tongji (China's Statistics).

Zhongguo tongji nianjian (China Statistical Yearbook).

Zhu, Ying and Campbell, Iain (1996) 'Economic Reform and the Challenge of Transforming Labour Regulation in China', *Labour and Industry*, Vol. 7, No. 1, pp. 29–49.

Zhuhai laodong bao (Zhuhai Labour News).

Zweig, David (1995) 'Developmental Communities on China's Coast: The Impact of Trade, Investment, and Transnational Alliances', *Comparative Politics*, Vol. 27, No. 3, pp. 253–74.

15

The Challenges and Opportunities for the Trade Union Movement in the Transition Era: Two Socialist Market Economies – China and Vietnam

YING ZHU and STEPHANIE FAHEY

Economic reforms and an open door policy have led to significant changes in the socialist market economies such as China and Vietnam. The emergence of new interest groups, the inflow of foreign capital and the diversity of ownership of enterprises, and a large and floating population moving from the countryside to the cities, have accentuated conflicts of interest and require a more relevant industrial relations system to cope with these challenges. Under the current globalization process and internal transformation, the trade union movement in the two countries is facing both challenges and opportunities to transform itself from a welfare organization (with the major function of administration) to a new body with the role of participation and representation.

In the past, trade unions in all communist societies presented conceptual difficulties for industrial relations analysts. If trade unions were defined as organizations of workers, which bargain freely and collectively, then they might not be considered as unions at all. So far, two development trends emerge among these communist societies: one is in the Eastern European countries and the former Soviet Union with the direction towards Western democracies and trade union activities; another is in the so-called 'socialist market economies' such as China and Vietnam where trade unions are still fundamentally different from the unions in Western democracies. If we simply use the analytical concept of structural-functional analysis, unions in China and Vietnam have little or no 'subsystem autonomy'.

However, from a practical point of view, though the situations in China and Vietnam are not unique, there are more opportunities for trade unions in the two countries to be involved in policy formation at national level and participation in collective bargaining and dispute mediation at enterprise level. In addition, trade unions in both countries play a more significant role on a wide range of social issues as a major social actor. Therefore, this chapter aims to identify the major challenges and opportunities for trade unions in China and Vietnam under their special political, social and economic systems in the transition period towards the twenty-first century in an era of globalization.

This contribution is divided into the following sections: the second (next) section reviews the issue of 'globalization'; the third illustrates the function of the trade unions in both countries, such as representing workers and protecting workers' interests in different enterprises with different ownership systems; the fourth examines the new legal framework of industrial relations in relation to the challenges of the market-driven economy and labour market developments; the fifth examines the ongoing problems and dilemmas associated with the changes to the system of labour regulation and trade unions. In conclusion, we identify the major issues concerned by the trade unions in relation to globalization and the possible direction for the development of the trade unions in both countries.

GLOBALIZATION AND GLOBAL CIVIL SOCIETY

Globalization refers to the development of an economy and forms of governance that span much of the world (Betcherman, 1996; Cox, 1994; Stubbs and Underhill, 1994; Water, 1995; Hirst and Thompson, 1996; Hoogvelt, 1997). Such developments reflect three processes: (1) the integration of financial and currency markets across the entire world; (2) the integration of production, trade and capital formation across national boundaries in global corporations; and (3) the emergence of functions of global governance that partially regulate national economic, social and environmental policies. The fusion of finance, corporations and other organizations also reflects the decisions that permit, promote or execute enhanced connexion between these organizations (Stubbs and Underhill, 1994; Bradley *et al.*, 1994; Water, 1995; Hirst and Thompson, 1996; Hoogvelt, 1997). Cox (1994) identifies three key aspects responsible for the phenomenon of globalization: the structural power of capital, the restructuring of production and the role of debt. As for the structural power of capital, international capital is the dominant influence over the state's economic decisions. Since states are overdependent on investment and capital, the power of capital forces states to create 'favourable' environments for investment. In other words, the state is constrained by the structural power of capital from following an independent economic development plan. Tighter control of labour and restrictions on trade unions, maintaining low wages and long working hours, and lack of regulations to protect workers' rights can be seen as part of the outcome.

As for the restructuring of production, Cox (1994: 45–59) suggests that the 'globalization process' has been accelerated by the emergence of a new model of production that shifted from Fordism to post-Fordism. The new model is based on a core–periphery structure of production in which the core functions with a small number of employees who handle research and development, technological organization and innovation. The periphery is responsible for the production process itself and, because it is more loosely linked to the overall production process, its components can be called into action according to the corporation's needs. The consequences of the new model of production can be identified in two aspects: one is the weakness of the power of trade unions and the strengthening of the power of capital within the production process; another is that it makes business operation less controllable by an individual state authority.

A third factor is the role of debt. Since the 1980s the increasing dependency on borrowing in foreign currencies, and the burden of servicing that debt, have made governments and corporations more accountable to external bond markets than to their own public. Governments are constrained in their fiscal and monetary policies from pursuing their own programmes of economic development. Associated with the problem of servicing the debt, states have also to deal with financial manipulators who have made finance an independent power over the real economy. Because these manipulators' short-range interests are in immediate financial gain, this can lead to the destruction of jobs and productive capital, seriously harming the industrial development of the countries (ibid.). The recent Asian regional financial crisis has reflected these problems.

All these factors, according to Falk (1992), have resulted in a significant loss of control by the states over national economic policy. This is defined as 'globalization from above' (ibid.). In contrast, transnational social forces that have managed to establish links between local action and global campaigns, such as international human rights movements and labour movements, are promoters of 'globalization from below' (ibid.). These transnational social movements push for the establishment of a global civil society (Hyden, 1997). In this new global environment, a serious challenge is confronting the state and trade union movement. There is little doubt that trade unions are the most important forces for developing a global civil society. In addition, its establishment relies on the development of individual countries' civil society, especially in developing countries such as China and Vietnam, where trade unions are facing this challenge.

THE FUNCTION OF TRADE UNIONS IN TRANSITION

The birth of trade unions in both China and Vietnam was closely associated with imperialism and anti-imperialist revolution, as was the case in many countries in East and South East Asia. According to Leninist principles, trade unions have a dual role in the process of socialist construction: one is to participate in the management of state enterprises; the other is to represent workers' interests. However, under the Stalinist approach, the emphasis on dualism was diminished as theoretically there was no division between the interests of the state and the workers (Pravda and Ruble, 1986).

The Role of Trade Unions

In both China and Vietnam, the traditional role of trade unions as a 'transmission belt' between party and 'masses' was even enhanced after the Communists took power. As Ng and Warner (1998) claim, trade unions have four main official functions: (1) protecting the interests of the whole country, but at the same time safeguarding the legitimate rights and interests of the workers; (2) helping their members participate in the management of their own work units; (3) mobilizing the labour force to raise productivity and the economy's performance; (4) educating the workers to be better members of society.

Therefore, the trade unions in China and Vietnam represent different functions from those in Western economies and the transition economies in Eastern Europe. In these two countries, union representatives are vetted by the party. The relationship between the trade unions and the party is merely ancillary. If trade unions are defined as organizations of workers that bargain freely and collectively, then the trade unions in both countries cannot be considered unions at all. Yet, it is possible to argue that the collusive nature of the enterprise socio-political coalition ensured an increasing standard of living and improved working conditions through the 1990s.

In China, the All-China Federation of Trade Unions (ACFTU) was the only official union representative (there was a period of abeyance during the Cultural Revolution) (Warner, 1995). According to its Constitution, the ACFTU and the National Congress of Trade Unions are the highest leading bodies over the trade unions, and the Executive Committee of the ACFTU is elected by the National Congress, which meets every five years. As for the structure of trade unions, they were tightly integrated into party structures and indeed even into management structures, and in fact the key trade union personnel owed their appointments to their links to these structures (Zhu and Campbell, 1996). By 1997, there were 16 industrial unions and 30 provincial trade union federations under the leadership of the ACFTU (see Ng and Warner, 1998: 44).

The ACFTU enjoys a strong numerical position and claimed a membership in 1996 of 102 million amongst the urban workforce, with 40 per cent women membership among 585,937 grass roots union organizations (CSPH, 1997). Union density in this sphere is likely to be around 90 per cent, but mainly in state-owned enterprises (SOEs) and collective-owned enterprises (COEs) and not much in domestic private enterprises (DPEs) and foreign-invested enterprises (FIEs). In 1996, the number of trade unions in DPEs and FIEs was 2,272 and 10,536 respectively, which constitute 0.39 per cent and 1.8 per cent of the total number of union organizations (ibid.).

In Vietnam, the role of trade unions was confirmed in the 1980 Constitution Article 10, which stipulated that:

> The Vietnam Federation of Trade Unions (VFTU) is the largest mass organization of the Vietnamese working

class, a school of communism, of economic management, and management of the state. Within its power, the trade unions take part in state affairs and supervise the work of state bodies, and participate in the management of factories. (Constitution of Vietnam, 1980)

The organization of trade unions in Vietnam is extremely complex, based on an industrial-sector basis in association with geographically established trade union councils to form a dual system of authority. The VFTU has a permanent secretariat, which represents the executive committee of the VFTU between congresses held every five years. The National Branch Trade Union represents workers under the same ministry in larger localities. The FTU of a province, city and special zone represents workers in a locality. The Local Branch Trade Union represents workers at the more local levels of district, prefecture, provincial capitals and cities and is under the direct guidance of the trade union of the provincial city and special zone. The company group and unified enterprise trade unions are above the grass roots level and are organized on the basis of factories in the same sector under the guidance of the National Branch Trade Union. The primary trade union organization at enterprise level is the basic unit. Below this is the trade union section and small group. Since 1988, the number of industrial unions has increased from 17 to 26 with the new type of unions in the private sector called professional and trade or occupational unions. These include the banking union, public sector union, petroleum workers' union, and unions for the police, aviation, commerce and tourism, medical workers and sailors. In 1997, some unions merged due to the changes of ministry structure (for example, the Ministries for Light and Heavy Industry merged to form the Ministry for Industry) and now there are only 18 industrial unions.

The Internal Structure of Trade Unions

At enterprise level, unions in both countries chose the union leadership on Leninist lines (Pravda and Ruble, 1987; Warner, 1993). The bottom-up selection of union cadres and representatives takes place from the primary union level through nomination and election. In that sense, 'mass participation' has been encouraged (ibid.: 69). Certainly, both party and management play a primary role in the process of selection.

In China, among a large number of SOEs and COEs, both trade unions and the union-guided Workers' Congresses are the major bodies representing the organized workers at enterprise level since the 1980s (Zhu and Campbell, 1996: 42). The Workers' Congresses have been linked into the trade union structure, with the trade union committee at enterprise level turned into a standing body of the Workers' Congress to deal with routine duties, such as supervising occupational health and safety in enterprises, training workers, and mediating disputes between workers and enterprises (ibid.).

Trade unions in SOEs and COEs normally have one to two full-time officials, depending on the size of production and number of employment. Union members contribute 2 per cent of their wages as union fees. Following further enterprise reform in the 1990s, the representative role of the unions at enterprise level has emerged as part of the campaign of promoting democratic management. Trade union leaders are members of three important decision making bodies at the enterprise level, namely the 'directors' committee', 'shareholders' committee' and 'supervision committee'. Hence, unions are not only being informed about decisions, but also participate in the decision making process. In addition, according to the new Labour Law, labour disputes should be handled at the enterprise level by the enterprise mediation committee, which is composed of management, trade union leaders and workers' representatives. Union leaders are the chairs of such committees and play the most important role in the mediation process. In relation to the complaint process, union leaders have an influential communication role between management and workers.

In recent years, two new issues have emerged that require trade unions to play a crucial role: the development of collective bargaining – collective negotiation and collective agreement (CNCA) in Chinese terms that avoid using the sensitive term 'bargaining' – and the mass layoff of workers and unemployment. At a recent trade union congress, the ACFTU raised the importance of trade unions at the enterprise level in playing a safeguard role to protect workers' rights, especially those being laid off under the wave of SOE restructuring (*Guangming Daily*, 1998).

As for the DPEs and FIEs, trade unions do not have such an influential role as in SOEs and COEs. There are several reasons for this. First is the low union density in these enterprises (for example, just 30 per cent of FIEs and less than ten per cent of DPEs had established unions by 1995) (Zhu, 1995). Second is government policy, which did not push for unionization at the FIEs and DPEs in the period of early reform. Third is the lack of union leadership independence, due to formation and selection processes. For example, union leaders in these firms are chosen by the management, and some may be the relatives or friends of owners or managers. This personal kinship prevents the union from representing workers and protecting workers' interests effectively. However, there are some formal union organizations at relatively large DPEs and FIEs, where unions are similar to those in SOEs and COEs. One to two full-time union officials take charge of union activities. In recent years, CNCA has been practised in a very small number of FIEs as an experiment. Some FIEs with CNCA practices would invite union representatives to negotiate and sign collective agreements. However, for the majority labour force in DPEs and FIEs, CNCA cannot be implemented because of the lack of union representation.

In Vietnam, in the past, the party leader and administrative director carried the most power. Often, the trade union representative was either the deputy party representative or deputy director, and in this respect was seen as closely linked to management. In fact, union leaders took their major task as assisting management to meet enterprise production targets and assuring the enforcement of government labour laws and policies. The priorities of the union were to participate in administration, to educate workers and to defend workers' rights. In contrast, their new set of priorities reverses this order, with the primary role being to protect the material interests of its members.

Since *doi moi* (economic renovation) started, with broadened autonomy in state run enterprises, the trade unions were given responsibility to determine the methods for the distribution of the factory's income. The responsibilities of the trade unions were expanded from wages, bonuses, housing, medical care and treatment, public welfare in factories and localities, labour safety, social security, and the household economy, to more far-reaching problems such as markets and prices, control of goods and commodity funds, supplying and selling of necessities at stable prices, employment, and the distribution of the national income.

Trade unions could deduct two per cent of the real salary of workers for the union, and no state body could dismiss or transfer any worker without the permission of the union. Since 1991, unions have direct control over the Social Insurance Fund. Every year the trade unions are granted five per cent of the total fund of wages of workers and employees for payments for social security, illness, labour accidents and childbirth. In reality, trade union leaders have more of a role as mediators between workers and management. For example, in a dispute at the Viet Than tailoring company the trade union requested the director to take disciplinary action against a supervisor who insulted a worker, and asked the workers for restraint (*Vietnam Investment Review*, 1993a). Other actions by trade unions have been to persuade employers to increase allowances for hazardous work, lunch and relief; to strictly adhere to minimum wage levels and work and rest hours; and to allow the formation of trade unions.

The drive for the right to strike has come from the workers rather than the VFTU, which appears keen to use strikes as a last resort and to maintain Vietnam as an attractive climate for FDI. Advice given to the VFTU through their international affiliations has warned of the dangers of transnational corporations, but it is the Federation's intent to encourage transnational investment. Nguyen Van Tu, chairman of the VFTU, stated that the role of trade unions was 'to protect the worker's legal rights without causing bad influences to the economic development and political stability of the country' (*Vietnam Investment Review*, 1993b). In fact, earlier in the debate Tu argued against the right to strike, fearing it may be abused for political purposes. Apparently, some workers are reluctant to support trade unions, as they believe that officials are too easily coopted by company bosses.

Generally speaking, union density is relatively high in SOEs with 84 per cent union membership (ibid.). However, non-SOEs (including DPEs and FIEs) have a very low level of union density of just 14 per cent (Fahey, 1997). The low membership in the private sector is because both the employee and employer see little effective outcome from union involvement in labour relations (*Vietnam Investment Review*, 1993a).

The Challenges for Trade Unions

The major challenge that faces the trade union movement in China and Vietnam concerns the globalization process and market-driven economic reform. How can a trade union obtain credibility in its representation of labour (a challenge not unlike that which faces the party-state as a manager of the so-called 'socialist market economy')? Does the trade union movement need to be independent from the party-state to be effective? Could the trade union movement be financially viable or enjoy its current level of freedom of expression without party-state support? How will it continue to fund its activities with declining membership in the state sector due to closure, layoffs, etc., combined with no compensation for improving membership in non-state sectors? These questions will need to be resolved in the coming years.

In both China and Vietnam, trade unions are in the process of renewing their organization and activities to perform the function of workers' representatives in protecting their rights and interests. In the past, they existed only as part of the state sector and were organized to promote political unity. There are various options for reinventing unions, as described by Pravda and Ruble (1986: ix, 18–19). Unions are moving away from the 'classical dualism' in which they both protect the interests of the workers and promote production. Alternatives include 'corporatist dualism', usually supported by officials from the union and party-state who desire more effective policymaking. 'Participatory dualism' attracts union officials, party officials and skilled workers who desire continued economic reform. Finally, 'adversarial non-dualism' is driven by the grass roots. These challenges would require greater union democracy, which would allow the 'bottom-up' model to replace the 'top-down' one over time and also allow safety-valves to be built into it. This means taking a bold step, perhaps in the context of wider and pragmatic political reform. Which direction union reform takes in both countries appears to vary in terms of different geographical location, ownership of enterprises and industrial sectors.

THE NEW LEGAL FRAMEWORK

The legal and regulatory framework is one of the weakest areas of reform in China and Vietnam. This is particularly true in the sphere of labour regulation in China, where regulatory regimes have failed to catch up with the proliferation of new conditions. The process of the establishment of a legal framework so far has gone through three stages: lack of legislation in the early stage, some temporary regulations later, and finally union and labour legislation (such as the Trade Union Law and Labour Law or Code).

In the early stages of reform in both China and Vietnam there was limited legislation on labour issues. Since the late 1980s, some temporary regulations have been implemented, reflecting the objectives of the state to reform the labour system. In China, some of the so-called labour regulations issued by provincial authorities or ministries have been implemented as 'internal regulations', 'minimal law or 'semi-law'. For instance, the temporary regulations on labour contracts, discharging employees and social insurance played an important role in the 1980s and early 1990s (Zhu, 1995). In Vietnam, a number of minor ordinances have been issued on labour regulations since 1990, with the major piece being a temporary ordinance on labour contracts issued in September 1990 (Norlund, 1993).

The most important pieces of recent legislation refer to labour and trade unions. In China, the new Trade Union Law was adopted in 1992 (Biddulph and Cooney, 1993). The new law represents a substantial revision of the law of 1950. Although it covers formal powers, structure, rights and duties of trade unions, its objective is not the reform of existing practice but to ensure the application of principles governing trade union activities and regulating labour so as to advance economic development and maintain social stability in the long term. A contradiction emerges in the tasks of trade unions: on the one hand, they are expected to represent the workers' interests in the enterprise; on the other hand, they have to work for the collective welfare of the enterprise, as well as for the general interests of workers and the state. In Vietnam, the Law on Trade Unions (1990) contains chapters on rights and obligations of trade unions and guarantees concerning trade union activities. Although the law is an initial step in the direction of establishing independent unions, which can defend the interests of workers *vis-à-vis* employers and the state, their level of independence is still questionable. The recently promulgated Labour Law in China and Labour Code in Vietnam reflect that the government is seeking to establish more relevant and universal labour legislation in order to cope with the changes in the industrial relations system.

There are many common issues between the Chinese Labour Law and the Vietnamese Labour Code, such as the employment contract, the relations between enterprise, union and the state, minimum wages and conditions, health, safety and training, minimum working age and the conditions for women, the social insurance system, and the opportunity for collective bargaining. Although both sets of legislation address the issues of mediation and arbitration, the system in China is within the Labour Bureau administrative system. In contrast, the Code in Vietnam sets up an independent legal arbitration system. However, in reality, the function of the mediation and arbitration system is more effective in China than in Vietnam, especially in the Special Economic Zones (SEZs) and other open cities. For instance, about 2,000 cases were considered through the mediation and arbitration system in Shenzhen SEZs in 1995 (authors' survey). In contrast, although the legislation has been established in Vietnam, it is still in the early stage of implementation and the mediation and arbitration system has not been used effectively. Another difference between the Chinese Labour Law and the Vietnamese Labour Code refers to the right to strike. The right to strike has not been raised in the Chinese Labour Law (since the last revision of the constitution in 1982, in which the right to strike was dropped). It has been introduced in Vietnam, despite many restrictive conditions. These differences suggest that the Chinese Labour Law is relatively conservative and that it does not conform to the International Convention of Labour.

CONTINUING PROBLEMS

Both China and Vietnam appear to have managed the transition away from a command economy more successfully than Eastern Europe, where economic change corresponded with a collapse in political structures and was more dramatic and sudden. Both countries have maintained impressive rates of economic growth (see Tables 1 and 2) in contrast to the experience of Eastern Europe after 1989, though they started from a higher base. At the same time it is clear that the transition in China and Vietnam is not yet complete, and that policymakers continue to be confronted by difficult problems and dilemmas with respect to labour regulation and the role of trade unions which can be traced back to the political sphere. The dismantling of the political legitimacy of the Communist party in both countries in many economic spheres may turn out to be a decisive factor in determining the outcomes of the current changes.

TABLE 1

GDP GROWTH IN CHINA SINCE 1978

Year	GDP (100 Million Yuan)	Real GDP Growth (%)
1978	3,624.1	11.7
1980	4,517.8	7.8
1985	8,964.4	13.5
1987	11,962.5	11.6
1988	14,928.3	11.3
1989	16,909.2	4.1
1990	18,547.9	3.8
1991	21,617.8	9.2
1992	26,638.1	14.2
1993	34,634.4	13.5
1994	46,759.4	12.6
1995	58,478.1	10.5
1996	68,593.8	9.6
1997	74,772.0	8.8
1998	76,396.0	7.7
1999	82,054.0	7.1

Source: China Statistical Yearbook (1997), China Yearbook (*Zhongguo Nianjian*), (1998–99), and National Statistics Bureau, January 2000.

TABLE 2

GDP GROWTH IN VIETNAM SINCE 1986

Year	GDP (Billion Dong)	Real GDP Growth (%)
1986	510	–
1987	2,470	–
1988	13,270	–
1989	24,310	–
1990	41,955	5.0
1991	76,707	6.0
1992	110,535	8.6
1993	136,571	1.3
1994	170,258	8.8
1995	222,840	9.5
1996	226,094	9.3
1997	313,624	8.1
1998	361,468	5.8
1999	399,942	4.8

Source: ADUKI (1994–97), and Statistics Department of Vietnam, 2000.

One of the major elements of globalization in the two countries is FDI, which has been an important force for high economic growth and job creation. The inflow of FDI has been growing rapidly in recent years and its positive impact can be identified as generating revenue, introducing new technology and higher quality standards, and creating employment opportunities. At the same time, problems also exist within a large number of FIEs: low levels of unionism, lack of basic hygiene facilities, frequent industrial accidents, overcrowded working environments and exposure to pollution, high temperature and noise without protection, physical abuse, long working hours, low wages and delay of payment.

One reason for the development of such a situation in both China and Vietnam could be that in their enthusiasm for seeking FDI, some government officials might have been less than energetic in the supervision and regulation of FIEs. Second, a wide range of corruption among officials and public servants in both countries creates an environment for foreign investors to avoid punishment under these officials' protection. Third, the means open to workers' organizations to protect workers may well be inadequate. At present, union density in FIEs is still very low. Finally, rapid changes have occurred over a short time, leaving legislation far behind reality.

However, in recent years, labour conflicts in the FIEs have escalated, and more and more strikes have occurred in both countries. The governments are aware that such tensions could lead to social instability and block further economic reform. These concerns have led to a reorientation in favour of regulation through encouragement of trade unionism and more intensified inspection. The problems in the FIEs are relatively manageable. The more intractable problems and dilemmas concern the SOEs and DPEs.

The pressures SOEs are facing arise from excessive employment and accumulated debts that make them vulnerable in competition with recently established private sector firms (both domestic and foreign). In China, the SOEs have started to lay off 'superfluous' employees, and female workers are most affected. After the recent 15th CCP Congress, the central government pushed for further SOE and COE reform. One important step is the speeding up of the process of bankruptcy and reorganization of inefficient enterprises. By the end of 1998, over 17 million SOE workers had been laid off (*xia gang*), representing more than one in five employees, and urban unemployment has been estimated at eight per cent in 1998 (Wilnelm, 1999: 12). Taking into account unemployment in both urban and rural areas, the unemployment rate would be somewhere between 21 and 23 per cent (Biffl, 1999: 5). This level of unemployment places tremendous pressure on the government, trade unions and industries (both public and private sectors) to create new jobs, to train and re-skill the workers who had been laid off and to develop a fully functional labour market and social insurance system.

In Vietnam, since there is a different economic structure compared with China – for example, a shorter history of economic development and less industrialization (a lack of heavy industry with large size production capacity and employment) – redundancy in the SOEs has proceeded on a more substantial scale. Over 25 per cent of those employed in the SOEs have been made redundant. Between 1989 and 1993, 1.5 million SOEs' employees became unemployed, retired or reduced to part-time work as a result of the dissolution or restructuring of 2,000 SOEs to form half that number (*Vietnam Investment Review*, 1993b). Although the government carries out different programmes (such as the Work Creation Schemes and Resettlement Schemes) to assist redundant workers to transfer to other sectors, and provides 'start-up loans' for new small business and training programmes for re-employment, so far they have met with little success mainly due to financial shortages and the lack of training know-how and materials.

In fact, the worst situation in terms of working conditions and respecting labour's rights is in DPEs, and many of them are not even registered. Most employees are peasants from rural areas and the rest are superfluous labourers retrenched from the state sector. DPEs are often the only employment alternative. Therefore, DPEs take advantage of these workers with low wages, long working hours, terrible working environments (exposure to noise, pollution and unsafe working practices), lack of health and safety insurance, and sometimes even physical abuse. In addition, the rate of unionization is very low in DPEs. People employed by DPEs are more concerned about maintaining their jobs, so they do not dare 'make trouble' by organizing unions or challenging employers. Under these circumstances, the government enforcement of labour regulation is necessary.

DISCUSSION

At the crux of the transition from a central planning system to a market-orientated economy in both China and Vietnam is the changing position of labour and the contradictions faced by the trade union movement. The trade unions are clearly now at a crossroads and further political reform is needed to adjust to the structural economic change that has already been implemented and is likely to continue. The industrial relations system in both countries requires a further transformation which allows a more federal, independent and reconstructed trade union organization to evolve further as well as find a way for excluded representational forms to find a constructive role in the system.

The trade union movement in both countries had its roots in organized political opposition to colonialist oppression. As a consequence, and in line with Leninist notions, unions emerged as locality-based and vertically organized. Within the planned economy, trade unions represented the interests of labour in their role of management of SOEs, which were theoretically owned by the workers. Furthermore, unions were responsible for the social welfare of workers through such means as sickness benefits, pensions and holidays. The challenge for the union movement in the process of socialist transition is to transform their role from one of management in which they ensured that labour met its production targets, to one where they become advocates on behalf of labour in the new society.

A major economic as well as political problem that faces the two countries is the high level of unemployment. The strategy of the party-state is that as the SOEs are rationalized, COEs, DPEs and FIEs will emerge to soak up the unemployed, which keeps social unrest at bay. To a large extent this strategy has been successful. However, following the recent regional Asian financial crisis, both countries have experienced the decline of FDI and exports. More difficulties will emerge in the near future.

One problem for trade unions, for instance, is the emergence of FIEs and DPEs as the major sites of employment with their very low union density. Those in the private sector rarely organize in the form of unions. In contrast, the tendency of private domestic capital has been to employ labour within a pseudo-family structure in which employees and the employer are obliged to honour the cultural expectations imbued within this relationship. As a consequence, labour is largely unrepresented in most DPEs and FIEs.

Curiously, a legal framework is largely in place which should protect labour. The new labour legislation (including the Trade Unions Law and Labour Law/Code) promulgated in the first half of 1990s strengthened the position of trade unions by making it obligatory for larger firms to have some form of worker organization. Both the English and local language press are filled with stories of 'wildcat' strikes as a consequence of worker abuse, mainly in FIEs, and in some SOEs and DPEs. Yet, these strikes do not follow the prescription of the labour legislation and are rarely led by the trade unions. In this context, trade unions in both countries are attempting to redefine their role in order to obtain support from the grass roots. On the other hand, at the enterprise level, under the growing market and institutional reforms, unions will need to position themselves so as to be able to constrain the excesses of management and to provide a degree of empowerment to workers. This will require a more representative role for trade unions. The introduction of collective bargaining provides the opportunity for trade unions to make this transition. These developments will lead to the establishment of a new industrial relations system, which strikes at the heart of the socialist market economy and the successful transformation.

CONCLUSION

The cases of China and Vietnam provide a lesson for other developing economies. Under current globalization, states cannot become overdependent on foreign capital and market forces but must appropriately use them for national development. The recent regional financial crisis has taught us that, without protection, not only can development not be sustained, but also political and economic chaos can erupt and cause severe damage.

A gradualist transition is likely in China and Vietnam, from traditional methods of social control to ones commensurate with a 'civil society', the rule of law and a pluralist framework for negotiations among the state, capital and workers. These 'Chinese and Vietnamese characteristics' under the current globalization process would benefit other developing countries if they stand up and work together for developing an open and equal global society.

REFERENCES

Betcherman, G. (1996) 'Globalization, Labour Markets and Public Policy', in R. Boyer and D. Drache (eds), *States against Markets*. London: Routledge, pp. 250–69.
Biddulph, S. and Cooney, S. (1993) 'Regulation of Trade Unions in the People's Republic of China', *Melbourne University Law Review*, Vol. 19, No. 2, pp. 253–92.
Biffl, G. (1999) 'Unemployment, Underemployment and Migration: A Challenge for Labour Market Policy in China'. Paper presented to Workshop, The Melbourne Institute of

Applied Economic and Social Research, University of Melbourne, 8 March.

Bradley, S.A., Hausman, J. and Nolan, A. (1994) *Globalization, Technology and Competition: The Fusion of Computers and Telecommunication in the 1990s.* Cambridge, MA: Harvard Business School Press.

Cox, R.W. (1994) 'Global Restructuring: Making Sense of the Changing International Political Economy', in R. Stubbs and G.R.D. Underhill (eds), *Political Economy and the Changing Global Order.* New York: St Martin's Press, pp. 45–59.

CSPH (1995–1996) *China Labour Statistical Yearbook, 1995–1996.* Beijing: China Statistical Publishing House.

Fahey, S. (1997) 'Vietnam and the 'Third Way': The Nature of Socio-Economic Transition', *Journal of Economic and Social Geography*, Vol. 88, No. 5, pp. 469–80.

Falk, R. (1992) *Explorations at the Edge of Time: The Prospects for World Order.* Philadelphia: Temple University Press.

Guangming Daily (1998) 'The 13th ACFTU Congress Opens in Beijing', 20 Oct., p. 1.

Hirst, P. and Thompson, G. (1996) *Globalization in Question.* Cambridge: Polity Press.

Hoogvelt, A. (1997) *Globalization and the Postcolonial World.* Baltimore: Johns Hopkins University Press.

Hyden, G. (1997) 'Building Civil Society at the Turn of the Millennium', in J. Burbidge (ed.), *Beyond Prince and Merchant: Citizen Participation and the Rise of Civil Society.* New York: Pact Publications.

Ng, S.H. and Warner, M. (1998) *China's Trade Unions and Management.* London: Macmillan.

Norlund, I. (1993) 'The Creation of a Labour Market in Vietnam: Legal Framework and Practices', in C.A. Thayer and D.G. Marr (eds), *Vietnam and Rule of Law.* Canberra: Australian National University, pp. 173–89.

Pravda, A. and Ruble, B.A. (1986) *Trade Unions in Communist States.* Boston: Allen and Unwin.

Stubbs, R. and Underhill, G.R.D. (eds) (1994) *Political Economy and the Changing Global Order.* New York: St Martin's Press.

Vietnam Investment Review (1993a) 'Trade Unions: A New Role in Vietnam', 16–22 Aug., p. 18.

Vietnam Investment Review (1993b) 'Right to Strike Likely under New Labour Law', 8–14 Nov., p. 5.

Warner, M. (1993) 'Chinese Trade Unions: Structure and Function in a Decade of Economic Reform, 1979–89', in S. Frenkel (ed.), *Organized Labour in the Asia-Pacific Region.* Ithaca, NY: ILR Press, pp. 59–81.

Warner, M. (1995) *The Management of Human Resources in Chinese Industry.* London: Macmillan.

Water, M. (1995) *Globalization.* London: Routledge.

Wilnelm, K. (1999) 'Cover Story: China', *Far Eastern Economic Review*, 18 Feb., pp. 10–16.

Zhang, Q. (1994) 'Labour Relations in Foreign Invested Enterprises'. Paper presented at China–Japan Labour Relations Conference, Beijing, 24 March.

Zhu, Y. (1995) 'Major Changes Under Way in China's Industrial Relations', *International Labour Review* Vol. 134, No. 1, pp 37–50.

Zhu, Y. and Campbell, I. (1996) 'Economic Reform and the Challenge of Transforming Labour Regulation in China', *Labour and Industry*, Vol. 7, No. 1, pp. 29–49.

16

Globalization, Labour and Prospects

CHRIS ROWLEY and JOHN BENSON

This collection has examined and analysed some of the aspects of globalization, an area where 'the rhetoric of the globalizers is wide of the mark' (Hirst and Thompson, 1999: 37). We focused on globalization's impacts on workers and labour organizations and their possible responses across a broad and diverse range of economies in the Asia Pacific. This has provided a wealth of detail and research evidence on the situation. While on the one hand some of the results may well have been expected, such as some weakening of worker organizations, on the other hand some results were less expected, are paradoxical, and serve as a clarion call for further work and research.

MAIN CONCLUSIONS

The diversity of the countries and issues studied has allowed several broad conclusions to be reached. Four will be emphasized here.

Universalism and Determinism

First, we should continue to remain sceptical about universalism and determinism in the globalization area (as in many others). Indeed, the Asian crisis of 1997 should serve as a reminder that development along one projected path is not always a foregone conclusion. Views that globalization must produce a neoliberal response as the only possibility are similarly misplaced. This is not to say that there are no significant impacts from globalization, but rather that these vary and can be mediated. Globalization is more contingent, with differential effects on, and responses from, states, economies, workers and organized labour. Not only are there clear inter-economy differences in these, but the picture is further blurred as there are intra-economy, sectoral and organizational size and ownership variations.

For example, globalization can result in diversity of outcomes even in one economy. Not only the 'host' context, but also the 'home' nationality of capital have impacts. As Bhopal and Todd[1] show, the behaviour of multinational corporations (MNCs) varied within a common Malaysian context. Australian and Japanese MNCs were willing to work with trade unions, unlike the more anti-union stance of US MNCs. Thus, there is no 'inevitable production logic', a key underpinning of universalists, but rather management 'philosophy' appears to be driving outcomes and preferences. These were in turn affected by range of contingent variables, which included: (1) 'home' perceptions, knowledge and competence in dealing with unions; (2) experience of unions in host environments; (3) MNC power; (4) host environment political formations; and (5) union responses. These created a 'zone of manoeuvre' open to contest at micro and macro levels.

Likewise, the varied responses of unions both between and within economies indicates that universalism is limited. Globalization can also produce paradoxes for labour organization. Globalization via foreign direct investment (FDI) can erode existing industrial relations (IR) practices and systems. Yet, overseas capital can also internationalize work regulation and rules, making IR more international, complex and formal, even producing a 'window of opportunity' for unions to recruit. Similarly, for Hadiz, Indonesia's globalization via its greater integration within the world economy through light manufacturing had spurred both the growth of a larger, maturing industrial workforce with a greater propensity to organize, and some pressure for reform in policy and frustration at the state-backed labour federation. However, an accommodation with labour making some form of Western-style unionism possible was unlikely, as he believes workers as a social force remained constrained and repression over negotiation or co-optation was more likely to be maintained. Likewise, Kim *et al.* believed Korean worker rights were increased to meet global standards imported via globalization. This may represent, however, the first stage of the 'global subordination of workers'. Yuen and Lim argued that Singaporean unions gained in stature and influence in providing for training and helping workers cope with consequences of globalization (retrenchment and recession).

In short, it may be argued that 'national economies continue to exist ... world market forces are not beyond governance' (Hirst and Thompson, 1999: 36). It is clear that despite globalization, the impacts of institutions, national labour markets and culture remain (see Rowley, 1997).

Deregulation and Labour Markets

Second, we should not simply absorb rhetoric or nostrums about deregulation and labour market rigidities. Deregulation does not automatically and unequivocally equal 'free'. Rather, it can actually mean 'less free', as seen in China's 'bonded' labour market analysed by Chan. Also, rigidities can actually enhance flexibilities (see Dore, 1987) and encourage routes to competition (Bae *et al.*, 1997). There can also be a requirement for strong states to exist for free markets to be forged. This can be seen in the Thatcherite UK labour market experiments in the 1980s (see Gamble, 1988). Hong Kong also provides examples, as shown by Ng and Rowley, of deregulation producing more regulation.

Labour's Role in Competitiveness

Third, the role of labour, particularly its wages and costs in global capital's calculation of 'competitiveness', is not a simple issue. One strand sees low wages as the only way in which economies can remain attractive destinations for mobile capital. This is mistaken, short sighted and unsustainable over the long term. Firstly, it is important to distinguish in globalization impacts on the tradeable sector, where developed economies cannot compete on wages, from impacts on the non-tradeable sector (which includes many private services), where driving down wages actually depresses domestic demand, output and employment. Secondly, where does such 'bidding down' of pay and conditions end? As is often pointed out, it is frequently feared that labour costs in one economy are higher than in others. The outcomes of weak regulatory regimes are also witnessed in the litany of abuses catalogued in China by Chan. These should serve as salutary reminders of the continued capriciousness and carelessness of capitalism and becoming engaged in any 'race to the base'. Thirdly, arguments based on wages as determinants in competitiveness also take much for granted, not least management foresight, coherence (see Hyman, 1987, for a critique of this), ability and even belief in 'the evidence' on these matters – the facts may not always 'speak for themselves'. Other key elements in competitiveness include productivity and currency exchange rates. One example of this was Thailand's linking of its currency so that when the US dollar rose it made exports uncompetitive. It may be that rather than wages and worker compliance, other factors, such as political uncertainly and corruption, are the cause of problems. For example, fear among ethnic Chinese business people who dominate the Indonesian economy caused capital flight of £10 billion in 1998 (Sheridan, 1999). Hadiz argued that in Indonesia there are few robust indicators that its 'attractiveness' as an investment destination was being eroded solely because of rising wages and labour unrest. Rather, any weakening in Indonesia's 'desirability' was more due to its 'high cost economy' created by inefficiencies and widespread corruption. Fourthly, there are alternative, sustainable upgrading means to competition (see Rowley and Bae, 1998), though other supportive elements are needed. One constraint, however, would be skill shortages, making the introduction of more sophisticated technology difficult. Nevertheless, this is not determinism in action, but political choice.

Labour Organization: Micro and Macro Aspects

Fourth, globalization's impacts have produced problems for labour organization. This is in terms of the need not only to organize and protect local workers in increasingly fragmented employment and increased levels of unemployment following the Asian financial crises of 1997, but also to act as 'fraternal' agents for guest workers. For example, following the crisis, the Labour Congress of Thailand lost 10,000 of its 160,000 members by late 1998 (Grumian, 1998b). Indeed, Linard (1998) reports guest workers in low paid jobs in difficult working conditions and suffering discrimination of all kinds. It was recently estimated that there are 42 million migrant workers worldwide, not including illegal migrants or countries where figures are rarely recorded, while China alone has 80 million internal economic migrants (David, 1998b). Guest workers include three million Filipino women working as maids, including those working in Hong Kong, Taiwan and Japan (Blain, 1998a). In Thailand there were some one million 'illegals' in 1997 (*The Economist*, 1998). In Malaysia over 20 per cent of the workforce is 'foreign', with 800,000 illegal Indonesian immigrants (ibid.), with two million migrants at a very high density in some sectors such as construction, where they comprise 80 per cent of workers (David, 1998a). It has been estimated that one million Burmese are working as illegal migrants in Thailand, attracting large numbers of garment manufacturing workshops to the border region (Grumian, 1998a). There are instances of Burmese working in construction for $3–$4 per day, or of factories where two people earn $6 per day for producing 1,000 pairs of slippers and sandals, of garment factories paying $40–$50 per month but with no free days, and frequent accidents and fines for those who refuse to work more than eight hours per day (ibid).

One only has to look at the common protectionist posturings of US, UK and European unions to try to halt job relocations, or Hong Kong unions' ambiguity towards guest worker entry, to witness this intra- and inter-union tension. This conflict is not only over the search for cheap labour. Benson and Debroux provide a clear example of conflict between public and private unions in Japan. Deregulation, a major outcome of globalization, has seen potential gains split unevenly. Japanese public sector unions fearful of substantial membership loss have resisted change. This resistance is seen by private sector unions, particularly those in manufacturing, as a major cause of the increasingly uncompetitive state of Japanese industry. Nevertheless, there are some rays of light in the gloom. These can be at both micro and macro levels.

Micro Levels

There are some examples of union successes, even in adverse conditions. These include the foreign (mainly Korean, Japanese, Taiwanese) plants in 'export processing zones' where the Trade Union Congress of the Philippines (with 1.5 million members) managed to gain 7,500 recruits (Blain, 1998b). Harcourt indicated that trade unions could protect workers in the face of globalization and, in proving their worth to fearful workers, raise recruitment. The possibilities and strategies included domestic ones (such as industrial campaigns, as in textiles with its 'fair wear campaign'), industry inquiries, and labour market responses (for example, award restructuring to raise skills to increase productivity). Similarly, Burgess outlined the need for unions to adapt to globalization's impacts with various tactics and strategies. Hall and Harley contrasted the strategic response of unions in Australia by orientation on two dimensions. First, the relative emphasis on either narrow sectionalism or integration and articulation with the broader labour movement. Within this there are two opposing orientations. One is 'articulated institutional unionism', an integration of unions (or sections) with others – confederations, peak bodies or political parties – and the pursuit of ends through political/institutional means as well as industrially. The other is 'militant economistic unionism', an emphasis on sectionalism and a narrow concern with the affairs and membership of one's own union (or section). The second dimension is the relative extent to which unions adopt traditional industrial tactics or a range of practices associated with a 'servicing' model – 'managerialist service unionism'. Different unions engage in different kinds of strategy, partly because globalization has differential impacts on parts of the economy and labour markets. Also, while union responses are conditioned by political, institutional, economic and industrial forces, the characteristics and predicament of membership also imposes a critical influence. On the one hand blue-collar unions face continued erosion and may intensify their use of traditional tactics and emphasis on solidaristic approaches, while on the other white-collar and service unions may be more prepared to market themselves as 'service orientated' organizations. Therefore, concerted and united political action that draws on the resources and strengths of the labour movement as a whole and on the capacity of individual unions to see themselves a part of a political movement, is important.

Macro Levels

It has been pointed out that globally mobile capital requires international regulation via labour standards (Mehmet *et al.*, 1999), structures and organization, and legal instruments (Linard, 1998). Indeed, Harcourt's second group of union response strategies are international, such as international labour cooperation (as in shipping, airlines) and international trade instruments (including policies and bodies). Other examples of labour cooperation internationally include dock work, where the UK and Australia are high profile examples (see Lambert, 1999). Indeed, unions in some sectors, such as media, and in some regions, such as Australia–Asia, are stepping up activities of coordination to the point of creating supranational bodies with a certain degree of authority and resources (Leisink, 1999).

Price outlined the Asia Pacific Economic Cooperation (APEC) forum and its Human Resource Development Working Group, a regional union body meeting with management and government, though it is constrained at present. Abbott contended that globalization processes of integration may allow regional trade unions to transform. However, regional union bodies (such as the Asian Pacific Regional Organization) were confined to moral, logistical and educational support to member organizations that were unwilling to cede the authority and resources necessary for coordinated cross-border campaigns. So, there was a lack of organizational mechanisms that would enable it to bring pressure and intervention to bear on MNCs and transnational polities operating in the Asia Pacific. Abbott concludes that this situation is unlikely to change while regionalism in the Asia Pacific is driven by commonly held free market ideals and notions of minimal state action, and while entrenched national parochialism remains a major constraint upon the possibility of supranational institution-building. At the same time, union inabilities to act transnationally remain desirable among MNCs and powerful economic and political interests in the region.

Nevertheless, interesting examples of unions creating international linkages and forging a 'new internationalism' are provided by Lambert (1999). He notes that with increasing competition from low wage Asian economies, Australian unions did not choose a purely protective posture but a longer term strategy to sponsor building local unions in the Asian economies so that they would be able to oppose exploitation, demand fair wages and conditions, and reduce discrepancies within the Asian region, from which Australian workers would also benefit in the long run. These linkages between unions in the Asia Pacific region forged in the 1990s were now receiving widespread international support from the established international union movement through the International Confederation of Free Trade Unions and various International Trade Secretariats.

The main characteristics of this new internationalism are that it was regionally initiated. Its dimensions are as follows. Firstly, 'regional linkages': linking workers across a region with extremes of regulatory and production regimes to grow unionism where rights are denied. Secondly, 'militant internationalism': the internationalism that emerged out of these linkages exploits the vulnerability created by globalization, while economic integration increases the level of trade and communications dependency of nations, enhancing possible boycott pressure to the extent unions are organized in these sectors. Thirdly, 'global social movement unionism': engagement in international action results in moves to create global unionism, requiring union leaders and members to internationalize a deep and sophisticated internationalist culture – to understand working class issues in other nations, which is partly an organization question, for example by using a rotating exchange of delegate level leaders and cultural symbols. Fourthly, 'new working class politics': this is needed to challenge the neoliberal model of globalization that many unions have adopted (ibid.).

CONCLUSION

The debates on globalization's meanings and effects will continue. Globalization will have impacts on states, economies, labour and work, although the exact nature and magnitude of these is less clear. What this collection has shown is that globalization's terrain is uneven and contested: MNCs are not undisputedly 'the masters of the universe', and states ultimately retain considerable power. This is one arena where labour needs to (re)build its linkages and influences. This can be seen within Hall and Harley's ideas of 'articulated institutional unionism'. Indeed, perhaps the recent Asian crisis will be an impetus for change and greater social dialogue. For instance, Korea and Thailand established tripartite dialogue that involved unions in the search for solutions. Undoubtedly, labour and trade union organization have been weakened in some places. Yet, at the same time there have been some counter-currents (Korea, Singapore) and attempts to build a more globalized union movement to match capital. There are also ideas of 'social movement unionism' (Lambert, 1999).

In sum, while labour's road will be full of obstacles and tricky to navigate, this has often been the case for unions in the past and should not prevent developments towards globalization. It needs to be remembered that in these circumstances it is a question of *vis unita fortior* (united strength is stronger).

NOTES

1. From now on, undated citations of authors refer to their contributions to this volume.

REFERENCES

Bae, J., Rowley, C., Kim, D.H. and Lawler, J. (1997) 'Korean Industrial Relations at the Crossroads: The Recent Labour Troubles', *Asia Pacific Business Review*, Vol. 3, No. 3, pp. 148–60.

Blain, D. (1998a) 'Migrant Workers: Marissa's Choice', *Trade Union World*, No. 3, March, p. 17.

Blain, D. (1998b) 'The TUCP Makes a Breakthrough', *Trade Union World*, No. 3, March, p. 17.

David, N. (1998a) 'Migrants Made the Scapegoats of the Crisis', *Trade Union World*, No. 2, Feb., pp. 24–5.

David, N. (1998b) 'Migration and Globalization: The New Slave Trade', *Trade Union World*, No. 7–8, July–Aug., pp. 16–17.

Dore, R. (1987) *Flexible Rigidities*. London: Athlone.

Economist, The (1998) 'Asia's New Jobless: The Unwanted', 28 March, p. 75.

Gamble, A. (1988) *The Free Economy and The Strong State*. London: Macmillan.

Grumian, S. (1998a) 'The Harsh Reality of the Thai Eldorado', *Trade Union World*, No. 7–8, July–Aug., pp. 13–15.

Grumian, S. (1998b) 'The Hidden Face of the Crisis', *Trade Union World*, No. 9, Sept., pp. 6–7.

Hirst, P. and Thompson, G. (1999) 'Globalization – Frequently Asked Questions', in P. Leisink (ed.), *Globalization and Labour Relations*. Cheltenham: Edward Elgar, pp. 36–56.

Hyman, R. (1987) 'Strategies or Structure? Capital, Labour and Control', *Work, Employment and Society*, Vol. 1, No. 1.

Lambert, R. (1999) 'Australia's Historic Industrial Relations Transition', in P. Leisink (ed.), *Globalization and Labour Relations*. Cheltenham: Edward Elgar, pp. 212–48.

Linard, A. (1998) *Migration and Globalization: The New Slave Trade*. ICFTU.

Leisink, P. (1999) 'Introduction', in P. Leisink (ed.), *Globalization and Labour Relations*. Cheltenham: Edward Elgar, pp. 1–35.

Mehmet, O., Mandes, E. and Sinding, R. (1999) *Towards a Fair Labour Market: Avoiding a New Slave Trade*. London: Routledge.

Rowley, C. and Bae, J. (eds) (1998) *Korean Businesses: Internal and External Industrialization*. London: Cass.

Rowley, C. (1997) 'Comparisons and Perspectives on HRM in the Asia Pacific', *Asia Pacific Business Review*, Vol. 3, No. 4, pp. 1–18.

Sheridan, M. (1999) 'Indonesia's Future Imperfect', *The Sunday Times*, 20 June, p. 3:4.

Notes on Contributors

Keith Abbott is a Senior Lecturer in the School of Business and Law at Deakin University, Australia, and is currently the unit chair of Employee Relations. He has written a number of articles on European industrial relations and regional trade union theory.

Johngseok Bae is Assistant Professor of Management, Hanyang University, Seoul. He is the author of several articles on international and strategic HRM/IR and Korean management, and was co-editor, with Chris Rowley, of *Korean Businesses: Internal and External Industrialization*, a special issue of *Asia Pacific Business Review*.

John Benson is a Reader in the Department of Management at the University of Melbourne. From 1994 to 1997 he was a professor of economics and industrial relations at Hiroshima City University. He has published a number of articles on Japanese, Chinese and Australian labour issues and is currently researching the effects of globalization on Japanese manufacturing enterprises.

Mhinder Bhopal is a Senior Lecturer at the University of North London. He has published on the impact of US MNCs on Malaysian trade unionism and has forthcoming publications on ethnicity, state, labour and capital in Malaysia.

John Burgess is Associate Professor in the Department of Economics, University of Newcastle, Australia. His research interests include EEO and employment equity, employment restructuring, employment policy, employment rights and workplace bargaining.

Anita Chan is an Australian Research Council Senior Research Fellow hosted by the Australian National University, and co-editor of *The China Journal*. Her research focuses on management styles, worker–management relations in Chinese enterprises, and Chinese trade unions. She is author of *Children of Mao*, co-author of *Chen Village under Mao and Deng*, and editor of *China's Workers under Assault* (forthcoming).

Philippe Debroux is a Professor of international business at Soka University, Faculty of Business Administration. He has lived and worked in Japan for most of the past 25 years. Prior to his academic career he worked as a management consultant for a Tokyo-based Japanese firm. He has published a number of articles on Japanese and Chinese human resource management and is currently researching changes in Japanese management systems.

Stephanie Fahey is Professor and Director of the Research Institute for Asia and the Pacific at the University of Sydney. She has several research projects in Vietnam, including the development of the private sector, labour relations and the changing position of women, and has published widely on these issues.

Vedi R. Hadiz teaches in the Department of Sociology at the National University of Singapore. He was formerly a Research Fellow in the Asia Research Centre, Murdoch University. He has written extensively on labour as well as on the politics of industrialization and social change in Indonesia, and is currently co-authoring a book on the reorganization of economic and political power in that country.

Richard Hall is Senior Researcher in the Australian Centre for Industrial Relations Research and Training (ACIRRT) at the University of Sydney. He was formerly a Senior Lecturer in the Labour Studies programme at the University of Queensland. His research interests lie chiefly in the areas of comparative labour law, comparative political economy and trade union strategy.

Tim Harcourt is a Research Officer/Advocate with the Australian Council of Trade Unions (ACTU). He has worked in the private, public and union sectors in Australia, the UK, Israel and the USA. His research interests include macroeconomic policy, labour markets, international trade, trade unions, collective bargaining and international relations.

Bill Harley is Senior Lecturer in the Department of Management at the University of Melbourne. His main research interests are in the areas of trade unions, employer labour use strategies and changing patterns of work organization in the advanced economies.

Dong-One Kim is an Associate Professor at Korea University. His research interests include workplace innovations and comparative industrial relations. His articles have been published in many labour relations, HRM and sociology journals.

John Lawler is Professor of Labor and Industrial Relations at the University of Illinois at Urbana-Champaign. His research interests focus primarily on human resource management practices in East and South East Asia.

Changwon Lee is a Research Fellow at the Korea Labor Institute, a government-sponsored research unit. His academic interests include the social foundation of labour markets, unemployment and poverty issues, industrial relations, and trade and labour rights. His publications include *Changing Approaches to Industrial Relations in the Asia-Pacific Area* (Allen & Unwin, forthcoming) co-edited with O. Bamber, F. Park and P. Ross.

Lim Ghee Soon is a Senior Lecturer at the National University of Singapore. His teaching and research cover human resource management, labour–management relations and organizational behaviour.

Ng Sek Hong is a Reader in the School of Business at the University of Hong Kong. His area of research deals largely with labour, employment and human resource management issues. He has also published in the field of Chinese management.

John Price teaches history at the University of Victoria, British Columbia, Canada. He is the author of *Japan Works: Power and Paradox in Postwar Industrial Relations* (Cornell University Press, 1997).

Chris Rowley is a Senior Lecturer at City University Business School, London. He researches and publishes in the areas of employee relations, human resource management, technological change, flexibility and Asia Pacific business.

Chokechai Suttawet is associated with the Pridi Banomyong Institute in Bangkok. He has been a lecturer at Thammasat University in Bangkok and has served on the National Labour Development Advisory Council of Thailand. His research interests include labour issues, international social security and social insurance in Thailand.

Patricia Todd is a Senior Lecturer at the University of Western Australia. She has published articles and a book on trade unions in Peninsular Malaysia. She has a particular interest in Malaysian and South East Asian Industrial Relations.

Ying Zhu is Senior Lecturer in the Department of Management at the University of Melbourne. His research interests are industrial restructuring and industrial relations in East Asia, and his main publications are in journals covering Asian economies, labour, industry and human resource management.

Yuen Chi Ching is Associate Professor at the National University of Singapore. Her current research interests include conflict management, negotiation and human resource management.

Index